lonely planet

Denmark & the Faroe Islands

Thomas O'Malley, Abigail Blasi, Laura Hall

Klakkur (p264), the Faroe Islands

CONTENTS

Tivoli Gardens (p56)

Egeskov Slot (p166)

Christiansø (p140)

DENMARK & THE FAROE ISLANDS

THE JOURNEY BEGINS HERE

Researching this new edition took me through the pleasant lands of Denmark's South, a watercolour of wheat fields, summerhouses and sailboats. Wildflowers bloom, ferries join the dots between islands. It's all so beautifully formed, so wholesome. Huts on the roadside sell jars of honey and strawberries – you just pop money in a box. There's history here too. I ducked inside the vestiges of a Viking ship burial; hunted for Bronze-age petroglyphs; marvelled at church murals. The weather mostly obliged, but after hiking the cliffs of Møns Klint, I was ambushed by a storm. The nearest refuge? A shack of a bar called Klap Hesten ('slap the horse'). Nothing for it but to hunker down with the locals, have a beer or three, and wait for it to blow over. Wonderful.

Thomas O'Malley
eatmywordz.com

An inveterate wanderer and unashamed fan of Danish street hot dogs, Thomas has worked on over 20 Lonely Planet guidebooks.

My favourite experience is taking the boat from Bornholm to **Christiansø** (p140). A tiny, time-warp isle adrift in the Baltic, it has a single inn, a few dozen residents and a whole lot of serenity.

WHO GOES WHERE

Our writers and experts choose the places which, for them, define Denmark.

JONATHANFILSKOV-PHOTOGRAPHY/GETTY IMAGES ©

Our second flat in Copenhagen overlooked **the Lakes** (pictured; p63): it was a surprise to me how close this tranquil spot was to the centre of the city, and it was a sheer joy to overlook the water, with statuesque joggers and cyclists making use of its paths, swan pedalos bringing a touch of whimsy, the sunset spreading across the dusky sky, and fireworks reflected in its waters every New Year's Eve.

Abigail Blasi

@abi.where/abiwhere

Abigail Blasi is a travel writer whose Italian husband worked in Copenhagen for several years: she still spends as much time there as she can.

ADWO/SHUTTERSTOCK © ARTIST: HANS PAULI OLSEN

The **Kópakonan** (pictured; p265) statue on Kalsoy is a powerful sculpture of a fierce sealwoman coming to wreak revenge on the local people because of how they have treated her family. With wild seas behind it, and jagged mountains as a backdrop, it's the personification of the force of nature on the Faroe Islands and how closely people here live alongside it. It's also something to think about: that we are part of nature, not apart from it.

Laura Hall

@laura_hall_copenhagen

Laura Hall is a travel writer and author specialising in Scandinavia and the Nordics.

The Faroe Islands
Kalsoy
Kunoy
Viðoy
Svínoy
Eysturoy
Borðoy
Streymoy
Vágar
TÓRSHAVN
Sandoy
ATLANTIC OCEAN
Suðuroy
0 20 km
0 10 miles
The Faroe Islands (550km) (see inset)
Faroe Islands
Turf-topped homes and otherworldly landscapes (p242)
Silkeborg
Bathing lakes and ancient bog-bodies (p214)
Jutland's West Coast
Raw and remote, a water-sports playground (p223)
Ribe
Medieval history and a wild tidal coastline (p184)
Billund
Family-oriented global home of Lego (p219)
Ærø
Delightful, quintessentially Danish island (p172)
Hirtshals
Tornby
Hjørring
Løkken
Brønderslev
Østerv
Tranum Strand
Aabybro
Hjallerup
Hanstholm
Fjerritslev
Nørresundby
Aalborg
Klitmøller
Thisted
Limfjord
Nibe
Stenbjerg
Støvring
Nykøbing Mors
Fur
Aars
Skørping
Agger
Farsø
Hurup
Mors
Hadsund
Nissum Bredning
Hobro
Mariage
Skive
Handest
Lemvig
Struer
Vinderup
Viborg
Randers
Nissum Fjord
Holstebro
Bjerringbro
Ulfborg
Karup
Silkeborg
Aarhus
Ringkøbing
Herning
Ikast
Ry
Hvide Sande
Ringkøbing Fjord
Kibæk
JUTLAND (JYLLAND)
Skanderborg
Skjern
Odder
Nørre Nebel
Give
Horsens
Henne Strand
Jelling
Juelsmind
Billund
Vejle
Varde
Fredericia
Bogense
Oksby
Holsted
Esbjerg
Bramming
Vejen
Kolding
Middelfart
Sønder
Fanø
Jels
Årup
Ribe
Glamsbjer
Vojens
Assens
Vadehavet
Skærbæk
Toftlund
Haderslev
Hårb
Rømø
Lille Bælt
Faabor
Løgumkloster
Aabenraa
Nordborg
Højer
Tønder
Tinglev
Fynsh
Als
Sønderborg
Mommar
Padborg
Flensburg
GERMANY
NORTH SEA
0 50 km
0 25 miles

Skagen
Art and nature where two seas collide (p233)
Aarhus
Denmark's loveable second city (p206)
Helsingør
Hamlet's castle and harbour vistas (p102)
Copenhagen
Culture-rich playground with cutting-edge design (p46)
Bornholm
'Sunshine island' adrift in the Baltic (p132)
Møn
Towering sea cliffs and dark starry skies (p142)
Skagen
Ålbæk
Frederikshavn
Sæby
Vesterø Havn
Østerby Havn
Læsø
Byrum
Asaa
Göteborg (Gothenburg)
Aalborg Bugt
Anholt
Kattegat
SWEDEN
Auning
Grenaa
Rønde
Ebeltoft
Gilleleje
Helsingør
Humlebæk
Rungsted
Hundested
Frederiksværk
Odden
Rørvig
Hillerød
Isefjord
Frederikssund
Lyngby
Ølstykke
Hellerup
Sælvig
Samsø
Sejerø Bugt
Kalundborg
Holbæk
COPENHAGEN
Malmö
Jyderup
Roskilde
Tissø
ZEALAND (SJÆLLAND)
Store Bælt
Otterup
Gørlev
Køge
Køge Bugt
Sorø
Ringsted
Odense
Store Heddinge
Nyborg
Slagelse
FUNEN (FYN)
Korsør
Fakse Ladeplads
Ørbæk
Næstved
Rødvig
Kværndrup
Fakse Bugt
Lohals
Korinth
Præstø
Svendborg
Vordingborg
Stege
Tåsinge
Smålandsfarvandet
Møn
Ærøskøbing
Rudkøbing
Nørre Alslev
Bornholm (40km) (see inset)
BALTIC SEA
Ærø
Nakskov
Sakskøbing
Falster
Maribo
Nykøbing Falster
Lolland
Bagenkop
Rødbyhavn
Gedser
Bornholm
Christiansø
Sandvig
Allinge
Gudhjem
Hasle
Svaneke
Rønne
Nexø
Åkirkeby
0 20 km
0 10 miles

MUSEUM MAGIC

Denmark is a master of museums, crafting engaging, artistic, affecting, even thrilling exhibitions at every level, from a small-town history museum to a cutting-edge national institution that rivals the world's best. Whether you're into modern art, ceramics, dinosaurs, WWII, the Vikings or something quirkier like the history of camping, Denmark has a museum for it, and it's bound to be brilliant. Bringing history to life through costumed reenactments is another Danish speciality.

Modern Art

It's easy to indulge your artist's soul in Denmark, with a cache of impressive modern-art museums covering contemporary classics to the truly avant-garde.

Romancing the Past

Born in the wrong era? Don't fret – drop into one of Denmark's many open-air museums and see if life as a 16th-century blacksmith would have suited you better.

Natural Wonders

While Denmark's countryside may seem serene, its natural wonders are vividly showcased in museums covering everything from geological processes to ecological diversity.

FROM LEFT: STIG ALENAS/SHUTTERSTOCK ©, LEV LEVIN/SHUTTERSTOCK ©, DIEGO GRANDI/SHUTTERSTOCK ©

BEST MUSEUM EXPERIENCES

Discover marvellous modern art at the iconic ❶ **Louisiana Museum** (pictured far left, p93), where the coastal views and sculpture gardens are also masterpieces.

Experience the closest thing to time travel at ❷ **Den Gamle By** (pictured left, p211), a live-action recreation of a Danish town from different eras.

Meet mummified Grauballe Man, long-term resident of a Danish bog, and see Viking hoards at the high-tech ❸ **Moesgaard Museum** (p212).

Nuke whole cities (yes, it's weird) with hands-on exhibits before descending into a once-secret cold war bunker at ❹ **REGAN Vest** (p229).

Explore the world of the 'Viking Sorceress', a powerful and prophetic fortune teller, at the ❺ **National Museum** in Copenhagen (p59).

Amager Bakke (CopenHill; p77)

DESIGNER DENMARK

Characterised by its clean lines, minimalism and functional beauty, Danish design is rightly celebrated around the world. And the Danes themselves go absolutely mad for it – is there another country where the creators of chairs and lamps are household names, as are the chairs and lamps themselves?

Brilliant Buildings

Inspiring architecture is all around, from modernist gems like Arne Jacobsen's Danish National Bank to Amager Bakke (pictured above), a waste-to-energy plant with rooftop park.

Design Houses

Wandering the streets of central Copenhagen reveals active workshops and independent gallery-shops that showcase the latest from Denmark's talented designers.

BEST DESIGN EXPERIENCES

Explore the wildest flights of designer fancy at ❶ **Designmuseum Danmark** (p67).

Question what you know about architecture at the ❷ **Danish Architecture Centre** (p60).

Visit the immaculate ❸ **Finn Juhl House** (p92), designed by the esteemed architect.

Get creative at ❹ **Lego House** (p219), an interactive temple to the most famous design toy.

Traverse Olafur Eliasson's rainbow panorama topping ❺ **ARoS Aarhus Kunstmuseum** (p206), then explore art below.

A FAMILY AFFAIR

Denmark is family holiday perfection: relaxed, easy to get around, and packed with theme parks, historical reenactments, zoos and child-friendly beaches. Museums are typically free for little ones, and most have dedicated children's areas and activities. But be ready, pangs of envy come easily when meeting put-together Danish parents and their equally coiffed kids.

Fresh Air Fun

When schools are out for summer, legions of family-filled camper vans hit the road and park up alongside Denmark's many fine beaches, forests, parks and playgrounds.

Amusement Parks

Home to two of the world's oldest amusement parks, Denmark has got funfairs down to a splashy, squealy, ice-cream-sticky science.

Play for Free

Families can save kroner by visiting Copenhagen's free staffed playgrounds like Skydebanehaven, where playworkers help kids engage in creative games and explore nature.

BEST FAMILY EXPERIENCES

Forge fond childhood memories at Copenhagen's picture-perfect ❶ **Tivoli Gardens** (p56) theme park.

Push, pull, play, build and blow bubbles at ❷ **Experimentarium** (p84), a hands-on experience centre.

Amble through knee-high Lego towns, then whizz past icebergs aboard a speeding snowmobile 'coaster at ❸ **Legoland** (p221).

Climb above the tree canopy on the remarkable, all-wood ❹ **Forest Tower** (p124), then hit the high ropes course for more thrills.

Drive through the Danish savannah at ❺ **Knuthenborg Safari Park** (p149), home to free-roaming zebras, giraffes, rhinos and even retired circus elephants.

THE DANISH TABLE

Over the past couple of decades, Denmark's food scene has risen up out of the doldrums like a textbook soufflé. Today many visitors come just to eat – almost unthinkable not so long ago! This culinary transformation is anchored around the seasonal and sustainable New Nordic concept, championed by an ever-growing cast of Danish farmers, chefs, brewers, bakers and even vintners, and it's all here waiting to be tasted.

Fine Dining for All

Though the New Nordic movement coalesced around the fine-dining scene, its flavours and philosophy are widespread, tickling taste buds on tighter budgets, too.

Flavourful Farmsteads

Denmark's raw ingredients are the root of its culinary renaissance, and many rural farmsteads operate their own shops and cafes – perfect for an epicurean afternoon.

Casually Delicious

When this New Nordic philosophy marries a street-food sensibility, the results are thrilling – taste them at the food markets sprouting countrywide.

BEST FOODIE EXPERIENCES

Give in to temptation at ❶ **Torvehallerne KBH** (p52), where vendors sell Danish and international dishes alongside farm-fresh fruit and veg.

Indulge in a selection of Denmark's legendary pastries on our ❷ **bakery walking tour** (p71) through Copenhagen's ever-burgeoning upscale baking scene.

Admire the artful deliciousness of traditional Danish smørrebrød (open sandwiches), made with a modern twist at Copenhagen's ❸ **Selma** (p68).

Join the ❹ **oyster harvest** (p189) at Wadden Sea National Park, then pair the fruits of your foraging with crisp champagne.

Taste sparkling wine, whites and rosé at ❺ **Dyrehøj Vingaard** (p116), Denmark's largest winery and distillery.

Trawl the menus at the dozen-plus dockside restaurants of ❻ **Skagen Harbour** (p233), then pick your catch of the day.

GONZALES PHOTO/ALAMY LIVE NEWS ©

Icona Pop performing at SmukFest (p33)

HANDS IN THE AIR

Home to one of Europe's biggest music festivals, it's no secret that Denmark is Scandinavia's wild child. Swedes and Norwegians love to journey south for the party, letting loose at a huge variety of events in the packed Danish festival calendar, which covers everything from indie rock to esoteric electronica.

Culture

It's not all about partying, of course – Denmark hosts plenty of more mild-mannered gatherings centred on food, film, art, design and even Viking reenactment.

Summer Socialising

Danes know to make hay while the sun shines, meaning that summer is positively packed with fairs, fests and feasts, big and small. Absolutely join one if you can!

BEST FESTIVAL EXPERIENCES

Party to folk music at ❶ **Tønder Festival** (p192) for four days each August.

Experience ❷ **Smukfest** (p33), 'Denmark's most beautiful' pop and rock festival.

Get your rocks off at ❸ **Roskilde** (p113), a city of 130,000 souls including music fans from around the globe.

Join the party parade at ❹ **Copenhagen Pride** (p284), Denmark's largest LGBTIQ+ festival.

Immerse yourself in a world of theatre and music at the ❺ **HC Andersen Festival** (p160), held every August in Odense.

ISLANDS OF ADVENTURE

With 443 named and 72 inhabited islands, Denmark is a true archipelagic nation. Ranging in size from Zealand with nearly 2.5 million people to a handful of tiny skerries that count a single, solitary resident each, flitting between islands (ideally utilising plenty of scenic ferries) is a fabulous way to experience the real Denmark.

Ferry Fun

The boat trip can be half the fun! Some of the smaller routes use lovely vintage ferries with wood panelling and on-board bars.

Island Etiquette

Some of these islands are truly tiny, so be aware of the effect your presence can have, both environmental and social. And book ahead!

Invisible Island

You might not have noticed, but the north of Jutland is itself also an island, the country's second largest. In 1825, the Limfjord broke through during a particularly violent storm.

BEST ISLAND EXPERIENCES

Wander (or bike) the gentle country lanes of idyllic ❶ **Ærø** (p172), a microcosm of rural Denmark at its most enchanting.

Set sail (or fly) to Denmark's sunshine island of Bornholm, then carry on to the clutch of scenic fort-islands at ❷ **Christiansø** (p140).

See the smoke and steam of the saltworks at ❸ **Læsø** (p239), first fired up in the 12th century.

Ramble the plunging chalk clifftops, uncover medieval church murals and stay overnight for Denmark's darkest skies at ❹ **Møn** (p146).

Strap into a blokart and race over the beaches of ❺ **Rømø** (p192), a summertime hotspot near the German border.

VIKING ENCOUNTERS

From the 8th to 11th centuries, Viking raiding parties in their longships were the scourge of northern Europe, but their story is far richer than mere plunder. The Vikings were not just raiders but successful traders, skilled mariners and daring explorers. Denmark proudly embraces its Viking heritage, making it easy to immerse yourself in this fascinating era. A wealth of Viking-centric attractions include archaeological sites, longship workshops, museum exhibits and kid-oriented Viking experience centres.

FROM LEFT: STIG ALENAS/SHUTTERSTOCK ©, NEKTOFADEEV/SHUTTERSTOCK ©, SOUTH FJORD MEDIA/SHUTTERSTOCK ©

Life in a Longhouse

The Danes have a seemingly limitless enthusiasm for dressing up and recreating history, especially when it comes to the Vikings. Get involved at outdoor museums and Viking camps around the country.

Modern Mariners

Roskilde's boat builders are doing some of the most exciting Viking work of all: building and sailing faithful longboat reconstructions using only the tools and building techniques of the time.

Awesome Earthworks

Most structures from the Viking Age have long since perished, but you can see the scale of Viking-era settlements by visiting the remains of ring forts.

Jelling (p222)

BEST VIKING EXPERIENCES

Savour the aroma of fresh timber in the King's Hall at ❶ **Sagnlandet Lejre** (p115), Denmark's most exciting Viking reconstruction project.

Relive the Viking Age at the ❷ **Ribe VikingeCenter** (p188), where staff in tunics demonstrate cooking, crafting, blacksmithing, sword fighting and archery.

Marvel at real Viking ships recovered from the Roskilde Fjord, and delve into interactive exhibits on Viking life at the ❸ **Viking Ship Museum** (p113).

See the legendary Viking runestones at ❹ **Jelling** (p222), telling how Harald Bluetooth conquered, Christianised and unified the Danish lands.

Wander between weathered stone grave markers at ❺ **Lindholm Høje** (p227), a Viking burial ground preserved under shifting sand for centuries.

Bicycles, Bornholm (p138)

FUN ON TWO WHEELS

Denmark and cycling are practically synonymous, and thanks to an extensive national network of cycle routes (with dedicated lanes even in countryside), and a flat-to-undulating landscape, it really might be the world's best country for biking. The Danes are cycle-mad, so if you want to get under the country's skin, start by getting on a bike.

Ride the Cities

Copenhagen in particular is known for its world-class bicycle infrastructure. Several of the recent harbour bicycle bridges have even become attractions in themselves.

Cruise the Countryside

Denmark has 11 national cycle routes, each roughly 300km to 500km long, plus oodles of regional and local routes. All are suited to recreational cyclists, including families.

BEST CYCLING EXPERIENCES

Cycle through craggy ❶ **Bornholm** (p138) on 235km of bike trails.

For thrills and spills, hit the heights of ❷ **Rold Skov** (p231), one of the best mountain-biking spots.

Explore Copenhagen's inner waterways on the ❸ **bike bridges** (p60), cruising past Nyhavn.

Tour Jutland's wild ❹ **West Coast** (p223), past miles of beaches and scenic dunes.

Hire a bike on ❺ **Ærø** (p172) to pootle through rural landscapes.

Embark on a ride along Den Grønne Sti, a parkland route from ❻ **Frederiksberg** (p86) to Nørrebro.

CASTLES & ROYAL RETREATS

Denmark's regal pedigree is easy to see – there are dozens of grand castles dotted around the country, along with hundreds of lesser manors and estates. The finest of these are a big part of what lends Denmark its famous fairy-tale allure, making a visit to at least one of these enchanting relics a must for every traveller.

FROM LEFT: GUSTAVO MS_PHOTOGRAPHY, TRABANTOS/SHUTTERSTOCK ©

Royal Rights

Denmark is, of course, still a monarchy, so many of the country's royal castles and palaces remain in active use, such as Amalienborg and Fredensborg.

Sleep Like a Queen

Many estate homes and castles operate as upscale hotels, while others are involved in agro-tourism. The Danske Slotte og Herregaarde association lists participating properties.

No Gods, No Masters

'Gods' is Danish for an estate or manor, and the countryside is littered with these former noble homes. Today many are involved in organic agriculture.

BEST CASTLE EXPERIENCES

Try to remember your Shakespeare as you explore the crypts at Hamlet's (fictional) stomping ground, ❶ **Kronborg Slot** (p104).

Meet the gaze of hundreds of portraits at ❷ **Frederiksborg Slot** (p109), a lakefront Renaissance marvel with magnificent gardens.

Explore ❸ **Egeskov Slot** (p166), a castle so beautiful it graced the cover of the previous edition of this guide!

Spot scenes from hit show *Borgen* at ❹ **Christiansborg Slot** (p53), the Danish parliament's HQ.

Admire the architectural interplay of old and new at ❺ **Koldinghus** (p194), creatively renovated after a devastating fire.

SAND, SEA & SURF

With so many kilometres of coast – 7314 to be exact – Denmark's shore-to-size ratio is ridiculously generous, and blessed with another geological treat to boot: miles and miles of pristine, powder-puff beaches. Of course, this is still Scandinavia, and the weather can be...uncooperative with would-be beachgoers, but if there's even the slightest hint of summer in the air, Danes hit the sand as fast as they can for a dose of sea salt and vitamin D.

FROM LEFT: PHILIPP SALVETER/SHUTTERSTOCK ©, METTE JOHNSEN FOR VISIT DENMARK ©, ROBIN SKJOLDBORG//GETTY IMAGES ©

Safe Swimming

Across something like 1300 registered beaches, lifeguards are comparatively rare – only about 60 have them, and typically only between mid-June and mid-August.

Winter Swimming

All swimming in Denmark requires a touch of bravado, but winter swimming takes a bucketload. That said, it's popular, and even has an annual festival in Skagen.

Check the Weather

Weather systems in Denmark can be highly localised. So if it's cool and cloudy in Copenhagen, you might still have sun on Zealand's north coast.

Surfer, Hvide Sande (p224)

BEST BEACH EXPERIENCES

Harness the wind at ❶ **Hvide Sande** (p224), Denmark's kite-surfing and windsurfing capital where beginners learn the ropes on the placid Ringkøbing Fjord.

Escape the capital at ❷ **Amager Strandpark** (p50), an urban beach where you can kick back on the sand or splash in the shallow lagoon.

Stand on the shore where two seas meet in ❸ **Skagen** (p235), then journey back across the dunes by tractor-bus.

Rub elbows (and sun cream) at ❹ **Hornbæk** (p108), one of Denmark's most popular beaches barely an hour from Copenhagen.

Find your own patch of pristine white sand at ❺ **Marielyst Strand** (p152), part of a 14km-long unbroken beach on the island of Falster.

REGIONS & CITIES

Find the places that tick all your boxes.

Aarhus, Central & Northern Jutland

PRISTINE COUNTRYSIDE, EPIC DUNES, BRILLIANT MUSEUMS

Denmark's second city has none of Copenhagen's name recognition, but all of the charm, from the iconic rainbow atop its art museum to the cobbles and cafes of the Latin Quarter. Head north across the Limfjord to Skagen, where two seas meet, or south for Lego fun in Billund.

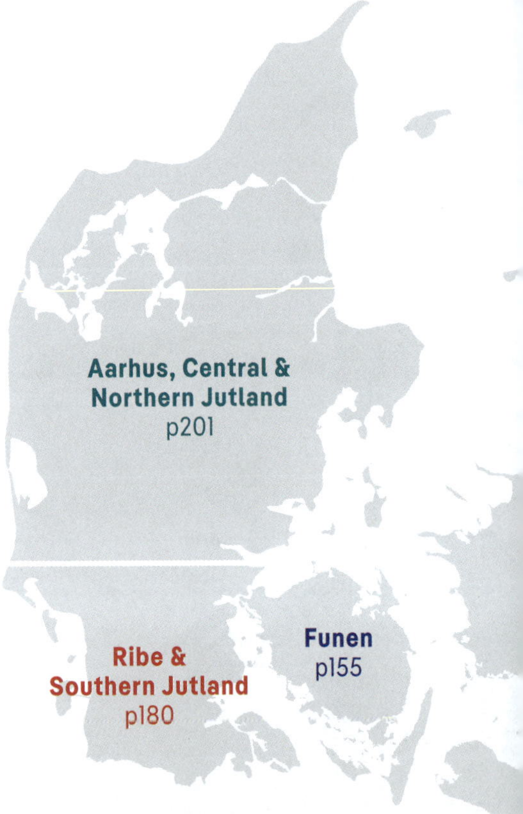

Aarhus, Central & Northern Jutland
p201

Ribe & Southern Jutland

OLD TOWNS AND THE SEA

Spot seals and seabirds at the Wadden Sea, Denmark's biggest national park, then forage for oysters over the tidal flats, or take a one-of-a-kind tractor ride to the island of Mandø. Soak up a bit of history in ancient Ribe, and discover edgy art and architecture in Kolding.

Ribe & Southern Jutland
p180

Funen
p155

Funen

FAIRY TALES, CASTLES AND GLITTERING ISLES

Half-timbered homes, harbourside villages and a certain HC Andersen together define Denmark's third-largest island. Throw in a couple of historic castles, and you'll wonder why it's so overlooked. Cross the water to uber-hygge Ærø, where thousands of lovebirds flock every year to tie the knot in the snuggest of settings.

The Faroe Islands

UNTAMED NATURAL BEAUTY AND SUBLIME ISOLATION

Marooned in the unpredictable squalls of the North Atlantic, this otherworldly corner of the Danish realm packs all the drama that the mainland lacks into one tiny package. Sheep nibble on turf-roofed houses, mountains tumble hundreds of metres into the sea, and flavours as wild as the landscape top tables at Ræst.

Copenhagen

SUPREMELY STYLISH, LIVEABLE CITY

Elegant, eclectic, designed-for-life Copenhagen is a foodie-focused, design-forward, cycle-friendly joy. Start the day with a lovingly crafted pastry, explore wonderful museums, swim in the sparkling harbour, graze on food and culture, and take your pick from cocktails, street food, craft beer, live music, fireworks and whimsical rollercoasters.

Zealand

BEACHES, UNESCO SIGHTS AND NATURAL WONDERS

Zealand is home to an enviable smorgasbord of nature and culture, where you can splash (or splash out) on the beaches of the north coast, inhale the woody scents of the reconstructed Viking hall at Lejre, and savour a Michelin-starred meal in tiny Præstø, all within a couple of hours of the capital.

Bornholm & the South Sea Islands

ISLAND LIFE WITH AN ARTISTIC TWIST

Just the mention of Bornholm, Denmark's 'sunshine island', can send Danes into song. This Baltic getaway is a hiking and biking paradise, with absurdly good crafts and culinary chops. Denmark's ancient chalk underbelly is spectacularly exposed at Møns Klint, while on Lolland-Falster, enigmatic standing stones gaze stoically out to sea.

Møns Klint (p142)

ITINERARIES

Danish Classics

Allow: 7 days **Distance**: 525km

Join the dots between Denmark's two biggest cities via a detour to the dramatic cliffs of Møns Klint. This itinerary gives you a taste of Zealand, Jutland and Funen, and can easily be extended with extra days in Copenhagen and Aarhus, further exploration on Jutland or a ferry trip to the South Sea Islands.

1

COPENHAGEN 2 DAYS

Get to know Scandinavia's **coolest capital** (p46), where quality of life has been honed to a fine art. The museums and cuisine are world-class, the waterfront setting (including a city harbour clean enough to swim in) is perfectly picturesque, and the cultural scene is as lively as anything you'll find north of Berlin. And all of it is easily navigated on foot or by bike.

2

MØN 1 DAY

The island of **Møn** (p142) lays claim to one of Denmark's natural wonders, the 120m-high chalk cliffs at Møns Klint. Follow trails that wind along the forested top before descending on endless stairways to the sea. Plan ahead to see the cliffs from the water, either by boat tour or guided SUP excursion.

Detour: *Spare a couple of hours to seek out Møn's medieval church murals and 5000-year-old tunnel graves.*

3

ODENSE 1 DAY

Famous as the birthplace of fairy tale maestro Hans Christian Andersen, **Odense** (p158) is a living tribute to Denmark's literary treasure, with all roads leading to high-concept HC Andersen Hus, a museum and children's centre in the heart of town. Chocolate-box lanes, riverboat rides, a railway museum, and a creative cache of cafes and eateries are yet more good reasons to make a day of it.

4 KOLDING ⏱1 DAY

Nestled at the end of its namesake fjord and overlooking the Little Belt, likeable **Kolding** (p194) is an ideal first stop on Jutland. The city's crown jewel, Koldinghus fortress (pictured), has weathered centuries of destruction and renewal, and now stands as a stunning architectural blend of old and new. Equally captivating is the Trapholt museum, a tribute to contemporary art and design.

5 BILLUND ⏱1 DAY

Who wouldn't be excited to visit the birthplace of Lego? Based here since the 1930s, you could say that Lego built **Billund** (p219) brick by brick. Major attractions include Legoland (pictured), Denmark's biggest tourist pull after Copenhagen, where carousels and coasters glide past detailed Lego landscapes. Across town, Lego House is an interactive play centre celebrating the toy.

6 AARHUS ⏱1 DAY

Known for its art, festivals, food and shopping, Denmark's student-filled **second city** (p206) never fails to win over all who 'discover' it. Between world-class art galleries, design-forward museums and the cobbled, cafe-filled Latin Quarter, you could comfortably spend two or three days here. Aarhus airport has onwards flights around Europe, or travel back to Copenhagen in style by taking the seaplane.

Kronborg Slot (p104)

ITINERARIES

Zip Through Zealand

Allow: 7–10 days **Distance**: 275km

Many of the highlights surrounding Copenhagen are within easy striking distance on public transport, so it can make sense to base yourself in the capital rather than hopping between accommodation. And what highlights! Hamlet's castle in Helsingør, Roskilde's dramatic cathedral and Viking ships, the impressive Louisiana museum and many more.

1 COPENHAGEN 2 DAYS

Eat, drink, and be merry - and do it all by bicycle. Denmark's **capital city** (p46) is not only a gastronomic mecca, but its bars and nightlife have for decades attracted Nordic neighbours looking to get a bit Dionysian. Throw in some world-class cultural attractions and a wonderful waterfront and you'll be wishing you could stay for another round.

2 HELSINGØR 1 DAY

Though best known for Hamlet's existential ponderings, **Helsingør** (p102) and its crown jewel Kronborg Slot aren't just for lovers of literature. Stroll the medieval city centre and admire the crooked half-timbered homes, dive into the maritime museum or enjoy a ferry trip across the Øresund to Sweden.

Detour: *Head just 10km down the coast from Helsingør to spend a day at Louisiana modern art museum.*

3 ROSKILDE 1 DAY

A trip to Denmark's old capital **Roskilde** (p111) reveals the majesty of Roskilde Cathedral (pictured), Denmark's finest religious building and royal burial place. Nearby on the edge of Roskilde Fjord, relics salvaged from its waters are on display at the Viking Ship Museum.

Detour: *The nearby town of Lejre is home to Lejre Land of Legends, which brings the Viking Age to life with historical reenactments.*

Kattegat
0 50 km
0 25 miles
Danish Riviera
5
Gilleleje
Tisvildeleje
2 Helsingør
Louisiana art museum
1hr
Frederiksborg Slot
1¼hr
Roskilde 25min
3
Lejre
1 Copenhagen
START/END
SWEDEN
Hässleholm
Karlshamn
Kristianstad
Hanöbukten
Lund
Malmö
1¼hr
Ystad
Trelleborg
1¼hr
Køge Bugt
Køge
1hr
Store Heddinge
ZEALAND
4 Stevns Klint
Fakse Ladeplads
Fakse Bugt
Præstø
Møn
Stege
Falster
Bornholm
6
Rønne
BALTIC SEA
GERMANY

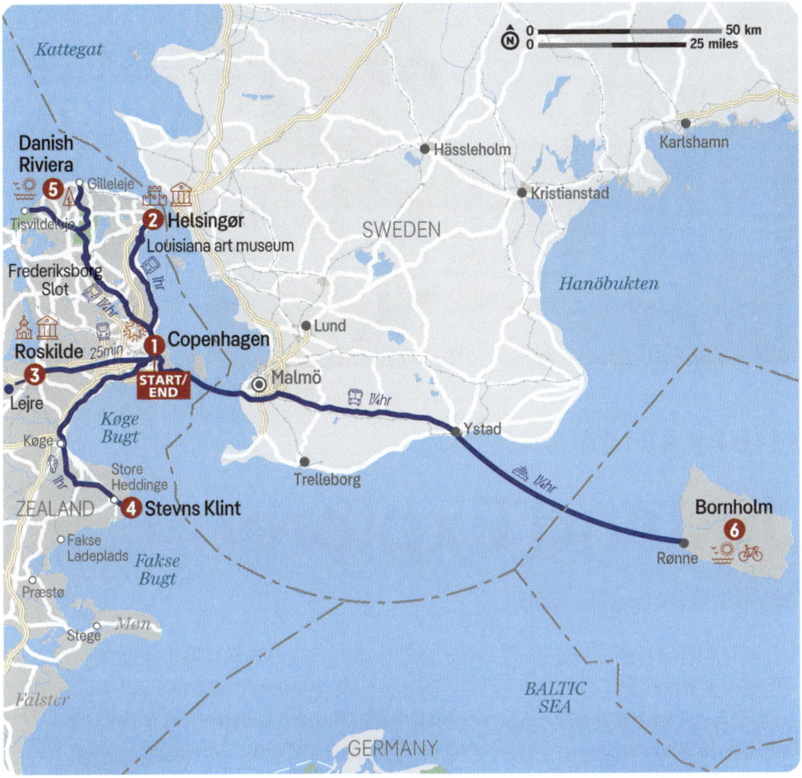

4

STEVNS KLINT 1 DAY

For Zealand's most dramatic landscapes, head for these 40m-tall chalk cliffs that plunge into the sea south of Copenhagen. A 22km footpath with beautiful views winds along the clifftop. The UNESCO-listed site has a visitor centre that explains why the exposed stratifications of **Stevns Klint** (p121) are one of the best places in the world to understand the fate of the dinosaurs.

5

THE DANISH RIVIERA 1 DAY

Head up to North Zealand for a day at the beach in **Tisvildeleje** (p110) and Gilleleje, both popular Danish summer getaways. If lounging on the sand doesn't do it for you, have a wander through cosy streets, flit between restaurants or take a hike through coastal forests.

Detour: *Consider making a stop at the impressive Frederiksborg Slot in Hillerød along the way.*

6

BORNHOLM 3 DAYS

Venture across the Baltic Sea for a blissful few days on Denmark's hidden holiday isle of **Bornholm** (p132). Though it's 150km off the Zealand coast, there are myriad daily connections by air and sea, putting stunning landscapes, ancient ruins and arty seaside villages within easy reach. It's also one of the best places in the country to saddle up for a bicycle tour.

Ribe (p184)

ITINERARIES

Jutland Explorer

Allow: 8 days **Distance**: 825km

Cheap European flights to airports in Billund, Aarhus and Aalborg means starting and ending your trip in Jutland is easy and affordable. There's more than enough to keep you busy in Denmark's largest region, from Lego fun in Billund to arty, well-heeled Skagen amid the dunes of Denmark's far north.

1 BILLUND ⏱ 2 DAYS

Superb for families, tiny **Billund** (p219) packs in some big sights, all within a few kilometres of the airport. The original Legoland theme park is great for kids from toddler age up to young teens, while Lego House sparks young minds with its Lego-building games and detailed dioramas. Lalandia waterpark (pictured) nearby is also a ridiculous amount of fun. Live the Lego dream by overnighting in a Lego-themed hotel or campsite.

2 RIBE ⏱ 1 DAY

Founded in the 9th century, **Ribe** (p184) is Denmark's oldest town and positively creaks with antique atmosphere. A walk through the cobbled streets around Ribe's Romanesque cathedral (pictured), whether by day or on the famous Nightwatchman Tour, is like travelling back to medieval Europe. Ribe is also the jumping-off point for nature excursions into the Wadden Sea National Park.

3 THE WEST COAST ⏱ 1 DAY

Denmark's windswept North Sea coast is lined with sweeping sand dunes, summerhouses and crumbling concrete bunkers left over from WWII (pictured). It's a supremely scenic drive up the coast and through Thy National Park, stopping at remote seaside communities like Hvide Sande and **Klitmøller** (p230) – the latter set on a stretch of coast charmingly known as Denmark's 'Cold Hawaii'.

4

SKAGEN ⏱ 1 DAY

Skagen (p233), at Denmark's northernmost tip, perches at the exact point where the Baltic and the North Sea collide. This fishing community became a haven for 19th-century painters drawn to the ethereal seaside light. Today it's an iconic Danish holiday destination, and its picture-book neighbourhoods heave with visitors in summer.

Detour: *On your way south stop at the new REGAN Vest bunker museum.*

5

AARHUS ⏱ 2 DAYS

After artsy-but-isolated Skagen, **Aarhus** (p206), Denmark's youthful second city, will feel like a full-on metropolis! Two days is just enough time to dip into world-class museums and vibrant art galleries, indulge in some waterside fun, and eat and drink at some of the city's top-rated restaurants, bars and cafes. Put ARoS Art Museum and Den Gamle By (pictured) at the top of your sightseeing list.

6

SILKEBORG ⏱ 1 DAY

Silkeborg (p214) sits astride Denmark's Lake District – a connected chain of idyllic lakes where you can swim, paddle-board, kayak or just take a scenic boat tour. Stop en route to climb the grandiosely named Himmelbjerget ('Sky Mountain'), one of the country's highest peaks at a whopping 147m. Back in town, visit the 2400-year-old Tollund Man, exhumed from a bog and on display at the Silkeborg Museum.

Svendborg (p168)

ITINERARIES

Southern Island Hopping

Allow: 8 days **Distance**: 390 km

See a different side to Denmark on this jaunt from Copenhagen through the South Sea Islands all the way to the eastern edge of Jutland. Taking it slow on rural roads, you'll pass through the islands of Møn, Falster, Lolland, Langeland and Funen, before setting sail to idyllic Ærø.

1 COPENHAGEN 2 DAYS

Dive into hundreds of years of history at one of **Copenhagen**'s (p46) impressive museums and royal palaces, where you can learn about everything from wartime history to the crown jewels. Then fast forward to the present at edgy galleries and boutiques, and get on-trend with the latest fashion and design innovations being dreamed up in workshops all over the city.

2 MØN 1 DAY

Take in some of Scandinavia's inkiest nights on **Møn** (p142), recognised as an International Dark Sky Park for the thrilling starscapes that paint pitch-black skies. Combined with the soaring sea-cliff geography of Møns Klint, and woodlands filled with wild orchids (pictured) and butterflies, the island's wonders are hard to beat. For culture and history, seek out Møn's muraled medieval churches.

3 LOLLAND-FALSTER 1 DAY

These twin islands meet in the middle at the town of **Nykøbing Falster** (p151). On the Falster side of the sound is the safari park of Knuthenborg (pictured), while in Lolland you'll find Middelaldercentret, a recreated 15th-century village peopled by costumed craftspeople. From there, take the ferry to Langeland and its fascinating Cold War Museum, then onwards to Funen.

Kattegat
Skanderborg
Odder
Horsens
Juelsminde
Samsø
Fredericia
Middelfart
Otterup
Søndersø
Odense
Årup
Funen
Nyborg
Ørbæk
Hårby
Lille Bælt
Egeskov Slot
Faaborg
Als
6
Fynshav
1hr
6 END
Sønderborg
5
Ærø
4 Svendborg
1hr
Rudkøbing
Langeland
2hr
Nakskov
Maribo
3
Lolland
Femerbælt
GERMANY
Odden
Sejerø Bugt
Kalundborg
Store Bælt
Jyderup
Gørlev
Korsør
Slagelse
Sorø
Ringsted
Frederiksværk
Isefjord
Holbæk
Roskilde
valeriiaarnaud
ZEALAND
Helsingør
Hillerød
Frederikssund
Copenhagen
START 1
Køge
Køge Bugt
Store Heddinge
2hr
Næstved
Fakse Bugt
Præstø
Smålandsfarvandet
Vordingborg
Møn 2
1½hr
3 Falster
Nykøbing Falster
BALTIC SEA
Gedser
0 50 km
0 25 miles

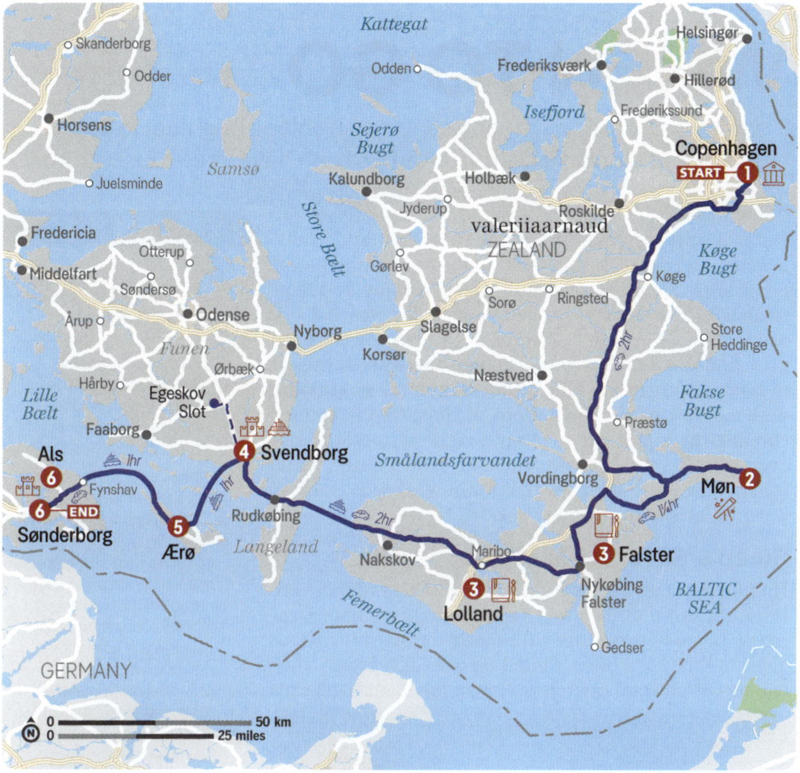

4

SVENDBORG 1 DAY

Breathe the sea air in **Svendborg** (p168), home of Denmark's sailing fraternity and the main gateway into the South Funen Archipelago. Admire modern yachts and antique schooners bobbing in the harbour, then go aboard the vintage *M/S Helge* for a lazy loop around the Svendborgsund.

Detour: *Try to squeeze in a trip to the 16th-century Egeskov Slot, one of Denmark's most beautiful castles.*

5

ÆRØ 2 DAYS

A contender for the title of Denmark's loveliest island, **Ærø** (p172) is peppered with thatched-roofed, half-timbered houses set along sleepy country roads tailor-made for cycling trips. Cobbled Ærøskøbing (pictured) is Ærø's nicest town, full of folksy museums and food shops selling artisanal produce. Bed down in a historic inn, or skip town and sleep in a shelter under the stars.

6

ALS & SØNDERBORG 1 DAY

Depart from Ærø on a different ferry, this time towards the island of Als. Straddling the Als Sund between Als and Jutland, the town of **Sønderborg** (p197) has changed hands frequently between Denmark and Germany, and the German influence here remains strong. Visit Sønderborg Slot (pictured) to learn about the region's past, then plan your next steps now you've made it to Jutland.

WHEN TO GO

It comes as no surprise that Scandinavia shines brightest in the summer, but Copenhagen and Aarhus both have year-round appeal.

Copenhagen sees 17 glorious hours of daylight on the summer solstice, while all summer long Denmark's trails, beaches and parks throng with ramblers, swimmers and picnickers. Shoulder seasons (March to May and September to November) can be chancier for weather but are much less crowded. Winter does tend towards the grey and gloomy, but Danes have time-tested, hyper-hyggefied ways of warding off the winter blues, starting with candles, cakes and gallons of *gløgg* (mulled wine). Outside the major cities, many tourist attractions and even restaurants shutter completely over winter, while others may limit offerings to certain weekends, such as during Christmas and New Year.

Sleep & Save, Danish Style

Holiday cottages are a national institution, and there are thousands of rental cottages available throughout Denmark. If you're travelling with family or planning a longer stay (they are often rented on a weekly basis), they can represent good savings over an equivalent hotel stay.

Holiday cottages, Løkken (p238)

I LIVE HERE

SUMMER SECRETS

Trine Hahnemann *(@trinehahnemann)* is owner of Hahnemanns Køkken and author of *Copenhagen Food*.

'When I was a child, my father had a sailboat moored at Copenhagen's Skudehavn marina in Nordhavn. It's still one of my favourite spots for a sunny summer picnic, and one of the few secrets still left in Copenhagen, full of quirky DIY fishermen's shacks overlooking the sea. I'm always reminded of my father relaxing on board – sharing a beer with the locals, talking about the weather, the boat or just sitting and saying nothing.'

SEASONS

Danes traditionally measure seasons of the year by calendar month rather than astronomically between equinox and solstice. Therefore spring *(forår)* is considered to start on 1 March, summer *(sommer)* on 1 June, autumn *(efterår)* on 1 September and winter *(vinter)* on 1 December.

Weather through the Year (Copenhagen)

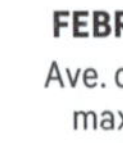

JANUARY	FEBRUARY	MARCH	APRIL	MAY	JUNE
Ave. daytime max: **3°C**	Ave. daytime max: **4°C**	Ave. daytime max: **7°C**	Ave. daytime max: **12°C**	Ave. daytime max: **17°C**	Ave. daytime max: **20°C**
Days of rainfall: **15**	Days of rainfall: **11**	Days of rainfall: **14**	Days of rainfall: **12**	Days of rainfall: **11**	Days of rainfall: **12**

WATER, WATER EVERYWHERE

Denmark is defined by water: you're never more than 50km from the sea. But take note of the temperature before hitting the beach: the water tops out at a refreshing 20°C in July/August, but averages nosedive to around 4°C come January/February.

Major Festivals

Electro-fied revellers throng the streets and clubs of Copenhagen (p46) during **Distortion**, a rowdy summer dance-music festival, where the subwoofers shake to the latest from Danish and international DJs and rappers. **June**

With 130,000 attendees, the legendary **Roskilde Festival** is one of Europe's largest, and for a week each year Roskilde (p111) becomes Denmark's fourth-largest city – sorry Aalborg. **Late June–early July**

Denmark's number two festival, **Smukfest** unfolds in a beautiful beech forest outside of Aarhus (p206). With a diverse line-up and sweet forest troll for a mascot, this is a magical, musical gathering with a cosy Danish twist. **August**

One of Denmark's best **Christmas fairs** is held in Aarhus' Den Gamle By (p211). Shop for gift-worthy handicrafts and indulge in *æbleskiver* (spherical pancakes) and *gløgg* (mulled wine). **Mid-November–December**

Quirky Celebrations

Dress up and join the street party as **Aalborg Carnival** marks the arrival of spring. Scandinavia's largest carnival draws up to 80,000 revellers in fancy dress. **May**

Every summer, **sand sculpture festivals** come to Hundested on Zealand (p110) and Søndervig on Jutland's west coast. Metres-high creations depict everything from mythical creatures to famous landmarks. **May–October**

Part funfair, part concert, part Europe's largest horse market, **Hjallerup Market** is a celebration of rural Denmark that's been held in northern Jutland since 1744. **June**

Learn about the Denmark of legend at **Viking festivals** in Højbjerg and Jelling (p222), where tunic-clad smiths, weavers and leatherworkers show off traditional crafts, and visitors can enjoy horse rides, Viking-age music and storytelling. **July**

I LIVE HERE

WINTER WATERS

Copenhagen-based **Laura Hall** writes about Scandinavia and documents her swimming around the region *@hello_laura_hall.*

'Winter bathing has gotten really popular in recent years in Copenhagen. It's an electrifying experience, daring to dip in the incredibly cold water and coming out with pink skin and a new zest for life. I've never regretted an ice-cold swim. If you've never tried it before, go with a friend or do it as part of a sauna experience.'

Winter bather

POWERFUL WINDS

Denmark produces about 50% of its energy from wind power – the highest proportion in the world. Be ready for unexpected gusts and gales anywhere in the country, but West Jutland is especially notorious. It's also a great spot for kitesurfing.

JULY	AUGUST	SEPTEMBER	OCTOBER	NOVEMBER	DECEMBER
Ave. daytime max: **22°C**	Ave. daytime max: **22°C**	Ave. daytime max: **18°C**	Ave. daytime max: **13°C**	Ave. daytime max: **8°C**	Ave. daytime max: **4°C**
Days of rainfall: **12**	Days of rainfall: **12**	Days of rainfall: **14**	Days of rainfall: **15**	Days of rainfall: **15**	Days of rainfall: **15**

FROM LEFT: JACEK CHABRASZEWSKI/SHUTTERSTOCK ©, LIFESTYLE PICTURES/ALAMY STOCK PHOTO ©

Copenhagen

GET PREPARED FOR DENMARK

Useful things to load in your bag, your ears and your brain

Clothes

Trainers: For Denmark's topography, a pair of trainers covers most bases. Be warned: heeled shoes are no friend of cobbles.

Everyday wear: Danes tend to dress casually but stylishly. Think jeans, trainers and good quality sweaters. Accessories like scarves complete the look. When in doubt, go head to toe in black.

Water-resistant shoes/boots: Very welcome outside of summer when it gets wet and muddy in the countryside.

Rain gear: Danish weather is fickle, so pack a water-resistant outer layer. An umbrella wouldn't go amiss, either.

Knitwear: A cosy sweater is worth its weight in gold throughout most of the year.

Manners

Be on time. If you make a plan with a Dane, they'll be on time, and so should you. Fashionably late is not the look.

Don't walk in the **bike lanes**.

Danes are not big on **small talk**. Minding the privacy of others is considered a way to show respect, so people don't usually pour their hearts out (or comment on the weather) to fellow passengers at the bus stop.

Layers: Layering is key. Even in summer you'll be glad of an extra garment for cool evenings and coastal winds.

Swimwear: For that impromptu harbour dip, if you dare.

READ

The Complete Fairy Tales (Hans Christian Andersen; 1874) These tales have shaped childhoods worldwide for over 150 years.

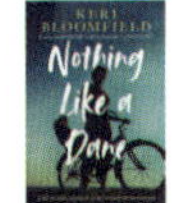

Nothing Like A Dane (Keri Bloomfield; 2022) A witty take on life in Denmark from a Kiwi who moved to Copenhagen with her young child.

Miss Smilla's Feeling for Snow (Peter Høeg; 1992) This progenitor of Nordic noir explores Danish-Greenlandic tensions.

The Old Man and His Sons (Heðin Brú; 1940) As the Faroe Islands' isolation begins to fade, families are torn between tradition and modernity.

Words

Danes are top-notch Anglophones (though they're sometimes shy about speaking), but a few words can go a long way in breaking the ice. As you struggle with the pronunciations, remember that Danes themselves will tell you their language sounds like someone speaking with a hot potato in their mouth – so *værsgo* (vass-go; here you go):

'**hej**' (*hi*) is easy enough for English speakers to assimilate, but say it twice – '**hej hej**' – and it becomes an informal goodbye.

'**tak**' (*tahk*) 'thank you'.

You've got a few options for 'you're welcome': '**selv tak**' (*sel tahk*) means 'thank you, too', while '**det var så lidt**' (*de vah so lit*) works as 'it was nothing'.

'**vær så venlig**' (*ver soh ven-lee*) is the equivalent of 'please', but it's used much less frequently than in English.

'**undskyld**' (*un-school*) is the word if you would like to get someone's attention, or bump into them.

'**hygge**' (*hoo-geh*) is the Danish catch-all for a good time spent with good people. Loosely translated as 'cosy', Danes describe any number of things as hygge, and tell each other '**tak for en hyggelig dag/aften**' (*tahk fuhr een hoo-gili dai/ahfen*) – 'thanks for an enjoyable day/evening'.

'**tak for sidst**' (*tahk fur seest*) is a bit unusual in English, used when first seeing someone you hung out with previously to say 'thanks for last time'.

'**vi ses**' (*vee seis*) is another informal goodbye: 'see you'.

'**hjælp**' (*yelp*) is if you need urgent assistance.

WATCH

Another Round (Thomas Vinterberg; 2020) Oscar-winning comedy about teachers trying to spice up their lives with booze.

Matador (Erik Balling; 1978–82) Beloved TV series following small-town drama in the 1930s and '40s.

Borgen (Søren Kragh-Jacobsen, Rumle Hammerich; 2010–22) The hit came back in 2022, with Birgitte Nyborg as foreign minister.

Flee (Jonas Poher Rasmussen; 2021) Oscar-nominated animated documentary about a gay Afghan refugee who flees to Denmark.

Babette's Feast (Gabriel Axel; 1987) Oscar winner about two stifled sisters and their cook.

LISTEN

Midt Om Natten (Kim Larsen; 1983) Sweet singalong pop from Denmark's biggest rock star. Learn a few words and you'll be friends with the whole bar.

Carnival (Gilli; 2022) Brazilian-inspired album from one of the loudest voices on the Danish rap scene – a favourite among teens with Bluetooth speakers.

I Danmark Er Jeg Født (Natasja; 2007) Danish dancehall star Natasja died unexpectedly after hitting it big, but her tunes live on as party-starters.

Slør (Eivør; 2015) Ethereal vocals and spacey beats build a dreamscape from prolific Faroese songstress Eivør; there's an English version too.

ULF SVANE/LONELY PLANET ©

Seafood, Copenhagen

THE FOOD SCENE

Two decades of innovation combined with local inspiration have seen Denmark go from culinary backwater to gastronomic powerhouse.

When the first edition of this guidebook was published in 1996, there were five Michelin stars in the whole country – today there are nearly 40. This dramatic change of fortunes really began in 2004, when a symposium of Nordic chefs came together and drafted a 10-point manifesto defining what they saw as the philosophy and aims of their work. They declared New Nordic cuisine to be defined by seasonality, sustainability, local ingredients and produce, and the use of Nordic cooking methods to create food that originally and distinctly reflects Scandinavian culture, geography and history.

From this ambitious framework, a movement was born, which has changed the face of food in Denmark and well beyond. It has also meant that traditional Danish cuisine, with pork, potatoes, fish and rye bread as its core ingredients, has enjoyed a resurgence, where classic meals are prepared not only according to habit, but with the care and attention of accomplished chefs,

Best Danish Dishes

TARTELETTER
Baked tartlet shells filled with a savoury chicken and asparagus sauce.

FLÆSKESTEG
Roast pork served with boiled and caramelised potatoes, plus red cabbage.

HAKKEBØF
Beef burger with fried onions, served with potatoes, brown sauce and beets.

KARBONADER
Breaded pork and veal patties served with a creamy pea-and-carrot sauce.

dedicated to drawing out all the beauty and flavour of their Nordic tradition and terroir.

New Nordic

No one has flown the New Nordic flag higher than Copenhagen's world-famous Noma restaurant and its owner-chef René Redzepi, renowned for playing with modest, often-overlooked ingredients and digging up long-lost food traditions. Noma earned the title of best restaurant in the world on five occasions between 2010 and 2021, before announcing that, after ushering in a new era of fine dining, the Noma space was to transform into a food research lab from 2025. You can still taste the Noma magic at roving residencies around the world (Kyoto in late 2024) and at their burger spin-off in Copenhagen, POPL.

Multiple waves of Noma alumni have also gone on to found restaurants of their own, so the Noma–New Nordic ripple effect continues to expand, and is slowly becoming more accessible as well.

Traditional Fare

Classic Danish grub tends towards the carnivorous, with pork (*flæsk* or *svinekød*)

Stegt flæsk med persillesauce

Tivoli Food Festival

FOOD FESTIVALS

Copenhagen Cooking *(copenhagencooking.dk)* Tables spill onto the streets for this collaborative August cook-off.

Tivoli Food Festival *(tivoli.dk)* May sees Tivoli Gardens fill up with food stalls, tasting events and themed workshops.

Food Festival *(foodfestival.dk)* Aarhus hosts this educational showcase focused on teaching cooking using high-quality local food.

Sol over Gudhjem *(sogk.dk)* Denmark's biggest cooking competition takes place in June on Bornholm, as chefs compete using island produce.

Nordjysk Madfestival *(nordjyskmadfestival.dk)* Taste flavours beyond the Limfjord at this north Jutland event showcasing local producers.

Mikkeller Beer Celebration Faroe Islands *(mikkeller.com/events/mbcfi)* A global line-up of breweries converges on Tórshavn in October for two days of hoppy fun.

STEGT FLÆSK MED PERSILLESAUCE
The national dish, fried pork belly served with boiled potatoes in a creamy parsley sauce.

RØDGRØD MED FLØDE
Classic of stewed berries and cream, and perhaps Denmark's worst tongue-twister.

BRÆNDENDE KÆRLIGHED
Means 'burning love' – this bacon-onion sauce with mashed potatoes is as homely as it gets.

WIENERSCHNITZEL
Made with pork and garnished with *dreng* – lemon, capers, anchovies and grated horseradish.

LEFT: MARIDAV/SHUTTERSTOCK ©, RIGHT: ALAN MALTA LEITAO/SHUTTERSTOCK ©

Smørrebrød

in particular found everywhere, served as *flæskesteg* (roast pork), *mørbradbøf* (pork tenderloin) and comfort-food favourite *frikadeller* – fried minced-pork meatballs commonly served with boiled potatoes and red cabbage. Crispy *flæskesvær* (pork crackling or rind) is a favourite salty snack.

Thousands of kilometres of coastline mean there's also no shortage of excellent seafood options. *Sild* (herring) is a staple, often served pickled and flavoured with sherry, mustard or curry; it's also commonly served smoked or fried. *Laks* (cured or smoked salmon) is also prolific, a favourite dish being *gravad laks*, cured or salted salmon marinated in dill and served with a sweet mustard sauce.

Smørrebrød

These elaborate, universally loved open sandwiches are Denmark's most famous dish – they've even starred on their own Danish postage stamps! With their roots in late 19th-century Copenhagen beer halls, these spruced-up bar snacks soon took on a life of their own, ultimately becoming one of the cornerstones of Danish cuisine.

The basic smørrebrød comes in a number of configurations, starting with a slice of rye bread and topped with anything from roast beef or pork to juicy shrimps, pickled herring, liver pâté, potatoes or a fried fish fillet, artfully assembled and looking (almost) too good to eat.

Specialities

Smørrebrød

Kartoffelmad Sliced new potatoes, mayo and crispy/raw onions.
Med fiskefilet Breaded fried plaice with Danish remoulade and a squeeze of lemon.

Sweet Treats

Kanelsnegle Cinnamon roll, sometimes frosted.
Wienerbrød A 'Danish' abroad is ironically known here as *wienerbrød* – Viennese bread.
Tebirkes Flaky pastry filled with a marzipan spread and sprinkled with poppy seeds.
Hindbærsnitter Frosted raspberry bars, like a classy Pop-Tart.
Koldskål Summer treat of sweet vanilla-flavoured buttermilk topped with crunchy biscuits called *kammerjunkere*.
Risalamande Christmas rice pudding with whipped cream, chopped almonds and cherry sauce.

Street Food

Rundstykke Bread roll, often multigrain, served with butter, cheese or jam.
Pølse Iconic Danish hot dog, served with mustard, ketchup, Danish remoulade, crispy onions and pickles.

Koldskål

Dare to Try

Sild Pickled herring comes in several varieties like *kryddersild* (with warm winter spices), *karrysild* (with curry), and *marinerede sild* (the 'classic' with vinegar and onion.
Akvavit Danish version of this Scandinavian spirit favourite is closely associated with Aalborg and flavoured with caraway seeds.
Øllebrød Old rye bread soaked in beer overnight and blended into a breakfast porridge with cream and sugar.
Lakrids Danes will sneak liquorice into just about anything – up to and including ice cream.

MEALS OF A LIFETIME

Geranium (p60) The 16-course menu at three-Michelin-starred Geranium is an artistic tour de force.
Alchemist (p79) Now that Noma is hanging up its chef's whites, here is a brilliant substitute, crafting food odysseys over 18 courses.
Kadeau (p136) It's worth the price of passage to Bornholm to dine at this remote, Michelin-starred outpost of Copenhagen's esteemed restaurant.
Henne Kirkeby Kro (p223) A west Jutland redefinition of the Danish country inn, serving meat, veg and dairy from its own smallholding.
Ræst (p250) Traditional Faroese delicacies with a modern twist, served in one of the most historic buildings in Tórshavn.
Substans (p211) High-tech New Nordic tasting menus. Big views over Aarhus harbour.

THE YEAR IN FOOD

SPRING

Springtime is defined by the fresh flavours of tender new potatoes served on *kartoffelmad* smørrebrød or in potato salad with fresh dill, flaky tartlets filled with asparagus and chicken, and foraged *ramsløg* (wild garlic, pictured).

SUMMER

Summer is pure zest. Strawberries and cream (pictured) are sunshine in a bowl, while buttermilk *koldskål* is a refreshing ice-cream alternative. Fizzy *hyldeblomstsaft* (elderflower cordial) tastes like a picnic.

AUTUMN

Savoury flavours return, with foragers heading to the woods for Karl Johan (porcini) mushrooms, chanterelles and sour sea buckthorn (pictured). Kale, beetroot and squash start to appear.

WINTER

The *julebord* (Christmas table) defines the season, with hearty flavours from sweet, buttery *risengrød* (rice porridge, pictured), roast pork and duck, red cabbage and brown gravy all de rigueur.

SOREN SVENDSEN/GETTY IMAGES ©

Mountain biking, Copenhagen

THE OUTDOORS

Look elsewhere for extremes: Danish nature is as bucolic as it comes, and the countryside is easily accessible by foot, pedal or paddle.

First of all, leave the skis at home (except at CopenHill). Denmark's highest peak doesn't scratch 200m, but there are still loads of low-altitude adventures on offer. Danes are avid cyclists, and the gentle terrain is ideal for a bicycling break. All those fjord systems invite scenic kayak, SUP or canoe safaris, while the blustery North Sea Coast is a world-class wind-surfing and kite-boarding destination. Or simply ramble through idyllic forests, fields and along miles of scenic coast.

Cycling

It's hard to think of a better country for cycle tourism than Denmark. The infrastructure is excellent, the terrain favourable and the local attitudes fully supportive. Throw in 12,000km of signposted cycle routes and relatively quiet country roads, and you're in pedalling paradise.

There are 11 national cycling routes in excellent condition, as well as a smorgasbord of regional and local routes to choose from. The routes are well suited to recreational or occasional cyclists, including families with kids.

Most major city roads and central areas have dedicated bike lanes (with their own signage), and bicycle racks are found everywhere. Danish cyclists also enjoy favourable rights in traffic, and cyclists and drivers coexist well – likely because many of the drivers are frequently cyclists themselves.

Furthermore, distances are small, rentals are common and bikes are allowed on most

More Outdoor Action

HORSE RIDING
There are many places to go horse riding, from coastal beaches and dunes near **Skagen** (p233) to **Thy National Park** (p230).

ROCK CLIMBING
Bornholm's (p132) rocky geology, from granite outcrops to sea cliffs, makes it Denmark's best climbing spot.

MOUNTAIN BIKING
In place of mountains, the trail-scarred glacial hills of **Svanninge Bakker** (p174) are a top spot for mountain bikers.

FAMILY ADVENTURES

Time-travel at the **Sagnlandet Lejre outdoor museum** (p115), where hiking paths in the surrounding fields detail local archaeological finds.

Go cycling, kitesurfing or boating at **Ringkøbing Fjord** (p223), an extraordinary windswept landscape.

Hop between islands in the **South Funen Archipelago** (p172), riding tiny ferries and licking birch-juice ice cream.

Cut loose on the sand at Copenhagen's **Amager Strandpark** (p50), an artificial lagoon with kid-friendly shallow water and playgrounds.

Spot seals lolling on sand banks and watch the wonder of starling murmurations with a **Wadden Sea Visitor Centre** (p189) wildlife tour.

Go surfing in the wavy waters of Denmark's 'Cold Hawaii' at **Thy National Park** (p130), or have a blast exploring dunes.

trains, some buses and all ferries. Helmets are not mandated.

Swimming & Watersports

The temperatures can certainly be bracing, but Danes love an excuse to get in the water – and with 7314km of coastline, 406 islands, and dozens of beaches with clean water and silky-soft sand, they've got plenty.

July and August are the top months for swimmers, and the calm Baltic is generally a bit warmer than the wilder North Sea – where you should watch out for strong currents. Jutland's wind-lashed west coast attracts surfers of all stripes. Gnarly Klitmøller (p230) has become known as Denmark's 'Cold Hawaii', while at Hvide Sande (p224) you can take wind-surfing and kite-surfing lessons on the placid fjord just inland. Stand-up paddle boards can be hired from harbours and beaches all over Denmark, and both Copenhagen and Aarhus have wakeboarding/water-skiing cable parks.

Inland, canoeists and kayakers can paddle for hours or even days along scenic rivers and lakes, such as near Lyngby (p92) or through Jutland's Lake District (p214).

Canoeing, Lake District

Walking & Hiking

Denmark has bags of nature but very little of what you might call wilderness. Still, there are plenty of lovely trails and forests for a good romp through the woods, and any tourist office will be able to point you towards walking trails – udinaturen.dk has an impressively thorough index and map as well.

There are also a couple of 'Camino' pilgrim-inspired trails; the most popular being the 127km Camøno on Møn, and also the 27km Amarmino across Copenhagen's outlying island of Amager.

In Jutland, hikers gravitate towards Thy National Park and the Lake District, while the 220km Øhavsstien (Archipelago Trail; p176) goes through Funen and its archipelago. There are also shorter hikes and trails around landmarks like Møns Klint, Stevns Klint and the Grenen sand spit, or Hammeren on Bornholm.

SKATEBOARDING

Skate parks for a variety of skill levels can be found in Copenhagen's **Refshaleøen** (p78) and Fælledparken – and at Ebeltoft.

SAILING

Denmark has more than 350 marinas, and the sailing gene is strong in this archipelago nation. Try it at **Svendborg** (p168).

BIRDING

The Faroe Islands' **Vestmanna bird cliffs** (p254) are one of Europe's most extreme birding sites, with a 600m drop into the sea.

STARGAZING

The entire island of **Møn** (p142) has been named an International Dark Sky Park thanks to its crystal-clear night skies and brilliant starscapes.

The Faroe Islands

National Parks

1. Nationalpark Kongernes Nordsjælland (p108)
2. Skjoldungernes (Scyldings Land) National Park (p114)
3. Wadden Sea National Park (p189)
4. Mols Bjerge National Park (p216)
5. Thy National Park (p230)

Cycling

1. Bornholm (p132)
2. Thy National Park (p230)
3. Copenhagen's bike bridges (p60)
4. Rold Skov (p231)
5. Nysted (p150)
6. Copenhagen to Helsingør (p103)
7. Nordkystruten (p110)
8. Ærø (p172)

Kitesurfing/ Windsurfing

1. Lynæs (p110)
2. Hvide Sande (p224)
3. Klitmøller (p230)
4. Marielyst (p151)
5. Klintholm Havn (p144)

NORTH SEA

0 50 km
0 25 miles

ACTION AREAS

Where to find Denmark & the Faroe Islands' best outdoor activities.

Walking/Hiking

1. Archipelago Trail (p176)
2. The Camøno (p146)
3. Stevns Klint Trampesti (p121)
4. Tjørnuvík (p255)
5. Mols Bjerge (p216)
6. Thy National Park (p230)
7. Møns Klint (p142)

Kayaking/Canoeing

1. Møns Klint (p144)
2. Central Copenhagen (p60)
3. Silkeborg & the Lakes District (p214)
4. Esrum Sø (p108)
5. Svendborg (p169)
6. Faaborg (p175)

DENMARK

THE GUIDE

Chapters in this section are organised by hubs and their surrounding areas. We see the hub as your base in the destination, where you'll find unique experiences, local insights, insider tips and expert recommendations. It's also your gateway to the surrounding area, where you'll see what and how much you can do from there.

Stevns Klint (p121)

Copenhagen

SUPREMELY STYLISH, LIVEABLE CITY

Copenhagen hosts candy-coloured half-timbered houses, historic ports and palaces, and is one of Europe's best-designed and most people-centred modern capitals, with some of the world's finest places to eat.

The Danish capital is regularly ranked on global indices as among the best places in the world to live, but it wasn't always thus. In the late 1990s, industries and families had moved out of the city, and many of the people who remained were those who couldn't afford to leave. The canals were dirty and harbourside was not a place you'd want to wander. Many homes didn't have bathrooms, with many apartment blocks having a shared toilet in the backyard, and local *badeanstalter* (communal baths) providing washing facilities. The city needed to attract people back, to bring investment, so they took out loans to improve the city centre. The waterways were cleaned in the early 2000s, making it possible to swim, and urban regeneration saw areas turn from no-go to go-to areas.

Ever since, Copenhagen has been on the up, and this charismatic harbour town is today likely to tempt you to start dreaming of a Scandi life, whirring along on your bicycle, dressed in tastefully muted colours with a a bunch of sunflowers in your basket. There are the obvious attractions, such as Tivoli Gardens, the Little Mermaid statue, the royal palaces and canals, but it's the people-centred design and architecture that are the allure. It's the well-thought-out museums, the free harbour baths where you can swim in the clean canal water, the nightlife in Nørrebro and Vesterbro, and the bohemian flavour of Christiania. Cuisine and beer are other areas where the Danes took the ordinary and made it extraordinary, with 22 stars spread across 15 Michelin-starred restaurants (and hundreds of more affordable others).

JRMARSH/SHUTTERSTOCK ©

With nine centuries of royal history, some enlightened city planning (2023 to 2026 UNESCO World Capital of Architecture, anyone?) and a seemingly ever-growing wave of grassroots creativity, this elegant and egalitarian city on the water seems set to continue reinventing itself.

THE MAIN AREAS

CENTRAL COPENHAGEN & THE OLD CITY
The city's hygge and historical heart. p52

NYHAVN, ROYAL COPENHAGEN & THE PARKS
Palaces, parks and museums. p65

CHRISTIANSHAVN & THE INNER HARBOUR
From hippy haven to high culture. p73

For places to stay in Copenhagen, see p94

NICK N A/SHUTTERSTOCK ©

Left: Christiansborg Slot (p53); Above: Nyhavn (p65)

NØRREBRO & ØSTERBRO
Neighbouring hoods; one diverse, one swanky. p81

VESTERBRO & FREDERIKSBERG
Edgy and hip meet posh. p86

BEYOND CENTRAL COPENHAGEN
Suburban grandeur and great museums. p91

Find Your Way

Other than finding your way blocked by a canal or the harbour, Copenhagen is pretty simple to navigate. The streets in the old city can be a bit of a tangle, but it usually doesn't take long to find a square or major street.

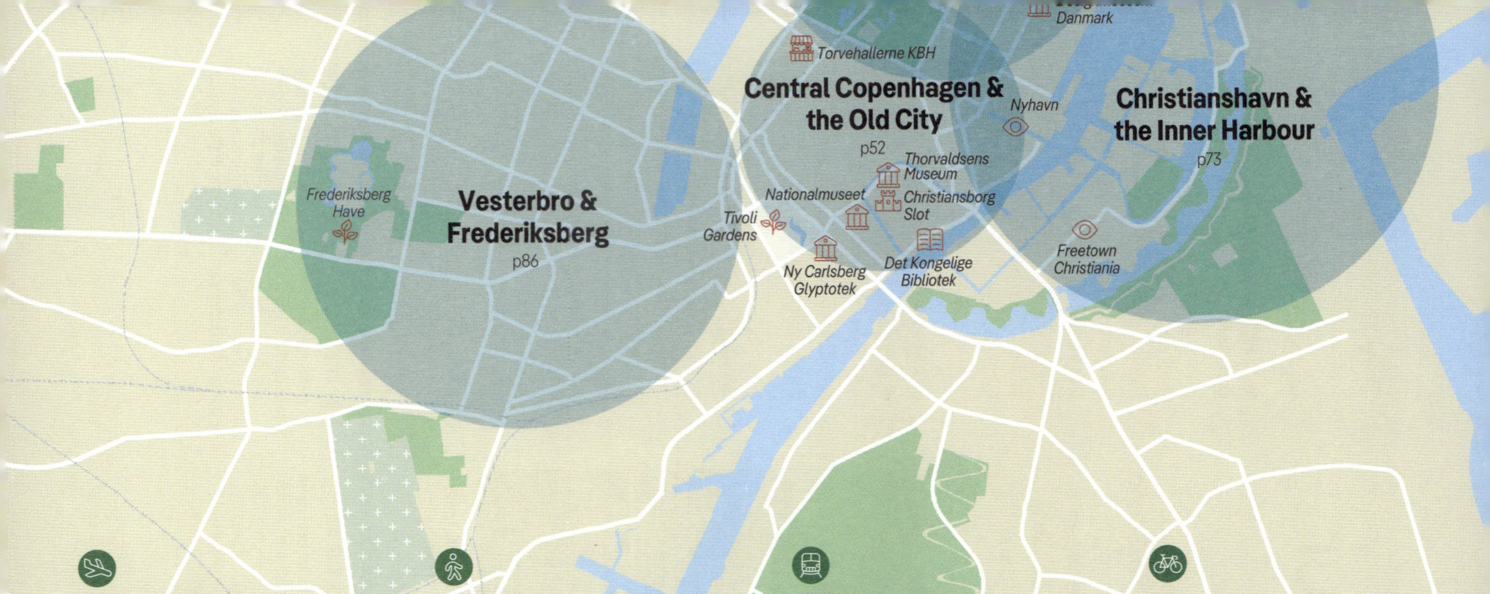

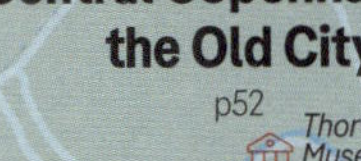

Danmark

Torvehallerne KBH

Central Copenhagen & the Old City

p52

Nyhavn

Christianshavn & the Inner Harbour

p73

Thorvaldsens Museum

Nationalmuseet

Christiansborg Slot

Tivoli Gardens

Det Kongelige Bibliotek

Ny Carlsberg Glyptotek

Freetown Christiania

Frederiksberg Have

Vesterbro & Frederiksberg

p86

FROM THE AIRPORT

Getting in from Copenhagen airport is a breeze. There are frequent train and metro connections to the centre – check which goes closest to your destination. It's 20 minutes to the central station (Hovedbanegård) by train; 15 minutes to Kongens Nytorv by metro.

WALK

Copenhagen must be one of the world's most walkable cities. There are no hills, and other than the unreliable weather, the occasional wonky cobblestone is your biggest nemesis here. And the distances are small: Tivoli to Nyhavn is just 1.5km through the historic old centre.

METRO

Copenhagen's metro system is relatively new, fresh, driverless, and still expanding. Line 2 brings you to and from the airport, while line 3 does a big loop around the central neighbourhoods.

BIKE

Flat, with great infrastructure, and separate cycle lanes most of the time, Copenhagen is one of the world's best cycling cities. There's nothing more Copenhagen than jumping on a bike.

Plan Your Days

In a city with pastry this good, skipping breakfast is a sin. Spend the rest of your day burning it off on foot or by bike between Copenhagen's canals, castles, museums, makers and markets.

LINGBEEK/GETTY IMAGES ©

Palmehus, Botanisk Have (p69)

Day 1

Morning

● Walk through the **Latin Quarter** (p61), pick up a pastry from legendary **La Glace** (p71), then stop at **Nyhavn** (p65) to get *the* classic Copenhagen photo. If travelling with kids, head to **Tivoli Gardens** (p56). Hop on a **boat tour** (p67) from Nyhavn, which will take you to see the **Little Mermaid** (p72) en route.

Afternoon

● Have a burger at Noma's takeaway sibling, **POPL** (p80) then take a tour of magnificent **Christiansborg Slot** (p53).

Evening

● Walk down **Vesterbro's** rough-round-the-edges **Istedgade** (p87) to see old and new Copenhagen mix; have dinner and drinks at the ever-hip **Kødbyen complex** (p88).

You'll Also Want to...

See what Copenhagen is cooking up – there's a treat around every corner in the Danish capital.

SEE THE ART

The glorious **Louisiana** (p93) museum is a short trip from the city with a beautiful seaside sculpture park and children's wing.

HIT THE BEACH

Go to **Amager Strandpark** for coastal sand dunes and lagoons between the airport and city centre.

TAKE A BIKE TOUR

Hop on a themed bike tour with a local expert, whether it's food, architecture or just taking in the sights.

Day 2

Morning

- If the weather cooperates, start with a pastry at **Hart Bageri** (p75) and swim at **Islands Brygge Havnebadet** (p73). If it doesn't, go to **Ny Carlsberg Glyptotek** (p53) or the **National Museum** (p59).

Afternoon

- Head to **Freetown Christiania** (p75) and mooch around the colourful lanes of this famously autonomous neighbourhood, then climb the dramatic spiral tower at the **Vor Frelsers Kirke** (p75). The extraordinary **CopenHill** (p77) power-plant-ski-hill combo (bar on top!) is just up the road.

Evening

- Carry on to **Refshaleøen** (p78) for diverse food and drink at Scandinavia's largest street-food market, **Reffen**, right on the harbour.

Day 3

Morning

- Head to Copenhagen's multicultural heart in **Nørrebro** (p83) for breakfast at **Ali's Bageri** (p83). Take in the boutiques on **Jægersborggade**, and **Assistens Kirkegård** (p81), a favourite strolling spot.

Afternoon

- Go traditional with smørrebrød (open sandwiches) at **Torvehallerne KBH** (p52) and carry on to the Botanisk Have and **Palmehus** (p69) nearby. From here, **Rosenborg Slot** (p69), or the **Statens Museum for Kunst** (p70) and **Østre Anlæg**, are both right next door.

Evening

- Go to **Tivoli Gardens** (p56) and see what's been keeping Danes coming back to this magical theme park since 1843.

GET UNDERGROUND

Frederiksberg's dank underground **Cisternerne** (p89) are a one-of-a-kind contemporary-art space.

VISIT A BREWERY

Copenhagen runs on craft beer from microbreweries like Brus/To Øl, Flying Couch and Christiania Bryghus – or go on the high-tech **Home of Carlsberg brewery tour** (p89)!

PICNIC IN THE PARK

Frederiksberg Have (p88) is particularly scenic, with sedate ponds and a grandiose palace.

DABBLE IN DESIGN

Start at the **Designmuseum Danmark** (p67) and continue to the **Dansk Arkitektur Center** (p60).

Central Copenhagen & the Old City

THE CITY'S HYGGELIG HISTORICAL HEART

GETTING AROUND

The best way to get around is by bike, and downloading the Donkey Republic app allows you to pick up bikes all over the city as you need. If you're fairly confident on a bike you'll find it easy, as there are lots of cycle lanes and it's largely flat. Metro and buses are very well-connected and efficient, and the city is fairly compact, so you can walk to a lot of attractions.

The tangled web of streets spreading east and north-east of Tivoli is the oldest part of Copenhagen, with crooked, timbered, ochre and chalky blue- and green-painted buildings. The 800-year-old settlement here is a historical, cultural and architectural treasure chest, overflowing with world-class museums, compelling buildings and culinary delights.

Barely 1.5km across, it's eminently walkable, with the central pedestrianised shopping street, Strøget, and the Danish knack for thoughtful design coupled with historical preservation are on full display – notice how some of the uneven cobbles have been discreetly shaved down to allow a smoother ride for cyclists.

The city went through a series of devastating fires in 1728 and 1795, and even a British bombardment in 1807, which destroyed much of the medieval city centre. While some older buildings survive, much of the city had to be rebuilt after these cataclysms, with a lot of the construction dating to the 18th and 19th centuries. Today it's an active and atmospheric introduction to this proud and pretty capital city.

TOP TIP

A Copenhagen Discover Card *(copenhagencard.com)* lasts one to five days (24 to 120 hours), and includes entrance to almost 90 attractions (including Tivoli, Christiansborg and the National Museum), as well as public transport and attractions all over Zealand. Get it before you come and activate on arrival so you cover transport from the airport.

Torvehallerne KBH

Superb covered food market

On the site that was Copenhagen's vegetable market until the 1950s, **Torvehallerne KBH** (Market Halls) represents a return to form for one of the city's most central squares. Opened in 2011, it's one of Copenhagen's established gastronomic hubs, open from 10am to 7pm Monday to Friday (to 6pm Saturday and Sunday). Buy fresh fish and meat here, and there are lots of high-end street food places where you can sample anything from Argentinian empanadas and Korean *hotteok* pancakes to traditional Danish pickled herring and smørrebrød from one of the 80 vendors. The vegetable market is back too, beautifully set outside between the twin glass halls.

TRABANTOS/SHUTTERSTOCK ©

Christiansborg Slot

Great Art & a Glass-Domed Indoor Garden

See sculpture at Ny Carlsberg Glyptotek

Based on early Carlsberg brewing magnate Carl Jacobsen's private art collection, it's sheer joy to wander the **Ny Carlsberg Glyptotek** *(glyptoteket.com; adult/child 125kr/free)*, from the Greek meaning 'sculpture collection' – though it contains paintings as well – which has been open since 1897. At its centre is the palm-filled, glass-domed winter garden, with pools and fountains: this was a museum intended to be lit only by natural light. There is classical sculpture from Rome, with heads put on different bodies where necessary as Carl wanted them to look complete, in a Roman-style, colonnaded atrium. There's *The Kiss* by French sculptor Rodin, and paintings by Gauguin. Cézanne, Van Gogh, Pissarro, Monet and Renoir, plus Egyptian mummies and Roman death mask paintings. The indoor terrace cafe, shop and an outdoor terrace are other treats in store.

Seat of Government: Christiansborg Slot

Made famous by TV's *Borgen* – the Danish government

Home to the Folketinget (Danish parliament), Prime Minister's office and the Supreme Court, **Christiansborg Slot**

continues on p58

THE DISASTER OF THE STOCK EXCHANGE

In April 2024, a fire destroyed parts of Copenhagen's historic Old Stock Exchange building, also known as Børsen – a shock to the city comparable to the fire at Nôtre Dame in Paris. You'll see the stark, fire-blackened remains close to Christiansborg Slot. The grey-stone 400-year-old building was gutted by the fire, which most devastatingly, caused the collapse of its spiralling 52m spire shaped like four dragon tails. The roof, originally made of lead, had been removed during the 1658 Swedish siege to be used for musket balls and replaced by copper. According to legend, the spire preserved the building from enemy attacks and fire, so it must have taken its eye off the ball. The building is undergoing restoration.

CENTRAL COPENHAGEN: BEST BAKERIES

Hart Bageri: By Richard Hart, formerly of Noma. The *tebirkes* (poppy-seed buns) are sublime, and the sourdough BMO is top-notch. *8am-6pm* €

Lido: Exquisite baked goods, breakfast, lunch and brunch, in a beautiful building. *8am-5pm Mon, Thu & Fri, from 9am Sat & Sun* €

Sankt Peders Bageri: The oldest bakery in the city, dating from 1652. Famed for its cinnamon rolls. *7.30am-5pm Mon-Fri, 8am-4pm Sat* €

Seks: Joyfully colourful, vegetarian bakery and brunch hot spot. *9am-6pm Thu-Tue* €€

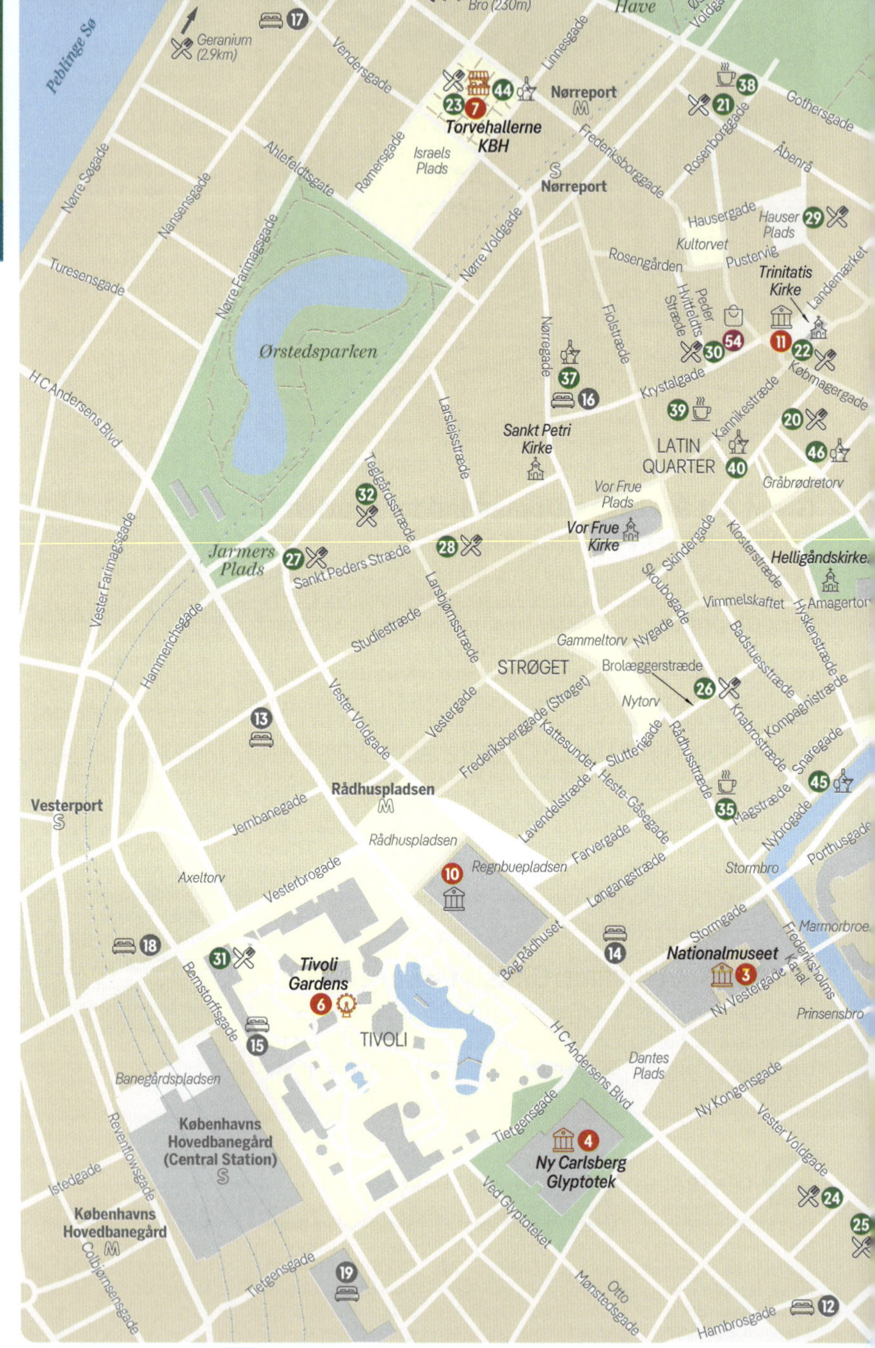
CENTRAL COPENHAGEN & THE OLD CITY
Dronning Louises Bro (230m)
Geranium (2.9km)
Peblinge Sø
Botanisk Have
Øster Voldgade
17
Vendersgade
44
23
7
Torvehallerne KBH
Nørreport
Linnésgade
Frederiksborggade
Israels Plads
Rømersgade
Ahlefeldtsgate
Nørre Søgade
Nansensgade
Nørre Farimagsgade
Nørre Voldgade
38
21
Rosenborggade
Gothersgade
Åbenrå
Hausergade
Hauser Plads
29
Kultorvet
Rosengården
Pustervig
Trinitatis Kirke
Landemærket
Peder Hvitfeldts Stræde
Turesensgade
Ørstedsparken
Nørregade
Fiolstræde
54
11
22
30
Købmagergade
37
16
Krystalgade
39
20
H C Andersens Blvd
Larslejsstræde
Sankt Petri Kirke
LATIN QUARTER
Kannikestræde
40
46
Gråbrødretorv
Vor Frue Plads
Teglgårdsstræde
32
28
Vor Frue Kirke
Jarmers Plads
27
Sankt Peders Stræde
Skindergade
Klosterstræde
Helligåndskirke
Skoubogade
Vimmelskaftet
Amagertorv
Vester Farimagsgade
Hammerichsgade
Studiestræde
Larsbjørnsstræde
Gammeltorv
Nygade
Hyskenstræde
Badstuestræde
STRØGET
Brolæggerstræde
26
Nytorv
Kompagnistræde
13
Vester Voldgade
Vestergade
Frederiksberggade (Strøget)
Kattesundet
Slutterigade
Rådhusstræde
Knabrostræde
Snaregade
45
Vesterport
Jernbanegade
Rådhuspladsen
Lavendelstræde
Heste-Gåsegade
35
Magstræde
Nybrogade
Rådhuspladsen
Farvergade
Stormbro
Porthusgade
Axeltorv
Vesterbrogade
10
Regnbuepladsen
Løngangstræde
Marmorbroen
18
31
Tivoli Gardens
6
Bag Rådhuset
14
Stormgade
Nationalmuseet
3
Ny Vestergade
Frederiksholms Kanal
Prinsensbro
Bernstorffsgade
15
TIVOLI
H C Andersens Blvd
Dantes Plads
Banegårdspladsen
Ny Kongensgade
Vester Voldgade
Tietgensgade
4
Ny Carlsberg Glyptotek
Københavns Hovedbanegård (Central Station)
Reventlowsgade
Istedgade
Ved Glyptoteket
24
25
Københavns Hovedbanegård
Colbjørnsensgade
Tietgensgade
19
Otto Mønstedsgade
Hambrosgade
12

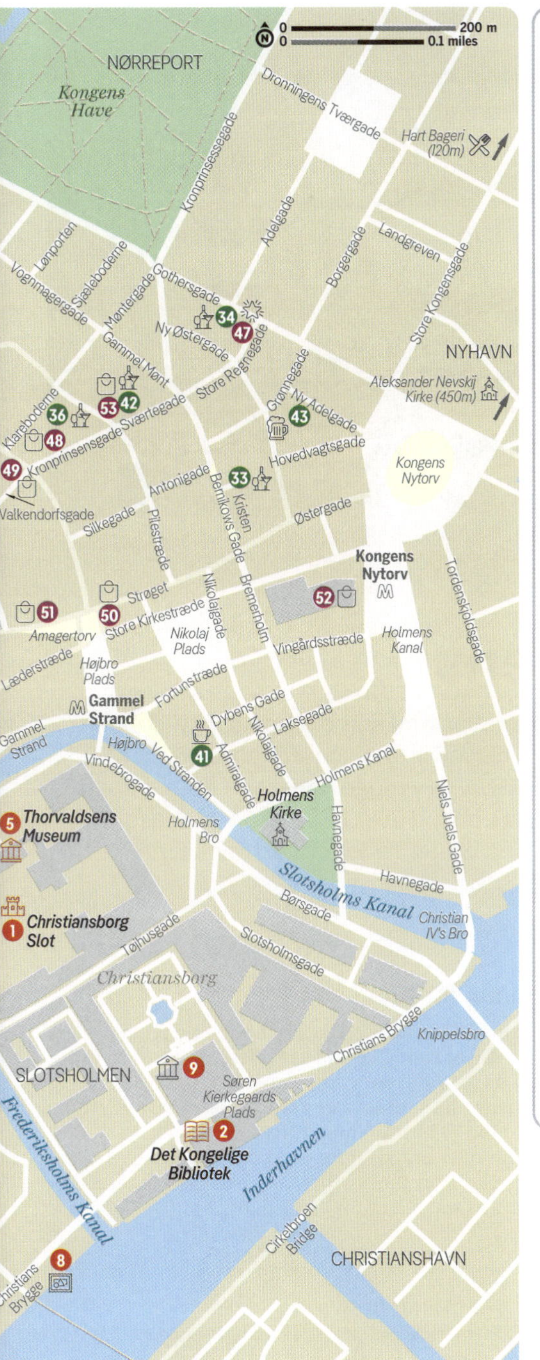

HIGHLIGHTS
1 Christiansborg Slot
2 Det Kongelige Bibliotek
3 Nationalmuseet
4 Ny Carlsberg Glyptotek
5 Thorvaldsens Museum
6 Tivoli Gardens
7 Torvehallerne KBH

SIGHTS
8 Dansk Arkitektur Center
9 Dansk Jødisk Museum
10 Rådhus
11 Rundetårn

SLEEPING
12 Danhostel Copenhagen City
13 Hotel Alexandra
14 Hotel Danmark
15 Hotel Nimb
16 Hotel Skt Petri
17 Ibsens Hotel
18 Radisson Collection Royal Hotel
19 Villa Copenhagen

EATING
20 Bar'Vin
21 Brdr.Price
22 DØP
● GRØD (see 7)
23 Hallernes Smørrebrød
24 Lido
25 Lillian's Smørrebrød
26 Restaurant Kronborg
27 Restaurant Mes
28 Sankt Peders Bageri
29 Schønnemann
30 Seks
31 Tivoli Food Hall
32 Venner

DRINKING & NIGHTLIFE
33 1105
34 Andy's Bar
35 Bastard Café
36 Bo-Bi Bar
37 Boulebar
38 Cafe Det Vide Hus
● Coffee Collective (see 7)
39 Democratic Coffee
40 Farfars Bodega
41 H A N S Coffee Bar
42 Moose
43 Palæ Bar
44 Pavillon de Verre
45 Ruby
46 Strøm

ENTERTAINMENT
47 Jazzhus Montmartre

SHOPPING
48 AC Perch's Thehandel
49 Arket
50 Hay House
51 Illums Bolighus
52 Magasin du Nord
53 Reseller
54 Time's Up Vintage

SURATWADEE RATTANAJARUPAK/SHUTTERSTOCK ©

Dragon Boats

TOP EXPERIENCE

Tivoli Gardens

One of the world's oldest operating amusement parks, city-centre **Tivoli Gardens** opened in 1843, and is genuinely enchanting. It's very Danish, whimsically pretty, with vintage rides, and details such as wandering peacocks and a boating lake. It has several seasons: Easter, summer, Halloween and winter, redecorated each time.

DON'T MISS

- Boating lake
- Rutschebanen ('Rollercoaster')
- Ferris wheel
- Flying Trunk
- Japanese pagoda
- *Æbleskiver* (doughnut-pancakes) and *gløgg* (mulled wine) at Christmas
- Outdoor ballet in summer

Attractions for All

Tivoli originally lay outside the city limits, covering around 15 acres of land outside Copenhagen's Vesterport (West Gate), and it still has 15 different garden areas, including the Japanese, Hanging and Vintage Car gardens, as well as Parterre, landscaped in 1943 by Gudmund Nyeland Brandt.

Lots of the rides are ideal for everyone, including the scenic Dragon Boats on the boating lake, especially as the daylight begins to wane and the fairy lights twinkle. The lake

PRACTICALITIES

Scan this QR code for prices and opening hours.

was formed out of what was once the city moat. The classic carousel is a vintage whirl, and the Ferris wheel takes you up for views across the gardens in small hot-air balloons, as it has since 1943. The Tivoli Aquarium is a 30m-long tank of exotic fish – around 1600 of them – and coral, including stingrays and reef sharks, and you can time a visit to coincide with their feeding (usually 1pm); however, there is an extra charge for visiting (50kr) if you don't have an unlimited ride pass. There are different light installations every season, and early evening projection shows over the Christmas period.

Rides for Younger Kids

Small kids will enjoy rides such as the whimsical Hans Christian Andersen ride, the Flying Trunk, where you ride past tableaux of the great storyteller's tales. There are multiple fun rides for younger visitors. Fatamorgana is a family affair where you can choose either a wild swing ride that hurls you around at a force of 2.5G, or the gentler family section has animal-shaped gondolas – a smooth ride with views from 43m over the gardens. On the Astronomer, you ride in a bright, steam-punk spaceship, aiming your telescope at the surrounding lampposts, which will twinkle when you make a direct hit, while on the Galley Ships you navigate your boat around a large pirate ship.

Rides for Thrill-Seekers

There's the Rutschebanen ('Rollercoaster'), built in 1914 and still roller coasting – it's so old-school that it still has an operator on board who has to control the brakes. Himmelskibet has swings that take you up high for a view over the city; on the Golden Tower, you're raised slowly upwards before dipping down at stomach-flipping speeds; the Demon is a rollercoaster with three loops; Aquila spins you upside down on giant eagles; and The Monsoon lifts you up 12m in various directions, next to a fountain. Villa Vendetta is a haunted house experience, for over 12s (with an adult) only: this is nothing like a creaky old Ghost Train experience; you walk through and actors in costume create heart-challenging jump scares.

Food & Drink

Food and drink includes street stalls – with hot dogs, of course. In winter *gløgg* (mulled wine) and *æbleskiver* (doughnut-pancakes) are sold. Tivoli food hall allows you all to choose different cuisines if you feel like it, from Indian to a Danish salad bar. In Tivoli's landmark Japanese pagoda, there's a changing roster of Michelin-starred chefs, or for slightly less high-end, try Brdr.Price, with home-style cooking in a light-filled interior, a restaurant part-owned by food critic Adam Price, who was a screenwriter and developer of *Borgen*.

ENTERTAINMENT

There are fireworks every Saturday night, and 'Fredagsrock' concerts take place on the outdoor Plænen stage on summer Friday evenings: these occasionally reach capacity, so go early. There's also the 1874 open-air Peacock Theatre, with ballet (sometimes with sets designed by Queen Margrethe), where you can catch a performance in the summer. Regular theatre shows are performed here, but usually in Danish.

TOP TIPS

- Tivoli is only open during set seasons: Easter, summer, Halloween and winter.
- It's open late, so you can save your visit for the evening, and eat here too.
- If you like rides, it's definitely worth splashing out on an unlimited day pass.
- In winter many of the outdoor rides are closed, but there are indoor entertainments and an ice rink, plus lots of Christmas shopping stalls.

BEST HARBOUR BATHS & POOLS

Islands Brygge Havnebadet: The first, designed by BIG Architects, with kids' and grown-ups' pools, plus a diving platform.

Kastrup Søbad: Snail-shaped swimming platform, close to Amager Strandpark metro.

Kalvebod Bølge: 'The Waves', facing Islands Brygge, with an undulating promenade, kayak slide and several pools. Year-round.

Havnebadet Fisketorvet: Close to Fisketorvet shopping centre, with children's, diving and swimming pools. May to March.

Sandkaj Badezone: Popular spot in Nordhavn. Year-round.

DGI-Byen: Indoor pool complex close to Copenhagen Central Station.

Øbro-Hallen: Denmark's first public swimming hall (1930) in Østerbro.

BALIPADMA/SHUTTERSTOCK ©

Det Kongelige Bibliotek

continued from p53

is familiar from one of Denmark's most loved exports, the TV series *Borgen*, but has been the seat of Danish political power since the 1400s. The king also has his state reception rooms here, and you can nose around chandelier-tapestry-and-stucco-decorated, opulent royal reception rooms, as well as the copper-pan-lined royal kitchen, royal stables with their the snow-white horses (a Czech pedigree that is born black) and palace chapel. You can also go underground to see the spookily lit 11th-century ruins of the former castle, used as foundations. Above ground, take the lift up to the tower for fabulous city views.

Black Diamond: Royal Danish Library

Old meets new at this waterfront icon

Better known as the Black Diamond (Den Sorte Diamant) for its angular facade clad in polished black granite, the harbourfront **Det Kongelige Bibliotek** *(kb.dk/en; free)* was completed in 1999, and was one of the first new buildings in the wholesale modernisation and redevelopment of Copenhagen's inner harbour. The soaring building elegantly bookends the 20th century, and the angular waterfront wing connects to the original library that dates from 1906. The transition from soaring glass atrium to the dark wood and green banker's lamps of

EATING IN CENTRAL COPENHAGEN: BEST BRUNCH & QUICK LUNCH

Tivoli Food Hall: 'Fast-gourmet' food court at Tivoli Gardens, but also accessible without a ticket. *11am-9pm Mon-Thu & Sun, to 11pm Fri & Sat* **€€**

Venner: Copenhageners love brunch, and this is a top choice for pancakes, sourdough and eggs. *10am-4pm Sun, Wed & Thu, to 9pm Fri & Sat* **€€**

GRØD: Denmark is known for making the ordinary extraordinary – this porridge bar is no exception. *7am-7pm Mon-Fri, 9am-6pm Sat & Sun* **€**

DØP: Not your average *pølsevogn*, this all-organic stand takes Danish hot dogs to the next level. *10.30am-7pm Mon-Sat, to 7pm Sun* **€**

TOP EXPERIENCE

Nationalmuseet

Denmark's dynamic **Nationalmuseet** is the repository for all manner of Stone Age tools, Viking weaponry, rune stones and medieval jewellery, with some incredible objects on display as well as cutting-edge major rotating exhibitions that change every couple of years and include themes such as Viking raids. It's great for kids, and there's a wonderful children's wing.

DIEGO GRANDI/SHUTTERSTOCK ©

Dollhouses

Delve into the Past

Start your voyage with extraordinary artefacts from the Iron Age and beyond, such as the 3500-year-old Trundholm sun chariot and the extraordinary Gundestrup Cauldron weighing 9kg, both discovered having been slung or sacrificed in peat bogs multiple millennia ago. Mesmerising Viking artefacts include huge rune stones, a well-preserved Viking warship, hefty gold hoards and intricate burial treasures.

The fabulous ground-floor children's wing is best for under-12s and offers the chance for kids to play at being a 19th-century school teacher or student, Vikings and shopkeepers.

From Colonies to Dollhouses

Discover personal stories from colonial history at the excellent Voices from the Colonies exhibition, which concentrates on the West Indies, India, West Africa and Greenland. You can also wander around Egyptian mummies, Assyrian reliefs, see the miniature worlds created in splendid dollhouses, and a 1970s Danish sitting room.

Viking Sorceress

A temporary exhibition running to 2027. Wear a headset and go through several rooms full of audio-visual thrills, narrated by a Viking sorceress. After this, there's a fascinating exhibition showing artefacts that evoke the times in which the *vølve* lived.

TOP TIPS

- Allow at least three hours to do the museum justice.
- The restaurant is great, serving tasty Danish cuisine.
- There are various free tours during the day, or you can download the free audio tour.

the reading room is a thrill, and there are great views down into the atrium from the top floor. Join a tour to explore the building in detail. Closed on Sunday.

Fun & Architecture at BLOX

The brilliant Danish Architecture Centre

You can't miss the BLOX building, on the harbour next to the Black Diamond. If you think its glass-block architecture looks not particularly Danish, you'd be right, it was designed by Dutch 'starchitect' Rem Koolhaas. It contains, as well as housing and a gym, the **Dansk Arkitektur Center**, with a permanent exhibition on the development of Danish architecture, alongside temporary exhibits. If it sounds like this is only for architectural fiends, it's fun for kids and the young-at-heart as well, with a 40m-long, spiralling Carsten Höller slide and a playground, as well as a rooftop cafe with views. DAC also runs regular 90-minute walking, running and cycling tours of the city's contemporary architecture.

Messing about on Boats

Tours and picnic boats

This is a city on water, so one of the best ways to explore is by boat. There are straightforward one-hour **Canal Tours** departing from either Nyhavn or Gammel Strand and taking in the Inner Harbour, Christianshavn, the Slotsholmen Canal and the Little Mermaid. Very different in atmosphere are the tours offered by **Hey Captain**, where your visit is with a local and you're encouraged to engage and talk, with the boat seating up to 12 (including the captain).

Another option is the **Harbour Bus** (Havnebus), a small ferry that's part of the public transport system (routes 991/992), making 10 stops between Teglholmen in the south and Orientkaj in the north. This is a particularly good way to get to/from Refshaleøen, and you can take your bike on board. Otherwise, **Kayak Republic** rents out kayaks and stand-up paddle boards on Slotsholmen, and even has a 'green kayak' scheme where your rental is free if you collect trash (grabby-arm provided) while paddling. They also offer guided kayaking tours.

COPENHAGEN'S BEST BIKE BRIDGES

Circle Bridge: Designed by Olafur Eliasson. Unusually, it has places to stop, to encourage people to slow down and look at their surroundings.

Bicycle Snake Cycle: Connects Vesterbro and Copenhagen H Station with Fisketorvet shopping mall, Bryggebroen and Islands Brygge Havnebadet.

Lille Langebro: The latest addition, close to the Dansk Arkitektur Center. Makes access to Christianshavn easier from the historic centre.

Inner Harbour Bridge: Controversial design, but handy to connect Nyhavn and Christianshavn/Holmen, with good harbour views.

Butterfly Bridge: Crossing Christianshavns Kanal and Trangraven, this has three spans that meet in the middle above the water.

EATING IN CENTRAL COPENHAGEN: BEST LEISURELY MEALS

Brdr.Price: Siblings Adam and James Price host a cult-status TV cooking show, focusing on quality comfort grub. *noon-10pm Mon-Sat* €€€

Schønnemann: This is where you go for a fancy lunch, with snaps (small shot of a strong alcohol) since 1877. *11.30am-5pm Mon-Sat* €€€

Restaurant Mes: Owned by Mads Rye Magnusson (former chef at Geranium); offers affordable high-end cooking. *5.30pm-midnight Mon-Sat* €€€

Bar'Vin: Rustic Mediterranean dishes at this bottle-lined wine bar. *noon-11pm Mon-Sat* €€

Geranium: The 16-course menu at three-Michelin-starred Geranium is a tour de force. *noon-3.30pm Fri & Sat, 6.30pm-11pm Wed-Sat* €€€

Restaurant Kronborg: Wood-beamed Kronborg serves up classic smørrebrød, served on Royal Copenhagen china. *11am-6pm* €€

Lillian's Smørrebrød: Tuck into a classic at this good-value open sandwich bar. *9am-2pm Mon-Fri* €

Hallernes Smørrebrød: Beautifully prepared smørrebrød, plus seasonal choices. *hours vary* €€

Harbour Bus

GoBoat and **FriendShips** offer you the chance to hire and drive your own eco-boat, or you can book one with a captain.

Views from Rådhus Tower

Gaze across the city

Close to Tivoli Gardens, the romantic 1905 **Rådhus** *(City Hall; kk.dk; tower 40kr)* soars above the main square and the Latin Quarter. To the right of the entrance inside is the eccentrically elaborate World Clock, designed by astro-mechanic Jens Olsen (1872–1945) and built at a cost of one million kroner. The interior of the town hall is magnificently of its time, but the main reason to explore is to take one of the regular tours to climb the 300 or so steps to the top of the 105m city-hall tower, for fabulous city views.

Secret Garden & the Zigzagging Jewish Museum

Innovative museum and inner-city oasis

Step inside the former Royal Boat House, an early-17th-century building once part of Christian IV's harbour complex, and

CENTRAL COPENHAGEN'S BEST SHOPPING

Reseller: Great place to hunt out designer clothes bargains while polishing your sustainable halo.

Hay House: A contemporary design success story, with affordable, practical homeware and furniture.

Illums Bolighus: Multistorey emporium of Danish design.

Time's Up Vintage: High-scale vintage boutique.

AC Perch's Thehandel: Beautifully packaged teas in this historic shop with attached tearoom.

Magasin du Nord: Huge, historic department store. Lots of local labels and design, plus the excellent Hallernes Smørrebrød on the top floor.

Arket: The flagship of this popular Scandi brand, part of H&M, in the former Post & Telegraph Museum.

DRINKING IN CENTRAL COPENHAGEN: BEST COFFEE

Coffee Collective: Sip perfect coffee at this outlet of Copenhagen's most respected roastery. *7am-8pm Mon-Fri, 8am-7pm Sat & Sun*

Cafe Det Vide Hus: This coffee shop is perfectly situated across from the King's Garden. *7am-6pm Tue-Fri, 9am-5pm Sat & Sun*

H A N S Coffee Bar: Superb coffee from Copenhagen Coffee Lab, plus delicious pastries. *7.30am-5pm Mon-Fri, from 9am Sat & Sun*

Democratic Coffee: A great place to sink espresso as well as V60-brewed coffee, with fresh pastries. *7.30am-5pm Mon-Fri, 9am-4pm Sat*

MEANDER THROUGH THE PRETTIEST POSTCODES

This walk visits the back-in-time port of Nyhavn, the grandeur and tranquillity of Christiansborg Slot, and the city's oldest streets, finishing at City Hall.

START	END	LENGTH
Nyhavn	Rådhus	2.7km; 2 hours

Start at 1 **Nyhavn** (p65), constructed by Swedish war prisoners in the 17th century to connect the harbour to 2 **Kongens Nytorv**. At the southern end stands 3 **Magasin du Nord** (p61). Continue south into Laksegade and turn right into Nikolajgade, which leads to church-turned-contemporary-gallery 4 **Nikolaj Kunsthal**. Head west down Fortunstræde to 5 **Højbro Plads**, backdrop to a statue of Copenhagen's founder, Bishop Absalon. Stop for a drink at winebar 6 **Ved Stranden 10**, then cross the canal to 7 **Christiansborg Slot** (p53), home to the Danish Parliament. Head through the archway left of the palace, then through the second archway on your left. Awaiting is the 8 **Royal Library Garden**, built on top of Christian IV's old naval port, Tøjhushavnen. Head back through the archway, continuing south to the 9 **Riding Ground Complex**, the only surviving remnant of the original Christiansborg Slot. The riding ground leads out to 18th-century 10 **Marble Bridge**. Cross it, turning right into Frederiksholms Kanal until you reach 11 **Magstræde**, Copenhagen's oldest street. Wander down here, turning left into Knabrostræde and then left again at Brolæggerstræde. The street spills into Nytorv, home to Copenhagen's pink-stucco courthouse 12 **Domhuset**. Head down Slutterigade to the left of the building, at the very end of which soars the architectural flourish that is 13 **Rådhus** (p61).

Assistenshuset dates from 1730 and was once a royal pawn shop, now housing the Ministry of Culture.

Børsen, Copenhagen's 17th-century Stock Exchange building with a distinctive dragon spire, burned down in 2024 and is currently being restored.

The zigzagging architecture of the **Dansk Jødisk Museum** (p63) was created to give the sense of escaping via boat as local Jews had to during WWII.

you'll find the **Dansk Jødisk Museum** *(Danish Jewish Museum; jewmus.dk; adult/child 100kr/free)*, with it arresting geometric design, by Polish-born Daniel Libeskind. The zigzagging floors and walls are intended to create the unsteady feeling of being aboard a boat. It takes you through history, as well as telling the story of how over 90% of Danish Jews were evacuated to Sweden over two nights in 1943.

Backdrops & Art at Thorvaldsens Museum

Exquisitely beautiful interiors

Michael Gottlieb Bindesbøll designed the Graeco-Roman-style **Thorvaldsens Museum** *(thorvaldsensmuseum.dk; adult/child 100kr/free; free last Wed of month)*, Denmark's first art museum, to house the work of his close friend, superstar Danish sculptor Bertel Thorvaldsen (1770–1844). After four decades in Rome, Thorvaldsen returned to Copenhagen and donated his private collection to the Danish public, and in return the royal family provided this site. The result was this dazzling museum, where Thorvaldsen's bone-white neoclassical sculptures are set against backgrounds of ochre, berry, mustard and royal blue, with zigzagged and patterned tiles, creating perfect tableaux at every turn. Don't neglect upstairs, which has the artist's collection of ancient artefacts.

Spiralling Walkway at the Round Tower

Climb a 17th-century ramp

The 35m **Rundetårn** *(Round Tower; rundetaarn.dk; adult/child 40/10kr)* was built as an observatory for astronomer Tycho Brahe in 1642. You reach the top by a spiralling ramp – making the walk gentler and more fun than many towers. Spend the walk up considering whether or not you think Peter the Great could have gotten his horse up here, as the legend goes.

Copenhagen's Tranquil Lakes

Pedalos, food and drink, joggers and sundowners

The streets straighten out and the city changes character slightly once you reach Nørreport and cross Nørre Voldgade,

STRØGET SHOPPING

Copenhagen's main pedestrian street, the 1.1km Strøget (struh-ul), runs between Rådhuspladsen and Kongens Nytorv. Pedestrianised in 1962, this was so successful that it spread to other central streets, including nearby Købmagergade and Fiolstræde. It's home to Danish design flagships, like Royal Copenhagen porcelain, Illums Bolighus design store and Georg Jensen silverware. Luxury brands are clustered by Amagertorv and Kongens Nytorv, while the end near Rådhuspladsen is a bit more downmarket. Parallel Strædet has interesting ceramics and antique shops, while Pilestræde has good independent fashion, and the beautifully verdigrised Stork Fountain (Storkespringvandet) has been the meeting point on Amagertorv since 1894.

DRINKING IN CENTRAL COPENHAGEN: BEST BARS & COCKTAILS

Jazzhus Montmartre: Since the late 1950s this has been one of Scandinavia's great jazz venues. *6-11.30pm Thu & Fri, to 11pm Sat*

Bastard Café: Come and play one of the hundreds of board games at this stalwart cafe-bar. *noon-midnight Sun-Thu, to 2am Fri & Sat*

Boulebar: Play a few rounds of pétanque, even in winter, at this indoor bar and boules court. *3-11pm Mon-Thu, noon-1am Fri, 10.30am-1am Sat*

Farfars Bodega: Three floors, including a dance floor in the basement. *4pm-2am Mon & Tue, to 3am Wed, to 4am Thu, 1pm-5am Sat & Sun*

1105: Head in before 11pm for a bar seat at this dark, luxe lounge. It's aimed at sophisticated over 30s. *6pm-2am Wed, Thu & Sat, from 4pm Fri*

Ruby: Gaze over at Slotsholmen from one of the leather chairs at this impeccable, intimate address. *4pm-2am Mon-Sat, 5pm-1am Sun*

Strøm: Get swept away in the art deco ambiance at this bar on Gråbrødretorv square. *6pm-1am Tue-Thu, 4pm-2am Fri & Sat*

Pavillon de Verre: Taste your own bespoke beverage at this flavour-forward cocktail corner. *10am-8pm Mon-Thu, to 9pm Fri & Sat, to 7pm Sun*

BEST CITY-CENTRE HISTORICAL CHURCHES

Holmens Kirke: Queen Margrethe II got married in 1967 at this 17th-century naval church.

Sankt Petri Kirke: Copenhagen's oldest surviving church (1400s) built for, and still serving, the city's German evangelical population.

Vor Frue Kirke: This 1829 neoclassical church hosts the Kunsthåndværker-markedet artisan's market every August.

Trinitatis Kirke: Attached to the Rundetårn and rebuilt in 1731, this Dutch Baroque-style church holds classical Friday concerts.

Helligåndskirken: Burned in the 1728 fire, this former monastery was rebuilt and today sits right on Strøget.

Aleksander Nevskij Kirke: Completed in 1883, golden-domed, granite-and-brick Aleksander Nevskij Kirke flaunts a Russian Byzantine style.

KIEV.VICTOR/SHUTTERSTOCK ©

Ørstedsparken

which is easily explained because this was for centuries Copenhagen's northern rampart and city gate – Voldgade just means 'Wall Street'. The ponds in pretty **Ørstedsparken**, as well as those in the **Botanisk Have** (p69) and **Østre Anlæg**, are remnants of the defensive ramparts and water features that once surrounded the city. And the set of rectangular ponds 500m past Nørreport started out as a dammed-up stream used for agriculture, eventually becoming incorporated into the city as it began to outgrow its original confines.

Today the Lakes, as they're known, are one of Copenhagen's most popular strolling, jogging and hangout (p83) spots, with a handful of restaurants and cafes dotted along the Nørrebro side, where there's a path (the other side has a road). A round-trip is about 6.5km. There are swan-shaped pedalos on the lake, and on the Nørreport side are the 'Potato Rows', houses built for workers in the 19th century and now some of the city's most sought-after real estate.

Crossing the Lakes, **Dronning Louises Bro** (Queen Louise's Bridge) is the hip summer spot to 'hænge ud' (hang out), and one of the world's busiest bike routes, with thousands of cyclists passing here daily. Any nice day will see it packed with people soaking up the sun – probably along with a six-pack.

DRINKING IN CENTRAL COPENHAGEN: BEST NO-NONSENSE BARS

Moose: Central but untouristy, covered in graffiti and open until 8am at weekends. Need we say more? *noon-7am, to 8am Fri-Sun*

Andy's Bar: Open since the 1930s and just as rowdy as the day it was born. *noon-2am Thu, to 4am Fri, to 6am Sat & Sun*

Palæ Bar: Soak up the living-room vibes at this cosy, warmly decorated bar and lunch spot. *11am-1am Mon-Wed, to 3am Thu-Sat, 4pm-1am Sun*

Bo-Bi Bar: Smoky (yes, you can smoke), flock-wallpapered, dimly lit dive bar that's full of cinematic atmosphere. *2pm-2am*

Nyhavn, Royal Copenhagen & the Parks

PALACES, PARKS AND MUSEUMS

Taking in the northern half of Copenhagen's Indre By (Inner City), the twin neighbourhoods of Frederiksstaden and Østervold stretch between the inner harbour and the Lakes. Here you'll find some of the city's most significant royal sites and delightful parkland, as well as two of Denmark's most iconic images: the richly colourful historical harbour of Nyhavn and the diminutive Little Mermaid statue.

Directly north from Nyhavn and the large Kongens Nytorv square, the royal quarter of Frederiksstaden is centred on the queen's waterfront residence, Amalienborg Slot, and the glorious Marmorkirken (Marble Church) dome just beside it. The quarter ends at Kastellet (the Citadel), a massive five-pointed, moated fort complex (also home to the famous mermaid), which forms the end of a string of parks and ponds that were originally part of Copenhagen's defensive walls and moats, and are today home to some of the city's finest museums.

GETTING AROUND

The closest metro stops to this area are Kongens Nytorv and Marmorkirken. Everything is concentrated in a fairly small and much pedestrianised area, so you can easily explore on foot.

Sugar-Bright Harbour: Nyhavn

Copenhagen's iconic dockside

If there's one defining image of Copenhagen – or even Denmark – it's probably **Nyhavn**. The line-up of perfectly pastel portside townhouses seems like it could have been created with the express purpose of looking phenomenal on a postcard. In reality, King Christian V had this 'New Harbour' dug by Swedish prisoners-of-war in 1673, to connect more easily to his newly cobbled plaza, **Kongens Nytorv** (King's New Square). Nyhavn's oldest surviving building, No 9, dates from shortly afterwards in 1681. Ironically, the southern side – which tends to mostly see tourists' backs these days – was long considered the 'good' side of Nyhavn, as the other was for years a notorious strip of sailor's bars and brothels; a far cry from the photogenic terrace cafes of today.

TOP TIP

The Park Museums *(parkmuseerne.dk)* now offer a joint ticket. For 295kr, this offers half-price admission to six participating museums, with a year to use it. It includes one admission each to the Statens Museum for Kunst (SMK), Rosenborg Slot, Natural History Museum, Palmehus, Hirschsprung, Arbejdermuseet (Workers Museum) and the David Collection (already free).

Dome-Topped Marmorkirken – Marble Church

Copenhagen's biggest dome

The enormous green-and-gold dome atop the rococo-style **Marmorkirken** *(Marble Church, aka Frederik's Church; marmorkirken.dk; dome adult/child 50kr/free)* is obviously the showstopper here *(dome visits: weekends at 1pm)*. Funding troubles meant the church was left half-built for more than a century after Frederick V laid the foundation stone in 1749, but a wealthy benefactor finally saw the project to completion in 1894.

Royal Life at Amalienborg Slot

Daily routine at the royal residence

The four identical palaces facing each other across the large cobbled square are the main residences of the Danish royal family. Completed in 1760, the somewhat austere **Amalienborg Slot** *(kongernessamling.dk/amalienborg; adult/child 125kr/free)* palaces are named after kings Frederik VIII, Christian VII, VIII and IX. The now-abdicated Queen Margrethe II has lived in Christian IX's palace since 1967, while the relatively new King of Denmark, Frederik X, and his Tasmanian wife, Queen Mary, live at Frederik VIII's palace. You can visit the palace of Christian VIII, which also serves as a guest palace for the 'spare' Prince Joachim and Princess Marie, when they visit from the US. You get to see some historic reconstructed royal studies, giving a sense of life behind the scenes, plus the changes in royal taste. It's worth heading to Amalienborg Slot to see the daily show when the Royal Life Guards, in tall bearskin caps, march from Rosenborg Slot at 11.30am to change the guard here at noon.

Epicentre of Design

Design treasure trove: Designmuseum Danmark

Close to the Marble Church, **Designmuseum Danmark** *(designmuseum.dk; adult/child 130kr/free)* houses a stupendous collection, from mesmerising Japanese samurai sword rests to the iconic chairs and lamps that are enduringly the benchmarks of good taste to be found in the majority of Danish households. Housed in a converted 18th-century hospital, the museum was originally designed by architects Ivar Bentsen and Kaare Klint, opening in 1926. It was renovated a few years ago, reopening in 2022 having been revamped by OEO Studio, who have retained the legacy of the former heavyweight designers, while bringing it up to date. This is a must for fans of the applied arts and industrial design, with its collection exploring the evolution of one of the world's most emulated design cultures, from the homespun practicalities of the early mid-century designers who are still Denmark's biggest design stars – Arne Jacobsen, Poul Henningsen, Nanna Ditzel and Finn Juhl – to exhibitions of designs answering the challenges of the future and sustainability. You could spend at least three hours here.

BEST COPENHAGEN TOURS

Cycling Copenhagen: Choose from highlight, waterfront or urban tours by bike, with informative guides.

Bike Copenhagen: City tours with funny, knowledgeable Mike. Cash only. Age 12 to 25.

Cykelkokken: Morten, a chef, takes visitors on his unique tour, cooking a gourmet meal on his kitchen bike en route.

Copenhagen Free Walking Tours: Free daily walking tours, with donations of what you feel like paying.

Hey Captain: Small group boat tours where you're encouraged to talk with your captain.

Stromma: Canal and harbour cruises, taking in the main sights with commentary.

Running Tours Copenhagen: Run (or jog) around town for a cardio-friendly sightseeing session.

EATING IN NYHAVN & ROYAL COPENHAGEN: BEST QUICK LUNCH

Lille Petra: Slip into this garden cafe for sandwiches and fresh bread in beautiful surrounds. *8am-5pm Mon-Fri, from 10am Sat* **€€**

Bobs: With just a few seats, a contender for Copenhagen's best burger. Delicious meat, and knives and forks are supplied. *11am-8.30pm* **€**

Gorm's: On the less-busy side of the Nyhavn canal, rustic Gorm's is a rare gem on this touristy strip. *5-10pm Mon-Thu & Sun, to 11pm Fri & Sat* **€€**

Gasoline Grill on Landgreven: The organic hamburger joint was founded inside this petrol station in 2016. *11am until sold out* **€**

BEST FREE THINGS TO DO IN COPENHAGEN

Little Mermaid: Love her or hate her, she's free to see.

Harbour baths: Swim for free. For a list, see p58.

Museums: Davids Samling is always free. Thorvaldsens Museum, Nikolaj Kunsthal and the Museum of Copenhagen are free the last Wednesday of the month.

Det Kongelige Bibliotek: Stunning architecture worth exploring.

Viewpoints: Christiansborg Slot tower and CopenHill rooftop offer free views.

Kastellet: Copenhagen's star-shaped fortress built in the 1600s.

Parks/gardens: Such as Kongens Have.

Changing of the Guard: Danish pomp at Rosenborg Slot (11.30am daily).

Churches: Wonderful Grundtvigs Kirke, Marmorkirken and more.

DENYS TETERNYK/SHUTTERSTOCK ©

Windmill, Kastellet

Fortified Gardens at Kastellet

Possibly the world's prettiest military base

This huge pentagonal bastion-and-moat **Kastellet** was built to guard the entrance to Copenhagen's inner harbour starting in 1626 under Christian IV, and expanded a few decades later by Frederik III. Even today, it's still administered by the Ministry of Defence, but mostly used as offices. The rest of the citadel site, including the 1703 church, is open for visitors, and the tree-lined bastions and ramparts today provide some of Copenhagen's most unique recreational space, full of joggers and picnickers taking in the harbour views. The Dutch-style 1847 **windmill** is particularly photogenic and even still works – some hobbyists put the sails on and grind flour from time to time.

Underground at the Museum of the Danish Resistance

Vivid, immersive WWII museum

The **Frihedsmuseet** *(Museum of the Danish Resistance; en.natmus.dk; adult/child 120kr/free)* has its entrance above the surface but is an underground bunker, vividly bringing

EATING IN NYHAVN & ROYAL COPENHAGEN: DANISH FAVOURITES

Toldbod Bodega: Serving up your grandma's favourite Danish classics since 1787. *noon-3.30pm & 5.30-8.30pm Tue-Sat, noon-5pm Sun* €€

Café & Ølhalle '1892': The cellar cafe at the Arbejdermuseet (Workers Museum) still parties like it's 1899, with smørrebrod and snaps. *11am-5pm* €€

Restaurant Amalie: Close to Amalienborg Slot, serving up traditional Danish fare in the cellar of a historic building. *11.30am-5pm Mon-Sat* €€

Selma: Swedish chef Magnus Pettersson creates beautiful smørrebrød (open sandwiches) for lunch. *11.30am-4pm Wed-Mon & 6.30-11pm Wed-Sat* €€

to life how it felt to live under Nazi rule and the resistance in Denmark during WWII, from the prewar period to Liberation Day – still commemorated across Denmark on 5 May. Follow the story of various characters, through a combination of projections, audio and real artefacts on display. It's a compelling representation of this awful time. En route you can try your hand at decoding secret messages, tapping phone calls and even printing an illegal magazine. It's a good one for kids as well as adults. The museum was destroyed in an arson attack in 2013, but its artefacts survived and so it was entirely rebuilt, reopening in 2020.

Magnificent Regal Gardens & Rosenborg Slot

From ramparts to fine arts

The magnificently manicured **Kongens Have** (King's Garden) is the oldest park in the city. Once Christian IV's vegetable garden, today it's the picture of elegance, crisscrossed by romantic paths and planted in fragrant roses. It faces the fairy-tale turrets and gables of the 1633 Dutch Renaissance-style **Rosenborg Slot**, which served as Christian IV's summer home (presumably for easy access to all those vegetables). The castle still holds Denmark's crown jewels; visit the basement treasury to see Christian IV's extravagant crown and Christian III's jewel-studded sword. Fifteen small stone pavilions ring the park, specifically reserved for independent/creative boutiques, as well as several greenery-enveloped cafes.

Botanical Tropical Escape

Glasshouses, butterflies and more

An ideal escape in the city centre, whether rain or shine, the 10-hectare **Botanisk Have** (Botanic Gardens) feel organic and indulgent after the elegant geometry of Kongens Have, and are a biodiverse (literal) hot spot, with around 10,000 plant species. The extensive outdoor gardens are free, but don't skimp on a ticket to the 1874 cast-iron-and-glass **Palmehus**, which includes a complex of glass houses. The dominant Palmehus was inspired by London's no-longer-standing Crystal Palace. It dates from the 19th century, and its dense collection of plants from continents as far flung as Australia make for a quick, steamy escape. The main circular section features wrought-iron spiral staircases leading to an elevated walkway with a bird's-eye view of the 'jungle' below. The butterfly house is a place of wonder, full of fluttering butterflies as well as incubators for glittering chrysalises.

DESTINATION: DESIGN

Mille Maria Steffen-Nielsen Smith is head of communications at Designmuseum Danmark. *@designmuseumdanmark*

Etage Projects: Beautiful art and design gallery with changing exhibitions (Borgergade 15). Marvel at lamps and vases by Danish artist FOS, unique ceramics by Karl Monies or tinted mirrors by Sabine Marcelis.

Danish design showrooms: There are many exemplary showrooms near the Designmuseum: House of Finn Juhl (Gothersgade 9), Montana Furniture (Bredgade 24) or File Under Pop (Esplanaden 6).

Design-forward cafes and bars: FRAMA's Apotek 57 (Fredericiagade 57) – great and very Instagrammable food in a beautiful space. Den Lille Blå might be the city's most beautiful wine bar.

EATING IN NYHAVN & ROYAL COPENHAGEN: BEST LEISURELY MEAL

Iluka: Innovative insider's seafood restaurant in the quiet streets south of Nyhavn. *5.30pm-midnight Tue-Sat* €€

Pluto: Popular bistro that hits the bull's eye between cosy vibe and creative menu. *5.30pm-midnight Mon-Thu, to 2am Fri & Sat, to 11pm Sun* €€

A Terre: This French restaurant purrs with chic, serving creative cuisine by French-Danish chef Yves Le Lay. *5-10pm Wed-Sat, noon-2pm* Sat €€€

Ambra: With high ceilings and soft lighting, excellent Italian cuisine is overseen by Michelin-starred Andreas Bagh. *5pm-1am, to 2am Fri & Sat* €€

BEST SHOPPING IN ROYAL COPENHAGEN

Klassik Moderne Møbelkunst: Valhalla for lovers of Danish design, with classics from Poul Henningsen, Hans J Wegner, Arne Jacobsen, Finn Juhl and Nanna Ditzel.

Tranquebar: Bookshop specialising in world literature, organised into countries and regions.

FRAMA: Beautiful, practical homeware and design for living the best life.

Botanisk Haves Butik: A small but rich collection of botanically themed gifts.

Statens Museum for Kunst: Denmark's museum shops are always top-notch, and the National Art Gallery is as good as it gets, with all sorts of high-end trinkets, art and gift items.

At the north end of the gardens, a new 1.2-billion kroner Natural History Museum is under construction, overrunning its planned 2024 opening date. The €155-million construction will have a glass dome in line with the nearby Palmehus and span three floors underground.

Glass-Walled Fabulous Art Museum

Dazzling National Art Gallery

Mostly known by its Danish acronym SMK, **Statens Museum for Kunst** *(smk.dk/en/section/visit-smk; adult/child 130kr/free)* is Denmark's largest art museum, with more than 9000 paintings and sculptures in its collection. At the southern end of Østre Anlæg park, its grand Italian Renaissance revival building has been turned into a modern marvel through the attachment of a modern wing with a glass wall overlooking the park. This inside-outside architecture and extraordinarily rich collection, including works by Mantegna, Munch, Ancher, Dürer, Modigliani, Hammershøi and PS Krøyer, makee it an especially good place to escape on a rainy day. The cafe and shop are both excellent.

Jewel-Like Gallery: Hirschsprung

Palatially housed Danish Classics

Dedicated to Danish art of the 19th and early 20th centuries, **Hirschsprung** *(hirschsprung.dk/en; adult/child 110kr/free)* is a little jewel box of a gallery, full of wonderful surprises for art lovers unfamiliar with the classic era of Danish oil painting. Originally the private holdings of tobacco magnate Heinrich Hirschsprung, it contains works by 'Golden Age' painters such as Christen Købke and CW Eckersberg, a notable selection by Skagen painters PS Krøyer, and Anna and Michael Ancher, and also works by the Danish symbolists and the Funen Painters.

Play & Learn at the Workers Museum

Surprisingly entertaining and fun for kids

A couple of steps across Gothersgade is the **Arbejdermuseet** (Workers Museum), where you can learn about the Danish labour movement. If this sounds a bit niche and not likely to appeal to non-Danes, think again. Like most Danish museums, it's imaginatively done, with reconstructed fin-de-siècle worker's interiors, and chances for kids to play at shopkeeping. Plus there's an authentic-feeling 1950s cafe in the basement.

DRINKING IN NYHAVN & ROYAL COPENHAGEN

Søhesten: Pub quiz Tuesday, live jazz Wednesday and DJ weekends. *5pm-midnight Tue & Wed, to 2am Thu, to 5am Fri & Sat*

Hviids Vinstue: The city's oldest bar, here since 1723. In winter *gløgg* is served from November. *10am-1am Mon-Thu, to 2am Fri & Sat, to 8pm Sun*

Brønnum: Take in this atmospheric lounge from the comfort of a velour barstool. *4pm-1am Tue-Wed, to midnight Mon, to 2am Thu, to 3am Fri & Sat*

Tipsy Mermaid: Craft beer on a boat at the mouth of Nyhavn. *noon-10pm Mon-Thu, to midnight Fri & Sat*

CARB ODYSSEY: BAKERY & SIGHTS TOUR

Danish pastries are in a field all of their own. This tour takes you to some of the city's most dazzling bakeries, passing some of the lesser-known highlights on the way.

START	END	LENGTH
Juno the Bakery	La Glace	5.5km; half a day

Start in Østerbro, at buzzing (usually with a queue) 1 **Juno the Bakery**, famous for its warm-from-the-oven BMO: *bolle med ost* (sourdough roll, generously buttered, with a slice of punchy cheese). Founded by a former Noma pastry chef, Emil Glaser, Juno is also famous for sumptuously good cardamon buns.

Walk south, through pretty squares, such as leafy Bopa Plads, seemingly populated by models, to reach 2 **Hart Bageri**, from another Noma baker, Richard Hart. The BMO are famously great here too, but the *tebirkes* are a must-eat. They're flaky, soft, with caramelised *remonce* (sugar, butter and marzipan filling), and topped with poppy seeds.

From here you can walk along the bank of the 3 **Lakes**, or continue to stroll. Stop at 4 **Bageriet Benji** in Nørrebro, from another Noma alumnus, Rasmus Kristensen, crossing. Walk along Frederiksborggade, then stop at 5 **Torvehallerne KBH** (p52), the food hall, which is always a sensational browse. You may have had your fill of BMO at this point, but their go-to bakery is Albatross & Venner. From here, walk through Ørstedsparken to 6 **Sankt Peders Bageri** (p53), Copenhagen's oldest bakery, dating from 1652. As a final stop, it's a five-minute walk around the corner to glittering 7 **La Glace**, with its windows full of fanciful cakes.

Close to the Lakes is the wonderful **Enigma Museum** (p84), well worth stopping off for an hour or two.

Dronning Louises Bro (p64), the bridge at the centre of the Lakes, is ideal for a photo op. It's a popular hang-out spot in the early evening.

If you fancy stopping along the Lakes for a drink, **Søernes Ølbar** has seats out by the lake, and local craft beers on tap.

SEAPLANE FLIGHTS

With a dock right next to tourist hot spots Kastellet and the Little Mermaid, one of Denmark's most unique means of travel is hiding in plain sight. **Nordic Seaplanes** *(seaplanes.dk/en)* runs several daily flights to and from Aarhus, with centrally located boarding/departure gates and seaplanes that take off from the open water just outside each city. The Copenhagen–Aarhus trip takes about 45 minutes each way, and one-way tickets start at 997kr. There are also purely sightseeing flights (797kr), which circle around both Copenhagen and Aarhus at 500m high, with 15 minutes in the air.

Use this QR code to book your Nordic Seaplanes flight

SERGII FIGURNYI/SHUTTERSTOCK ©

The Little Mermaid

Controversial? The Little Mermaid

Diminutive city icon

The **Little Mermaid** might be a modest monument, sitting out on her rock in the harbour, but she doubtless provokes strong feelings. Carl Jacobsen commissioned the statue in 1909 after being entranced by the ballet of the *Little Mermaid*. The ballerina, Ellen Price, who had played her, refused to pose nude for the artist, Edvard Eriksen, so his wife, Eline Eriksen posed for him, with the face modelled on the star.

She has frequently been the victim of vandalism, beheaded in 1964, having an arm severed (and then returned) in 1984, with another attempted beheading in 1990, then her head was cut off for the second time in 1998. In 2003 explosives blew her off her perch, but she was discovered in the harbour and put back in her spot. So if you find the 1.25m statue underwhelming, you can at least admire her awe-inspiring resilience.

Just past Kastellet on the Langelinie quay, you'll run into Bjørn Nørgaard's *Genetically Modified Little Mermaid*, a cheeky rejoinder to the persistent mermaid-mania.

Nyboder Yellow

Photogenic neighbourhood

Painted such a distinctively ochre-yellow colour there's even a term 'Nyboder yellow' in Danish, **Nyboder** is a quaint central neighbourhood of two-storey terraced houses. Built for naval personnel by King Christian IV, it's a rare example of workers' housing that was well built enough to last for centuries, and is still home to many military families. Most of the houses date from the second half of the 1700s, and their symmetrical layout around **Sankt Pauls Kirke** is particularly photogenic. It's usually pretty quiet, but the first house to be built, **Nyboders Mindestuer**, contains a display *(open 11am to 2pm on Sunday)*.

Christianshavn & the Inner Harbour

FROM NAUTICAL HEARTLANDS TO HIPPY HAVEN

Just across the water from Nyhavn, to which it has been connected since 2016 by the handy Inner Harbour cycle bridge, Christianshavn is built over a series of artificial islands and defensive structures sandwiched between 'mainland' Zealand and Amager Island. Constructed during Christian IV's 17th-century reign with more than a bit of inspiration from the Dutch, Christianshavn is the nautical heart of the city, cut through by numerous canals and moats where a quaint and quirky collection of houseboats are docked.

Today the radical, autonomous Christiania community and industrial-chic Refshaleøen to the north coexist in Christianshavn alongside government ministries and some of Copenhagen's most ambitious and prestigious building projects. Despite this increasing wealth and allure, there's still something just a bit salty in the air and the vibe here. The neighbourhood's sailor roots and decades as a working-class bastion fortunately can't be gentrified out quite so easily – there's still just enough room on the island for everybody.

GETTING AROUND

Metro Lines M1 and M2 stop at Christianshavn metro station.

Bus Catch westbound 2A or 37 for Tivoli Gardens, Ny Carlsberg Glyptotek and Central Station; westbound 350S for Nørrebro; and northbound 9A for the northern reaches of Christianshavn and Holmen.

Boat Harbour buses stop at Knippelsbro and Operaen. Catch a southbound service for Nyhavn and Det Kongelige Bibliotek, or a northbound service for Nordre Toldbod (Kastellet), and Refshaleøen.

Swimming at Islands Brygge Havnebadet

Copenhagen's harbourfront Hawaii

At Christianshavn's southern border, the **Islands Brygge Havnebadet** are the purest essence of summertime in Copenhagen. The complex, designed by Bjarke Ingels and Julien De Smedt of PLOT and JDS Architects, was the first to open after the harbour was declared fit for swimming in 2001, and has since inspired many others (p58). It remains wildly popular, with locals and visitors alike flocking to the five pools (two suitable for children) all summer. (Plus a few in the winter!) The long grassy park along the quayside is picnic perfection, and there are a couple of nearby fast-food places.

TOP TIP

The best way to reach Refshaleøen, other than by bike, is the Harbour Bus ferry, but note its last run of the night is usually between 8pm and 9pm.

CHRISTIANSHAVN & THE INNER HARBOUR

HIGHLIGHTS
1 Freetown Christiania
2 Refshaleøen

SIGHTS
3 Copenhagen Contemporary
4 CopenHill
5 Øens Have
6 Vor Frelsers Kirke

ACTIVITIES, COURSES & TOURS
7 Islands Brygge Havnebadet

SLEEPING
8 25 Hours Paper Island
9 CPH Living
10 Hotel NH Copenhagen
11 Kanalhuset
12 Sankt Anna B&B

EATING
13 Alchemist
14 Cafe Wilder
15 Christianshavns Færgecafé
● Connie-Connie (see 3)
16 Hart Bageri
17 Hart Bageri
18 Kanalen
● Kanalhuset (see 11)
19 La Banchina
20 Lille Bakery
21 Månefiskeren
22 Morgenstedet
23 Reffen

DRINKING & NIGHTLIFE
24 Christianshavns Bådudlejning & Café
● Eiffel Bar (see 14)
● Terrassen (see 23)

ENTERTAINMENT
25 Christiania Jazz Club
26 Den Grå Hal
27 Loppen
28 Nemoland

Tower with a View

Climb Vor Frelsers Kirke

You'll get a soul-feeding view from the top of the spiralling tower of 17th-century **Vor Frelsers Kirke**. Make the head-spinning 398-step ascent to the top – vertigo-sufferers take note, the last 150 steps run along the outside rim of the tower, narrowing to the point where they literally disappear at the top. Inspired by Borromini's tower of St Ivo in Rome, the spire was added in 1752 by Lauritz de Thurah.

Communal Dining at Kanalhuset

Get to know your neighbours

Kanalhuset is a fine old primrose-yellow canalside building dating from 1754, previously a boarding school for young sailors, a hospital and a museum. The founders of the Tiger retail chain, Lennart and Susanne Lajboschitz, started their community-centred ventures with Folkehuset Absalon in Vesterbro, but this is a more upmarket version. They live in the house, which also contains boutique hotel rooms and apartments. It's not expensive, however. You book ahead for a daily changing set menu (150kr) based on seasonal ingredients, and then turn up at 6.30pm to dine at 7pm, You'll be seated at long tables in the graceful dining room, and everyone is encouraged to talk to their neighbours. It's a great way to get to meet some Danes or other travellers, with a lovely warm atmosphere.

Hippy Vibes at Freetown Christiania

Out-there commune district

Encompassing a once-abandoned military barracks and surviving parts of Christian V's 17th-century Fæstningsringen (Fortification Ring) bastions, **Freetown Christiania** was established by squatters in the heady days of 1971. It has existed in an uneasy relationship with the Danish state ever since. It was long notorious for 'Pusher Street', where weed and hash were once sold openly, before a spate of gang-related violence led to a community-led crackdown. Pusher Street no longer hosts its eponymous dealers, and was dug up in 2024 in preparation for reestablishing the zone as a cultural centre. At present it has the feel of a traveller hangout somewhere like Nepal or the Khaosan Road, with an unpaved surface, fluttering prayer flags, and wooden buildings selling vegan meals, T-shirts and fridge magnets.

BEST MUSIC VENUES IN CHRISTIANIA

Unlike the rest of Denmark, cash is king in Christiania, so come prepared.

Nemoland: At the heart of 'downtown' Christiania, this bar, stage and restaurant complex puts on two daily Sunday concerts in summer.

Loppen: Lively, intimate music venue with a strong calendar of Danish and international acts.

Den Grå Hal: Live-music venue that also hosts a Christmas market in December.

Christiania Jazz Club: Small and sociable club where you might catch live jazz, hip-hop, comedy and more from Wednesday to Sunday. Cash only.

EATING IN CHRISTIANSHAVN: BEST BAKERIES & CAFES

Hart Bageri: Homely harbourfront bakery with sweets, sandwiches and a wine list; open evenings at weekends. *7.30am-6pm* €€

Månefiskeren: Simple coffees, cakes and sandwiches at this popular Christiania hangout. Cash only. *11am-7pm Tue-Sun* €

Lille Bakery: For gourmand Copenhagen visitors, Lille Bakery is worth a trip to Refshaleøen alone. *8am-5pm Wed-Sun* €

Morgenstedet: A homely, hippy vegetarian garden cafe in the heart of Christiania, Morgenstedet offers a short, simple menu. *noon-9pm Tue-Sun* €

BEST COPENHAGEN FOR KIDS

Playgrounds: Copenhagen has over 140 brilliant playgrounds. Unique is the Traffic Playground (Trafiklegepladsen) in Fælledparken: bikes and helmets are free for kids aged two to eight. Konditaget Lüders is on a rooftop in Nordhavn.

Paddling pools & swimming pools: The city has many *soppebassiner* (free water parks). For harbour baths with kids' pools, see p58.

Museums: The hands-on Experimentarium, Nationalmuseet, Enigma Museum, Aquarium, Louisiana and the War Museum.

Theme Parks: Tivoli is in the city centre, while Bakken is likewise magical and in the deer park.

Beaches: Amagerstrand is the nearest beach. Bellevue to the north is also popular.

Outside the centre, Christiania is a wild and wonderful place to wander, full of whimsical DIY homes, cosy garden plots, eateries, beer gardens, music venues, waterfront trails – and a tantalising taste of the slightly chaotic, countercultural frisson that perfectly coiffed Copenhagen sometimes lacks. Resident-led tours start at the Prinsessegade entrance at 3pm *(weekends year-round, daily July and August; 60kr cash)*. Many places don't accept cards, so take some cash.

Wander around to find **Green George**, one of Thomas Dambo's two famous giant wooden trolls to be found in Copenhagen, as well as **Gallopperiet** (Stadens Museum for Kunst), an upstairs gallery showing local Christiania artists. Stop at beloved, volunteer-run, hippy garden cafe **Morgenstedet**, with an enchanting, Hansel-and-Gretel vibe, serving a bargain menu of vegetarian treats.

DRINKING IN CHRISTIANSHAVN: BEST BARS

Eiffel Bar: Drop into this quirky, smoky dive for a glimpse back in time at the old Christianshavn. *noon-2am*

Christianshavns Bådudlejning & Café: This floating cafe-bar is a wonderful spot for drinks. *11.30am-midnight Jun-Aug, reduced hours rest of year*

La Banchina: Natural wines at this waterside bar, with a sauna (book ahead). *8am-11pm Mon-Sun May-Sep, reduced hours rest of year*

Terrassen: Beer garden in Reffen, with waterside seating and a laidback vibe. *10.30am-10.30pm Mon-Thu, to 11.30pm Fri & Sat, to 9.30pm Sun*

VIKTOR OSYPENKO/ALAMY STOCK PHOTO ©

Green George

CopenHill, a Rooftop Ski Slope

An audacioius surprise in Europe's flattest capital

Visible from around the city, **CopenHill** (aka Amager Bakke) is an undeniably creative – but equally controversial – monument to Copenhagen's sustainable ambitions. This architectural feat was designed by the Bjarke Ingels Group, who won a competition about how to use the rooftop of this waste-management plant. BIG's audacious solution was this 450m green-roof ski slope, plus the world's tallest climbing wall at 85m. Guests can rent skiing equipment, but most make do with the long walk up to the rooftop bar. Take the lift down to see inside the energy source for 90,000 households. The climbing wall is as tall as the building, and though the ski slope may be made of green plastic, there are lifts, slaloms and ski rental at the ready. Views from the cafe-bar are unassailable. It's free to walk the 450m to the top.

HEDONISTIC SUSTAINABILITY

Almost every new spectacular building project in Copenhagen seems to have been designed by the same architecture firm. This is the Bjarke Ingels Group (BIG), founded by Danish architect, Bjarke Ingels, who studied architecture at the Royal Danish Academy of Fine Arts. Ingels has become renowned for a playful approach that has been a move away from the traditionally functional, sober buildings of architects like Arne Jacobsen and Finn Juhl. Perhaps the most extraordinary of BIG's buildings is CopenHill, but you'll also notice two spiky towers, known as the cacti, which dominate the sky in Vesterbro. These projects and others reflect his philosophy of 'hedonistic sustainability', which focuses on fun and liveability while addressing environmental concerns.

EATING IN CHRISTIANSHAVN: LEISURELY DINING

Kanalhuset (p75): Come for a fresh and affordable communal dinner every evening at 7pm. *dinner 7pm, arrive at 6.30pm* **€€**

Christianshavns Færgecafé: Smørrebrød and other classics in a cosy canalside haunt. *11.30am-3.30pm daily & 5.30-9pm Mon-Sat* **€€**

Kanalen: Beautiful, modern Danish food and a canalside location. *11.30am-midnight Mon-Sat* **€€€**

Cafe Wilder: One of Copenhagen's oldest cafes, serving dainty smørrebrød. *11.30am-11pm Mon-Thu, to midnight Fri & Sat, to 10pm Sun* **€**

Reffen Street Food market

TOP EXPERIENCE

Refshaleøen

Marking the northern entrance to Copenhagen's harbour, the former shipyard island of **Refshaleøen** – home to the easier-to-pronounce 'Reffen' street-food market – is a hip, post-industrial creative campus, with a feel not unlike Amsterdam Noord or Rathenau-Hallen in Berlin. Since the shipyards closed in 1996, it has slowly become a centre of art, gastronomy, music, theatre, architecture and sport.

- Reffen
- La Banchina
- Copenhagen Contemporary
- Øens Have
- Hart Bageri
- Werkstatt
- CopenHill

Getting Here

You could cycle or take the bus to Refshaleøen. Cycling here is a scenic trip in itself, crossing Holmen island behind the Operaen, passing charming boat-bar Kontiki, skirting around Noma's organic farm and meandering through the delightfully rural north end of Christiania. A lovely way to reach here is by Harbour Bus.

PRACTICALITIES
Scan this QR code for more details.

Street Food Market

The focal point for most visitors is the Reffen Street Food market, Scandinavia's largest, covering an area of 6000 sq metres. There are over 50 stalls, with authentic cuisines from Afghanistan to Argentina, and a big Mikkeller beer bar attached. There's also a 4000-sq-metre area on the waterfront, where you can sit back on deckchairs with views over the harbour. When it gets too cold to do this, head to Werkstatt, a former machine hall, where bars and food stalls open year-round, and there's an ice rink and campfires outside.

Sights

There are still military facilities up this way, and the retired frigate boat *Peder Skram* is open to visitors in the summer. Once considered Copenhagen's distant periphery, Refshaleøen has shifted the city's cultural centre of gravity, and today the island is a choose-your-own-adventure book of culture, cuisine and more: Scandinavia's biggest urban farm? **Øens Have** – you can volunteer here to help with gardening and get a free lunch (made from the garden produce) in return. Modern art? **Copenhagen Contemporary**, with changing exhibitions in 7000 sq m of industrial halls. Theatre? Teaterøen. Climbing? Blocs & Walls. A short walk away is **CopenHill** (p77), the city's dry ski slope on top of a waste-processing plant: as well as skiing, there's a climbing wall, or take the lift to the top for superb views across Copenhagen and out to sea.

Other Eats

The double-Michelin-starred **Alchemist** can take you on a 50-course culinary journey, just around the corner. This is an artistic, holistic adventure, rather than a mere meal of a lifetime, with projections such as the Northern Lights, as you tuck into high-art, high-concept food, created by Rasmus Munk. For something more breakfast or brunchy, there's **Lille Bakery** (p75) or **Hart Bageri** for pastries and coffee, or eat at **Connie-Connie** at the Copenhagen Contemporary. **La Banchina** (p76) is housed in a kiosk on the waterfront, and is the place to go for a glass of natural wine and antipasti with a view.

Festivals

The island also hosts several annual festivals: metalhead favourite Copenhell, Karrusel for house and disco, and the Distortion festival's 'forest rave'.

Lynetteholmen

A new neighbourhood is planned for Refshaleøen. This is part of the enormous, and controversial, Lynetteholmen land reclamation project, in which a 275-hectare artificial island is being built to the north. The project broke ground at the end of 2021, and some 35,000 residents are expected to live here when it's complete – in 2070! The first residents are expected to arrive in 2035.

SWIM & SAUNA

The sauna cabin at La Banchina has a lovely view over the water, and you can book for private sessions, and then swim in the water in front. Nearby is Badezone Søndre Refshalebassin, another harbour bath. Both are deep water only and without a beach.

TOP TIPS

- You could also walk to Reffen, it's only around 20 minutes from Nyhavn.
- Be aware that most things close around 8pm or 9pm, including the Harbour Bus.

EXPLORE CENTRAL CHRISTIANSHAVN

Christianshavn's centre, cut through with canals and bobbing with boats, is easy to explore on foot or by bike.

START	END	LENGTH
Inderhavnsbroen	Lagkagehuset	3km; 2–3 hours

Start from the pedestrian-only 1 **Inderhavnsbroen**, aka Kyssebroen (the Kissing Bridge), after its two moveable halves that meet in the middle. To your left is 2 **Operaen** (Copenhagen Opera House), a 2.5-billion-kroner donation from shipping giant Maersk, and next to this is the 3 **Operaparken** green space, a new development above a huge, hidden multistorey car park. There's a nice cafe in the park. Closest to the bridge, the trapezoidal skyline of the 4 **Papirøen** (Paper Island) is one of the city's newer developments, home to a hotel, restaurants, flats and a Japanese-designed 'water-culture house' opening in 2025. At the foot of the bridge, get a coffee or a bite to eat at 5 **Broens Gadekøkken** street food market (which turns into an ice-skating rink in winter), or try Noma's burger spin-off, created during lockdown, 6 **POPL**. The 7 **Nordatlantens Brygge** (North Atlantic House), a historic warehouse turned culture and art centre, sits just behind, with rotating exhibitions from Iceland, Greenland and the Faroe Islands.

You can't miss the 8 **Vor Frelsers Kirke**, with its spiralling spire – stop for a climb if you feel like it. Have an afternoon pastry at the original canalside 9 **Lagkagehuset** (Layer Cake House) bakery, which is now preaching the Danish gospel as far afield as London and NYC.

Nørrebro & Østerbro

HALF BOHEMIAN, HALF BOUTIQUES

The twin 'bro' (bridge) neighbourhoods of Nørrebro and Østerbro are a bit like siblings who lead very different lives: Nørrebro went to art school, studied abroad and goes to protests at weekends, while Østerbro works in marketing or tech, prefers electoral politics and spends the weekends at a summerhouse on the Danish Riviera. They still get together from time to time, but don't have many friends in common.

So while Nørrebro's creative effervescence and funky international vibe is just the ticket for an artistic rendezvous or a wild party weekend, Østerbro will be there when you wake up on Sunday – a calm place to cure your hangover with exquisite coffee and croissants, or a cool dip in the harbour to clear your head, and ideal for picking up a gift for yourself or someone else on your way.

Both districts have a charm all their own, and a stroll along the Lakes that lie between the two takes in the best of both worlds.

GETTING AROUND

Nørrebro is more spread out than Østerbro, though it's served by several metro stops. Cycling is typically the easiest way to get around, though the ride up to Grundtvigs Kirke has something very rare in Copenhagen: a hill.

TOP TIP

Don't mix up Nørreport and Nørrebro stations. At the edge of the old city, Nørreport is the capital's second-busiest station, served by the Øresundståg, many S-tog lines, regional trains, and metro M1 and M2. Nørrebro is served by S-tog F and M3. Bus 5C connects the 3km between Nørreport and Nørrebro stations.

RIP VIPs

Nørrebro's haunted hangout

Visitors are often surprised to see **Assistens Kirkegård** listed among Copenhagen's top tourist destinations, but for a Dane, nothing could be more normal. Set behind a long yellow wall, this calm and leafy cemetery is a prime hang-out spot, with Danes of all ages strolling and relaxing in the forested grounds.

Formerly a pauper's graveyard, and before that a tobacco field, from the mid-1800s until today it has been the preferred cemetery for Denmark's leading cultural figures, such as philosopher Søren Kierkegaard (d 1855), writer Hans Christian Andersen (d 1875), physicist Niels Bohr (d 1962) and singer Natasja Saad (d 2007).

SIGHTS
1 Assistens Kirkegård
2 Enigma Museum
3 Superkilen

SLEEPING
4 Rye 115
5 Urban Camper

EATING
6 Ali's Bageri
7 Bæst
8 Durum Bar
9 Hidmona
10 Omar
● Send Flere Krydderier (see 3)
11 Turning Chicken
12 uGood

DRINKING & NIGHTLIFE
13 Barking Dog
14 Mikkeller & Friends
15 Mucki Bar
16 Pompette

Glorious Grundtvigs & Blossom Central

Modernist-Gothic and cherry trees

Just past Nørrebro, in the largely residential neighbourhood of Nordvest, **Grundtvigs Kirke** *(grundtvigskirke.dk)* is one of Copenhagen's architectural wonders, built from six million bricks.

Named after the hugely influential 19th-century minister NFS Grundtvig, it was designed by architect Peder Vilhelm Jensen-Klint, who also landscaped the surrounding area, creating a uniquely harmonious neighbourhood. He died before it was finished, and his son, designer Kaare Klint, completed it in 1940. Kaare also created the chairs. The soaring organ-pipe lines of the Expressionist facade give way to the 22m-high Gothic interior, and you can clearly see how it inspired Reykjavík's famous Hallgrímskirkja cathedral. Each column is built from 30,000 bricks.

The church also sits at the entrance to **Bispebjerg Kirkegård**, famous for its *Kirsebæralléen* (cherry alley), where dozens of Japanese cherry trees bloom every spring, attracting tens of thousands of visitors who come to see the vivid pink blossoms. The scenic lakes at **Utterslev Mose** sit just behind.

Getting to Know Nørrebro

Where the cool things are

On any number of 'coolest neighbourhood lists' Nørrebro is Copenhagen's hippest, densest, liveliest, foodiest, artsiest, most international district, full of 19th-century architecture and international eats from Ugandan to Persian.

Nørrebrogade is the main spine of the neighbourhood (all Copenhagen's 'bro' districts have a street like this, for example Vestobrogade). Most all of Nørrebro's highlights and hot spots are within a few blocks of this artery, and you can easily spend a day mooching and flâneuring your way around the mural-strewn streets.

BEST CLUBBING & MUSIC VENUES

Alice: Nonprofit venue focusing on global alternative and eclectic styles.

Christiania Jazz Club: Atmospheric club in Christiania.

Vega: Three halls showcasing Danish and international performers in a modernist building.

Pumpehuset: Central spot for everything from new Danish hip-hop to Chicago house and drag shows.

Spillestedet Stengade: Nørrebro venue with a diverse calendar, but especially known for rock and metal.

Culture Box: Fun in central Copenhagen, focusing on electronic music.

Bolsjefabrikken: Reggae-centred sounds at this off-beat, graffiti-covered place in Østerbro.

Werkstatt 167: Post-industrial bar-club on Refshaleøen.

EATING IN NØRREBRO: BEST INTERNATIONAL

Hidmona: Homely Ethiopian serving hearty stews over spongy, gently sour *injera* bread. *noon-10pm Tue-Sun, from 2pm Mon* €€

Ali's Bageri: Handy for Superkilen, counter-service Lebanese classics like *ful*, *fatayer* and *manakish*, plus a brunch combo. *9am-7pm* €

uGood: Hip outlet serving *rolex* – savoury Ugandan chapati roll-ups stuffed with omelettes and veg. *noon-9pm Tue-Sun* €

Bæst: Europe's best pizza, according to some pizzaiolo rankings. *5-10.30pm, plus noon-3pm Thu-Sun* €€

Turning Chicken: Rôtisserie, with the menu reflecting the migrant route of the Turkish-born owner Imam Gür. *hours vary* €

Send Flere Krydderier: Somali *sambusas*, Pakistani pakora and more at this delicious social enterprise. *hours vary* €€

Omar: Fun and eclectic bistro and wine bar with a tasting menu and hip-hop soundtrack. *noon-midnight Sun-Thu, to 1am Fri & Sat* €€€

Durum Bar: Arguably the king of Copenhagen kebabs, with fresh bread and big flavours. *11am-midnight Sun-Wed, to 3am Thu, to 5am Fri & Sat* €

DANISH DIVES

Morten de Fine Olivarius and **Carmen Mirea Robrahn** are documenting every bodega in Copenhagen. *@baggulegardiner*

We love the old and smoky bodegas of Copenhagen. There are around 200 of these bars left across the city. Besides the cheap beer and indoor smoking, they differ a lot. Some attract young people, some mostly have old regulars sitting around the bar. In some you can dance, in some you can barely hear the music. But the best thing: in here, the famously introverted Danes will have conversations with complete strangers. A few of our favourites:

Café Nick (city centre)
Café Viking (Nørrebro)
Jeppes Bodega (Nordvest)
Blomsten (Vesterbro)
Tingkroen (Amager)

Make a left down **Blågårdsgade** for a fun mix of greengrocers and terrace bars, or a right down **Elmegade** for fresh fashion.

Back on Nørrebrogade, competition is fierce between the dozens of kebab joints – there's even a Nørrebrogade Shawarma Championship – but duck behind the yellow walls of **Assistens Kirkegård** (p81) for a garden shortcut to **Jægersborggade**, which used to be as notorious as Pusher Street in Christiania, but now is the neighbourhood's artiest, foodiest drag.

From here continue 700m to **Superkilen**, a linear park and plaza running through the heart of Nørrebro. Connecting between Nørrebrogade and Tagensvej, it consists of three parts – the red square, black square, and green park. It's an eclectic community space filled with pop art, swings and skateboard ramps.

Breaking the Code

AI, deep fakes and vintage games

At the back of the former Post Office building, is the **Enigma Museum** *(enigma.dk; adult/child 140/55kr)*. From the impressive 1930s switchboard in the foyer, to the indoor playground full of telephone-themed fun, this is an absorbing meditation on the development of communications from the earliest telephones to AI and deep fakes.

In the basement are vintage arcade games and computer consoles, so kids can discover retro entertainment and older visitors might indulge in a spot of nostalgia. Charge up a card at reception to play the games.

Fun-Packed Joyous Science

Multistorey hands-on fun

The hands-on **Experimentarium** *(experimentarium.dk/en; adult/child 248/154kr)*, a short bus ride from Hellerup station, is a thrilling science museum in a beautiful building – its levels centre on a spiralling atrium, where you can step inside bubbles, have brainwave wars and practise moving cargo or go through a 'tunnel of the senses'.

DRINKING IN NØRREBRO

Barking Dog: Far from hostile, this Barking Dog is affable, unpretentious and not too loud. *6pm-1am Tue-Sat*

Mucki Bar: Classic bodega with a youthful vibe, immortalised in a 2022 Danish smash hit by Tobias Rahim. *2pm-1am Mon-Sat*

Mikkeller & Friends: Pale wood and Tiffany blue set the scene for over 40 artisanal draft beers. *2pm-11am Mon-Thu, from noon Sat & Sun, to 1am Fri & Sat*

Pompette: Duck into this rough-meets-refined *vinbar* bar just off of Nørrebrogade for a glass of natural wine. *noon-midnight*

BEST DESIGN ICON SITES

Finn Juhl's House: Part of the Ordrupgaard Museum in Charlottenlund, Finn Juhl's house is perfectly preserved.

Radisson Collection Royal Hotel: Designed by Arne Jacobsen, from the building to the teaspoons. One room is perfectly preserved. The concierge will usually let you look, for a fee.

Bellevue Beach: Near Klampenborg station, with lifeguard seats and changing rooms designed by Arne Jacobsen, as well as a nearby petrol station and theatre.

Designmuseum Danmark: Huge array of design classic chairs, as well as architecture a reworking of the original Klint design.

Dansk Arkitektur Center: Trace the development of Danish architecture and design.

NIELSKLIM/SHUTTERSTOCK

Bellevue Beach

Vesterbro & Frederiksberg

GENTRIFIED EDGY DISTRICT MEETS POSH

GETTING AROUND

Vesterbro is especially well connected, as it's close to Copenhagen's Central Station. Frederiksberg has a handy metro stop. You can walk from Vesterbro to Frederiksberg with ease, but you might want to jump on a bike. Carlsberg has its own S-train station.

If Nørrebro and Østerbro are chalk-and-cheese siblings, then Vesterbro and Frederiksberg are more like distant cousins. Vesterbro flows southwest from Central Station. Istedgade is one of Copenhagen's most (in)famous streets: centre of drugs and prostitution, and it's still a bit seedy, but not unsafe. The whole area was once synonymous with its red-light district and drug issues, where 70% of flats still didn't have a bathroom in 1989, until an influx of government funding turbo-charged gentrification. This wrought its usual work, creating a haven for independent businesses and artisanal coffee, while pricing out the original inhabitants. However, it has undeniably transformed the area, with its meatpacking district reinvented to become Copenhagen's buzziest evening haunt. The south is dominated by Kaktus Towers, a pair of two spikey towers – apartments built by Copenhagen's starchitects BIG. Old-money Frederiksberg – the less-complicated cousin – has some of the city's grandest housing, lush parks, the zoo, art-filled cisterns and the new Carlsberg district.

Vesterbro Vibes

Get to know Copenhagen's hippest hood

The hipster density climbs sharply as you head towards Enghave Plads – where the **Beat Cafe** does tapas and live gigs, and **Vega** does concerts – and the lovely neoclassical Enghaveparken, dating from the 1920s, with different zones: water features, a rose garden, a playground and more. The bandstand was designed by one of the godfathers of Danish modernism, Arne Jacobsen.

Halmtorvet/Sønder Blvd is the hippest of Vesterbro's three main streets. Its linear green space (a major hangout) runs almost 2km to Carlsberg in Frederiksberg.

Next along is candlelit craft-beer hub **Fermentoren**, followed by deluxe corner shop **Kihoskh**, where there's usually a lively crowd on the grass out front, or at **Litauens Plads** around

TOP TIP

Don't mix up Frederiksberg with Frederiksborg, the royal castle set in Hillerød, some 35km away (or Frederikssund or Frederiksværk or Frederikshavn for that matter).

HIGHLIGHTS
1 Frederiksberg Have

SIGHTS
2 Cisternerne
3 Copenhagen Zoo
4 Frederiksberg Rådhus
5 Frederiksberg Slot

SLEEPING
6 66 Guldsmeden
7 Andersen Hotel
8 Axel Guldsmeden
9 Bertrams Guldsmeden
10 Coco Hotel
11 Hotel Ottilia By Brøchner Hotels
12 Manon Les Suites
13 Scandic Falkoner
14 Steel House Copenhagen
15 Urban House Copenhagen by MEININGER
16 Zleep Hotel

EATING
17 Beyla
18 Bistro Pan Pan
19 Bjørnekælderen
20 Chicky Grill
21 Fasangården
22 Folkehuset Absalon
23 Granola
24 Hart Bageri
● Hija de Sanchez (see 20)
25 Italo Disco
● Le Gourmand (see 23)
26 Mielcke & Hurtigkarl
27 Sanchez
28 Warpigs

DRINKING & NIGHTLIFE
29 Ancestrale
30 Beat Cafe
31 Café Intime
32 Fermentoren
33 Home of Carlsberg
34 Jernbanecafeen
35 Kihoskh
36 Lidkoeb
● Prolog Coffee (see 24)

ENTERTAINMENT
37 Vega

SHOPPING
38 Samsøe & Samsøe

EATING IN VESTERBRO: MEATPACKING DISTRICT

Warpigs: Brewing and barbecuing on the spot; tender roasted meats are shovelled directly onto your tray. *hours vary* **€€**

Hart Bageri: Superb baked goods founded by Noma alumnus Richard Hart, with some of the best pastries in Denmark. *8am-6pm* **€**

Hija de Sanchez: Takeaway *taqueria* incarnation of Sanchez restaurant, serving a short menu. *11am-9pm Sun-Thu, to 10pm Fri & Sat* **€€**

Chicky Grill: Prices are low and portions generous, from fried chicken to classic Danish staples like *flæskesteg* (roast pork). *11am-10pm Mon-Fri* **€**

MEATPACKING DISTRICT

Once upon a time a massive abattoir complex, Copenhagen's **Kødbyen** (meat town) is today one of the city's biggest nightlife and creative clusters, and the beating heart of still edgy, but uber-hip Vesterbro. Known as the Meatpacking District in a nod to NYC's similarly revitalised butchers' quarter, it's divided into brown, grey, and white sectors based on the colour of the buildings. The brown and grey parts are older (the first buildings date from 1879), while the white's celebrated modernist halls were opened in 1934. Visit by day or night to take your pick from its buzzy, indie restaurants, visit the contemporary V1 Gallery or Bo Bjerggaard galleries, and continue the evening at its late-night bars.

the corner. Further still is **Folkehuset Absalon**, an ex-church turned community and games centre, where the 6pm daily communal dinner is the best, and most memorable, deal in town. The brainchild of Flying Tiger founders, Lennart Lajboschitz and his wife Suzanne, Absalon is always worth checking out, especially if you want to mingle with Copenhageners, with events such as silent discos and bingo aimed at bringing the community together. Closer to the station is **BaneGaarden** – a garden and event hub, converted from former railway sidings, with some street food and special events.

Little Paris: Værnedamsvej

Parisian vibes and designer boutiques

Straddling the border between Vesterbro and Frederiksberg, Værnedamsvej is barely 200m long, but is one of the city's most charming streetscapes. It's named after Werner Dam, a beer tapper who owned a pub on the corner of the street in the 18th century. Packed with designer boutiques, gourmet groceries and pavement cafes spilling into the street, it's also known as Copenhagen's 'Little Paris', and it's not hard to see why (the French school being here until 2021 probably also helped). Double-named designers **Samsøe & Samsøe** and **Wood Wood** are here, the **Granola** cafe has long been a local institution, and – when in Paris – go for wine and cheese at **Le Gourmand**.

Emerald-Green Gardens & Zoo

Frederiksberg's royal green heart

The hilltop **Frederiksberg Slot** dates to the beginning of the 18th century, built as a summer residence for King Frederik IV, and home to the Royal Danish Military Academy since 1869. It's surrounded by the expansive and atmospheric **Frederiksberg Have**, one of the finest gardens in Copenhagen for a scenic afternoon, cut through by meandering streams, islands and also home to the city zoo.

Approaching from the Lakes, follow either the tree-lined Frederiksberg Allé or the main shopping street, Gammel Kongevej. From the latter, you arrive first at the **Frederiksberg Rådhus**, notable for its Saturday flea market. Here, the gardens are just in from the street, as well as the fabulous (and smoky) living-room vibes of **Café Intime**. (Better still, arrive from Nørrebro on Den Grønne Sti cycle path.)

Enter the gardens and stroll around the bird-rich waterways, or take one of the idyllic 20-minute rowboat tours. You may

EATING IN VESTERBRO

Italo Disco: Intimate top-notch Italian, a neighbourhood restaurant with excellent fresh fish. *5.30pm-midnight Tue-Sun* €€

BaneGaarden: Street food stalls serve delicious fried chicken and other marvels in a courtyard. *9am-8pm Tue-Thu, Sun, to 10pm Fri, to 6pm Sat* €

Sanchez: Noma alumnus Rosio Sanchez modernises Mexican home cooking. *5pm-midnight daily & 11am-2pm Sat & Sun* €€€

Bjørnekælderen: Clever twists on Danish favourites in this century-old Bib Gourmand restaurant. *11.30am-10pm* Wed-Sat €€€

Polar bear, Copenhagen Zoo

even spot a pacifier tree *(suttetræer)* – a sweet Danish tradition where a child will symbolically give up their dummy by hanging it in a tree, sometimes with a note saying goodbye. Continue south to the back of **Copenhagen Zoo**, where you can check out the elephants without needing a ticket (but it's also worth a proper visit).

If you're here in midsummer, come for concerts and a bonfire on Sankt Hans Eve (*Sankthansaften*, June 23). South of the palace, the park is called **Søndermarken**, and worth a visit for the otherworldly **Cisternerne**.

Art-Filled Underground Wonder

Unparalleled art galleries

Beneath the grassy expanse of Søndermarken one of the city's strangest attractions sits right beneath your feet. **Cisternerne** (Cisterns) once served Copenhagen's water reservoir, holding up to 16 million litres. They were drained in 1981, and since 2013 have served as an utterly unique art exhibition space. The rotating presentations often involve water – so you might find yourself handed a pair of gumboots, seated in a rowboat or skirting around reflective pools.

Beyond the Carlsberg Curtain

Historic brewery tour

Even non-beer drinkers could get absorbed by the impressive **Home of Carlsberg** experience, housed in the whimsical

VESTERBRO'S ROOTS

Despite its social challenges, Vesterbro has been a culturally significant neighbourhood since long before the waves of gentrification first broke here in the 1990s. Life here was famously immortalised by treasured Danish author Tove Ditlevsen in her *Copenhagen Trilogy*, which chronicles the victories and agonies of growing up in a poverty-stricken part of city that now feels largely lost to history.

Vesterbro retains its historically seedy air, including a few strip clubs, in the blocks closest to the Central Station. At the edge of the Meatpacking District there's a harm-reduction, safe space for hard drug users, keeping them relatively safe while also keeping users off the streets.

DRINKING IN VESTERBRO

Jernbanecafeen: This feast-for-the-eyes, old-school bar near the Central Station is a must-visit for the decor alone. *7am-2am*

Lidkoeb: Blink and you'll miss this cosy multilevel cocktail and whisky bar hidden away in a backyard. *4pm-2am Mon-Sat, from 8pm Sun*

Ancestrale: Study up on natural wines with a few happy-hour glasses at this informal wine bar. *5.30pm-midnight*

Prolog Coffee: Perfectly refined roastery with superb coffee, snacks and outdoor seating. *7am-6pm Mon-Fri, from 9am Sat & Sun*

COPENHAGEN CRAFT COCKTAILS

Sebastian Høyer is the founder of the Gamble Cocktail Bar *(@gamble.cph)*. Here he tells us about what he loves about Copenhagen's active cocktail scene.

If you're willing to look, Copenhagen is littered with small amazing places hidden slightly off the beaten path, each with its own unique style. If I'm headed out in the city, some of my favourite addresses for a cocktail include:

Gensyn Bar: Welcoming and down-to-earth.
Pulp: Ideal for a livelier evening.
Bar Deco: Traditional vibes and top-end ingredients.

MINO SURKALA/SHUTTERSTOCK ©

Home of Carlsberg

19th-century buildings of the old Carlsberg Brewery, the heart of a developed neighbourhood that's dotted by restaurants and cafes. The flashy exhibition explores the history of Carlsberg, complete with family rifts and the obsessive approach that created this hugely successful business. At times it feels a bit corporate, but you get a tasting session. Best of all, a historical tour around the old site takes you into buildings such as a temple-like empty brewery and incredible underground cellars (part of 7km of tunnels).

Neighbourhood Secrets

Off-the-track harbourside neighbourhood

Beyond Vesterbro to the south, **Sydhavn** is another former industrial harbour area undergoing rapid redevelopment. Few visitors make it here unless they're riding the Harbour Bus to the end of the line (Teglholmen) – but the cruising views make it worth the trip. Hop off the boat and take a walk at **Sydhavnstippen** park, where you'll spot free-roaming alpacas, and maybe another troll if you're lucky. Or swim at Teglholmen Brygge or **Havnebadet Sluseholmen**, grab a couch and a panini at neighbourhood favourite **Rallys**, or watch the boats at **Café Slusen**, on the old harbour lock, where you might also catch a DJ at the weekend.

EATING IN FREDERIKSBERG

Fasangården: Beautiful restaurant in Frederiksberg Have. Delicious cuisine. *11.30am-4.30pm Tue, Wed & Sun, to 11pm Thu-Sat* €€

Beyla: Great vegan restaurant in the Carlsberg area, with incredible Korean fried mushrooms. *hours vary* €€

Mielcke & Hurtigkarl: In a former royal summer house adorned with murals; as ethereal as its menu is heavenly. *6-11pm Wed-Sat* €€€

Bistro Pan Pan: A zoo is not a place you expect to have a fancy meal, but this has great fusion-Asian food. A great place to recharge. *9am-6pm* €€

Beyond Central Copenhagen

Depart Denmark's capital to discover splendid palaces, world-class art galleries, glorious beaches and deer-filled forest parks.

Places

Copenhagen's outskirts, which tend to have larger houses and grander villas, spread north towards Helsingør and the Danish Riviera, and south towards Køge. The northern coastal areas are particularly affluent: the suburb of Hellerup, with its modernist villas and historic homes along the seashore, is synonymous with a wealthy lifestyle. But no matter which direction you go, there's plenty to see and do, from modern art to marine biology and Michelin-starred country inns, and nothing listed in this section is more than an hour from central Copenhagen. Malmö, Sweden's third-largest city, is just 35 minutes across the Øresund Bridge.

Charlottenlund & Klampenborg

TIME FROM CENTRAL COPENHAGEN: **35 MINS**

Seaside wonders to the north

These twin seaside suburbs 10km north of central Copenhagen (S-tog line C) are two of Denmark's wealthiest towns. Charlottenlund has a fine sandy beach backed by a former fort and small royal forest, from where it's 3km up the coast to Klampenborg. Here, the 700m **Bellevue Beach** has been a summertime magnet for decades; architecture fans will enjoy Arne Jacobsen's modernist apartments (1934), stripy lifeguard towers (1932) and Skovshoved petrol station (1937). It's a great place for a dip.

Forest theme park

Bakken *(bakken.dk; multi-ride wristband/ride and game fun card 329/199kr)* got its start with the discovery of a (still flowing) natural spring in 1583. The seemingly healthful waters began to attract thirsty crowds, and with them came an entourage of touts, traders and entertainers – the seed of what is today the world's oldest amusement park. While the rollercoaster, cotton-candy fun-fest at Bakken lacks some of Tivoli's dreamland charm, it still makes for a fun day out.

GETTING AROUND

A 24-hour City Pass (Large) allows you to travel on any bus or train in zones 1–99 (everything in this section). They're available from ticket machines and the Din Offentlige Transport app. A Copenhagen Card (p276) does the same but includes museum admissions.

DAN OLSEN/SHUTTERSTOCK ©

Dyrehaven

Deer spotting at Dyrehaven

Dyrehaven (Jægersborg Deer Park) is one of three UNESCO-recognised 'par force' (with horses and dogs) royal hunting estates in north Zealand. There are around 2000 deer in the park, and it's a lovely place to cycle.

Mid-century design home and masterpieces

Easily combined with a trip to the Deer Park, make time to see the wonderful Zaha Hadid–designed **Ordrupgaard** *(ordrupgaard.dk; adult/child 110kr/free)* collections of 19th- and 20th-century French and Danish art; a Snøhetta-designed underground exhibition wing opened in late 2022. The perfectly preserved former home of pioneering 20th-century Danish designer Finn Juhl is part of the museum.

Lyngby

TIME FROM CENTRAL COPENHAGEN: **18 MINS**

History comes alive alongside lakes

Lyngby (sometimes Kongens Lyngby) is 12km northwest of central Copenhagen, an easy trip and home to the enchanting **Frilandsmuseet** open-air museum. It showcases original Danish vernacular architecture and village life from 1650 to 1940 over a sprawling 40-hectare campus where actors and volunteers dress up in period costumes on school holidays (S-tog A/E or bus 184, Light Rail).

Hidden away west of Lyngby are three lovely lakes, **Lyngby Sø**, **Bagsværd Sø**, and **Füresø**, surrounded by a mix of forest, parkland and housing. **Baadfarten** runs three different one- two-hour historic boat trips here. The dock is a short walk from central Lyngby, and you can either buy a return or hop off at Farum (S-tog B), Bagsværd (S-tog B) or Holte (S-tog A/E) for the train home.

Lyngby also sits directly inland from Klampenborg; there's an 11km **walking trail** along the Mølleåen (Mill Stream) that takes you directly between the Øresund (via Raadvad/Dyrehaven) and Frilandsmuseet.

Humlebæk

TIME FROM CENTRAL COPENHAGEN: **40 MINS**

World-renowned Louisiana

An extraordinary museum of modern and contemporary art, **Louisiana** *(louisiana.dk; adult/child 145kr/free)* sits in a garden landscape facing the Øresund. Its maze of halls and glass corridors integrate seamlessly with the grounds outside, where there's a sculpture garden that includes works by Alexander Calder, Roy Lichenstein and Alicja Kwade. Architects studied the landscape for months before breaking ground in 1958, and it shows. There's access to the beach and Jean Nouvel-designed jetty, and you can swim from here, though if you want to return to the galleries, you need to go around to the front entrance.

The children's section is even aligned with current exhibitions, where kids can draw and paint in expert-led workshops. The museum shop is also a design treasure chest, and posters from here decorate seemingly half the flats in Copenhagen.

Kastrup

TIME FROM CENTRAL COPENHAGEN: **12 MINS**

Sculptural wonderland: the national aquarium

To the south of the city, only one stop from Copenhagen Airport, Copenhagen's aluminium-clad **Den Blå Planet** *(denblaaplanet.dk; adult/child 230/120kr)* is the largest aquarium in northern Europe. The space is divided into climatic and geographic sections, the most spectacular of which is 'Ocean/Coral Reef'; home to swarms of technicolour tropical fish, the exhibition features a massive four-million-litre tank brimming with sharks, stingrays and other majestic creatures. If possible, visit the aquarium on a Monday evening when it's at its quietest and most evocative.

MEET ME IN MALMÖ

Many Copenhageners rarely cross the Øresund, but underrated and walkable Malmö is only 35 minutes away, and they frankly don't know what they're missing! The Øresundståg drops you right next to the old city of Gamla Staden with the central square and Malmö Castle. Carry on to hip, multicultural Möllevången for fabulous falafel at **Jalla Jalla**.

On the water, you can sauna and swim at the delightfully vintage over-water **Ribersborgs Kallbadhus** bathhouse, and admire the view of Calatrava's Turning Torso building (second-tallest in the Nordics) from here. Finish the night with music at **Plan B**.

The Øresundstog runs all night, but remember to bring a passport, as there are irregular border checks.

EATING NORTH OF COPENHAGEN

Søllerød Kro: In Holte, this Michelin-starred restaurant occupies a 17th-century cottage. *noon-2.30pm & 6-9.30pm Wed-Sun* **€€€**

Den Røde Cottage: Serves a seasonal menu in a cottage tucked away in the forest behind Taarbæk. *noon-3pm Fri-Sun, 6-11.30pm Wed-Sun* **€€€**

Den Gule Cottage: In a rustic cottage, serving fresh-from-the-sea seafood behind Bellevue Beach. *noon-9pm Tue-Sun* **€€**

Kystens Perle: Cheerful restaurant serving brunch, burgers and Danish favourites next to Den Blå Planet. *11am-10pm Mon-Fri, from 10am Sat & Sun* **€€**

Places We Love to Stay

€ Budget €€ Midrange €€€ Top End

Central Copenhagen p52

Hotel Nimb €€€ Part of historic Tivoli Gardens, this boutique belle has antiques, contemporary comfort – especially in the new wing – and a rooftop bar and pool. Some suites have a terrace-with-a-view.

Hotel Danmark €€ Cosy hideaway near the action, with muted colours inspired by the nearby Thorvaldsen Museum. It's the epitome of boutique comfort, with heavenly beds, tactile fabrics and restrained, elegant Danish furniture.

Villa Copenhagen €€€ With a rooftop pool, this is between Tivoli and Copenhagen Central, and is a handsome conversion, purring with Danish style, of the palatial former Post & Telegraph Head Office.

Hotel Alexandra €€ The furniture of Danish design deities such as Arne Jacobsen graces the interiors of the crisp, refined yet homely Alexandra, with rooms themed for each designer, including a poppy Verner Panton.

Radisson Collection Royal Hotel €€ Arne Jacobsen designed everything here from the cutlery to the building; it's been renovated since, in rather more generic tasteful-hotel style, but room 606 has been left entirely intact (visits only).

Danhostel Copenhagen City € In a tower block overlooking the harbour just south of Tivoli (did we mention the views?); dorms and private rooms are all bright, light and modern.

Ibsens Hotel €€ Rooms are minimalist yet plush, with muted tones, designer fixtures and blissful beds.

Hotel Skt Petri €€ Former department store with a charcoal palette softened by blonde-timber flooring and rich splashes of colour. The best views are from the 4th floor and up.

Nyhavn & Royal Copenhagen p65

71 Nyhavn Hotel €€€ Housed in two striking 200-year-old canalside warehouses. Offers character, comfort and great views.

Babette Guldsmeden €€ The 98-room Babette is part of the superb Guldsmeden hotel chain, with the same (unexpectedly) harmonious blend of Nordic and Indonesian design aesthetics.

Bedwood Hostel € On Nyhavn waterfront, this cosy hostel, with six to 12-bed dorms, occupies a historic wood-beamed warehouse dating from 1756. Each bed has a nifty curtain for privacy and a bedside power socket.

Copenhagen Strand €€ In a converted 19th-century warehouse, the Strand overlooks Copenhagen Harbour. Pay more for a view of the water.

Christianshavn p73

Kanalhuset €€ Beautiful rooms and apartments in softly glowing colours, in an historic canalside building, converted by former Tiger owners. Book well ahead.

25 Hours Paper Island €€ In one of Copenhagen's newest developments, Papirøen (Paper Island), this quirkily decorated design hotel has a seaside feel, a stone's throw from the Opera House and its new harbourfront garden.

Sankt Anna B&B €€ A rustic little guesthouse (no breakfast, despite the name) in a historic property in the heart of picturesque Christianshavn, with plain yet charming rooms, some with terraces.

CPH Living €€ On a converted freight boat, Copenhagen's only floating hotel consists of 12 stylish, contemporary rooms with harbour and city views.

Hotel NH Copenhagen €€€ A glass-fronted office block,

formerly housing Nordea, has turned swanky hotel with great harbour views.

Nørrebro & Østerbro

p81

Rye 115 €€ Lovely location close to the lakes and the bars, boutiques and restaurants of Nørrebro, with simple, *hyggelig* (cosy) rooms and lots of charm.

Urban Camper € Hostel with indoor tents (bring earplugs?) and double rooms with shared bathrooms, some with two walls of windows.

Vesterbro & Frederiksberg

p86

Urban House Copenhagen by MEININGER € Cheery, central hostel with rooms sleeping from three to 10 people, all en-suite.

Steel House Copenhagen € Excellent hostel close to the Lakes, with pods providing a sense of privacy, plus facilities including a pool and gym.

66 Guldsmeden €€ Simple yet tasteful, with four posters, crisp white linen, snug blankets and artwork by the owner's talented father-in-law.

Coco Hotel €€ Chic hotel with a Parisian vibe, and fresh greens and blues in the rooms, some of which have views over the rooftops.

Scandic Falkoner €€ Handily near Frederiksberg metro, this is a comfortable, business-like hotel.

Hotel Ottilia By Brøchner Hotels €€ In the Carlsberg area, this style-conscious hotel has comfortable rooms, the best with round-window seats.

Zleep Hotel € Reasonably priced hotel with snug but comfortable rooms.

Manon Les Suites €€ Bali-styling and a jungle pool in a courtyard that genuinely feels tropical make for a refreshing surprise in Vesterbro.

Axel Guldsmeden €€€ Eco-hotel; Axel Guldsmeden puts a Nordic spin on Balinese chic. Has a lush spa.

Bertrams Guldsmeden €€ Part of the Guldsmeden group, Bertrams features raw stone, bare wood, crisp white linen, spectacular bathtubs and exotic Bali-style decor.

Andersen Hotel €€ White-on-white gives way to bold, playful design at the Andersen. We also love the Molton Brown bathroom accessories and complimentary evening wine (between 5pm and 6pm).

Hotel Sanders €€€ High-end, characterful place, with an air of sober luxury, featuring freestanding tubs and antiques, owned by an ex-ballet dancer.

Beyond Copenhagen

p91

Raadvad Vandrerhjem € Budget rooms in a historic building surrounded by the forest at the Raadvad mill complex, to the north of Charlottenlund.

Charlottenlund Fort € Eight kilometres north of Copenhagen, a friendly campsite in the sheltered grounds of an old, moat-encircled coastal fortification. Close to Charlottenlund Beach.

Hotel Alexandra

For places to stay in Zealand, see p125

TRABANTOS/SHUTTERSTOCK ©

Above: Frederiksborg Slot (p109); Right: Kitesurfer, Hornbæk Beach (p110)

THE MAIN AREAS

HELSINGØR
Maritime history and Hamlet's castle. **p102**

BEYOND HELSINGØR
Summerhouse coast with beautiful beaches. **p107**

ROSKILDE
Wild fests and Viking ships. **p111**

Zealand

BEACHES, UNESCO SIGHTS AND NATURAL WONDERS

More than just Copenhagen's backyard, Zealand is also Denmark's historical heartland, with castles, manors and mills dotted along the island's placid fjords, fields and coastline.

Copenhagen is not the end of this island's delights. Zealand takes barely two hours to drive across, but it contains five of Denmark's eight UNESCO World Heritage Sites, and two of the country's five national parks.

Head to North Zealand to see medieval Helsingør, home to the world-famous Kronborg Castle – Shakespeare's Elsinore – and the idyllic summerhouse territory of the windswept, dune-backed northern beaches. In Roskilde, about 35km west of Copenhagen, five ancient Viking ships (and many reconstructions) are displayed alongside the fjord they sailed nearly 1000 years ago. Elsewhere the west is a wide-open landscape dotted with manors, mills, vineyards and even Michelin-starred dining, plus honesty-box farm stands selling everything from honey and flowers to locally brewed beer.

JAKOB HELBIG/GETTY IMAGES ©

South of the medieval market town of Køge is Camp Adventure's spiralling Forest Tower, a glorious folly offering epic views above the tree canopy, below which there are zip lines galore. Zealand has more than 400km of shoreline, lined with dunes, heather and summer homes, but nowhere is more dramatic than the southern sea cliffs at Stevns Klint, where you can go for a hike and unravel mysteries of the ancient and more recent past.

Hop a train or put on your bike helmet – Denmark's largest island has much to explore beyond Copenhagen.

BEYOND ROSKILDE
The coast and countryside of Denmark's wild west. p115

KØGE
Medieval market town close to a Viking ring fortress. p118

BEYOND KØGE
Ancient geology meets modern geometry. p121

CAR

Exploring Zealand is ideal with a car. The driving is easy, and nothing is more than about 1½ hours from Copenhagen. With a car, you can crisscross the rolling countryside, stopping at farm stands, scenic spots and quirky local museums as you please.

TRAIN

The train network in Zealand is extensive, with most settlements of any size served by regional or local trains. Roskilde, Helsingør and Køge are all less than an hour from the capital by train.

BUS

Even small settlements have a regular bus service, though sometimes only a handful of daily departures. With planning, you can get out into more remote parts of the countryside without a car. Bus routes usually start and end at train stations.

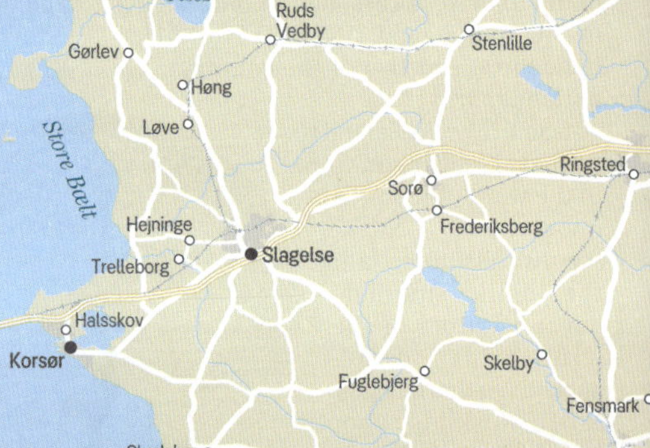

Find Your Way

Covering one-sixth of Denmark's area but home to 40% of its population, Zealand is a compact and compelling slice of the country, where half-timbered villages, royal castles and seductive beaches are within easy distance of Copenhagen.

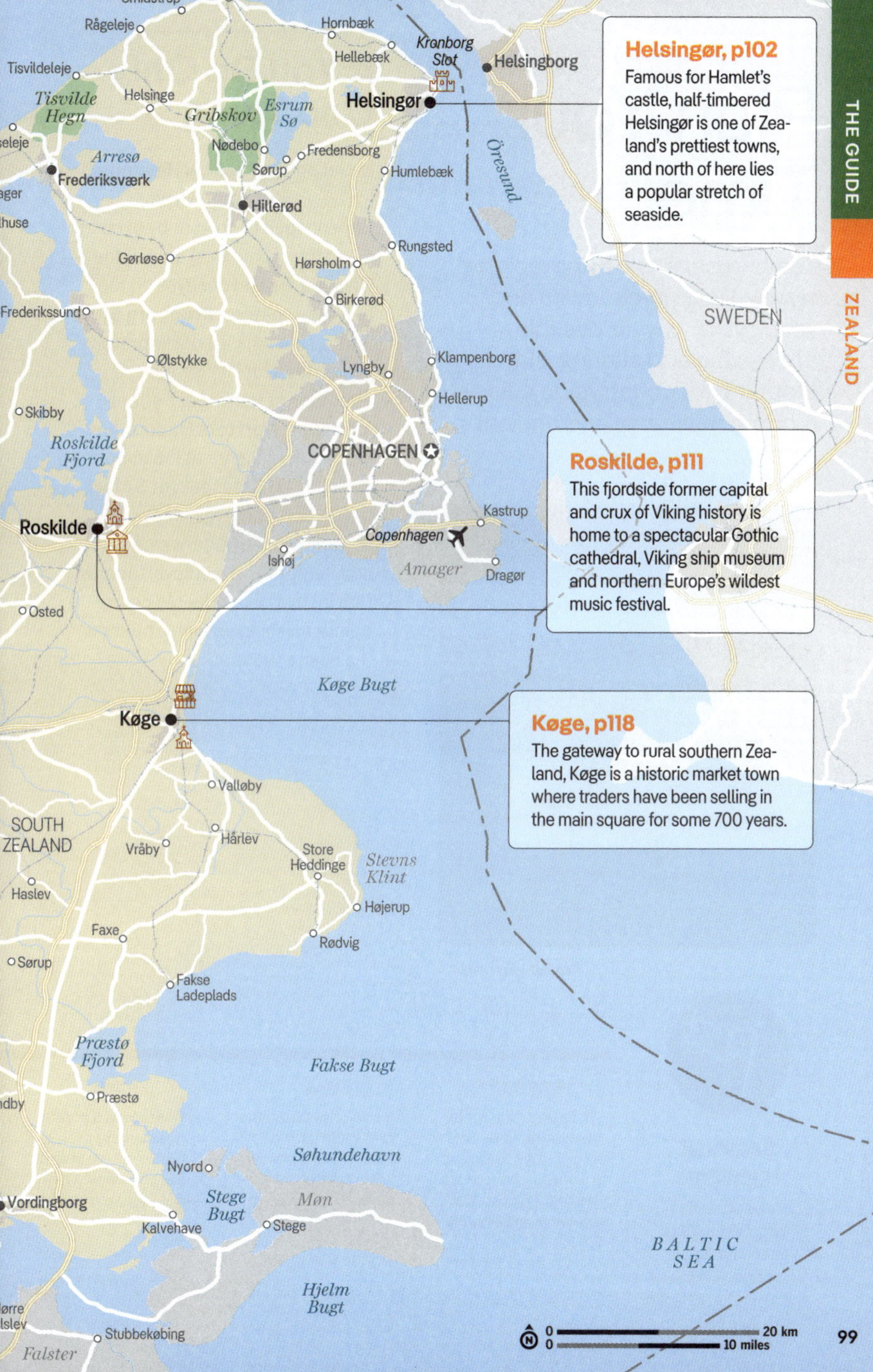
Helsingør, p102
Famous for Hamlet's castle, half-timbered Helsingør is one of Zealand's prettiest towns, and north of here lies a popular stretch of seaside.
Roskilde, p111
This fjordside former capital and crux of Viking history is home to a spectacular Gothic cathedral, Viking ship museum and northern Europe's wildest music festival.
Køge, p118
The gateway to rural southern Zealand, Køge is a historic market town where traders have been selling in the main square for some 700 years.
Smidstrup
Gilleleje
Rågeleje
Hornbæk
Hellebæk
Kronborg Slot
Helsingborg
Tisvildeleje
Tisvilde Hegn
Helsinge
Gribskov
Esrum Sø
Helsingør
Nødebo
Fredensborg
Arresø
Sørup
Humlebæk
Frederiksværk
Hillerød
Øresund
Rungsted
Gørløse
Hørsholm
Birkerød
Frederikssund
SWEDEN
Ølstykke
Klampenborg
Lyngby
Hellerup
Skibby
Roskilde Fjord
COPENHAGEN
Kastrup
Roskilde
Copenhagen
Ishøj
Amager
Dragør
Osted
Køge Bugt
Køge
Valløby
SOUTH ZEALAND
Hårlev
Vråby
Store Heddinge
Stevns Klint
Haslev
Højerup
Faxe
Rødvig
Sørup
Fakse Ladeplads
Præstø Fjord
Fakse Bugt
Præstø
Søhundehavn
Nyord
Vordingborg
Stege Bugt
Møn
Kalvehave
Stege
BALTIC SEA
Hjelm Bugt
Stubbekøbing
Falster
0 20 km
0 10 miles

Plan Your Time

Zealand begs to be appreciated slowly. Walk, cycle, swim and snack your way across this accessible and alluring island, stopping for countryside cuisine, modern museums and ancient artistry.

TRABANTOS/SHUTTERSTOCK ©

Trelleborg (p116)

If You Do Only One Thing

- Get an early start in **Helsingør** (p102), easily reached from Copenhagen by train or by cycling along the scenic west side of the Øresund. Feast your eyes on the fairy-tale spires of **Kronborg Slot** (p104), Denmark's most impressive castle, then fuel up for the afternoon at Helsingør's street-food spot, **Værftets Madmarked** (p102). Drop anchor at the maritime museum, **M/S Museet for Søfart** (p102). Spend the rest of the day admiring the age-warped architecture and medieval lanes of Helsingør's delightful old centre before finishing up with a beer on the main square.

Seasonal Highlights

Zealand shines brightest during midsummer, but late spring and early autumn offer a similar appeal.

FEBRUARY

Chase away the winter blues with Vinterjazz, which brings live music to a dozen-plus venues around Zealand and elsewhere in Denmark.

MAY

Sink your teeth into the year's first harvest of delicate new potatoes, best tasted on a ***kartoffelmad*** (open potato sandwich).

JUNE

Gather round a bonfire on Midsummer's Eve, when pyres are lit and music and singing carry on into the sunlit night.

Three Days to Travel Around

After a day in Helsingør, head west along Zealand's north coast to the white-sanded, windsurfer-dotted **Hornbæk** (p108) and **Gilleleje** (p108) beach resorts. Veer south to Hillerød to ogle the lakeshore opulence of **Frederiksborg Slot** (p109) before continuing to **Roskilde** (p111) for preserved Viking ships, Roskilde Domkirke (Denmark's most dramatic church) and next-door **Lejre** (p115) for a compelling reconstruction of a Viking village. Pass through the attractive small town of **Køge** (p118) on day three to reach the UNESCO-listed sea cliffs at **Stevns Klint** (p121), where you can walk the clifftops and find out what really happened to the dinosaurs.

If You Have More Time

Only two hours across by car, Zealand is your oyster. Ponder Viking life at the evocative **Trelleborg archaeological site** (p116), climb Camp Adventure's delightfully symmetrical **Forest Tower** (p124), learn to kitesurf in **Lynæs** (p110) or poke around the blissfully bucolic countryside, stopping to sample smoked fish at **Gilleleje harbour** (p108), biodynamic beer at **Herslev Brewery** (p114) and even local wine on the **Rosnæs Peninsula** (p117). For a taste of the really remote, hop on a ferry to one of Zealand's five **offshore islands** (p116), where life slows down to an Arcadian crawl.

JULY

Summer reaches its peak at the weeklong Roskilde Festival. Tisvildeleje and Gilleleje also put on big bashes with live tunes.

AUGUST

Spend an evening with the Bard at Helsingør's Shakespeare Festival, where Kronborg Castle makes for a dazzling mise en scène.

OCTOBER

October is harvest season at Zealand's growing number of vineyards, centred on Røsnæs Peninsula. Dyrehøj is the largest and the oldest.

DECEMBER

Christmas markets are dotted around Zealand. Head for Roskilde's shipping-container Musicon Julemarked for holiday hygge with an industrial twist.

Helsingør

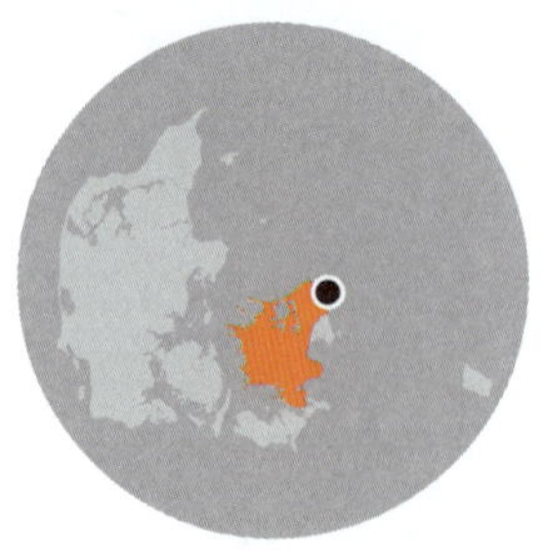

HISTORY | HAMLET | GASTRONOMY

GETTING AROUND

If you're driving to Helsingør, you can park by the station (two hours free, afterwards paid), next to the old centre, which is best explored on foot. Find 24-hour parking next to Værftets Madmarked. By train, Helsingør is well connected to Copenhagen (45 minutes), Gilleleje (45 minutes) and Hillerød (30 minutes). Trains run throughout the weekend nights and stop just after midnight on weekdays.

Once one of the most important maritime cities in Europe, Helsingør may no longer command the sea, but it still wears its nautical history on its sailor-tattooed sleeve. Guarding the passage between the North and Baltic Seas, Helsingør is strategically set at the Øresund strait's narrowest point – it's only 4km across to Helsingborg, Sweden – and its location has defined the city since its formal inception in the early 1400s. Both sides of the water were once Danish territory, making the kingdom fabulously wealthy thanks to the Sound Dues, taxes levied on ships passing through the strait. These glory days lasted until 1658, when Denmark lost one of its many wars with Sweden. The city took shape over this period, and Helsingør's medieval old centre, filled with narrow cobbled lanes and crooked half-timbered houses, is one of the city's main draws, alongside the spectacular Kronborg castle that broods at the water's edge, like its most famous (fictional) inhabitant, Hamlet.

Superb Subterranean Maritime Museum

BIG-designed M/S Museet for Søfart

Ingeniously built into a dry dock beside Kronborg Slot, the subterranean maritime museum **M/S Museet for Søfart** *(Maritime Museum of Denmark; mfs.dk; adult/child 135kr/free)* was designed by Denmark's starchitects, the Bjarke Ingels Group, and merits a visit as much for its innovative design,

EATING IN HELSINGØR

Strejf: Thrilling new Nordic seafood and setting inside Helsingør's Renaissance-style railway station. *11.30am-9.30pm Tue-Sat* €€

Rådmand Davids Hus: Where better to feast on Danish classics than a snug, red-beamed 1694 house? *10am-5pm Mon-Sat* €€

Værftets Madmarked: Food hall thick with the aromas of so-so global food – ideal, however, for a quick lunch stop. *11am-8pm, to 9pm Sat & Sun* €

Kulturværftet Spisehuset: A light-filled cafe in the Culture Complex on the harbourfront. *9am-7pm Mon-Fri, 10am-5pm Sat & Sun* €

HIGHLIGHTS
1 Kronborg Slot

SIGHTS
2 M/S Museet for Søfart

SLEEPING
3 Hotel Hamlet
4 Kagefryds Gæstehus

EATING
5 Kulturværftet Spisehuset
6 Rådmand Davids Hus
7 Strejf
8 Værftets Madmarked

DRINKING & NIGHTLIFE
9 Holger
10 Københavneren
11 Skum
12 Strandvejsristeriet

fitted into the dock, with internal, glass-lined interiors and access to outdoors as well. The multimedia exhibitions explore Denmark's maritime history and culture in dynamic, contemporary ways, as well as beautifully constructed model boats, often made by former sailors. Some of the most interesting sections look at slavery, trade and exploitation in Denmark's overseas colonies.

TOP TIP

Danish National Cycle Route 9 is an approachable and scenic ride, with 45km of mostly protected bike lane along the coast between Copenhagen and Helsingør. The route has many fine stopping points in the upmarket towns and villages in between.

Side Trip to Sweden

Visit another country

Many visitors to Helsingør pop over the water to Sweden's **Helsingborg**, and why not? The ferries run 24/7, and it's 20 minutes each way, costing 199kr return. Bring your passport. Sweden's ninth-largest city is worth a wander. Exit the ferry and head up **Stortorget**, stopping for a photo of the ornate 1897 **Rådhus** (City Hall). The 1400s Gothic **Sankta Maria Kyrka** (St Mary's Church) is about a block from here or continue uphill to the **Kärnan** watchtower and enjoy the views from the top (or from the scenic staircase below). The flower-filled **Sofiero Slott och Slottsträdgård** (Sofiero Castle and Gardens) sits 5km up the coast (take bus 8). In town, visit the strikingly designed **Dunkers Kulturhus** near the port.

DRINKING IN HELSINGØR

Strandvejsristeriet: In the yellow outhouses around Kronborg Slot, this spacious cafe has excellent coffee and snacks. *10am-5pm*

Københavneren: 'The Copenhagener' is lined by a massive decorative stein collection, serving Helsingør's own Wiibroe beer. *hours vary*

Holger: Named after Holger the Dane, who sleeps awaiting an emergency in Kronborg. A cosy place to drink draught ale. *9pm-2am Fri & Sat*

Skum: Modern-feeling beer bar with 20-odd drafts, plus terrace seating on a pretty plaza. *noon-midnight Sun-Wed, to 2am Thu, to 4am Sat & Sun*

TRABANTOS/SHUTTERSTOCK ©

Kronborg Slot

TOP EXPERIENCE

Kronborg Slot

Most famous in the English-speaking world as Elsinore castle, the setting for Shakespeare's 1602 play *Hamlet*, **Kronborg Slot** juts into the water at the Øresund's narrowest point. You can explore the grounds without a ticket, but it would be a shame to miss the inner palace, full of grand views and elaborate art. Even better is the descent into the spooky maze of casemates, subterranean dungeon passages barely lit by flickering paraffin lamps.

DON'T MISS

- Chapel
- Casemates
- Banqueting Hall

History

The building mostly post-dates Shakespeare's play, apart from the chapel and the dungeons. A star-shaped system of moats, walls and bastions surrounds this UNESCO-listed masterpiece, crowned with baroque green copper spires.

The fort, then known as Krogen, first took shape at the command of King Erik of Pomerania in the 1420s, and along with its counterpart of Kärnan in Helsingborg, got busy collecting the Sound Dues from passing ships. These tolls made

PRACTICALITIES
Scan this QR code for prices and opening hours.

Helsingør rich, allowing Frederik II to expand the castle in 1585. A 1629 fire destroyed most of the interior, bar the chapel. The castle took another blow when it was occupied by Sweden from 1658 to 1660, after which Christian V shored up the defences, but the Danish royals largely lived elsewhere. It served as a barracks from 1785 until 1924, when it took on its present-day role as a museum. The outhouses were used as barracks until 1991.

Royal Apartments

The Royal Apartments cover two floors. They're still furnished to give a sense of their use. You can visit what was, in 1585, the longest ballroom (62m) in Scandinavia. The decadent banquets held here were legendary: guests were equipped with buckets to purge their way through the 65-course marathons. Rooms nearby house the king's tapestries, some of which depict Danish kings through the ages.

The Chapel

The castle chapel dates from 1582 and is still used for Mass and concerts. It survived the fire of 1629, and so retains its Renaissance trappings. It was used as a powder magazine and fencing hall for a time, but restored in the 19th century.

Cannon Tower

Across the wide courtyard are entrances to the 145-step Cannon Tower. Climb to the roof, the former site of the castle cannons. There are big views from here over to Sweden.

Casemates & Ogier the Dane

Enter the dark, clammy casemates from the courtyard. As you enter these low-ceilinged dungeons, the temperature drops and you'll feel the chill on your neck in the dimly lit storerooms and soldiers' quarters that stretch into the gloom beneath the castle. Around 1000 soldiers could shelter down here, with supplies to last sieges of up to six weeks. Down here the legendary knight Holger Danske (Ogier the Dane) rests, in statue form. According to legend, he is awaiting a moment of national peril, when he will awake and defend the motherland.

SHAKESPEARE

Despite setting one of his most famous plays at Kronborg Slot, aka Elsinore, Shakespeare had never been to Denmark. It's thought that the setting for *Hamlet* (1602) was inspired by tales of the newly expanded castle, which were spread by travelling players as well as Danish nobles Frederik Rosenkrantz and Knud Gyldenstierne, who met the Bard in England in the 1590s. Their surnames might sound familiar – the two were written into the play as Hamlet's childhood friends. Hamlet was first staged at the castle in 1816, and you can see a performance for yourself every August when Kronborg hosts the open-air Shakespeare Festival.

TOP TIPS

- Visitors can wander the site as they please, but guided tours are available.
- Tour times are chalked up on a blackboard near the courtyard entrance.
- A mobile app also provides commentary.
- There's a nice cafe on the grounds of the site.

STROLL AROUND HELSINGØR'S HISTORIC CENTRE

Helsingør's compact and characterful city centre is packed full of fascinating things to see.

START	END	LENGTH
Kulturværftet	Gyldenstræde	1.3km; 1–2 hours

Start at the harbour, overlooked by the ❶ **Kulturværftet** (Culture Yard), with a useful tourist office, and home to the ❷ **Helsingør Bymuseum** (City Museum). In the same complex, the small, free ❸ **Værftsmuseet** (Shipyard Museum) delves into Helsingør's shipbuilding history, which dominated the town until the 1970s. Walk down ❹ **Hestemøllestræde**, a cobbled, colourful street. First you'll see street art by Eron – *Soul of the Wall*, a depiction of ❺ **Hamlet with Yorick's skull** that looks like it's been burned onto the wall with smoke – while to the end is a beautiful mural showing the ❻ **history of the churches**. Turning right, ❼ **Sankt Mariæ Kirke & Karmeliterklostret** is Scandinavia's best-preserved monastic cloister, ringed with photogenic arched brick arcades. Inside, you'll find outlandish animal frescoes and an impressive baroque organ. A block away, the Gothic ❽ **Olai Domkirke** dates from 1559 in its current form, with a tall, copper-capped spire and a 12m altarpiece. Before walking on, look down ❾ **Gammel Færgestræde**, a particularly atmospheric block. It's one more block to the Gothic ❿ **Rådhus**, dating from 1852. Cross to the parallel ⓫ **Stengade**, the pedestrianised main shopping street, walking on to ⓬ **Skyttenstræde**, then down ⓭ **Anna Queens Stræde** before turning onto ⓮ **Gyldenstræde**: these are some of the most atmospheric streets in the city centre.

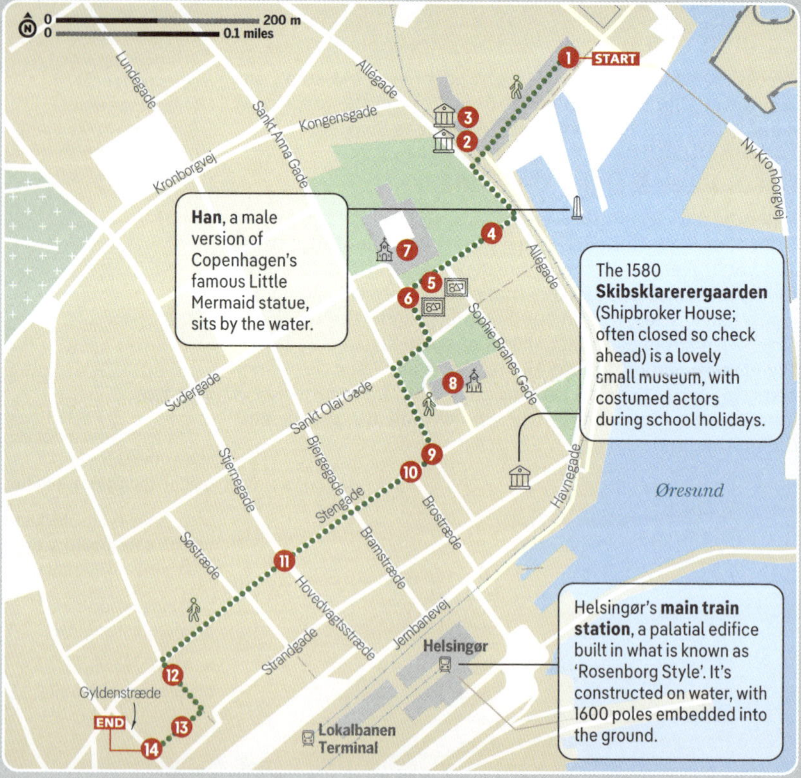

Han, a male version of Copenhagen's famous Little Mermaid statue, sits by the water.

The 1580 **Skibsklarerergaarden** (Shipbroker House; often closed so check ahead) is a lovely small museum, with costumed actors during school holidays.

Helsingør's **main train station**, a palatial edifice built in what is known as 'Rosenborg Style'. It's constructed on water, with 1600 poles embedded into the ground.

Beyond Helsingør

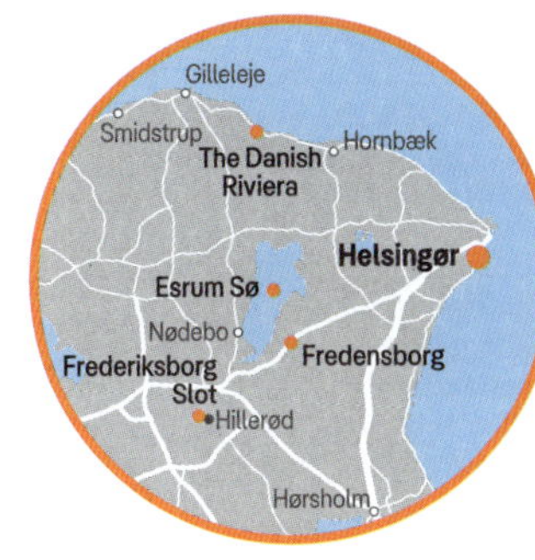

Do as the Danes do and escape to Zealand's seafront summerland, with days spent at cliffs, beaches and castles, sinking beers and dining on the catch of the day.

North Zealand is Mayfair on Denmark's Monopoly board, home to some of the most desirable real estate in the country. The landscape is a patchwork of forest, lake and heath, punctuated with groves of summer cabins and luxury villas dotted along lavish sweeps of beach. Also known as the Danish Riviera, this peninsula between the Øresund and Isefjord has long been a retreat for Copenhageners, including royalty, as the castles, palaces and manors attest – when Denmark's glitterati are not in Skagen in Northern Jutland, they're here. Towns of the north coast – Tisvildeleje, Gilleleje, Hornbæk – are synonymous with summertime for many Danes. Grab an ice cream or a surfboard and soak up the atmosphere in this low-key idyll.

Places

Fredensborg

TIME FROM HELSINGØR: **30 MINS**

Favoured royal palace

Fredensborg is a town whose focus is its palace, which is still the former queen's favourite royal abode.

Greenery-enveloped, 18th-century **Fredensborg Slot**, built in Italian baroque style, is a pleasure palace rather than a fortress. The building's unfortified architectural elegance reflects the more tranquil mood of the era, as Denmark had recently achieved peace with its Scandi neighbours, an abrupt contrast with the moat-encircled fortresses of Kronborg and Frederiksborg that preceded it. It has beautiful baroque gardens, with riding avenues radiating like sun rays from the palace. Beyond continue around 120 hectares of parklands, which stretch along Denmark's second-largest lake. The town nearby is tucked away like an afterthought.

The palace only opens to the public in July and early August, but it's still worth a visit at other times for peaceful greenery, swimming, boating and fishing opportunities. When the palace is closed, you can admire the gracious facade from the octagonal forecourt or from the back if you walk anticlockwise through the park. When the royals are in residence, guards in white-striped uniforms and bearskin hats perform a changing-of-the-guard ceremony at noon.

Year-round, the parklands are open free of charge, apart from private gardens immediately west of the palace, which

GETTING AROUND

Local trains connect Helsingør and Hillerød to north Zealand. From Helsingør, the 930R goes to Hillerød (via Fredensborg), and the 940R travels to Gilleleje (via Hornbæk). From Hillerød, the 950R connects to Gilleleje and the 960R to Tisvildeleje (both via Gribskov). The 920R/E goes to Hundested, from where you can take the ferry to Rørvig if you're continuing to Odsherred and northwest Zealand.

THE UNESCO-LISTED ROYAL HUNTING GROUND

Opened in 2018, the **Nationalpark Kongernes Nordsjælland** cuts a chequerboard pattern across the peninsula, but it's largely centred on Gribskov (Grib Forest) and Esrum Sø (Esrum Lake), north of Hillerød and Fredensborg. Gribskov and Store Dyrehave are excellent places for hiking and have been recognised by UNESCO as unique 'par force' hunting landscapes, featuring networks of radial avenues cut through the woods to allow access to all parts of the forest. Begun under King Christian V, royal hunts here were massive spectacles designed to project royal power. The denouement saw the king personally pierce the stag's heart with his *hirschfænger* dagger.

are only accessible through palace tours in July *(tours in English at 1.45pm and 2.45pm)*. The park is dotted with commemorative rocks, obelisks and statues, notably in a double circle called Normandsdalen featuring 70 life-sized statues of Norwegian and Faroese folk characters. These are based upon small wooden dolls of fishermen, farmers, soldiers and servants that were carved by an 18th-century postman. He sent them to King Frederik V, who liked them so much that he had them remade full-size in sandstone.

Esrum Sø

TIME FROM HELSINGØR: **30 MINS**

Boating around Esrum Abbey

At 17 sq km, **Esrum Sø** is Denmark's second-largest lake, and beautiful, hemmed by lush green forest. The most popular access point is about 1km west of the Fredensborg Slot gate via Skipper Allé. Here you'll find a lakeside restaurant, **Skipperhuset**, beside which (with advance booking) you can rent canoes and kayaks or take open-boat tours across to the protected former hunting forest of Gribskov.

Esrum Abbey & Millyard is near the north end of Esrum Sø. Established in 1151 as a Cistercian Catholic monastery, after the Reformation it was used as everything from a garrison to a tax office. The museum it contains has some small, VR-aided displays on medieval monastic life and the Reformation, but is fairly expensive for what it is. The gardens, however, are free, and you can sample various organic goods, on sale in the shop and cafe. Bus 362 connects the two and carries on to Gilleleje.

The Danish Riviera

TIME FROM HELSINGØR: **25 MINS**

Artsy seaside Hornbæk

West along the coast from Helsingør is the 'Danish Riviera'. A white-sanded, summerhouse territory, edged by the Kattegat strait, this is one of Denmark's sunniest spots. Artsy **Hornbæk** has a fine, dune-backed beach for swimming or kiting, plus a centuries-old coastal plantation forest east of town. There's a food court behind the beach – a fun place to eat with your toes in the sand.

Rudolph Tegners Museum and Statuepark

Don't miss the wild **Rudolph Tegners Museum & Statuepark** *(rudolphtegner.dk; adult/child 80kr/free)*, with 14 monumental, somehow ghostly bronze statues dotted across untamed moorland heath; the concrete museum houses more than 250 other pieces. It's around midway between Hornbæk and Gilleleje. If you take the bus from Hornbæk, it's a 2km scenic walk from Dronningmølle St, while the bus from Gilleleje passes 1km away.

OTHER UNESCO HUNTING LANDSCAPES

Jægersborg Dyrehaven (p92), north of Copenhagen, is the third element of the 'par force' hunting landscape and a popular excursion for a day of walking and deer-spotting. It's home to the elegant and photogenic 1734 Hermitage hunting lodge.

Seafood and fishing harbour at Gilleleje

Head to **Gilleleje** for its fish restaurants around the busy fishing harbour. The bobbing boats are

TOP EXPERIENCE

Frederiksborg Slot

Denmark's Versailles is a dazzling, gigantic, Dutch Renaissance-style fortress-palace, with the vision doubled by its position on the mirror-like lake-moat Slotsø. Unlike Kronborg, **Frederiksborg Slot** – completed in 1620 under King Christian IV – was built for enjoyment and not defence, and the interior is packed to the elaborate rafters with over-the-top artwork, including hundreds of portraits, tapestries, carvings and opulent furnishings.

TRABANTOS/SHUTTERSTOCK ©

Frederiksborg Slot and Slotshaven

Slotskirken

Especially dazzling is the Slotskirken (Chapel), where Danish monarchs were crowned between 1671 and 1840. It retains the original interior commissioned by Christian IV, one of the few areas to survive the 1859 fire. It's a deliciously ornate confection of gold and pink-cheeked cherubs, with the altar, font and pulpit overlooked by a priceless 1610 Compenius organ (played on Thursdays from 1.30pm to 2pm).

Interior Highlights

Other rooms in the castle were restored to their original appearances in the 19th century, most fantastically the richly embellished **Riddershalen**, a vast ballroom. The eye-boggling **Audience Chamber** contains trompe l'oeil details and a portrait of big-nosed Christian V styled as a Roman emperor. **The Museum of National History** is worth a look for its portrait gallery of kings, queens and VIPs.

Grounds

North of the castle is Slotshaven, extensive parklands. The formal baroque garden (open from 10am to sunset) is made up of perfect terraces. In the Romantic garden, Indelukket, 18th-century rigidity melts into a wilder 19th-century notion of gardening. North again is the oak wood of Lille Dyrehave. Complete your visit on the enchanting, diminutive Frederiksborg ferry.

TOP TIPS

- Allow at least three hours.
- The Frederiksborg ferry gives you a fantastic view.
- It's better to take the ferry from the castle, as if you arrive on land you enter through the grand main entrance.

DANISH RIVIERA BEST BEACHES

Hornbæk Beach: The best-known sandy stretch, dune-backed Hornbæk Beach is hugely popular for beach holidays and water sports.

Liseleje Beach: Blue Flag, this is a scenic, sandy, gently shelving, kid-friendly beach.

Gudmindrup Beach: One of the best beaches, this 500m-long shallow, sandy beach in Sejerø Bay is great for children.

Tisvildeleje Beach: Copenhageners have been coming here since the 1920s, and today the 5km of sand are enduringly popular.

Rågeleje Beach: Famous for its distinctive and picturesque striped beach houses.

Dronningmølle Beach: Attractive, greenery-backed family-friendly seaside resort.

STEFANO EMBER/SHUTTERSTOCK ©

Tisvildeleje

backed by a triangular arc of lawn, a big 1750 anchor, and a pretty mix of tiled and thatched old houses stretching east from the port area. Many Jews were smuggled on boats from here to Sweden during WWII.

Several nice hikes start here. Walking 2km west from the Nordre Strandvej/Vesterbrogade junction, pass clifftop gardens and the Badehotel to reach a memorial stone dedicated to the Danish philosopher Søren Kierkegaard. Or follow the easterly trail, accessed beside Hovedgade 51 (100m southeast of the church), leading 2.5km to a pair of 1772 lighthouses that originally had coal-burning beacons – one has a museum.

Water sports and a polar explorer

Tisvildeleje has the best swimming beach along here, backed by the sizeable Tisvilde Hegn and Troldeskoven forests. Ideal for a blissful day between wild waves and wizened woods.

Overlooking the entrance to the Isefjord, **Hundested** is best known for its harbour full of restaurants and fishing boats. On its outskirts is the thatched house of polar explorer Knud Rasmussen, which you can visit, with its beautiful views over the Kattegat.

Next-door village **Lynæs** is an increasingly popular destination for windsurfing and kitesurfing.

Hit the 65km **Nordkystruten** (North Coast Route, Danish National Cycle Route 47) to see the smaller villages like **Liseleje** (where there's the lovely Liseleje Badehotel) and the former bombing range moorland at **Melby Overdrev**.

EATING ON THE DANISH RIVIERA

Hornbækhus: Good-value smørrebrød lunches and celebrated communal meals at this hygge Hornbæk hotel. *social dinner 7pm* €€

Adamsens Fisk: Casual waterfront eats and big portions at this Gilleleje institution. *8am-5.30pm Mon-Thu, to 6pm Fri, to 5pm Sat, to 4pm Sun* €

Tinggården: This charming restaurant on the south side of Tisvilde Hegn does a great New Nordic menu. *from 6pm Thu-Sat, also Sun Jul & Aug* €€€

Fyrkroen: All the Danish hits in a gorgeous seaside setting near the lighthouse outside of Gilleleje. *noon-9pm Tue-Sun May–Aug* €€

Roskilde

MUSIC | VIKINGS | BOATING

Only 30km west of Copenhagen, Roskilde, founded by the legendary King Harald Bluetooth in 980 CE, has a riproaring Viking heritage. It contains the unparalleled Viking Boat museum, which displays, fjord-side, five well-preserved Viking boats, and has reconstructions in its harbour offering boat trips. It's also centred on its UNESCO-listed cathedral, an extraordinary resting place for Danish royalty, resembling a lavish indoor cemetery.

Roskilde is synonymous, for many, with its huge music festival, and its musical reputation doesn't quit when the festival packs up. The Musicon, a re-imagined post-industrial neighbourhood, is home to Ragnarock, an innovative and experiential museum of modern music, where you can dive into Danish and international pop culture from the 1950s until today.

GETTING AROUND

If you're driving, there's free unlimited parking in front of Museumsøen and the Viking Ship Museum. Roskilde is a significant rail hub, and you can connect to towns in west Zealand like Ringsted or Sorø (and onwards to Odense), or up to Holbæk and Kalundborg or Nykøbing Sjælland. Trains also run south towards Køge, Næstved and Vordingborg. Bike lanes run most of the way to Roskilde from Copenhagen.

Prestigious Tombs at Roskilde Domkirke

Roskilde's royal burial place

The ultra-fine Gothic spires of UNESCO-listed **Roskilde Domkirke** *(Roskilde Cathedral; roskildedomkirke.dk; adult/child 70kr/free)* pierce the sky in the city centre. Bishop Absalon laid the first bricks in 1170, building upon a previous wooden church, but the intervening centuries and a series of fires, renovations and the Reformation saw it rebuilt to take the form you see today.

This magnificent building is as much a religious and historical site as it is a living document of 850 years of Danish history, architecture and leadership. It's a regal cemetery, with 21 kings and 18 queens buried here. With your ticket, you get a pamphlet with information about all the tombs so that you can navigate.

Each chapel has a completely different style, from the cold, elegiac neoclassical tomb of **Frederik V** (d 1766) to the baroque trompe l'oeil and wrought-iron one of **Christian IV** (d 1648) and the seemingly organic fresco and marble of the **Magi**. Look out also for the three-sided 1560 **altarpiece** from Antwerp, the 15th-century carved choir stalls, the 1500 mechanical clock

TOP TIP

Accommodation is relatively limited in Roskilde because it's so simple to get to Copenhagen. If you're not able to get a room, frequent regional trains connect Roskilde with the capital. Trains run at night, but less frequently.

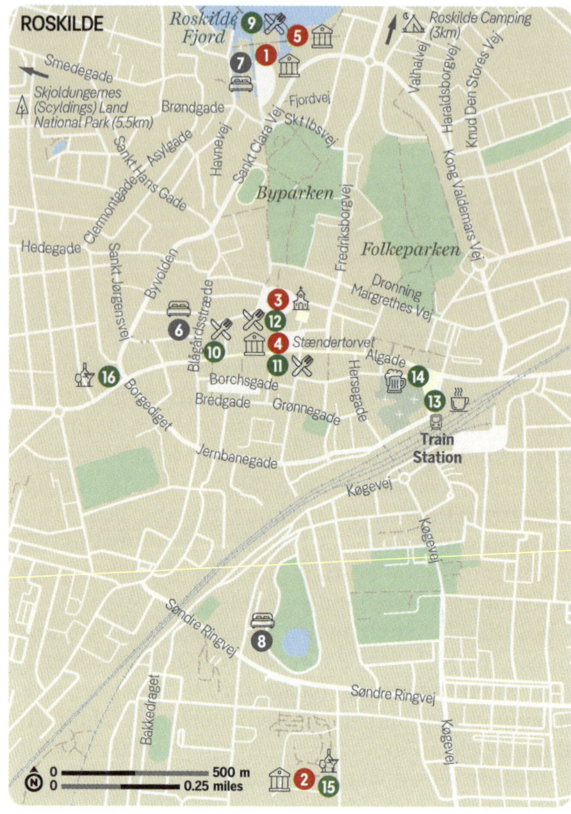

(every hour, St George kills the dragon and it lets out a death wail), and the strikingly elegant marble **tomb of Margrete I** (d 1412), who was the first monarch to be buried here after her body was controversially taken from Sorø Abbey. A tomb designed by artist Bjørn Nørgaard has already been prepared in one of the cathedral's 11 chapels for Queen Margrethe II, who abdicated after more than 50 years on the throne in 2024. (The tomb will remain covered until it's needed.)

Underground & Views at Sankt Laurentius

Above and below ground

In Stændertorvet square stands **Sankt Laurentius**, with its original bell tower from 1500. You can squeeze up a narrow spiral staircase for views through peepholes over Roskilde's main square. This is where the night watchmen used to sit, with jail cells on the level below. There's still a listening pipe so the watchman could eavesdrop on conversations. After you come down from the tower, descend into the basement to see the remains of a 12th-century church and a whole series of medieval graves – skeletons and all.

Viking Ships & Harbour

Five millennia-old Viking ships

Behind the incongruous brutalist exterior of the harbourside **Viking Ship Museum** *(vikingshipmuseum.dk; adult/child 160kr/free)* are five original Viking ships, which, set against a glass wall that faces the fjord, seem almost ready to float.

They were discovered at the bottom of a narrow channel of the Roskilde Fjord, where they had been weighed down with stones over 1000 years ago, possibly to form a blockade against invaders. Excavated in 1962, the five 'Skuldelev ships' (named after the place they were discovered) range from 25% to 75% preserved and have been painstakingly reassembled on frames. Skuldelev 3 is the best preserved. As if to showcase the Viking maritime range, there's an ocean-going trading vessel, a 30m warship for international raiding, a coastal trader, a 17m warship probably used around the Baltic, and a fishing boat.

Outside, at the **Museumsø** boatyard, replicas of the five classic longboats displayed in Roskilde's Viking Ship Museum are moored around this 'museum island' along with several other Scandinavian traditional wooden vessels rebuilt like their historical forebears. There are lots of activities here from June to September: sword fight, board a replica ship, and saw wood.

The Viking Ship Museum's highly amusing 50-minute trips provide the chance to propel a reconstructed traditional Nordic boat across the water by a mixture of sailing, rowing and ducking overhead ropes. A few tickets are available online, otherwise it's first-come, first-served. Departures are weather-dependent.

Rocking in Roskilde

Music festival city

Founded in 1971, the legendary **Roskilde Festival** is northern Europe's largest music fest, and the 100,000 attendees briefly make Roskilde Denmark's fourth-largest city, with its distinctive orange tent stage. Headliners have included Blur, Charlie XCX and – back in the day – Bob Marley. The Roskilde Festival runs for four days, with a four-day 'warm-up' period. Plan ahead if you want any hope of scoring tickets (2400kr for the whole fest) or sorting out camping arrangements.

Anchored by the dramatic neon-and-gold Lego-like building of the **Ragnarock** *(museumragnarock.dk; adult/child 110kr/free)* music museum, the factory-turned-neighbourhood of Musicon sits between Roskilde's centre and the Roskilde Festival fairgrounds. The district has summer concerts and cafes, plus eclectic galleries and workshops. Ragnarock has a

TROLL CHAPEL

The chapel close to the front door of Roskilde Domkirke with its distinctive troll-decorated doors served the Trolle family. Today it's the resting place for Queen Anna Sophie. The story behind this burial place is a case of particularly complicated family dynamics. Anna Sophie was Frederik IV's mistress, with whom he had a morganatic (a watertight prenup) marriage, while he was still married to Queen Louise. The day after his spouse's death, the king married Anna Sophie properly and soon had her crowned queen. She was expelled after Frederik's IV's death by her stepson, Christian VI, but he granted her wish to be buried under the same roof – Christian VI just ensured that the tomb was as far away as possible from his father's.

EATING IN ROSKILDE

Raadhuskælderen: Danish dishes in a pretty garden with views of the cathedral, or within the modernised cellar. *11am-9pm Tue-Sat* €€

PROP Vin og Tapasbar: Hidden-feeling, low-key tapas place in a lane off Skomagergade. *noon-10pm Mon-Thu, to midnight Fri & Sat* €€

Marcella Pizza: Friendly pizzeria with outdoor seating, good wood-fired pizzas and Italian music. *11am-10pm Tue-Sat, to 9pm Sun & Mon* €€

M/S Sagafjord: Lunch or dinner cruises around Roskilde Fjord on a 1950s ship serving Danish classics. *9am-2pm Mon-Fri* €€€

HOW DID THEY PRESERVE THE SHIPS?

Excavating 1000-year-old ships was an extremely complex process. First, a 2500 sq m cofferdam was sunk: water had to be drained step by step, as the level was reduced too much, the stones weighing down the boats would gain weight in air rather than water, and would damage the fragile boats. In addition, the cellulose in the wood had disintegrated and been replaced by water, which was allowing the remains to retain their shape. They had to be kept immersed in fjord water until this could be replaced by polythelene glycol so the shape would not collapse. The archaeologists also photographed the remains in situ, before removing them piece by piece and then reconstructing a very complex jigsaw puzzle.

OLIVER FOERSTNER/SHUTTERSTOCK ©

Roskilde Festival (p113)

Danish focus, but it's still spirit-lifting and this highly interactive museum delivers a multi-sensory, experiential and often humorous journey through the evolution of rock and youth culture from the 1950s to the present. There are music time capsules, and spin-to-hear turntables explain gramophones. Play with interactive musical lights, and practise dance steps on the hot-spot stage beside the 'world's biggest mirror ball'.

Mythical Parklands

Walking trails and cycle routes

The huge **Skjoldungernes (Scyldings) Land National Park**, named after the descendants of mythical Danish King Scyld Scefing and mentioned in *Beowulf*, covers 170 sq km across much of Central Zealand, including the gorgeous southern portion of Roskilde Fjord up to the half-forgotten Selsø Slot, as well as the fields, forests and gentle hills running south towards Lejre and Bidstrup Skovene beyond. Download the national park Skjoldungelandet app for mapped walking and cycling routes, as well as sites such as Slusehuset near Katinge Værk, on Roskilde Fjord, where you can take clinker-built dinghies out for free, unlocking them via an SMS.

One of the nicest ways to see the park starts in the 100-house village of Herslev, about 10km west of Roskilde through the Boserup Forest (take bus 207). In Herslev, pick up maps, snacks and local beer at the fabulous **Herslev Brewery & Cafe** before setting out for a countryside walk or cycle.

DRINKING IN ROSKILDE

Raven på Gimle: Popular, with friendly vibes at this live music venue and bar/cafe. *3-11pm Tue-Thu, to 2am Fri & Sat*

Kaffekilden: Get cosy with coffee and cake at this unpretentious cafe near the train station. *8am-8pm Mon-Fri, 9am-7pm Sat, 10am-7pm Sun*

Musicon Mikrobryggeri: Paninis and pints at this tiny container-built brewery. *2pm-midnight Mon-Thu, noon-2am Fri & Sat, noon-10pm Sun*

Klosterkælderen: Beer cellar stocking a long list of brews; puts on occasional live music. *2pm-midnight Mon-Thu, noon-2am Fri, 11am-2am Sat*

Beyond Roskilde

To travel into west Zealand is to venture deep into Danish country and coastal life.

Leave Copenhagen's commuter and summer cabin belt and you'll find a landscape of old mills and half-timbered farmsteads, windswept peninsulas, wildly unexpected wineries and active fishing villages with smokehouses on the docks. This region tends to get passed over by visitors zipping between Copenhagen and Odense, but lovers of country life should hit the brakes and dally in this little-visited side of Denmark. The rewards are sea cliffs, ferry trips, local crafts, a 'beer city' and even a couple of Michelin stars. Throw in two of Denmark's most important Viking sites at Trelleborg and Lejre, and you'll wonder why more people don't slow down and savour Zealand's wild west.

Places

Lejre p115
Zealand's Offshore Islands p116
Slagelse p116

Lejre

TIME FROM ROSKILDE: **6 MINS**

Where legends come alive

Set 10km west of Roskilde, Lejre village is home to helmet-loads of Viking history – even the name means 'tent' or 'camp'. It's best explored at the delightful **Sagnlandet Lejre** *(Lejre Land of Legends; sagnlandet.dk; adult/child 205/140kr)*, a fabulous open-air archaeological museum. A visit takes you through reconstructions of several historical eras, from a Stone Age campsite to a 1700s farmstead by way of Iron Age and Viking-era settlements, and even a sacrificial bog. Actors staff the reconstructions and show off their skills with technologies of the times. Most spectacular is the **King's Hall**. Using the largest Viking-era building ruins ever unearthed in Denmark – discovered in 2009 in a nearby field – as a template, the final product is a 61m-long, 650-sq-metre masterpiece of experimental archaeology, built from more than 1000 tonnes of Danish oak timber. A new 330m treetop boardwalk opens in 2025, with views over the countryside, dotted by wild boar and aurochs, a kind of cattle that has been reintroduced locally.

Check the daily programme online to plan your trip around whether you'd rather do pottery, archery, make fire with a flint, go canoeing or bake bread – all these activities are included.

There are trains here from Roskilde, met by a transfer bus (8 minutes) on weekdays.

A silver figure and Viking power base

Picturesque Gammel Lejre (Old Lejre) is a 2km walk from Land of Legends. It's worth walking over to visit the small but

GETTING AROUND

Most small villages have at least some regular bus service, but check *journeyplanner.dk* in advance. A service called Plustur provides affordable transfers *(adult/child 24/12kr on top of your initial ticket price)* if your destination is far from a bus stop. If it's an option for your journey, it will be offered and can be purchased as an integrated part of your itinerary using Journey Planner. Plustur must be booked two hours in advance.

VISIT MORE VIKINGS
Find another Viking king's hall reconstruction and museum at **Trelleborg** in west Zealand, as well as a new museum at the Viking Castle – **Vikingeborgen** (p119) – discovered outside Køge in 2014.

interesting **Lejre Museum** *(lejremuseum.dk/adult/child 50kr/free)*, which contains Viking relics discovered in the area, including a silver figure of Odin: just before you reach the museum, on the left, you'll see the outlines of the seven King's Halls discovered in the area – this was the legendary power base for the Scyldings dynasty, referenced in *Beowulf*.

Nearby you can explore the gardens (and zip line on summer weekends) at the 1745 **Ledreborg Slot**.

Zealand's Offshore Islands

TIME FROM ROSKILDE TO HAVNSØ: 1 HR

Island-hopping off Zealand

It's an offbeat adventure, especially in good weather, to take a ferry to one or two of the five tiny islands off west Zealand and have the place almost to yourself. Tourist infrastructure is limited but just about exists on each island – they're all flat and good to explore by bike, with some nice white-sand beaches.

The largest island is **Orø**, with 985 inhabitants, a 25-minute journey from Holbæk. It has accommodation, a zoo and several villages. **Sejerø** is long and narrow, an hour from Havnsø and home to around 300 inhabitants. **Agersø** is 15 minutes by ferry, while **Omø** takes 50 minutes with one ferry a day. Both have under 200 residents, but a few guesthouses and places to eat. Most sparsely populated is **Nekselø**, one of the prettiest of the islands, with fewer than 20 inhabitants. It's a 20-minute ferry from Havnsø.

ODSHERRED OENOLOGY

Based on the west coast of Odsherred, **Nina and Niels Fink** are the founders of Vejrhøj Vingård, which produces about 20,000 bottles of wine a year. Here they share their favourite Zealand wineries. *@vejrhojvingaard*

'At first sight, we decided this was the place for us to retire. What we didn't know was that the land we acquired was the perfect spot for a vineyard. We've been on a journey, uncovering the potentials of this – so far – rather unknown terroir of Danish wine.'

Dyrehøj Vingaard: Denmark's largest winery, on the Røsnæs peninsula.

Agerbo Vingaard: Our neighbours on the Nekselø Bugt.

Ørnberg Vin: A delightful setting on Sjællands Odde.

Slagelse

TIME FROM ROSKILDE: 1 HR

Bluetooth-built ring fortress

If you're fascinated by Vikings, the **Trelleborg** Viking fortress, built by King Harald Bluetooth in 980 CE, is a mesmerising landmark. It's one of the best-preserved Viking sites in Zealand, and the grounds are open 24/7. A large ring fortress, Trelleborg is essentially a perfectly circular raised earthwork, often covered in grazing sheep. The interior once contained 16 wooden longhouses, but only the foundations are indicated today. A king's hall (closed for restoration at the time of research) and a small reconstructed Viking village are near the small museum, which mainly contains artefacts found on the site. Come in July for a week-long Viking festival full of enthusiastic re-enactors in fancy period dress (admission is 150kr at this time). Getting here by public transporta is complicated.

Walking up onto the circular rampart you can readily grasp the precise geometric design of the fortress. Its grassy banks – 17m wide and 6m high – were originally topped by a wooden palisade. They protect a central space where two streets divided the circle into quarters. Each quarter contained a courtyard with four wooden longhouses, which have long since decayed away, but the post holes and gable ends have been identified and filled with cement to show the outlines of their foundations.

A DRIVE AROUND WESTERN ZEALAND

West Zealand's attractions are spread out, and ideal for a driving tour.

START	END	LENGTH
Ringsted	Sjællands Odde	200km; 1–2 days

Starting in the south, ❶ **Ringsted** has the Romanesque 1170 ❷ **Sankt Bendts**, Scandinavia's oldest brick church, and ❸ **Sorø** is home to the Sorø Akademi campus. Once one of Denmark's richest monasteries, established in the 12th century under Absalon, and later a knight academy, today it's a secondary school. The building you see today is a neoclassical edifice built in the late 18th century, but one of the gatehouses dates from the time of the monastery. Take in its fabulous lakefront location on a one-hour ❹ **boat tour**. The rest of central Sorø has a few half-timbered buildings and the ❺ **Sorø Kunstmuseum**, a contemporary art museum.

Head north towards half-timbered ❻ **Reersø** village and ❼ **Tissø** lake's observation tower on your way to ❽ **Kalundborg** for the five towers of the 1200s Vor Frue Kirke. Nearby ❾ **Rosnæs Peninsula** is the heart of Denmark's wine region, and you can hike out to the ❿ **lighthouse** with a cafe at the end. Keep north onto the ⓫ **Odsherred Peninsula**, recognised as a UNESCO Global Geopark for its unique end moraine landscape. Here, the wispy ⓬ **Sjællands Odde** juts 15km into the Kattegat, offering extraordinary views en route to the end (the ferry to Aarhus goes from here).

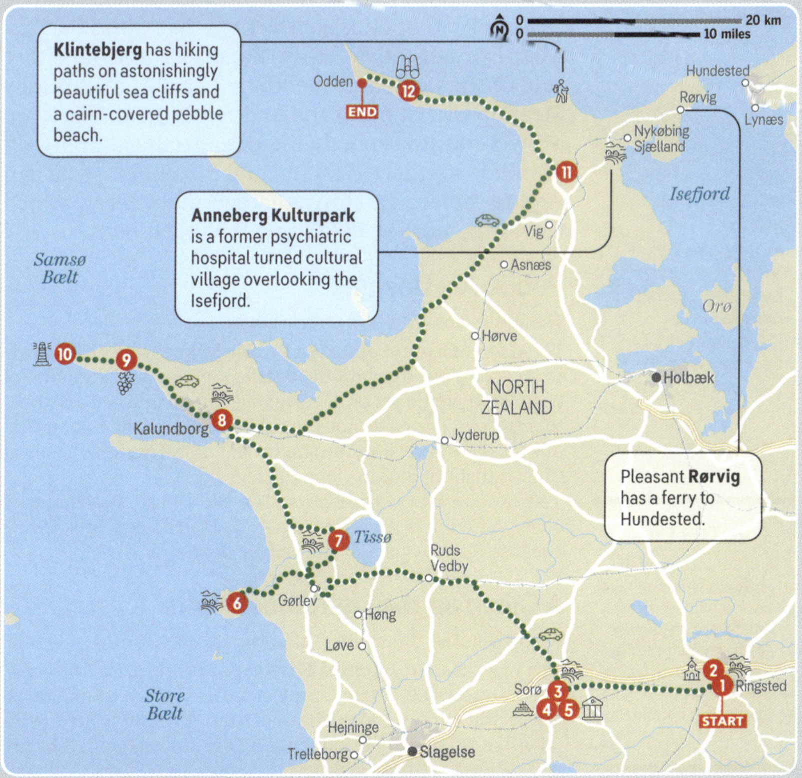

Klintebjerg has hiking paths on astonishingly beautiful sea cliffs and a cairn-covered pebble beach.

Anneberg Kulturpark is a former psychiatric hospital turned cultural village overlooking the Isefjord.

Pleasant **Rørvig** has a ferry to Hundested.

0 20 km
0 10 miles

Odden END 12 Hundested Rørvig Lynæs Nykøbing Sjælland 11 Isefjord Vig Asnæs Samsø Bælt Orø Hørve 10 9 Holbæk NORTH ZEALAND Kalundborg 8 Jyderup 7 Tissø Ruds Vedby 6 Gørlev Høng Løve Store Bælt Sorø 3 4 5 2 1 Ringsted START Hejninge Trelleborg Slagelse

Køge

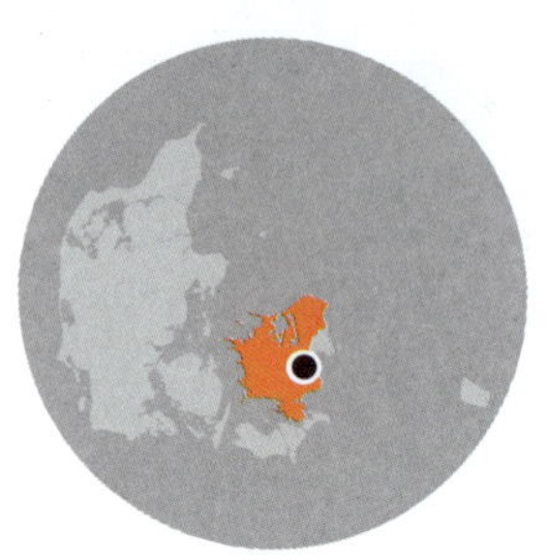

HISTORY | VIKINGS | MARKETS

GETTING AROUND

Køge is small and best explored on foot. It's just 40km to Copenhagen by bike, mostly following Danish National Cycle Route 9. By train, Køge is the southern terminus of S-tog lines A/E from Copenhagen. Local trains (110R/210R) continue from here and Rødvig (for Stevns Klint). For Ringsted and points west, trains go via Køge Nord station (accessible by S-tog lines A/E). To Roskilde, use Køge main station.

TOP TIP

Park the car east of the train station (paid) or take the roundabout along Værftsvej immediately north, where there's a large free car park facing the heat-and-power plant (follow signs for 'Køge Havn Gate 1').

With a medieval centre, Køge was recognised as an official market town in 1288 and its market still fills the huge town square (the largest in Denmark outside Copenhagen) every Wednesday and Saturday. It might be off the tourist trail, but you'll find a towering old church, a couple of intriguing museums, a Viking castle discovered in 2014 just outside of town, a trail that traces a witch hunt that took place here in the 17th century, and the moat-encircled Renaissance castle of Vallø, 7km south. Køge has two beaches, Køge Nordstrand and Køge Søndre Strand, on either side of the port, and the lovely beaches at Brøndby Strandpark, Ishøj Strand and Jersie Strandpark are a few S-tog stops north. Køge is also the jumping-off point for southern Zealand and Bornholm – you can explore before catching the overnight ferry, which leaves the port at 12.30am, arriving at 6am.

Public Art Designs

The ideas behind art in public spaces

The **KØS Museum of Art in Public Spaces** *(koes.dk; adult/child 90kr/free)* displays the drafts, sketches and scribbles of completed public art projects instead of the finished artworks themselves. The cavernous top floor contains the final mock-ups for the Bjørn Nørgaard historical tapestries on display at Christiansborg Slot in Copenhagen.

Next door, **Det Gamle Hus** (The Old House) is Denmark's oldest dated half-timbered house (1527). You can peek inside because it's now part of the city library.

A Climb up the Lighthouse Spire

Sankt Nikolai, the sailors' church

The brick **Sankt Nicolai Kirke** *(sanktnicolaikolding.dk)*, named after the patron saint of sailors, has a 43m church tower you can climb in summertime. In 1450 a little window-like brick projection (called Lygten) was added to the

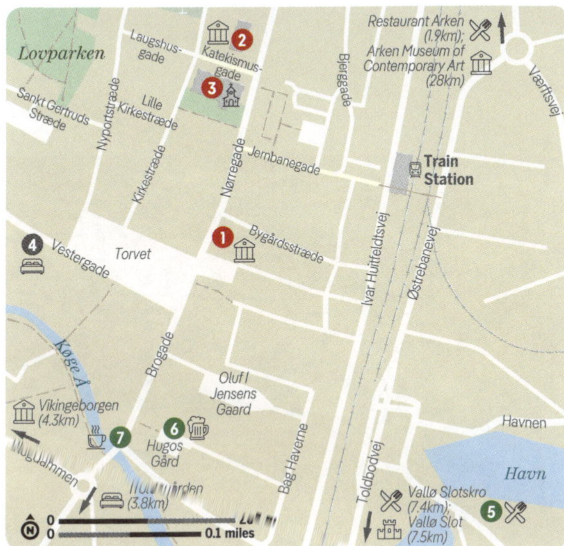

tower's upper eastern end to hang a burning lantern for guiding ships into harbour. It was from the top of this tower that Christian IV kept watch on his naval fleet as it successfully defended the town from Swedish invaders during the Battle of Køge Bay.

Grave Hauls & Witch Hunts

Fascinating artefacts at Køge Museum

Occupying a half-timbered 17th-century house, the **Køge Museum** *(koegemuseum.dk; adult/child 110kr/free)* has genuinely absorbing local history artefacts. One exhibit explores the 4000 BC Strøby Egede multiple-grave site, complete with a shockingly gory reconstruction. The museum is also home to Denmark's biggest coin hoard: a 32kg pile of 17th-century silver unearthed in the courtyard at Brogade 17 by two electricians in 1987. On the uppermost floor is an exhibition relating to the witch hunts of the early 17th century.

UNESCO-listed Ring Fortress, Køge

Vikingeborgen ring fortress

The ancient Vikingeborgen (Viking Castle) ring fortress, now one of five UNESCO-listed such fortresses, was only discovered in 2014, with the help of LiDAR (Light Detection and Ranging) imaging. Test excavations based on other ring fortresses in Denmark confirmed **Vikingeborgen** was indeed a lost fortress, and carbon dating placed it in the late 900s – the era of King Harald Bluetooth – just like the fortresses found in Trelleborg, Fyrkat, Nonnebakken and Aggersborg. At the time of research, construction of a new museum for the site

SIGHTS
1 Køge Museum
2 KØS Museum of Art in Public Spaces
3 Sankt Nicolai Kirke

SLEEPING
4 Centralhotellet

EATING
5 Braunstein

DRINKING & NIGHTLIFE
6 Hugo's Kælder
7 Kaffekælderen

CASTLE FOR 'SPINSTERS'

Around 8km from Køge, redbrick **Vallø Slot** looks like a castle should, with pointed metal-capped turrets and a moat filled with lily pads and croaking frogs. On her birthday in 1737 Queen Sophie Magdalene, who owned the estate, established a foundation that turned the castle into a home for 'spinsters of noble birth'. Unmarried daughters of Danish royalty unable to live in their own castles were allowed to live at Vallø, supported by the foundation and government social programmes. The last new residents arrived in the 1970s with the castle-estate's remit broadened since 1976 to one of a more general public charity. But a handful of ageing blue-blooded *stiftsdamer* (diocesan women) remain in residence. It's not open to the public, but you're welcome to wander the gardens.

TRABANTOS/SHUTTERSTOCK ©

Aerial view, Køge

was still ongoing, due to finish in 2025. It's about 5km west of Køge (take bus 260R).

Beachside Conceptual Art at Arken

Cutting-edge contemporary gallery

On the coast south of Copenhagen, the striking **Arken Museum of Contemporary Art** *(arken.dk; adult/child 115kr/free)* in Ishøj – take the train and then it's five minutes by bus from the station, or from late 2025 take the light rail direct to Ishøj Strand – hosts large-scale contemporary exhibitions of artists such as Anish Kapoor, with a smattering of its permanent collection as well. There's a good arty shop and a nice glass-walled restaurant with a view. The museum is surrounded by a moat on a barrier island facing the sandy Ishøj Beach; a popular escape on sunny days. The beach park is worth exploring – see if you can find the hiding troll.

EATING IN KØGE

Braunstein: Come for stone-oven pizzas and stay for microbrews and harbour views. *hours vary* €€

Kaffekælderen: Great coffee and cakes, but the top attractions are the time-twisted building and mini riverside terrace. *hours vary* €

Restaurant Arken: Overlooking the marina, 2.5km north of Torvet. Well-cooked seafood with top-quality ingredients. *11.30am-8.30pm* €€

Hugo's Kælder: Cosy 14th-century cellar bar, with candles on the tables, some 20 beers on tap and nibbles. *hours vary* €

Beyond Køge

Stevns Klint might be the star of the show, but you can also zip-line, climb the Forest Tower, bird-watch and much more.

Stevns Peninsula forms the southern edge of Køge Bay, ending at the UNESCO-listed Stevns Klint sea cliffs. These thrillingly beautiful high chalk cliffs run about 20km down the coast and are lovely for a clifftop walk, stopping off at the local niche museums. Keen geologists may even dig up fossils at the Faxe Kalkbrud limestone quarry nearby. Not far away, you can climb the vertiginous Forest Tower, a spiralling 45m lookout renowned for its design as much as its views. The unhurried Jungshoved Peninsula and the idyllic small town of Præstø nearby are pure rural bliss, featuring churches, farmhouses and fine country food. Zealand tapers towards its southernmost point near historic Vordingborg, just across the water from Denmark's South Sea islands.

Places

Stevns Klint

TIME FROM KØGE: **40 MINS**

Cretaceous cliffs

UNESCO-listed, the 40m-high, fossil-studded chalk cliffs of **Stevns Klint** are not only a beautiful place to walk along the clifftop, but they also present some of the best geological evidence for the asteroid-strike dinosaur extinction theory. The best way to see this rare stratification is to climb down the steep 110 steps beside the perilously perched old church in Højerup village. You'll be able to examine a thin layer of 'fish clay' that marks the asteroid strike thought to have taken out the dinosaurs.

A precarious church

Set on top of the cliffs at Stevn Klint is the jaw-droppingly precarious **Gamle Kirke** (Old Church), built around 1250 at Højerup. The continuously eroding cliffs finally had their way with the church in 1928, when the choir and part of the cemetery crashed into the sea. The reinforced remainder has a dramatic viewing platform where the altar once stood.

Walking and viewpoints

Højerup village is in the middle of the 22km coastal footpath (trampesti) that runs between Bøgeskov Havn in the north and Rødvig in the south; a beautiful walk in either direction.

Less than 10 minutes' walk north of Højerup car park along the footpath towards Stevns Fyr, Bråten is a clifftop perch with the best view down onto the Stevns Klint site.

GETTING AROUND

Local trains from Køge (110R/210R) connect to Faxe Ladeplads and Rødvig (change to bus 252 at Store Heddinge for Højerup/Stevns Klint). Danish National Cycle Route 7 follows southern Zealand's west coast from Næstved to Vordingborg, while Danish National Cycle Route 9 continues from Køge past Stevns Klint, Faxe and Præstø until crossing to Møn at Kalvehave. Although only 30km apart by car, it takes about two hours to get between Stevns Klint and the Forest Tower by public transport.

WHY I LOVE STEVNS KLINT

Sean Connolly, Lonely Planet writer

Having the spectacular seaside and cliffs of Stevns Klint more or less in your backyard as a Copenhagener is a chronically underused perk of living here. Spending a full day out hiking, taking pictures on the clifftops – where the white cliffs and blue seas make for reliably dramatic photos – and contemplating the mysteries of the ancient past is a life-affirming way to get your head out of the city and the day-to-day grind. The museums along the cliffs make fine stopovers too. There's plenty of time to savour your tired legs, and wind-chilled and sun-kissed cheeks on the way home, maybe even with a backpack beer as a reward for the journey.

If you head 1.5km north, you'll reach Stevns Fyr lighthouse, dating from 1878, which you can climb for an even better bird's-eye view.

To the south are the Stevns Klint Experience and the Koldkrigsmuseum Stevnsfort Cold War Museum.

Explaining the asteroid

The stylishly designed **Stevns Klint Experience** *(stevnsklint .dk/en; adult/child 140/70kr)* has minimalist looks that help it merge into the landscape, and this is the ideal place to come to understand fish clay, the asteroid theory and the geology behind the cliffs. There are fossils, dinosaur skeletons and interactive displays here.

Subterranean Cold War museum

This fascinating **Koldkrigsmuseum Stevnsfort** *(kalklandet. dk; underground guided tour adult/under 9s 195kr/free, above-ground tour only 85kr/free)* was a secret subterranean fortress used in the Cold War era, when countries felt the need to prepare for nuclear war in the bellicose stand-off between NATO and the USSR. Visits are by 90-minute guided tours (in Danish, but with audio guides available in English and German). You can explore the above-ground area without a tour and see vintage rocket launchers, mobile radar stations and container-box control rooms.

Quarry fossils

If you're after more geology, head west to Faxe Kalkbrud, a massive, active limestone quarry, where you can dig up 63-million-year-old fossilised sea creatures with a hammer and chisel from the **GeoMuseum Faxe** *(kalklandet.dk; axe rental 50kr, museum adult/child 95kr/free)* next door.

Zealand's Deep South

TIME FROM KØGE: **1 HR**

Slow-paced escapes

For a summer escape, **Karrebæksminde** and the nearby island of **Enø** have summer houses, beaches and fish shacks aplenty. Enø is joined to the mainland via its 'Grasshopper Bridge', made of recycled horseshoes, which opens to let sailboats through. It's well worth taking the **Rundfart Friheden**, a ferry that sails on the fjord, stopping at Næstved, Gavnø and Karrebæksminde. Go birdwatching at the pristine, waterside **Enø Overdrev nature reserve** or wine tasting at organic **Vesterhave Vingaard**.

WHERE TO EAT BEYOND KØGE

Traktørstedet Højeruplund: Seafront Danish buffet at the north end of the Stevns Klint footpath. *10am-4pm Tue-Fri, to 5pm Sat & Sun* €€

Villa Gallina: Deep-forest destination for smørrebrød, set on a pond in Haslev, a few kilometres from Camp Adventure. *noon-5pm Sat & Sun* €€

Fiskehuset Enø: This smokehouse, fishmonger and cafe is a winner for paper plates piled high with seafood. *hours vary* €

Vallø Slotskro: Just outside Vallø castle gate, this 200-year-old inn serves New Nordic dishes strong on local produce. *6-11pm Wed-Sat* €€

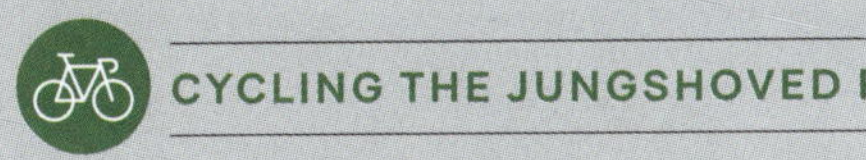

CYCLING THE JUNGSHOVED PENINSULA

The rural Jungshoved Peninsula juts eastwards into the Baltic. Take an hour or so or make a day of it cycling the country lanes and enjoying the wide-open views.

START	END	LENGTH
Præstø	Jungshoved Præstegaard	15km; 1–2 hours

Start in the picturesque tiny town of ❶ **Præstø** at the entrance to Præstø Fjord. Granted town privileges in 1403, Præstø was once a centre for the herring trade. The colourful and cobbled old town covers a few streets along an elevated ridge, with views down to the water on both sides. The solid old homes and commanding views make this little outpost with a population of 3857 feel bigger than it actually is. ❷ **Hotel Frederiksminde** overlooks the fjord and hosts an eponymous Michelin-starred restaurant.

About 1km northwest of town, the 1673 baroque ❸ **Nysø Manor** is home to the Thorvaldsen Collection (open weekends in summer), a small sculpture exhibition and counterpart to the Thorvaldsens Museum in Copenhagen (p63). At the southwest end of the peninsula sits the lonely ❹ **Jungshoved Kirke**. On first appearance, it's a whitewashed Danish church like many others, but the glorious waterside location sets it apart. Look inside for a beautifully carved pulpit and fading wall frescoes. Though it feels like a backwater today, for centuries it was a strategic location: enough so that a castle, ❺ **Jungshoved Slot**, and defensive works were built next door to guard the entrance to the inlet. You can even spend the night in the old rectory nearby at ❻ **Jungshoved Præstegaard**.

Roneklint Fyr, a former battery tower, with a beach and birdwatching.

Panorama Cycle Route 424 rings the peninsula.

Muldiverset farmhouse restaurant serves all-local cuisine for a gourmet but down-to-earth experience.

Præstø Fjord
Storeholm
Lilleholm
Maderne
Roneklint
Præstø
START
Øen Skovhuse
Lundegård
Ambæk
Togeholt
Øen Smidstrup
Stenstrup
Jungshoved By
Tjørnehoved
Stavreby
END
Allerslev
Rekkende
Bøgestrøm
0 2 km
0 1 mile

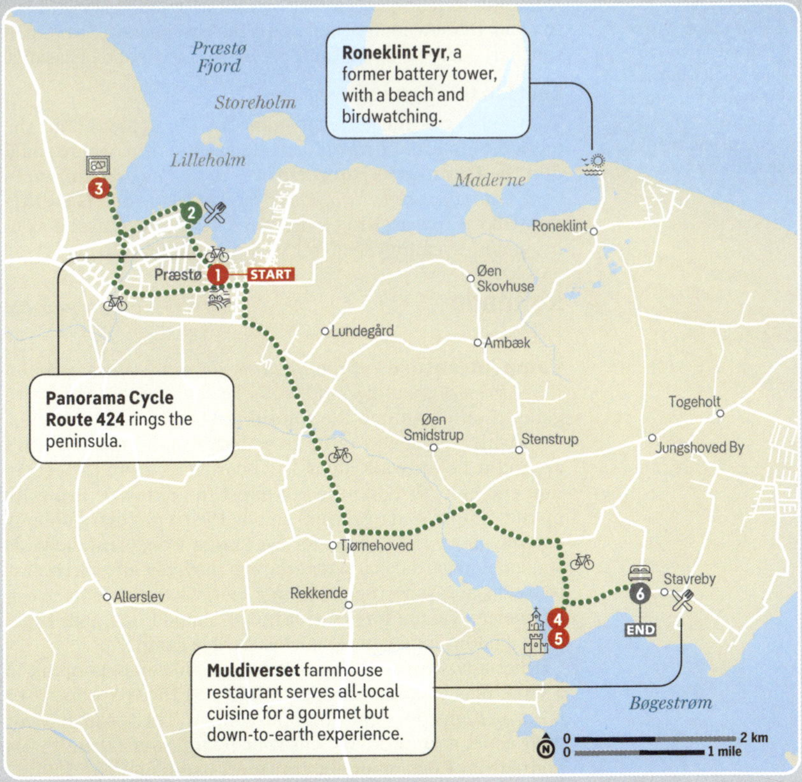

ZEALAND'S FORGOTTEN CASTLES

Næsseslottet: Regal neoclassical manor on a peninsula jutting into Furesø.

Selsø Slot: Even the signboards call this 1576 palace on the Hornsherred Peninsula 'the forgotten manor'.

Hirschholm Slot: This 1744 baroque palace was demolished in 1813. Today there's an 1883 church surrounded by the castle's large moats and gardens.

Søborg Slot: Queen Margrete I was born here in 1353, but the castle fell into disrepair in the 16th century, and even served as a quarry.

Forest Tower

Seal-spotting

A former airstrip, **Avnø Naturcentre** has repurposed the control tower as a birding lookout. There are good views over the Avnø Fjord to Avnø Røn, and this is the best place in Zealand to spot harbour seals, as well as ospreys, deer, geese and pheasants.

Boats to the island of Møn

Vordingborg is the transfer point for Møn (p142), and the town is built around an 1160 moated castle ruin, where you'll find the **Danmarks Borgcenter** *(Castle Centre; danmarksborgcenter.dk; adult/child 135kr/free)* museum and **Gåsetårnet** (Goose Tower), King Valdemar IV's architectural diss to his enemies, calling them all 'cackling geese'.

Rønnede

TIME FROM KØGE: **30 MINS**

The Spiralling Forest Tower

Camp Adventure *(campadventure.de; adult/child aged 3-6 175/85kr)* is a great day out if you like zip lines, but it's worth going if only to climb the spiralling Forest Tower (Skovtårnet), which rises above the trees like a modernist folly. It's around a 1.6km walk along the boardwalk from the reception and cafe, through the tall forest to the tower. You walk up the ramp, for many layers among the trees, then suddenly emerge above the canopy for ever more wonderful views as you loop upwards. Plaques at the top show the measurements to towns across Europe, with big views over the frilly green Denderup Vænge forest. Hourglass-shaped, it's 45m high, with a 650m-long wheelchair-accessible ramp.

Other adventures at Camp Adventure include glamping in a yurt, plus a sauna or zipping between the trees and over lakes on high-ropes and climbing courses. There's an outdoor food court and an idyllic cut-your-own flower farm. It's 1¼ hours from Køge on public transport (train and bus 630R).

Places We Love to Stay

€ Budget €€ Midrange €€€ Top End

Helsingør p102

Danhostel Helsingør € Set in an old manor on the beach a short walk from the centre.

Kagefryds Gæstehus €€ Light and stylish studio set above the central cafe and pâtisserie of the same name.

Marienlyst Badehotel €€€ Helsingør's grande dame is a large beachfront complex with a sea-facing spa and well-regarded restaurant.

Hotel Hamlet € This simple place has rooms with pleasant outlooks, is reasonable value and centrally located, with a restaurant downstairs.

Beyond Helsingør p107

Hotel Gilleleje Strand €€ An elegant pick at the centre of Gilleleje, with an attached restaurant.

Danhostel Hillerød € Popular budget pick in natural surroundings next to Store Dyrehave.

Gilleleje Badehotel €€€ This gently luxurious hotel, around 1km west of town, sits amid wooded gardens beside the clifftop path, with a direct passage down to the wild seashore below.

Fredensborg Store Kro €€ In a building that used to house palace guests, this is a historic and charming place to stay; the best rooms have balconies overlooking the lawns.

Liselængen Liseleje Badehotel €€€ Relaxed luxury only a few minutes' walk from the beach.

Roskilde p111

Danhostel Roskilde € Perfectly located budget option along the fjord and steps from the Viking Ship Museum.

Scandic Roskilde Park €€ Business hotel overlooking a pond between the city centre and Musicon.

B&B Roskilde City € Rooms in a central family home with a garden, shared kitchen and bath.

Roskilde Camping € Beautifully situated by a fjord-side beach, this has pitches, cabins and rooms.

Køge p118

Troldegården €€ Rural farmstead with a handful of individually decorated rooms just outside the city.

Vallø Slotskro €€ Rooms overlooking the castle pair well with a five-course dinner in the fantastic restaurant downstairs.

Centralhotellet €€ Neat modern rooms – excellent value in an old building next to Køge's main square. There's no breakfast but there are some help-yourself snacks and a coffee machine.

Beyond Køge p121

Norrmans Boutique B&B €€€ This design-forward country homestead is the prettiest accommodation near Stevns Klint; rooms come with dinner.

Bed & Boats €€ Spend the night harbourside in Kalvehave in your own little boat overlooking the bridge to Møn.

Danhostel Stevns € In Store Heddinge, this is the best budget option for sleeping close to the cliffs, about 5km away.

Rødvig Kro & Badehotel €€ Get a taste of the old days in this 1844 *kro* (country inn) – ask for a room with a view.

Bornholm & the South Sea Islands

ISLAND LIFE WITH AN ARTISTIC TWIST

Denmark's laid-back getaway islands are rustic places to slow down and unwind, with a scattering of historic small towns that attract artists, craftsfolk and creative chefs.

These bucolic islands are places to switch down a gear and soak up the silence, delve into arts and crafts, and experience fine food made with farm-fresh produce. In contrast to today's peaceful atmosphere, this richly agricultural region was once of great geopolitical importance. Sitting in the middle of the Baltic and accessible only by air or sea, Bornholm was the one small consolation prize reclaimed by Denmark from the swathe of lands lost to Sweden in 1658. It was also the only Danish territory occupied by the Soviet Union in a little-known footnote to WWII. In 2022, the island hit international headlines again when Russia's Nord Stream 2 natural gas pipeline was ruptured nearby in a suspected sabotage linked to the war with Ukraine.

Connected by bridges to Zealand and ferries to Germany, the South Sea Islands of Lolland, Falster and Møn grew wealthy on herring and sugar in the 19th century and then became important to NATO in the Cold War face-off with East Germany. Now, however, they are mostly idyllically calm, slow-paced backwaters that attract artists, nature lovers and holidaymakers seeking low-key beach getaways.

In this region, don't overlook the importance of choosing the right season to visit. July is briefly super busy, but from October or November to Easter, the vast majority of businesses close down.

THE MAIN AREAS

BORNHOLM
Crafty isle adrift in the Baltic. p132

MØN
Cliffs, dark skies and painted churches. p142

LOLLAND-FALSTER
Lakeland and dune-backed beaches. p147

For places to stay in Bornholm & the South Sea Islands, see p153

ROLF E. STAERK/SHUTTERSTOCK ©

Left: Svaneke (p137); Above: Møns Klint (p142)

Find Your Way

Lolland-Falster has road and rail links to the rest of Denmark and ferries to Germany. For Bornholm, fly or take a ferry from Køge, Ystad (Sweden) or Sassnitz (Germany). Bus-boat combos travel from Copenhagen.

CAR

Easy parking and pretty open roads make driving a pleasure. On Bornholm, having a car means you are rarely more than 30 minutes from anywhere else on the island, but in summer, book a hire car well ahead.

BUS

Bus routes cover virtually all of the main roads in Bornholm, including key sites and beaches. Day and multiday bus passes can prove cost effective. In the South Sea Islands, bus frequency and reach are limited.

TRAIN

Bornholm does not have a train network. Rail service is limited on the South Sea Islands, though Nykøbing Falster has a fast link to Copenhagen. The under-construction Fehmarnbelt tunnel project will eventually put Lolland-Falster on the Hamburg–Stockholm line.

Møn, p142
Chalk cliffs, orchids and birdlife come together at the eastern tip of Møn, while further west are medieval church murals and 5000-year-old tunnel graves.
Lolland-Falster, p147
Agricultural Lolland offers soothing lakelands, farm-fresh food and a latter-day Stonehenge, while neighbouring Falster has some of Denmark's best beaches.
Bornholm, p132
Out in the Baltic and nearer to Poland than Copenhagen, Denmark's sunniest island is a getaway for craftspeople, artists and gastronomes.
0 20 km
0 10 miles
Fensmark
Faxe
Fakse Ladeplads
ZEALAND
Præstø Fjord
Fakse Bugt
Køng
Lundby
Præstø
Nyord
Søhundehavn
Ørslev
Mern
Ulvshale
Vordingborg
Kalvehave
Stege Bugt
Keldby
Elmelunde
Stensved
Stege
Langø
MØN
Magleby
Orehoved
Farø
Tærø
Bogøby
Bogø
Klekkende Høj
Damsholte
Hjelm
Hjelm Bugt
Klintholm Havn
Nørre Alslev
Stubbekøbing
Næs
Ønslev
FALSTER
Hesnæs
Horreby
Nykøbing Falster
Idestrup
Væggerløse
BALTIC SEA
Bornholm (130km) (see inset)
Skelby
Bøtø Plantage
Gedesby
Gedser
Bornholm
0 10 km
0 5 miles
Sandvig
Allinge
Gudhjem
Hasle
BORNHOLM
Svaneke
Almindingen
Rønne
Nexø
Åkirkeby
BALTIC SEA

Plan Your Time

This region rewards a slow pace. Low-key exploration and minor discoveries trump must-see sights. While the sunny, artistic island of Bornholm takes a special effort to visit, the South Sea Islands are bridge-linked and accessible.

KENNETH BAGGE JORGENSEN/SHUTTERSTOCK ©

Fanefjord Kirke (p145)

Just Passing Through the Region

- If you're travelling between Copenhagen and Hamburg, Germany, tack on an extra day for some of the highlights of the South Sea Islands. Outdoorsy types might walk the grand woodland-topped cliffs of **Møns Klint** (p142), a slice of rare drama in the Danish landscape, or watch birds on the causeway that leads to the pretty hamlet of **Nyord** (p143). Families can choose between elephants and tigers while on safari at **Knuthenborg** (p149), or Europe's biggest croc at **Krokodille Zoo** (p149). One of Denmark's best beaches beckons at **Marielyst** (p151), while medieval Denmark is in full reenacted swing at **Middelaldercentret** (p151). To strike a more spiritual note, drop in on **Dodekalitten** (p147), a spellbinding sculpture of giant standing stones overlooking the sea.

Seasonal Highlights

Everything happens in midsummer. June and September are quiet, but facilities are still open. That changes from November.

MAY

Møn's wealth of rare orchids is in bloom, and you're well ahead of the busy tourist season.

JUNE

Bornholm accommodation is booked solid during Folkemødet, a series of political meetings that draw in some 100,000 Danes.

JULY

Peak of the short summer season brings activities, musical events and street markets that give Bornholm a jazzy vibe.

A Week on Denmark's South Sea Islands

● Instead of rushing through the islands' highlights, visit them at a slower pace. Extend your time at **Møns Klint** (p142) by taking on an energetic hiking trail that weaves up and down steep cliffside steps. After dark, gaze up at Denmark's **starriest skies** (p146) on Møn and Nyord, sample local beers in historic **Stege** (p145) before tootling around rustic back lanes in rural Møn that lead to offbeat ancient tunnel graves and medieval mural-decked churches like 13th-century **Fanefjord Kirke** (p146). From low-key **Maribo** (p148) explore its pretty lakeside setting on foot or boat, and then strike out on a road trip around Lolland, seeking out enticing farm shops, breweries and vineyards to sample artisanal farm produce and tart cherry wine.

Adding a Few Days on Bornholm

● Taste smoked herring, shrimp and salmon at Bornholm's most archetypal *røgeri* (smokehouse) in **Hasle** (p138) and then get a handle on the island's remarkable craft scene at **Grønbechs Gård** (p137). Explore the gigantic **Hammershus castle ruins** (p136), check out the pretty port hamlet of **Sandvig** (p137), then check in to charming lodgings in **Gudhjem** (p132). Spend a couple days visiting the town's art galleries and museums before setting off on a memorable boat trip to the tiny, time-warp island of **Christiansø** (p140). Don't miss the signature round church in nearby **Østerlars** (p133) or the craft shops and dining scene in **Svaneke** (p137). Stroll the picturesque older quarters of **Rønne** (p138) while waiting for your departing ferry.

AUGUST

Bornholm's Music Festival sees a month of classical concerts dotted about the island, notably at Aakirkeby, Allinge and Gudhjem.

SEPTEMBER

Bornholm hosts craft weeks and a 10-day culture fest. Roadside rowan trees turn scarlet with berries.

OCTOBER

Craft weeks continue on Bornholm. Æbletsdag (Apple Day) is celebrated in the orchard villages of western Lolland and Fejø island.

DECEMBER

Magical weekend Christmas markets pop up in Nexø on Bornholm. Lolland's Museumsbanen runs a festive steam train.

Bornholm

RUGGED ISLAND VISTAS | ARTISANAL CRAFT WORKSHOPS | VACATION VIBES

GETTING AROUND

DAT flights to Bornholm depart from Copenhagen year-round (40 minutes), and also from Aalborg and Billund (March to October), and Aarhus (June to August).

A catamaran car ferry (1 hour 20 minutes) sails to Rønne from Ystad (Sweden) – coach-ferry combo tickets use this routing from Copenhagen (2½ hours), some stopping at Copenhagen Airport. An overnight car ferry sails to Rønne from Køge south of Copenhagen, with free bunk beds in its 'resting areas'. A car ferry also links Rønne and Sassnitz (Germany), taking 3½ hours.

Once on the island, the BAT bus system is remarkably comprehensive. Car hire is available at the airport.

A distant dot way out in the Baltic Sea, sunny Bornholm is a geopolitical enigma, an artistic retreat and a summer holiday hot spot. The boulder-strewn island surprises cyclists with unexpectedly precipitous slopes where the undulating plateau swoops down to the northern coastal fringes, offering taxing gradients and glorious vistas. Ferries and flights arrive in patchily attractive Rønne, Bornholm's biggest town. Cosy Gudhjem, quaint Allinge-Sandvig and arty Svaneke all have more charm and historical pedigree, and make nicer bases for touring the island. Bornholm is small enough to visit anywhere from anywhere else, but large enough to offer days of discoveries, from mysterious standing stones to cutting-edge museums. In food terms, it punches well above its weight, with old-world smokehouses and a Michelin-starred outpost of Copenhagen's Kadeau.

In 1658, Denmark lost Bornholm and most of what is now southern Sweden to its Scandinavian neighbour. Bornholm alone was returned, however, hence its isolation from the rest of modern Denmark.

Culture on the Coast

The many charms of Gudhjem

Gudhjem brings together three of Bornholm's best attributes: scenery, art and good food. Compact, picturesque and thronged with visitors in summer, the town's photogenic commercial lane (Brøddegade/Åbogade) snakes steeply down from a prominent windmill to a pretty little port. The coastal strip features several cafes and ice cream parlours, and **Gudhjem Glasrøgeri**, Bornholm's oldest glass studio occupying a former smokehouse. Walk to Løkkegade to find the **Oluf Høst Museet** *(ohmus.dk; adult/child 95/25kr)*, a beautifully curated shrine to one of Bornholm's best-known artists. A few doors along is the vivid house-gallery of bold abstract artist **Søren Kent**.

On the town's upper heights, the **Gudhjem Museum** *(gudhjemmuseum.dk; 50kr, under-18s free, open Thu–Sun)* has set up shop

Footbridge to Sorte Gryde, Helligdomsklipperne

in a former train station, and focuses on local art and handicrafts. Around 1km southeast, **Melstedgård Frilandsmuseet** *(gaarden.nu; 100kr, under-18s free, open Wed-Sun)*, is a historic farmhouse turned museum complex. *Mad* means food, and the focus is on recreating 19th century-era agricultural production, with farm animals to pet and occasional food fairs.

Cruise into Art

Behold Bornholm's sanctuary cliffs

Several times a day in summer, the wooden cutter **M/S Thor** *(ms-thor.dk; roundtrip adult/child 140/90kr)* departs from Gudhjem's dainty harbour for a 30-minute cruise along a coastline etched with towering granite pillars and deep caves. The boat stops at a jetty beside the **Helligdomsklipperne** ('sanctuary cliffs'), once a place of pilgrimage. Disembark and climb rocky steps to the island's top art gallery, **Bornholms Kunstmuseum** *(bornholms-kunstmuseum.dk; 100kr, under-18s free, closed Mondays)*. The outdoor sculpture garden is free.

Just south of the museum, more steps lead down the cliffs to the sea, where you can shimmy into a cave called **Sorte Gryde** ('black cauldron'). Instead of returning to Gudhjem by boat, why not go via the popular **clifftop walk** (6km, 1½ hours), especially pretty at sunset.

Østerlars & Spiritual Bornholm

Round churches and sacred stones

Around 5km south of Gudhjem, **Østerlars Kirke** *(oesterlars kirke.dk; adult/child 25/10kr)* is the biggest and most memorable of Bornholm's four highly distinctive round churches from the 12th and 13th centuries. With heavy buttresses, conical spires and 2m thick walls, they are different to any other churches in Denmark. At Østerlars, visitors can squeeze through a claustrophobic staircase to the upper levels, where slot-like shooting-holes support the theory that these churches

continues on p136

TOP TIP

Valid for one week, Bornholm's Museum Pass is a remarkable bargain. The 170kr version includes entry to the splendid Bornholms Kunstmuseum; Bornholm Museum, Hjorths Fabrik and Erichsens Gård in Rønne; Melstedgård (aka the farming museum), and the highly-rated NaturBornholm.

THE BORNHOLM UPRISING

In 1658, after Denmark lost a series of wars, it was forced to cede large swathes of territory, including Bornholm, to Sweden. The island's residents, fiercely loyal to Denmark and unhappy with Swedish rule, soon rebelled. Led by local leader Jens Pedersen Kofoed, they launched a coordinated uprising on 8 December, 1658, assassinating the Swedish commander, Johan Printzensköld, and overwhelming the small garrison. Recognising the headache of holding Bornholm and its limited strategic value, Sweden chose not to reconquer the island. By 1660, under the Treaty of Copenhagen, Bornholm alone was officially returned to Denmark, an isolated outpost just off the coast of what had become, and remains, southern Sweden.

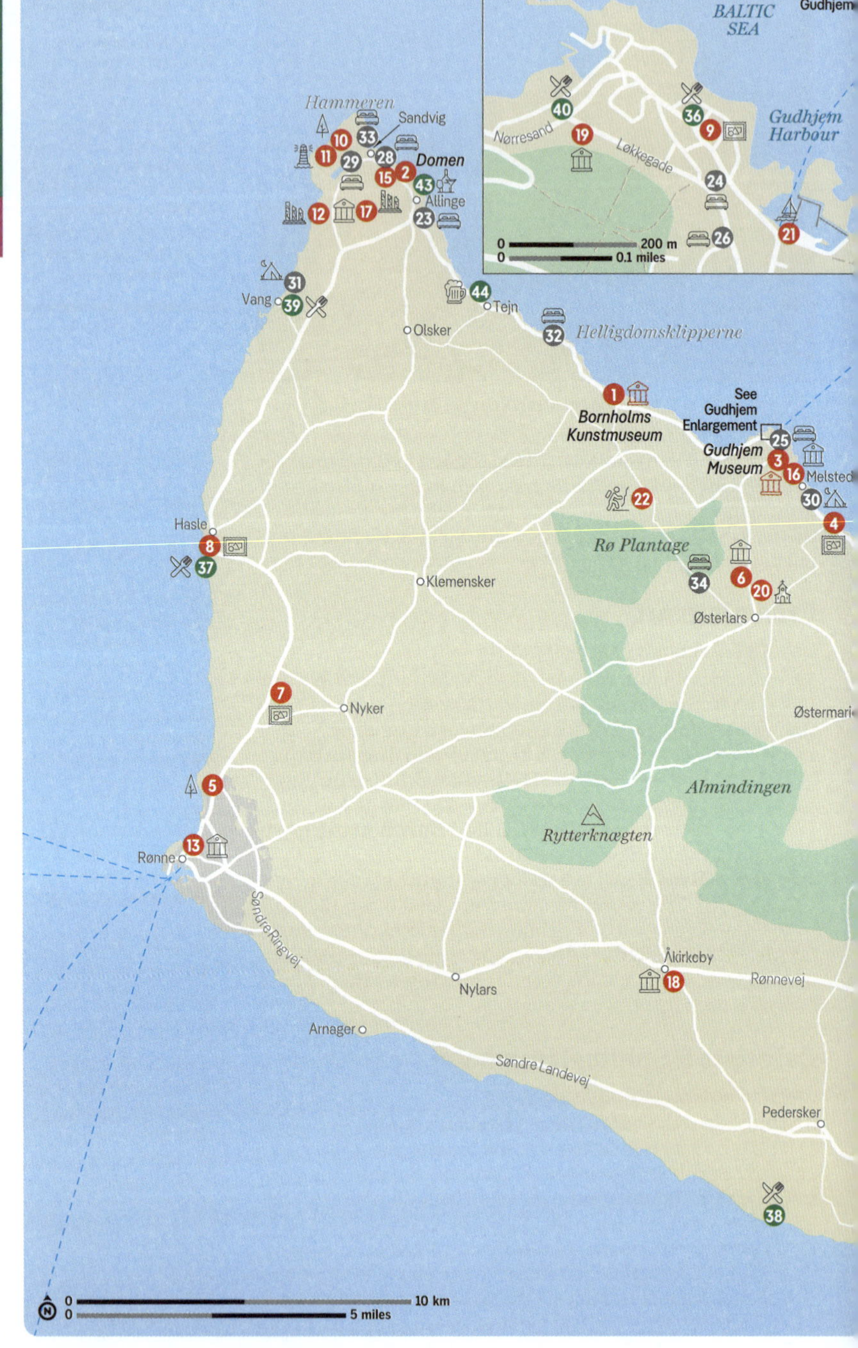
BORNHOLM
BALTIC SEA
Gudhjem
Gudhjem Harbour
Nørresand
Løkkegade
0 200 m
0 0.1 miles
Hammeren
Sandvig
Domen
Allinge
Vang
Tejn
Olsker
Helligdomsklipperne
Bornholms Kunstmuseum
See Gudhjem Enlargement
Gudhjem Museum
Melsted
Hasle
Rø Plantage
Klemensker
Østerlars
Nyker
Østermarie
Almindingen
Rytterknægten
Rønne
Søndre Ringvej
Ålirkeby
Rønnevej
Nylars
Arnager
Søndre Landevej
Pedersker
0 10 km
0 5 miles

HIGHLIGHTS

1 Bornholms Kunstmuseum
2 Domen
3 Gudhjem Museum

SIGHTS

4 Baltic Sea Glass
5 Blykobbe Plantage
6 Bornholms Middelaldercenter
7 Cassius Clay
8 Grønbechs Gård
9 Gudhjem Glasrøgeri
10 Hammeren
11 Hammeren Fyr
12 Hammershus Slot
● Helligdomsklipperne (see 1)
13 Hjorths Fabrik
14 Louisenlund
15 Madsebakke
16 Melstedgård Frilandsmuseet
17 Moseløkken Quarry Museum
18 NaturBornholm
19 Oluf Høst Museet
20 Østerlars Kirke

ACTIVITIES, COURSES & TOURS

● BornPark Minigolf (see 6)
21 M/S Thor
22 Nature Park Bornholm

SLEEPING

23 Allinge Badehotel
24 Gudhjem Vandrerhjem
25 Hotel Klippen
26 Jantzens Hotel
27 Myregaard Bed and Breakfast
28 Nordlandet
29 Pension Lindesdal
30 Sannes Familiecamping
31 Shelterplads Finnedalen
32 Stammershalle Badehotel
33 Strandhotellet
34 Yggdrasil Guest Lodge

EATING

35 Bornholms Ismejeri
36 Gudhjem Røgeri
37 Hasle Røgeri
38 Kadeau
39 Le Port
● Nordbornholms Røgeri(see 23)
40 Norresan
41 Svaneke Røgeri

DRINKING & NIGHTLIFE

42 Mikkeller Aarsdale
43 Ølstauan
44 Penyllan Brewery
45 Svaneke Bryghus

SHOPPING

46 Matter - House of Craft
47 Svaneke Chokoladeri

BORNHOLM'S SMOKEHOUSES

Buildings in Bornholm with distinctive upturned Y-shaped chimneys were originally smokehouses (*røgerier*, singular *røgeri*) for curing herring using alder-wood smoke. Locals insist that 19th-century Scottish visitors to Christiansø introduced this method, which later became an economic mainstay. Gudhjem became known as the '100-chimney town' for its many smokehouses, and across Denmark, it's still associated with a classic smørrebrød (open sandwich) of smoked herring on rye bread with chives and raw egg yolk called *Sol over Gudhjem* ('sun above Gudhjem'). The name is also given to a major national gastronomic contest held here in June. Despite the West Baltic fishing ban, Bornholm has a dozen working *røgerier* smoking herring imported from Jutland. Hasle's *røgeri* still uses century-old equipment.

Salomons kapel

continued from p133

were originally used as defence towers to guard against raiders. Slavonic Wends from Rugen, off Germany, attacked regularly before 1169. Another theory proposed in the book *The Templars' Secret Island* claims that the churches doubled as watchtowers and fortified storehouses for provisioning Crusaders who were sent in waves against pagan Estonia between 1164 and 1219. Whatever the truth is, Østerlars is a must-see. Across the lane is a **farmhouse cafe** and shop.

Far older than the round churches are Bornholm's various standing stones. Some are natural 'erratics', such as *rokkestenen*, rocking boulders that pivot miraculously. Other stones were erected at Iron Age and Viking-era gravesites, most impressively at **Louisenlund**, hidden in woodlands 4km east of **Østermarie**. On **Madsebakke**, a hill behind **Allinge**, bronze-age petroglyphs etched on to boulders depict curvaceous boats, footprints and sun wheels, evidence of a ritualistic culture engaging in spiritual practices on Bornholm some 3500 years ago.

Hammer of History

Medieval fortress and majestic views

At Bornholm's northern tip, the gargantuan ruins of **Hammershus Slot** *(free)* loom ominously over the windblown coast like a set from *Game of Thrones*. A beautifully designed visitor centre explains the history of the 'hated castle' that symbolised the imposition of power on Bornholm by tyrannical outsiders. Serving

Silent discos in summer! Check their FB page

EATING IN BORNHOLM: SEA-VIEW GASTRONOMY

Kadeau: Bornholm's Michelin-starred wunderkind is remote, and boasts sustainability credentials. *6-11.30pm Thu-Sat* **€€€**

Nordlandet: Attached to a hotel, Allinge's take on contemporary Nordic cuisine offers swoon-worthy sea views. *11am-9pm* **€€€**

Norresan: In a Gudhjem smokehouse by the water, enjoy lavishly-assembled smørrebrød, home-baked cakes and house-infused rhubarb gin. *noon-9pm* **€**

Le Port: High above the little harbour at Vang, set menus of modern Danish fare are accompanied by sea views. *noon-3pm, 6-11pm Tue-Sat* **€€€**

burgers, beer and smørrebrød, the incorporated cafe-restaurant has super castle-view tables inside and out. Car parking costs 40kr, or several buses stop here. You could also hike in from Sandvig, a fairly easy 3km on a path passing **Hammersø**, Bornholm's largest lake with zip-lining in the adjacent quarry pond. Longer and more taxing but more interesting alternatives loop around or over the windswept craggy headland called **Hammeren**. With a car, you could drive right to Hammeren's highest point, **Ørnebjerget** (Eagle's Hill), for panoramic vistas towards Sweden from **Hammeren Fyr** lighthouse.

More easily reached is **Hammerodde Fyr**, a supporting lighthouse to Hammeren on a less dramatic perch just up the coast from Sandvig. Paths continue west to **Salomons kapel** (Salomon's Chapel), the sea-facing ruins of a 13th century chapel built to serve local herring fishermen.

Back along the coast, the northern twin towns of Allinge-Sandvig are a delight, with chocolate-box cottages, classy seaside hotels, a wealth of summer dining options and two working smokehouses. The building that looks like an exploding wooden globe is the **Domen** concert hall and cultural centre, the epicentre of the Folkemødet political rallies that flood Bornholm with visitors for around a week in mid-June.

Island of Creativity

Europe's first 'World Craft Region'

What draws so many artisanal craftspeople, chefs, artists and nature lovers to Bornholm? Maybe it's something in the light, the draw of the earth, the colours of the Baltic Sea foam or the purity of the produce. Bornholm's clay certainly inspires ceramicists, and glass-making is a particularly well-established art form, so much so that Denmark's Royal Academy runs its glass and ceramics programme on the island. The World Crafts Council bestowed the title of 'World Craft Region' on Bornholm, the planet's first island community to receive it.

For a comprehensive introduction to the craft scene, start by visiting **Grønbechs Gård** *(groenbechsgaard.dk; 75kr, under-18s free)*, a one-stop crafts showcase housed in a restored 19th-century warehouse in Hasle, with possibly the best craft shop on the island. If you want to explore a single village on a relaxed craft-based day out, a good choice is the loveable harbour town of **Svaneke**. A central cluster of venues includes artist studios, shops selling glassware and jewellery, and hands-on workshops. Even the chocolate shop on the main square, **Svaneke Chokoladeri**, has artisans at work, while a few doors away, sticky confectionery and liquorice is

SPECIALIST CRAFT OUTLETS

Baltic Sea Glass: This widely admired studio 3km south of Gudhjem produces gallery-worthy glass masterpieces as well as characterful drinking vessels and vases. No expense spared.

Cassius Clay: In farm buildings between Rønne and Hasle, the wood-fired ceramics of Anne Mette Hjortshøj and Ann-Charlotte Ohlsson have earned a worldwide cult following.

Hjorths Fabrik: Rønne's 150-year-old ceramics workshop-factory still produces stoneware using traditional methods, and doubles as a museum and craft shop.

Matter - House of Craft: Part of the ongoing regeneration of Nexø's once gruesome port area, Matter is a gorgeous showroom selling work by leading Bornholm designers including Oh Oak and glass from Zelmer Olsen.

EATING IN BORNHOLM: TRADITIONAL SMOKEHOUSES

Live music most nights in July and August

Hasle Røgeri: Great value all-you-can-eat buffet. Sit inside or on a lovely sea-view lawn. Potently smoky/salty. *10am-9pm* **€€**

Svaneke Røgeri: Indulge in smoked mackerel, trout and *fiskefrikadeller* (fishcakes). Picnic tables overlook the old cannons. *10am-7pm* **€€**

Gudhjem Røgeri: Serves fish and salads, including the classic smørrebrød topping known as Sol over Gudhjem. *11am-9pm or later* **€€**

Nordbornholms Røgeri: In Allinge, this smokehouse serves a buffet of locally smoked fish, ice-cream dessert included. *11am-10pm* **€€**

BORNHOLM FOR KIDS

NaturBornholm: *(naturbornholm.dk; adult/child 150/75kr)* A museum that brings the science of geology alive brilliantly. A giant dinosaur peeps its head into the museum's gift shop, and the alligators in the prehistoric pool are in fact real.

BornPark Minigolf: *(bornpark.dk; adult/child 96/70kr)* Close to Østerlars Kirke, this 18-hole outdoor minigolf course is lovingly modelled on Bornholm, with each stage themed after one of the island's beauty spots.

Nature Park Bornholm: *(naturepark.dk; adult/child 299/225kr)* Superb network of assisted tree climbs, canopy walks and forest ziplines, 2km southeast of Rø.

Bornholms Middelaldercenter: *(bornholmsmiddel aldercenter.dk; adult/child 125/75kr)* Sneak past the 'guard geese' to find medieval buildings with costumed reenactors and educational play activities.

theatrically crafted by hand. Another sweet spot is **Bornholms Ismejeri**, credited with making the island's best ice cream. On Wednesday and Saturday mornings, **Svaneke Torvedage** market fills the central square. At the top of town, the bizarre three-legged concrete pyramid is in fact a surrealist **water tower** from 1952 by Danish architect **Jørn Utzon**, who would go on to design the Sydney Opera House.

For craft-minded visitors, Bornholm is a thrilling place to explore, but a little planning goes a long way. Many workshops have limited opening times and/or require appointments even during the Craft Weeks in September and October when the calendar is filled with open studio days and hands-on learning events. Check out *Maker's Island* magazine *(makersisland.bornholm.dk)* for information.

Cyclists' Delight

On your bike in Bornholm

Bornholm has many great cycle paths *(cykelvej)*, but none beat the northwestern coastal route for variety, dramatic Baltic views and the odd climb. In **Rønne**, you can hire a bike from behind the tourist office. Outside the city, cross **Blykobbe Plantage**, a shady forest planted in 1819 to prevent coastal erosion. Snack at Hasle's classic smokehouse before continuing north on a coast-hugging lane, passing the quaint hamlets of Helligepeder and Teglkås. Beyond Kystshelter Ginesminde, a hut-shelter on a tiny beach cove, there's an ascent so steep that for around 120m, the middle of the path is set with steps for those who need to get off and push. In summer, refreshments are available at a kiosk named after a nearby cliff called **Jons Kapel** (accessing the cliff requires dismounting and descending a long stairway). The bike route continues via **Vang**, a village with a gallery and choice of eateries, and passes close to **Shelterplads Finnedalen**, a rough camping spot and one of around 20 places in Bornholm where you can sleep for free in a first-come-first-served wooden box-shelter (one night at a time only, bring your own sleeping mats; see *udinaturen.dk*). You're now riding across Slotslyngen, raised heathland that slopes down towards the fortress ruins at **Hammershus** (p136), which is well worth a detour, before crossing the island neck to charming Allinge via the little **Moseløkken Quarry Museum**.

Bornholm has plenty of other great cycle routes averaging around 25km in length, and with five days, you could circumnavigate the whole island. You can always pop your bike on a bus if you're running out of steam. Detailed maps are available on *bornholm.info*.

DRINKING IN BORNHOLM: BEER & BREWERIES

Svaneke Bryghus: Sup your way through a quality line-up of beers, some brewed on the premises. Delicious Danish food. *11am-8.30pm*

Penyllan Brewery: Relax on mismatched couches by the harbour in Tejn for craft beers brewed by a husband-and-wife team. *11am-8.30pm*

Ølstauan: Taste all of Bornholm's homegrown beer on tap at this friendly little locals' bar in Allinge. Outdoor tables face the harbour. *11am-10pm*

Mikkeller Aarsdale: Showcasing beers from Copenhagen brewery Mikkeller, this harbour-side spot is housed in a former icehouse. *11am-10pm*

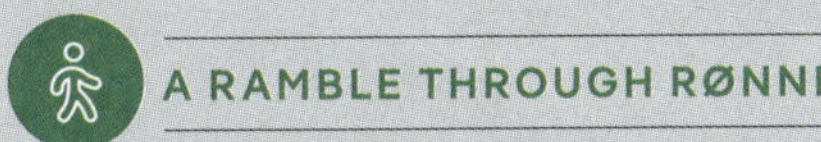

A RAMBLE THROUGH RØNNE

While you're waiting for the ferry, have a stroll through Rønne's old quarter, which forms a ring of charm around the modern centre rebuilt after WWII.

START	END	LENGTH
Rønne Tourist Office	Rønne Tourist Office	3km; 3 hours

Whether you travel by air or sea, Rønne is where you'll start and end your island experience. Though lacking the charm of smaller communities like Gudhjem, Bornholm's biggest town has plenty of facilities, including a theatre and museums.

You can leave bags in 20kr lockers at the helpful 1 **Tourist Office**. Cross the car parks and climb Lille Søstræde. Head south down Grønnegade, doglegging onto Storegade just before reaching the 2 **Sjøgaarinj** craft galleries. Raised above the harbour is 3 **St Nicholas Church**, after which Vimmelskaftet swings east between some of the town's most attractive half-timbered cottages. As you reach the colourful 4 **'Rainbow Cottage'** (Almegade 1), turn left and grab a classic Danish snack and a drink at 5 **Gamle Posthus Hotel**.

Next, take Klokkegade and then Lille Madsegade to reach 6 **Bornholms Museum** with its absorbing WWII exhibits recalling when Rønne and Nexø were bombed by Soviet aircraft in 1945. Continue via Rolighedsgade, sidestepping west down Magsttæde to Laksetorvet with its flurry of cafes. A little way along Laksegade, the pretty old cottages return, most impressively with lantern-fronted 7 **Erichsens Gård**, a 19th-century merchant's house that's now a museum. Drop in to 8 **Hjørths Fabrik**, a ceramics studio/museum before looping back using Kåsegade and Lillegade.

A few minutes' walk from the harbour, the sizeable **Tourist Office** is stacked with brochures and also souvenirs.

The garden is open Monday to Saturday but the house can only be entered on Friday and Saturday.

In August, **St Nicholas Church** invites internationally acclaimed organists to perform concert recitals.

Beyond Bornholm

If you thought Bornholm was remote, jump on the little passenger ferry from Gudhjem to discover tiny Christiansø.

Places

Adrift 18km into the Baltic from the north Bornholm coast, the magical little island of Christiansø is Denmark's easternmost point. With no cars and a population of around 90, the time-warp buildings here have changed little in three centuries. Unusually for Denmark, fig trees thrive in local gardens, but before fertile soil was imported, the land had been almost entirely barren. The first residents were prisoners, who arrived in 1684, sent in chains to build a fortress for King Christian V. Nowadays, Christiansø has its own school, public library, church, GP and microbrewery. Sleepy for much of the year, in summer the port fills with sails and the *kro* (inn) does a roaring trade with visitors.

GETTING AROUND

The 55-minute boat ride from Gudhjem on Bornholm can be idyllic or exhilarating depending on how fiercely the wind is blowing. In peak season, the ferry, *Ertholm*, sails up to three times a day every day of the week, while at other times crossings are made on *Peter*, the mail boat, once a day on weekdays. Return tickets cost 240kr (130kr for children) in summer, cheaper at other times. Book ferry tickets at *christiansoefarten.dk*.

Christiansø

TIME FROM BORNHOLM: **55 MINS** 

Bornholm's baby brother

A historic naval fortress turned close-knit island retreat, Christiansø is a blip in the Baltic that swells with tourists over the short summer season. Most people stay for just three hours on the 500m-long island, which is enough time to explore the massive granite **bastion ruins** that still defend its perimeter, seek out the **Doctor's House** to buy local Chrøøl beer, grab a quality coffee at the **Sirenehuset** shop/tourist office, sample marinated herring from **Ruths Kryddersild** and perhaps eat lunch at the **Kro** village inn. The latter's outdoor terrace seats gaze across the natural harbour towards the 'hat-topped' **Lille Tårn** defence tower. To enter and view the tower's military and maritime-themed exhibits, buy a 40kr ticket from the **village shop**. The same ticket also gets you into **Store Tårn**, a larger fortress tower turned lighthouse whose interior has been converted into an engaging museum and gallery space.

Pre-bookable with your ferry tickets, **guided tours** of the island's main settlement are available at 11am from the port (in English on Fridays from April to October, except July), which explain the island's history and give insights into the peculiarities of local life on these inaccessible specks of land that are still owned by the Ministry of Defence.

Though the name is widely used to refer to the whole group, technically Christiansø is only one of three main islands in

KENNETH BAGGE JORGENSEN/SHUTTERSTOCK ©

Aerial view, Christiansø

the mini-archipelago of Ertholmene. The western area across the pedestrian bridge, home to Lille Tårn, is on the separate island of Frederiksø. Further out, a barren area of rock called Græsholm is a bird sanctuary that's not open to visitors. From early April to mid June, the eider duck breeding season gets in full swing, with lines of ducklings quacking about delightfully in gardens and along island paths.

A night on the island

Staying overnight on Christiansø offers a rare glimpse of island life after the daytrippers have left. **Christiansø Gæstgiveri**, the island's inn, has six double rooms available above the restaurant, while **Ballonen** is a 'five-cell' hostel set in the island's former prison. A secluded **campsite** in the middle of Christiansø is open between May and September, with room for around 30 tents. All accommodation must be booked through *christiansoe.dk*. See the website for more choices including mini-apartments with fold-out sofa beds in the historic barracks buildings.

Another option is to stay late on the island for dinner, returning to Bornholm the same evening on a special 7.30pm sunset departure only sailing on Tuesdays, Wednesdays and Thursdays in high season. Order a dinner package when you book ferry tickets, which automatically reserves you a table at the inn for 6pm. The food punches well above its weight for such a remote spot, and the terrace setting is delightful as the sun dips.

TOP TIP

In the summer months it's wise to book ahead for ferry slots, guided tours and meal reservations at the village inn *(christiansoe.dk)*.

BRIEF HISTORY OF CHRISTIANSØ

The island's history as a strategic military outpost began in 1684 when King Christian V of Denmark established a naval fortress to protect Danish interests in the Baltic during the wars with Sweden. The fortification, named after the king, hosted around 500 people at its peak – not just soldiers but craftsmen, labourers, and other workers necessary to maintain the defences and the community. A protected harbour served as a base for the Danish fleet, allowing for control over vital shipping routes. In 1808, during the Napoleonic Wars, Christiansø was attacked by the British Navy in an attempt to weaken Danish sea power. Despite the bombardment, the island's defences held. By the mid-19th century, the fortress's significance had diminished, and in 1855 it was decommissioned.

Møn

SPECTACULAR CLIFFS | STARRY SKIES | MEDIEVAL MURALS

GETTING AROUND

There is no railway on Møn, but trains arriving at Vordingborg in southern Zealand are linked with Stege, Møn's main transport hub, by a connecting bus service.

Ponderously slow buses from Stege continue hourly via Kelby and Elmelunde to Klintholm Havn, where some connect to a Møns Klint service, but not in winter.

Your own wheels are essential for discovering the island's back lanes. Bikes can be rented in Stege and Klintholm Havn. Note that cyclists are not allowed on the Farø bridges that link Møn to Falster – take the summer-only car ferry via southern Bogø.

The magical island of Møn is synonymous with Møns Klint, a span of chalk-white limestone cliffs soaring to an imperious 126m above the waves. Looking like a giant, half-scooped tub of vanilla ice cream, the cliffs offer rare elemental drama in the otherwise genteel Danish landscape. The nearest settlement to Møns Klint is Klintholm Havn, a marina-village with good eating options and some attractive beaches within walking distance of its small fishing port. Otherwise, Stege is Møn's main hub and appealing little capital, with a brewery and burgeoning art scene. In between lie the settlements of Elmelunde and Keldby, whose village churches are picture-books of medieval murals. A third such church southwest of Stege at Fanefjord is just as impressive, and the peaceful lanes nearby wind through pretty undulating terrain passing several 5000-year-old tunnel graves. At Møn's northwestern tip, the island of Nyord is a delight for old-world charm, ornithology and local spirits.

Getting High at Møns Klint

Clifftop trails and tortuous stairs

Crowned by a lustrous forest of towering beechwood trees, the cliffs at Møns Klint are etched with trails and scenic lookouts, while well-maintained wooden stairways zigzag down to the shore – though it's no mean feat huffing back up again. Keen hikers can tackle longer trails like the 14km **Klintekongens Rige** ('Kingdom of the Cliff King', *klintekongensrige.dk*), which takes around six hours, though be aware that sporadic landslides can put paths and stairways out of commission.

The trailhead for most routes, and the main parking spot, is **GeoCenter Møns Klint** *(moensklint.dk; adult/child 155/100kr)*, the area's epicentre and a kind of hi-tech museum with cafe. Exhibits take visitors through millions of years of geological evolution, with wall animations of primordial forests and dinosaur-era underwater predators. Check timings for 3D film screenings and other videos in the 'ice cave', spot

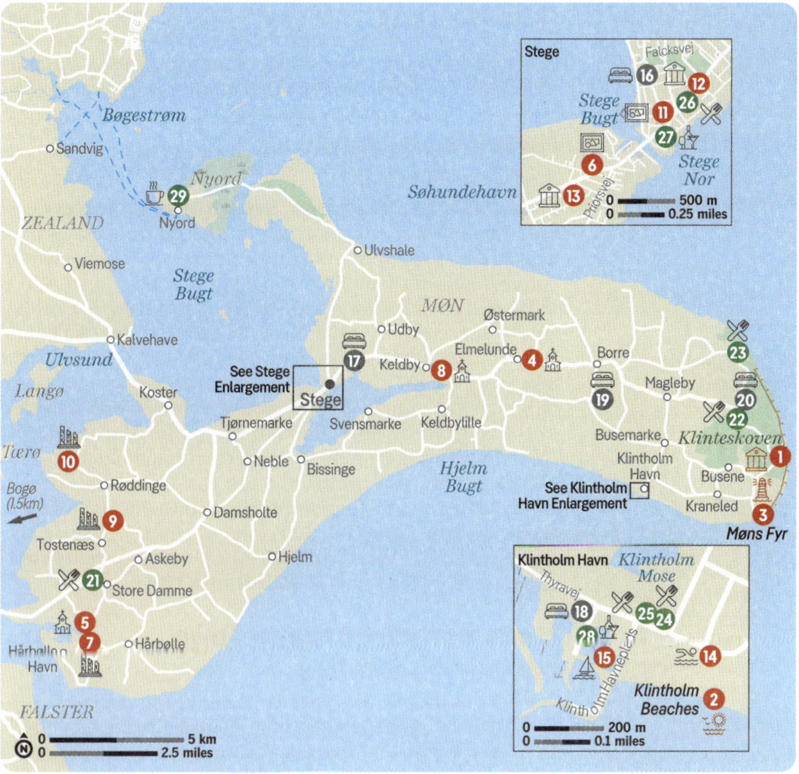

HIGHLIGHTS
1 GeoCenter Møns Klint
2 Klintholm beaches
3 Møns Fyr

SIGHTS
4 Elmelunde Kirke
5 Fanefjord Kirke
6 Glashytte
7 Grønsalen
8 Keldby Kirke
9 Klekkende Høj
10 Kong Asgers Høj
11 Liza's Gallery
● Mølleporten (see 12)
12 Møns Museum
13 Thorsvang

ACTIVITIES, COURSES & TOURS
14 Møn Surf
15 Sejlkutteren

SLEEPING
16 Hotel Residens Møen
17 Hotel Stege Nor
18 Klintholm Marina Park Cabins
19 Tiendegaarden
20 Villa Huno

EATING
21 Damme Kro
22 Dark Sky
23 Liselund Ny Slot Cafe & Restaurant
24 Portofino
25 Restaurant ND122
26 Slagter Stig Støberiet

DRINKING & NIGHTLIFE
27 Det Gamle Bryghus
28 Klap Hesten
29 Noorbohandelen

INFORMATION
● Tourist Office (see 12)

'thunderbolt fossils' and dinosaur feather-fluff preserved in amber, and play with water and sand to see erosion in action. Most exciting are the VR experiences: flying like a peregrine falcon attempting to catch pigeons, or a game in which visitors circumnavigate a dizzyingly high chalk pillar. The GeoCenter entrance fee includes a guided walk that starts at 11am or 2pm, plus a trio of tree-climbing and treetop walking options in summer only.

Rather than paying to park at the GeoCenter, you could leave your vehicle near **Møns Fyr**, the lighthouse at the island's

TOP TIP

Download the app Oplev Møn ('Experience Møn') to access a range of GPS-enabled hiking trails around Møns Klint, as well as info on the island's burial mounds and camping shelters.

ORCHIDS & BUTTERFLIES

Growing throughout **Klinteskoven**, the woods behind Møns Klint, are 18 species of wild orchid, the greatest variety anywhere in Denmark. Particularly beautiful is the pyramidal orchid *(Anacamptis pyramidalis)*, whose flower heads form conical mounds of pink-purple sub-blooms. Also notable is *Epipactis atrorubens*, a dark red helleborine with oval leaves, tall stems and many crimson flowers. The classic place to seek them is **Høvblege**, a shrubby area just west of Busene village. It's also one of only two places in Denmark where you can see the 'large blue' butterfly (*Sortplettet blåfugl* in Danish) with delicate dots in July.

far southeastern corner. From there, walk along the clifftop (around 40 minutes) or along the base of the cliffs (one hour, landslides and tides permitting), climbing the P348 stairway to link the two routes via the GeoCenter.

Møns Klint by Water

Best views of the cliffs

From mid-April to September, **Sejlkutteren Discovery** *(sejlkutteren-discovery.dk; adult/child 200/100kr)* operates popular cruises to view Møns Klint from the sea in an open-top cutter from Klintholm Havn. Booking your place (advised) is only possible by phone *(+45 21 40 41 81)*. Bring warm clothing and/or sunscreen as you'll be out in the open for two hours. You can also take your own food on board. Be aware that sailings are cancelled in bad weather, and that payment is by cash only – almost unique in Denmark (a cash machine is hidden in the courtyard seating area of Klintholm Marine Park, a four-minute walk from the boat departure point).

Alternatively, you can paddle the cliff-facing waters on a guided SUP excursion organised by Klintholm Havn's **Møn Surf** *(moensurf.dk; from 500kr per person)*. The same outfit also offers SUP and surfing lessons, and has a cute **surf-shack cafe** by the beach in **Klintholm Havn**.

Møn's Marvellous Market Town

Highlights of historic Stege

During the Middle Ages, Stege was one of Denmark's wealthiest provincial towns, thanks to its lucrative herring industry. In 1534, citizens who supported a mutinous army destroyed Stege's castle, and the town's walls and gatehouses were torn down in the 17th century. Some sections of rampart and moat remain, most notably the **Mølleporten** ('Mill Gate'), dating back to the 1430s. The adjacent **Møns Museum** weaves historical tales with the aid of audio sets, and has one room entirely dedicated to smells. Stege's characterful shops and eateries include **Slagter Stig Støberiet**, equal parts butcher-deli-restaurant, where you can pair unusual meat and game with Møn gin, or a glass of Brut de Møn sparkling wine, whose creators spent a decade in Burgundy. Tucked into the pretty Luffes Gård yard, **Det Gamle Bryghus** is the original site of the Møn Brewery and now a restaurant serving gourmet-style burgers, smørrebrød and local beer.

In a beautiful old merchant's house behind the church, **Liza's Gallery** exhibits the striking work of Liza Krügermeier,

EATING IN MØN: BEST SPOTS NEAR MØNS KLINT

Liselund Ny Slot: Set north of Møns Klint, this castle hotel serves smørrebrød lunches and a set menu for dinner. *noon-3pm, 6.30-9pm* €€€

Restaurant ND122: Klintholm Havn's most original eatery serves a seafood and simple lunch options. *noon-2.30pm, 6-9pm Tue-Sat* €€€

Portofino: Italian spot in Klintholm Havn cooks up tasty risotto and stays open later in the season than the competition. *5-9pm Wed-Mon* €€

Dark Sky: This basic restaurant attached to a campsite serves surprisingly good pizzas, best enjoyed in the garden with a cold beer. 5-8pm €€

Stege

an artist who has committed herself to painting a new work every day for the rest of her life. Across the main bridge in the regenerated old sugar factory is the fascinating **Glashytte** where glassblower Jesper Jensen turns old wine bottles into glasses, bowls and more.

Some 400m further west, **Thorsvang** is a collectors' museum that conjures up mid-20th century nostalgia by recreating shops and businesses crammed with the products and fittings of yesteryear. You don't have to buy an entry ticket to dine on the daily-changing **lunch buffet** *(noon-3pm)* of traditional Danish fare, which draws in locals from far and wide, especially on summer Sundays when live jazz accompanies meals.

MASTER OF MURALS

Several of Møn's churches have their vaulted ceilings covered in remarkable 15th-century frescoes. Depicting Bible stories like *Adam and Eve* and *The Last Judgement*, these artworks were a means of teaching the Bible to illiterate peasants, and their cartoon-like clarity still gets the message across today. Most were painted by the same artist, whose exact identity is a mystery but who is known as Elmelundemesteren (the Elmelunde master) after the church of the same name. That they have survived is thanks to Lutheran ministers, who thought the frescoes too Catholic and whitewashed over them in the 17th century. Ironically, this preserved the artwork from soiling and fading, allowing the whitewash to be successfully removed 300 odd years later.

Mysterious Møn

Tunnel graves and painted churches

Intriguingly, several of Møn's village churches are emblazoned with vivid, sometimes gruesome murals across their vaulted ceilings, illustrating biblical scenes for the benefit of the illiterate medieval congregation. Although **Keldby Kirke** and especially **Elmelunde Kirke** are more famous, the most

DRINKING ON MØN: OUR PICKS

Klap Hesten: Meaning 'slap the horse', Møn's liveliest summer bar is at Klintholm Havn. Live music at weekends. *2-11.30pm*

Det Gamle Bryghus: In a cobbled yard in Stege, this cafe-restaurant doubles as the tasting bar of Bryghuset Møn. *noon-4pm, 5-8pm*

Damme Kro: Classic village pub that's remained unchanged for years. It's kitsch rather than historic, yet all the more fun for that. *Thu-Sun 5-8pm*

Noorbohandelen: In Nyord village, this endlessly tempting booze shop and cafe is full of local beers and home-crafted hooch. *11am-5pm*

DENMARK'S DARK SKY REGION

What this part of Denmark lacks in nightlife, it makes up for with a captivating night sky. The whole island of Møn, along with causeway-linked Nyord, has been declared one of the world's 125 Dark Sky Parks, making it a great place to gaze skyward at the galaxy-filled heavens. It's also a Dark Sky Community, where local people make dedicated efforts to reduce light pollution. While the island doesn't have any observatories, visitors staying in Klintholm Havn need only walk a few minutes up the beach to see the full sky show. On Nyord, a one-hamlet islet with B&Bs in loveable little old-world farmhouses, you can book two-hour dark sky tours with local guides *(darkskymoen.dk)*.

engaging is the 13th-century **Fanefjord Kirke**, thanks in large part to the meditative appeal of its fjord-view setting. It's also worth the trip for what lies in a nearby field. Over 100m long and studded with 145 hefty boulders, **Grønsalen** is one of Denmark's longest megalithic barrows. It's fascinating to interpret these 5500-year-old graves as a kind of early expression of land ownership, at a time when hunter-gatherer clans were transitioning into settled farming communities.

Seeking similarly ancient mounds is a great excuse to tour the undulating farmlands of western Møn, where you're more likely to see pheasants on the roads than vehicles. In a field around 6km north of Fanefjord, **Klekkende Høj** is a neolithic tumulus unusual for its terraced lower levels. The twin entrance holes are barely 1m high, so you'll have to crawl in. Less problematic for claustrophobes is a two-for-one site 3.5km further northwest. A small parking area serves both Sprovedyssen (an excavated dolmen) and **Kong Asgers Høj**, the biggest of Denmark's hemispherical passage-graves.

Hiking Camønoen

Ten-day pilgrimage around Møn

If the Møns Klint cliff walk has whetted your appetite for hiking, it's possible to continue looping all the way round Møn on the 175km Camønoen. The name's a pun on Caminoen, the Danish translation of the famous Camino pilgrimage routes to Santiago de Compostela in Spain. The route is broken into 10 day-hikes of varied lengths, each ending at a rest stop (*Camønopause*), where you can get water, find shelter and stamp your *Camønopas* (Camønoen passport), available for purchase at **Stege Tourist Office**. Find the hiking sections, each with a name and nominal theme, online at *museerne.dk/en/camonoen/about-camonoen/about-the-hikes*. For insight from local guides and nature experts, check *dengroenneport.dk*.

Ferry into the Past

A trio of vintage voyages

Built in 1958, **Ida** *(idasvenner.dk; adult/child 39/28kr)* is a rare part-wooden car ferry that still lumbers between Bogø and Stubbekøbing on Falster *(bogoe-stubbekoebing.dk)*. The 12-minute crossing is handy for cyclists, but for drivers, it's a trip that's more nostalgic than practical as it's generally quicker to travel via highway bridges.

Two other historic boats that were once ferries also still operate on Møn, albeit now for tourist excursions. **Postbåden Røret** *(nyord.nu; adult/child 70/35kr)* was the post boat that linked Nyord to Stege from 1902 to 1967, a route it now reprises for tourists two or three days a week in summer.

The most vintage of the three, **Færgen Møn** *(faergenmoen.dk; adult/child from 220/125kr)* is the oldest preserved steel-riveted ferry in Denmark. These days, it runs 50-minute summertime bay tours from Stege, including one that loops around Lindholm Island and nips under the Queen Alexandrine Bridge, the very structure that originally put it out of a job back in 1943.

Lolland-Falster

WHITE SAND BEACHES | WILDLIFE PARKS | COUNTRYSIDE DRIVES

The twin isles of Lolland-Falster are some way off Denmark's mainstream tourist trail, and will appeal to travellers seeking slow-paced sojourns through a tapestry of fields, fruit orchards and scattered historic manors. Richly fertile Lolland is the biggest of Denmark's Sydhavsøerne ('South Sea Islands'). Giant farming manor-estates (called *gods*) grew wealthy from sugar-beet production in the late 19th century (the town of Nakskov has a sugar museum), but many have since diversified by providing top-quality organic produce or turning to wine and beer. The brilliant Fuglsang art museum and the vast tunnel-building project at Rødbyhavn are challenging the island's somewhat backward reputation. To the east, the dagger-shaped island of Falster is best known for the wide sandy beaches that grace its wooded eastern flank. The workaday town of Nykøbing Falster, the region's largest, spans both islands at the Guldborgsund, a narrow strait separating Lolland and Falster.

GETTING AROUND

Nykøbing Falster from Copenhagen by train takes 1¼ hours direct via Roskilde. Once the Fehmarnbelt Tunnel is complete (around 2029), direct trains will run through to Germany, but for now, the line to Rødby is being rebuilt. The Rødby-Puttgarden ferry across to Germany takes 45 minutes, with crossings every half-hour, day and night.

Local trains take 30 minutes to trundle between Nykøbing Falster, Sakskøbing and Maribo. From Nykøbing Falster, a 12-minute hop on Sundby-bound bus 702 crosses the bridge to the Middelaldercentret in Lolland. A car is pretty much essential for exploring more widely throughout Lolland-Falster.

Discover Denmark's Stonehenge

Modern megaliths and ancient mounds

You can't help but feel moved at first sight of **Dodekalitten** *(dodekalit.dk)*, a ring of monumental stone megaliths on a lonely meadow overlooking the sea. Artist Thomas Kadziola has been working on this modern-day Stonehenge since 2010, and in 2024 was just two stones short of a dozen – the sculpture's name stems from *dodecalith*, meaning 'Twelve Stones' in Greek.

Standing 7m-tall and each weighing 25 to 45 tonnes, the megaliths are carved with placid human faces, looking something between an Easter Island *moai* and an ancient Greek *herma*. An underground sound system plays curious new-age groaning hums and semi-musical AI-created sounds whose real-time composition is influenced by the sea and weather conditions.

HIGHLIGHTS
1 Dodekalitten
2 Fuglsang Kunstmuseum
3 Marielyst Strand

SIGHTS
4 De Gamle Huse
5 Frederiksdal Vineri
6 Knuthenborg Safari Park
7 Krenkerup Bryggeri
8 Krokodille Zoo
● Maribo Domkirke (see 4)
9 Museum Obscurum
10 Østergaard Vinmageri
● Stiftsmuseum Maribo (see 4)
11 Tågerup Kirke
● Vandtårnet (see 9)

ACTIVITIES, COURSES & TOURS
● Anemonen (see 4)

SLEEPING
12 Bandholm Hotel
● Hotel Nørrevang (see 3)
13 Hotel Saxkjøbing
14 Marielyst Sleep'n Go
15 Pederstrup Bed and Breakfast
● PilgrimsHuset (see 4)
16 Skelby Gammel Praestegaard

EATING
● Bandholm Badehotel (see 12)
● Café Vin og Brød (see 4)
17 Det Gamle Pakhus
18 Oreby Kro
● ViGGo N (see 2)

ENTERTAINMENT
19 Middelaldercentret

Access is from Kragenæs Havn. Park up by the harbour and walk 1km on a footpath that skirts around a campsite. Note that the few parking spaces close to the site are for visitors with accessibility needs only. By bus, get off at the Rævegade stop and walk through the Klinkesov Forest on any of the converging footpaths.

Dodekalitten is located in an area of Lolland playfully dubbed the 'Lollandian Alps' – gentle undulations in the otherwise level landscape, with extra bumps courtesy of Bronze-Age burial mounds. In the field next to Dodekalitten is 5m-tall **Glentehøj** (3200 BCE). Climbable roadside **Bavnehøj** is one of Denmark's biggest (7m-tall) marking the 'summit of the Alps'. Enjoy panoramic views from the top at a dizzying altitude of 30m. Other nearby tumuli include one in the churchyard at **Birket Kirke** in Lindet, whose disconnected bell tower is thought to be Denmark's oldest wooden structure.

Lolland on Safari

Lions, tigers and crocs, oh my!

The vast woodland safari park of **Knuthenborg** *(knuthenborg.dk; adult/child 279/189kr)* is a great place to bring the family. Residents, which include four elephants and Keni the 300kg Siberian tiger, are generally 'retired' here into sprawling enclosures after performance careers in circuses. In 2023, three lions arrived, evacuated from a zoo in war-torn Ukraine.

One of the park's main draws, the savanna area (car-only) has rhinos, zebras, camels, moose and many more free-roamers. Don't miss the theme park with its fiendishly steep log-flume, or the Dinosaur-skoven, a fabulous woodland full of dinos that actually move and roar. A fun way for families to experience Knuthenborg is to sleep in one of the 'camp' apartments that back onto wildlife enclosures. You might have wolves howling behind your window and buffalo wandering about outside your door.

Over in Falster, **Krokodille Zoo** *(krokodillezoo.dk; adult/child 189/99kr)* claims to have the world's largest collection of crocodiles – 150 in all, ticking off all known crocodilian species. Look out for Sobek, a Nile giant over 5m long and weighing 600kg. Apparently he's the largest croc in Europe. The zoo is also home to giant tortoises, pythons, monkeys and big cats. Krokodille Zoo participates in breeding programmes, and a portion of the ticket fee goes towards conservation charities.

Maribo's Lakeland

Shoreline strolls and nature trails

Lolland's low-key provincial centre of Maribo has a lovely lakeside setting beside **Søndersø**, a spirit-calming body of water that gives a distinctive setting to Maribo's austere **cathedral**. The freshwater lake is the biggest of four at the heart of the **Maribsøerne Nature Park**. Several sections of lakeside are private, but walkable paths include the stroll from **De Gamle Huse** *(museumlollandfalster.dk; 90kr, under-18s free)*, an open-air museum-village just beyond Maribo's campsites, to

TOP TIP

Falster's beaches are at their busiest in July and early August, but if you don't mind a reduced bar buzz, the shoulder seasons of mid-June and late August offer acres of empty sand yet relatively good weather.

DEEP DIVE TO GERMANY

The small ferry port town of Rødbyhavn in the south of Lolland also happens to be the site of one of Europe's largest infrastructure projects, the **Fehmarnbelt Tunnel**. When finished around 2029, it will be the world's longest immersed tunnel at 18km, connecting Lolland with the German island of Fehmarn and completing a motorway and rail link between Hamburg and Malmö (Sweden). The project involves major land reclamation along Lolland's coast, with plans for a lagoon, a beach, a hotel and an 8-hectare wetland lake to encourage birdlife. The tunnel sections, 217m long and 73,000 tonnes each, are being constructed in a harbour factory then floated out to sea, submerged, and carefully aligned in a gigantic dredged trench.

MEMORY OF WOE IN MARIBO

Maribo's cathedral has a sanctified history linked with the talented Countess Leonora Christina (1621–1698). A daughter of King Christian IV, she spent 22 years as a political prisoner but lived out her later years in Maribo, where she completed her celebrated autobiography, *Jammers Minde (Memory of Woe)*. Written secretly during over two decades of solitary confinement in a royal dungeon, it vividly details her dramatic life, including her marriage to Corfitz Ulfeldt, a prominent nobleman whose political actions led to their downfall. Ulfeldt's efforts to overthrow the monarchy resulted in Leonora Christina's imprisonment, accused of being complicit in his treasonous activities. The book provides a first-hand account of the political and social intrigues of the day and has left a lasting impact on Danish literature.

Nysted

a waterside bird hide on the edge of the Kidnakke forest. In July and August (plus some weekends), a relaxing way to enjoy the landscapes from the water is a gentle cruise on the **Anemonen** *(naturparkmaribo.dk; adult/child 100/50kr)*, a boat that launches from a jetty just outside the cathedral. Some trips stop at **Borgø island**, where visitors search the woodlands for traces of the former Revshaleborg fortress. Ornithologists, keep a watch for sea eagles.

Countryside Driving

Maribo to Nykøbing

An appealing back-road jaunt between Maribo and Nykøbing starts with stops at the fine estate-church at **Engestofte** and the **Røgbøllevej picnic spo**t with its lakeside bird hide. Explore the little port of **Nysted**, not missing the charming street of **Slotsgade** that's part cycle path with views towards an imposing but private sea-facing castle. **Det Gamle Pakhus** is a characterful inn-restaurant on Nysted's attractive main street.

Some 10km northeast, on the **Fuglsang Herregaard** historic estate, are free-to-visit walled gardens, an opulent mansion restaurant/B&B and the superb **Fuglsang Kunstmuseum** *(fuglsangkunstmuseum.dk, 100kr; under-26s free)*, an impressive, purpose-built gallery showcasing Danish art's development from the 1830s to today. Helpfully for those new to the subject, the gallery exhibits chronologically and has clear explanations on genres, trends and developments. The includes a number of Møns Klint landscapes – clearly an inspiring subject in the 19th century. On one side of the building, a giant picture window turns the sheep-nibbled meadowlands outside into a vast real-life work of landscape art. You'll also find changing temporary exhibitions, a cafe and a small gift shop.

If driving between Maribo and Rødby, stop at little-known **Tågerup Kirke**, a church with fabulous 15th- and 16th-century frescoes. It's especially worth the minor detour if you don't have time to get to similar churches at Elmelunde or Fanefjord on Møn.

History Comes Alive

Time travel to the middle ages

On the Lolland side of Nykøbing Falster, **Middelaldercentret** *('Medieval Centre'; middelaldercentret.dk; adult/child 165/90kr)* invites families to travel back to the days of damsels and knights by recreating an early 15th-century community. Costumed craftspeople populate a reconstructed Middle-Age village and put on demonstrations of archery, jousting and the firing of a brutal-looking trebuchet (siege catapult). The most picturesque spot is an old merchant's house with its own harbour and boats. Kids love the many hands-on play experiences, and the imaginative restaurant (Gæstgiveri Den Gyldne Svane) has food and decor based on medieval originals.

Vandtårnet & Vampires

Spooky stop in Nykøbing Falster

Nykøbing F, as the city is often abbreviated, is a friendly if threadbare sort of place with some lively pubs and minor attractions, but where historical remnants are relatively sparse. Of the once vast castle-palace of 17th-century Dowager Queen Sophie, only a wall stump outside the modern cinema on Slotsgade remains.

Rising up 43 metres above the central streets, **Vandtårnet** is a century-old water tower which you can clamber up past art exhibitions to a panoramic viewing floor. Top billing in town, though, goes to the mind-bending **Museum Obscurum** *(museumlollandfalster.dk; 90kr, under-18s free, closed Sundays),* which exhibits what purports to be the collection of an obscure occult investigator. Many of the exhibits are delightful oddities of the type found in a Victorian cabinet of curiosities, but things take a weird turn when you find skeletons of tiny devils and a vampire defence kit.

Miles of White Sand

Falster's forest-backed beach

Falster's celebrated stretch of dazzling white beach is backed by reed-grass dunes and forests running almost straight for much of its 14km from an ornithological hub at Denmark's southernmost point. The main beach access for holidaymakers is at **Marielyst**, a low-key resort town that's invisible

VINEYARDS, BREWERIES & FARM SHOPS

Frederiksdal Vineri: Stop at the gorgeous Frederiksdal Estate for a bottle of *kirsebærvin*. It's made with the 'grape of the North' - the small Danish sour cherry.

Krenkerup Bryggeri: Hidden within a moated farm-estate 'castle', Lolland's regal brewery crafts unimpeachable pilsner and other beer styles.

Østergaard Vinmageri: Lolland's fine soil and mild climate produce some of Denmark's best grapes, fruit and berries, put to work in this small vineyard's products, for sale in their farm shop.

Hotel Saxkjøbing: Visit this farm shop attached to a hotel for a culinary tour of Lolland-Falster: organic fruit and veg, wine, beer, juice and sourdough.

EATING AROUND LOLLAND: OUR PICKS

Bandholm Badehotel: Hotel restaurant with a chef bringing together local knowledge and Michelin-starred experience. *hours vary* €€

ViGGo N: Smart-casual manor-house restaurant at Fuglsang Herregaard. Dishes meld Danish and European cuisine. *Tue-Sun 5.30-9pm* €€€

Oreby Kro: Set in a rural 1847 estate-mill 3km from Sakskøbing, serves high-quality Danish fare with beautiful views. *noon-10pm Thu-Sat, to 4pm Sun* €€

Café Vin og Brød: A top spot in Maribo, this swish cafe-bakery bakes great cardamom buns along with tasty paninis and smørrebrød. *6am-9pm* €

LOLA: A CHEW STORY

One of the biggest stars in this part of Denmark is Lola, who first hit the headlines in 2018 despite being almost 6000 years old. During excavations for the huge sea tunnel project between Lolland and Germany, archaeologists found a prehistoric piece of birch-bark 'chewing gum', from which was miraculously extracted an entire human DNA sequence. It revealed a girl with dark brown skin, dark brown hair and blue eyes, who had recently eaten duck and hazelnuts. Her genetic profile suggests she was more closely related to hunter-gatherers than to the farming populations that were starting to spread through Europe at the time. Learn more about Lola at Stiftsmuseum Maribo *(museumlolland falster.dk; 90kr, under-18s free)* beside the town's train station.

Middelaldercentret (p151)

from the sea despite being mere yards away behind the raised sandy dike-dunes. A broad pedestrian boardwalk cuts inland through Marielyst from the beach, connecting restaurants, bars with happy-hour deals, ice-cream parlours, mini-golf and family-sports outfits. Spread widely throughout the woodlands are hundreds of holiday homes, most working on weekly rentals, along with one or two guesthouses and hotels. Further out, a few inland villages have charming family B&Bs.

Follow the coast of Falster all the way down and you'll reach Denmark (and Scandanavia's) southernmost point, a windlashed bluff marked by the **South Stone** (Sydstenen), a boulder facing the sea. In the other direction north of Marielyst, a cycle path follows Falster's thickly wooded east coast all the way to the little port hamlet of **Hæsnes**, which has a popular bakery-cafe. The cycle path also passes the highly rated, middle-of-nowhere **Pomle Nakke** cafe. En route is the village of **Ulslev**, where the beach forms an idyllic curl with just a single camping site nearby. After the historic thatched gazebo called **Generalens Lysthus**, take a short detour up Tromnæs Alleen to **Corselitze**, where the fine manor gardens are free to visit. Don't miss the thatched ice house. Another minor diversion reveals **Halskov Vænge**, ancient woodlands full of dolmens.

Places We Love to Stay

€ Budget €€ Midrange €€€ Top End

Gudhjem, Bornholm p132

**Gudhjem Vandrerhjem € ** Half-timbered hostel with fabulously central coast-facing location. Dorms aren't available in high season.

Sannes Familiecamping € On the road south of Gudhjem, this camping ground has pitches and cabins, plus a pool, sauna and bikes for hire.

Jantzens Hotel €€ Cosy and welcoming hotel opened in a building from 1872. Guests get to savour fine art, old-world touches and a lovely garden.

Hotel Klippen €€ Gently stylish midrange rooms, most with sea-facing shared balconies that overlook a rocky cove and Gudhjem's harbour.

Allinge-Sandvig, Bornholm p137

Pension Lindesdal € Family-friendly B&B overlooking Hammersø, the lake at the western end of Sandvig. Geared up for cyclists.

Strandhotellet €€ Historic sea-facing hotel in Sandvig given a loving makeover by its recent husband-and-wife owners. Great quality meals served.

Allinge Badehotel €€ Dating from 1770 and renovated in 2020, this black-beamed farmhouse perches right on the water in Allinge. Request a sea-facing (not road-facing) room.

Nordlandet (p136) **€€€** Opened by the folks behind Michelin-starred restaurant Kadeau, splurge on this classy seafront getaway raised above rock pools south of Sandvig.

Around Bornholm

Myregaard Bed and Breakfast € Down south, this charming countryside B&B offers rural serenity and generous travel intel from its American/Danish owners. You'll need a vehicle.

Yggdrasil Guest Lodge € Feeling some way from civilisation (but close to Østerlars Kirke), this pristine guesthouse has a long terrace facing nothing but cornfields. English owner cooks up fried breakfasts on request.

Stammershalle Badehotel €€€ One of Bornholm's top choices is this imposing, early-20th-century bathing hotel overlooking a rocky stretch of coast between Gudhjem and Tejn. Excellent restaurant. Book well ahead.

Near Møns Klint, Møn p142

Klintholm Marina Park Cabins € Super clean rooms with harbour-facing porches and shared bathrooms. Free SUP use, but BYO sheets.

Tiendegaarden €€ A family-run oasis of peace and quiet, with some rooms in the 1916 farm mansion. Dark skies here are begging for star-spotters.

Villa Huno €€€ Contemporary aparthotel with giant windows for lake gazing, lovely outdoor walks and a gourmet dinner when you get back.

Stege, Møn p144

Hotel Stege Nor €€ Elegant, unfussy rooms in a converted 1824 mill overlooking rural marshlands 1km east of Stege.

Hotel Residens Møen €€ Polished apartment-hotel with strong eco-credentials that faces central Stege's waterfront.

Lolland p147

PilgrimsHuset € Budget accommodation in a glorious location, set in a lakeside garden by Maribo's cathedral.

Pederstrup Bed and Breakfast € Budget self-catering spot with generous facilities for families (sports, games, toys, etc), self-serve draught beer and a barbecue area. Excellent breakfast.

Hotel Saxkjøbing (p151) **€€** Half-timbered hotel in Sakskøbing offers classy comfort in an authentic old inn owned by celebrity chef Claus Meyer.

Bandholm Badehotel €€€ Lolland's top option is this luxurious old bathing hotel set beautifully on grassy lawns that lead to the sea. Some rooms come with their own private garden patios.

Falster p147

Marielyst Sleep'n Go € Unusually characterful make-your-own-bed option, with a games room, free bike hire and a hearty breakfast.

Hotel Norrevang €€€ Design-chic meets classic thatched-roof kro (inn) at this central spot close to Marielyst's bars, restaurants and beach shops.

Skelby Præstegaard €€ In the former priest's house at Skelby, this idyllic spot has bright-white, apartment-style accommodation perfect for families.

For places to stay in Funen, see p179

TIM GRAHAM/CONTRIBUTOR/GETTY IMAGES ©

Above: Egeskov Slot (p166); Right: Tea pavilion, Valdemars Slot (p171)

Funen

FAIRY TALES, CASTLES AND GLITTERING ISLES

Picture-book coastal towns and a fairy-tale city break up Funen's inviting patchwork of fields and farmsteads. Slow down and explore.

Danes love to joke that Funen is little more than a bump in the motorway between Zealand and Jutland. Often overlooked in favour of its bigger neighbours, this underrated middle island is one of Denmark's loveliest regions. Take the time to explore and you'll discover bucolic countryside, thatched farmsteads, grand castles and inviting islands. Funen is home to half a million Fynbos, as the locals are known, who speak with a singsong accent and are among the warmest Danes you'll meet.

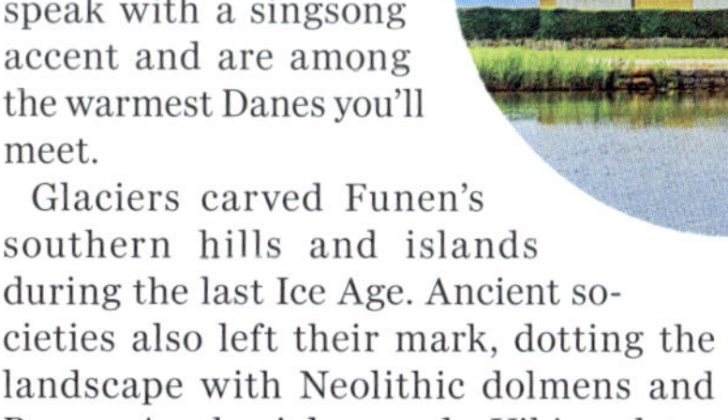

Glaciers carved Funen's southern hills and islands during the last Ice Age. Ancient societies also left their mark, dotting the landscape with Neolithic dolmens and Bronze Age burial mounds. Vikings later founded settlements, including Odense, Denmark's third-largest city and Funen's commercial centre and cultural heart. Odense has eclectic museums and plenty to entertain families, but its biggest drawcard is its status as the birthplace of Hans Christian Andersen, author of 158 fairy tales. Down south, Funen's harbour towns are steeped in seafaring tradition, and travellers can sail, kayak and hike the yacht-filled archipelago.

Funen is known as Denmark's garden, and much of the landscape is given over to rolling fields of wheat, barley and rapeseed. Fruit and flowers are big business, while medicinal cannabis is a fledgling crop. Along the roadside, farm stalls sell local produce, and endearingly, honesty boxes are still the way to pay. Keep cash handy!

THE MAIN AREAS

ODENSE
Birthplace of Hans Christian Andersen. **p158**

SVENDBORG
Archipelago gateway and maritime centre. **p168**

Find Your Way

Denmark's middle island is packed with sights, and its compact size makes it easy to get around. Odense is a great base to explore the northern highlights, while Svendborg is the gateway to Funen's beautiful southern archipelago.

Odense, p158

Fall into the fairy-tale world of celebrated storyteller Hans Christian Andersen and explore top-notch museums in Funen's cultural capital.

Svendborg, p168

Hit up the restaurants, bars and museums of this historic seafaring hub before striking out on boat trips around the South Funen Archipelago.

CAR

Having your own set of wheels is the most convenient way to travel. Journey times by road are relatively short, and you have more freedom to explore harder-to-reach gems scattered throughout the countryside.

PUBLIC TRANSPORT

Funen has decent regional bus links *(fynbus.dk)*, while trains *(dsb.dk)* connect Odense with Svendborg, Nyborg and Middelfart. Ferries depart from Svendborg and Faaborg to several islands including Ærø.

TRABANTOS/SHUTTERSTOCK ©

Hans Jensens Stræde, HC Andersen's birthplace near HC Andersens Hus

Plan Your Time

Divide your Funen trip into two parts: an activity-packed city break in Odense and then time to unwind on the southern coast.

If You Only Do One Thing

- Dive straight into **Odense** (p158) and immerse yourself in fairy tales at **HC Andersens Hus** (p158). Explore the city's heart on our **walking tour** (p161) that takes in cobbled streets, a cathedral and multiple museums. Sample the city's pub and bar scene and then tuck into street food at **Storms Pakhus** (p160) or sit down for a multicourse meal at **HOS** (p160).

3 Days or More

- Once you've explored Odense, visit spectacular **Egeskov Slot** (p166) before continuing south to **Svendborg** (p168). Wander around and then take the ferry to **Ærøskøbing** (p175). With more time, cycle **Ærø's scenic countryside** (p172) or make a side trip to quaint Kerteminde and its **Johannes Larsen Museum** (p163) and **Vikingemuseet Ladby** (p164).

Seasonal Highlights

SPRING

The countryside is full of wildflowers, making it a perfect time to tackle Funen's Øhavsstien (Archipelago Trail).

SUMMER

Funen springs to life as holidaymakers head to the coast. Harbours bustle and festivals are in full swing.

AUTUMN

Seasonal attractions have shuttered, but the harvest is under way. Pick up a punnet from a roadside stall.

WINTER

Nights draw in, festive lights come on and Christmas markets sprakle. Brave locals go winter bathing.

Odense

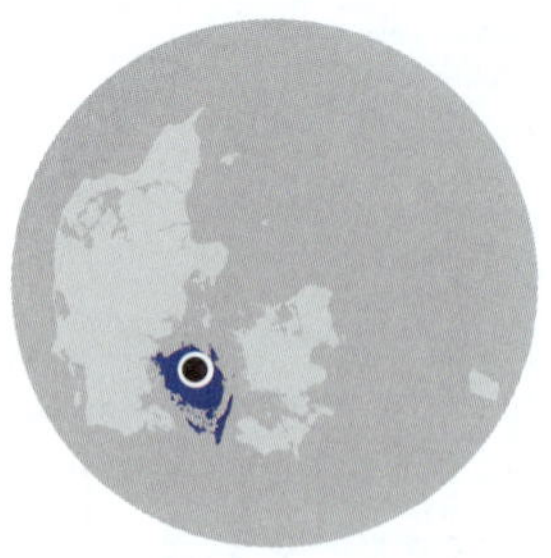

FAIRY-TALE FLOURISHES | MARVELLOUS MUSEUMS | BARS & BEER HALLS

GETTING AROUND

Direct trains run at least hourly from Copenhagen to Odense (1¼ to 1¾ hours), and from Aarhus in the other direction (1½ hours). The train station, a cafe-filled complex called the Odense Banegård Center is a five-minute walk north of the city centre. From the adjacent bus station catch bus 151, 153 or 55 for the zoo or bus 35 for Den Fynske Landsby.

Few hotels in Odense offer free parking. Underground Q-Park car parks cost around 220kr for 24 hours.

The tram is a commuter service and not very useful for tourists.

TOP TIP

It's a good idea to book tickets for HC Andersen Hus online. Entry is by timed 30-minute slots and visitor numbers are limited.

Once upon a time in Odense, a boy by the name of Hans Christian Andersen rose from a life of poverty to become one of the world's most cherished storytellers. Denmark's third biggest city is a living homage to its favourite son, referencing the writer in everything from street art to the lights at pedestrian crossings, which blink with Andersen in silhouette.

After major construction work, this former ugly duckling has re-emerged almost swan-like. At its heart is the showpiece HC Andersen Hus, built in 2021 and surrounded by a spruced-up historic district that is largely traffic-free. A 14km tramline opened in 2022, but most of the city's attractions are easily reached on foot or via sightseeing boats that ply the Odense River.

Top billing in the city's cultural calendar is the annual Tinderbox Music Festival, a three-day event held in June. Performers in 2024 included David Guetta, Janelle Monáe, Camila Cabello and Lenny Kravitz.

Fairy Trails in Odense

Discovering Hans Christian Andersen

A modern-day temple to Denmark's biggest cultural export, **HC Andersens Hus** *(hcandersenshus.dk; 165kr, under-18s free)* is a wonderful and, well, weird tribute to one of the world's greatest storytellers. Japanese architect Kengo Kuma, known for blending architecture with nature, designed the complex of curvaceous wood pavilions, spiralling gardens and subterranean gallery spaces, into which visitors embark on a high-concept, tech-forward sojourn into Andersen's life and writings. Helped by clever headsets, it's enormously creative, replete with visual illusions, puppetry, ambitious sculptural pieces and a dose of abstract eeriness. Embracing the malevolence that imbues Andersen's tales, there are one or two creepy moments, and kids under six might find the experience unsettling. For that age group, consider skipping the main exhibition and heading straight to **Ville Vau**, a beautifully designed play town with costumes to dress up in.

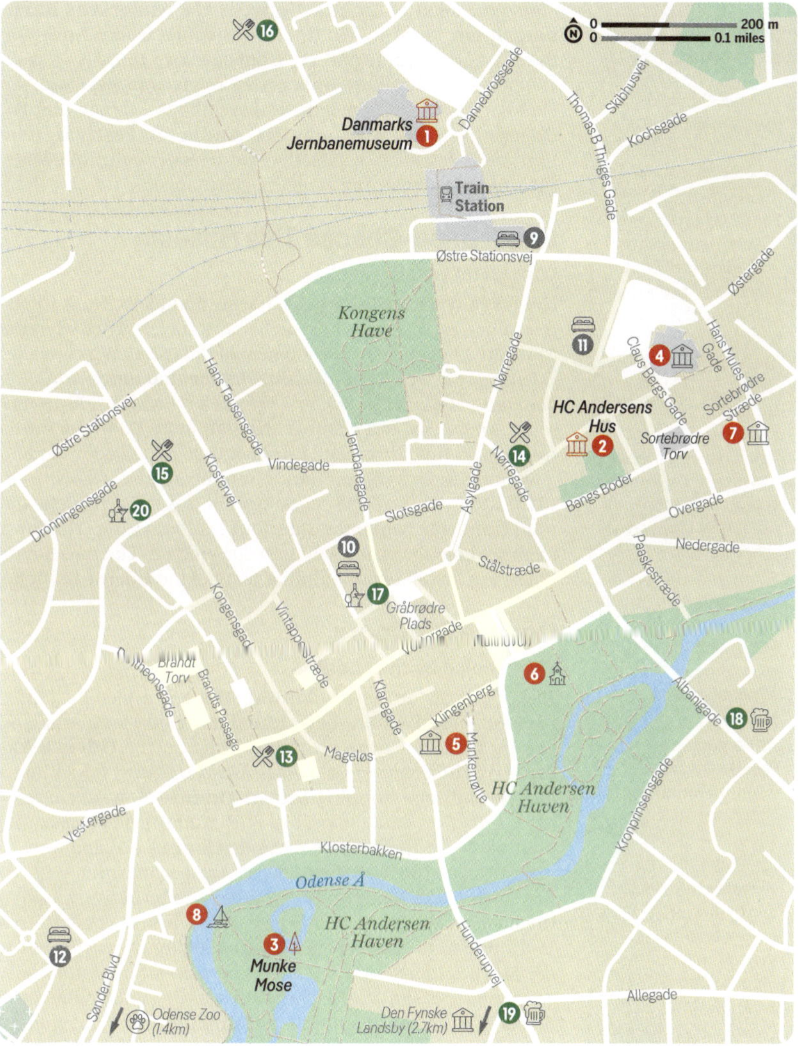

HIGHLIGHTS
1 Danmarks Jernbanemuseum
2 HC Andersens Hus
3 Munke Mose

SIGHTS
4 Carl Nielsen Museum
5 HC Andersens Barndomshjem
6 Odense Domkirke
7 TID Museum

ACTIVITIES, COURSES & TOURS
8 Odense Aafart riverboat

SLEEPING
9 Cabinn Odense Hotel
10 First Hotel Grand
11 Hotel Odeon
12 Villa A Hotel

EATING
13 Cafe Kosmos
14 Oluf Bagers Gård
15 Restaurant HOS
16 Storms Pakhus

DRINKING & NIGHTLIFE
17 Amy's Bar and Winehouse
18 Anarkist Beer & Food Lab
19 Carlsens Kvarter
20 Den Smagløse Café

SCULPTURE SPOTTING

On your Odense wanderings, keep watch for these public art pieces:

Treenigheden: Bjørn Nørgaard's sculpture 'Trinity' is a bizarre orgiastic trio of bronze granddads, supposed to represent the three aspects of Hans Christian Andersen's talent.

Oceania: This astonishing female figure reclines naked on Odense's central square, furnished with a classical face and a six-pack stomach.

Stoppenålen: Should represent the 'darning needle' from HCA's eponymous short story, though it looks altogether more phallic.

Andersen on a Bench: Outside the Comwell Hotel, Hans Christian himself sits with a top hat awaiting selfies.

Tinsoldaten: Next to a branch of Nelle's cafe-bar is the one-legged Tin Soldier, hero of an Andersen tale.

Download a map of 16 HCA-related sculptures at *visitodense.dk*.

Also included in the ticket price is **HC Andersens Barndomshjem**, the tiny childhood residence where Andersen lived in considerable poverty from ages two to 14. It's a well-signposted, ten-minute walk across town from HC Andersen Hus, set inside a yellow half-timbered house. In late August, Odense hosts the week-long **HC Andersen Festival**, celebrating its favourite son with child-friendly cultural events, theatre, workshops and street performances.

Choo-Choo-Choose This Museum

Love letter to rail travel

Not just a writer of fairy tales, poems and plays, Hans Christen Andersen was an avid traveller and travel writer who was captivated by the early development of rail travel. Which makes Odense an apt location for **Danmarks Jernbanemuseum** *(jernbanemuseet.dk; 140kr, under-18s free)*, a rollicking railway museum where you can clamber through more than two dozen trains including Christian IX's plush 1900 royal saloon car and a working replica of Denmark's first locomotive, ODIN, from 1846. Kids will love the mock station, toy train models and mini train ride, while the InterRail exhibition is a trip down memory lane for visitors of an older vintage. The museum is housed in an old depot building just behind Odense Station.

Odense Outdoors

Sightseeing by river boat

Just south of the centre, **Munke Mose** is a picnic-friendly park furnished with a playground, riverside footpaths and rowing boats for hire. From here, hop on the **Odense Aafart riverboat** *(aafart.dk; adult/child 115/85kr)* for an hour-long round trip stopping first at **Odense Zoo** *(odensezoo.dk; adult/child 230/130kr)*, one of Denmark's best. Spanning both banks of the Odense River, enclosures are home to giraffes, tigers and kangaroos, while the oceanarium, with its penguins and manatees, is a highlight. Alternatively, taking the boat to its second and furthest stop brings you within a 15-minute walk of **Den Fynske Landsby** *(denfynskelandsby.dk; 145kr, under-18s free)*, a nostalgic open-air museum where costumed 'peasants' role-play 19th-century village life amid flocks of geese and genuine period buildings transplanted from all around Funen. Note that the above attractions, like many in Funen, have patchy off-season opening hours, so check websites for scheduling.

Organic farmers' market on Wednesday afternoons

EATING IN ODENSE: TOP PICKS

Restaurant HOS: Modern restaurant serving spectacular smørrebrød and set menus with optional wine pairing. *hours vary* €€€

Storms Pakhus: Get your food truck fix at this converted warehouse hawking craft burgers, curries and other global eats. *11am-11pm* €

Oluf Bagers Gård: In a 16th-century building, this French-inspired Nordic place is known for its small-plate dinners. *noon-3pm, 5.30-10pm Mon-Sat* €€€

Café Kosmos: Organic, sustainable vegan dishes served in cosy, low-lit surrounds. Great coffee and cocktails. *noon-8pm Tue-Thu, to 9pm Fri-Sat* €

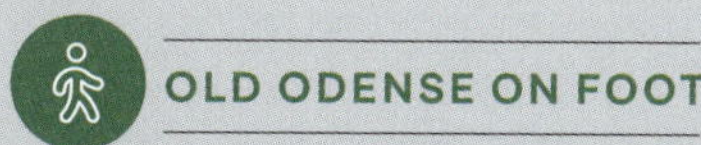

OLD ODENSE ON FOOT

Take in the best of the city's historic centre and cultural highlights on this walking tour.

START	END	LENGTH
HC Andersens Hus	Kunst Museum Brandts	2.5km; 1½ hours

Meander through the topsy-turvy gardens around ❶ **HC Andersens Hus** before tracking down the ❷ **Andersen mural**. Stroll around the compact old quarter, taking in the cute cobbled streets and historic houses along Bangs Boder and Ramsherred. Stop for a photo at the ❸ **Andersen sculptures** outside the Comwell Hotel and then head to the ❹ **TID Museum**, packed with facts about Funen from its early history to the modern day. Detour along quaint Nedergade, calling into museum-like bric-à-brac shop ❺ **Kramboden**.

Vestergade, the city's main shopping street, leads to the Italianate ❻ **Rådhus**. A few steps away is ❼ **Odense Domkirke**, an imposing 14th-century Gothic cathedral. Duck inside to see the skeletons of King Knud II and his brother in a crypt behind the altar. A couple of minutes' walk southwest is ❽ **HC Andersens Barndomshjem**, the storyteller's childhood home, where you can learn about his early life. Return to Vestergade and detour up Vintapperstræde, a narrow pedestrianised alley lined with bars and eateries. Return to Vestergade once again then take Brandts Passage, where a former textile mill is now a thriving cultural hub, home to a cinema, cafe and ❾ **Kunst Museum Brandts**, an excellent art museum. Go inside to admire works by renowned Funen Painters, as well as cutting-edge photography exhibitions and shows by internationally acclaimed artists.

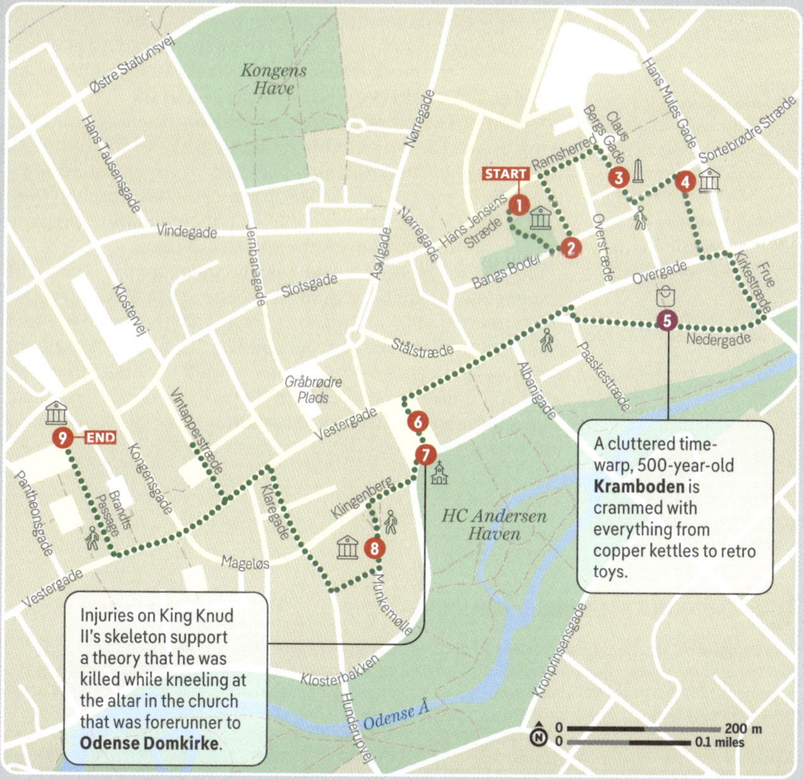

A cluttered time-warp, 500-year-old **Kramboden** is crammed with everything from copper kettles to retro toys.

Injuries on King Knud II's skeleton support a theory that he was killed while kneeling at the altar in the church that was forerunner to **Odense Domkirke**.

THE PECULIAR QUIRKS OF HC ANDERSEN

His stories have captivated readers worldwide, but Andersen himself was a fascinating and complex character worthy of his own tale. Riven by neuroses and obsessions, one of his most peculiar habits was carrying a nine-foot-long piece of rope wherever he went, in case he got caught upstairs in a burning building. Terrified of being buried alive, Andersen kept a note by his bed that read, 'I only appear to be dead'. Andersen never married, though he had intimate infatuations with both men and women. By his own accounts he remained a virgin and engaged sex workers merely for conversation. Beyond writing, Andersen was remarkably accomplished at paper-cut art, delighting children and friends with his exquisite creations. A selection are on display at HC Andersens Hus.

LIYA_BLUMESSER/SHUTTERSTOCK ©

Odense Domkirke

Skeletons & Saints

Tracing the town's turbulent history

Meaning 'Odin's Shrine', millennium-old Odense was named after the Viking god, but it was during the early days of Christianity that the city's fortunes took a turn. In the chilly crypt of **Odense Domkirke** *(free)* you can peer at the 900-year-old skeleton of Denmark's patron saint, King Knud (Canute) II, lying beside the bones of his younger brother Benedikt. Both were killed in 1086 during a peasants' revolt. Canonised by the Pope in a bid to help shore up the Catholic Church in Denmark, Knut's bones became the object of a popular pilgrimage, bringing considerable wealth to the town.

The rise of medieval and Renaissance Odense, the city's golden age, can be explored at the **TID Museum** *(tidmuseum.dk; 100kr, under-18s free)*, partly installed in a nobleman's townhouse from 1646. A newer section of the complex takes visitors on a thematic walk through Funen, examining major twists in world history through a local lens. The adjoining **Children's Museum** is three-floors of hands-on fun for little ones.

DRINKING IN ODENSE: TOP PICKS

Den Smagløse Café: Hip dive bar crammed with ephemera, from disco balls to vintage toys. *noon-midnight or later, to 10pm Sun*

Anarkist Beer & Food Lab: Beer hall with 20-plus choices and windows overlooking the production line. *3-11pm Wed, noon-midnight Thu-Sat*

Carlsens Kvarter: Ale aficionados adore this old-school bodega with countless beers on tap and in bottles. *noon-1am Mon-Sat, to 7pm Sun*

Amy's Bar and Winehouse: Among a cluster of bars, this buzzy hangout stands out for its wines, cocktails and tapas. *noon-midnight or later*

Beyond Odense

Regal castles, a Viking-era ship grave and dreamy countryside drives lie in wait just outside Funen's capital.

There's a lot going in the countryside around Odense. Make a trip northeast to explore quaint Kerteminde's artistic side, stopping off at the hamlet of Ladby to discover Denmark's only Viking-era ship grave, the final resting place of a 10th-century chieftain. A short train ride from Odense brings you to Nyborg, a former medieval stronghold on Funen's east coast. Riding the rails in the other direction leads to Middelfart, an appealing, arty town that offers opportunities to spot both street art and whales swimming in the strait between Funen and Jutland. Top billing in these parts though goes to Egeskov Slot, a 16th-century fairytale castle complete with moat, manicured gardens and fantastic museums.

Places

GETTING AROUND

Odense has regular train connections to Nyborg on the busy Copenhagen line, and to Middelfart in the opposite direction.

Local buses travel between Odense Station and Kerteminde, but it's better to go by car if you plan to also visit the ship burial at Ladby, which is 5km from Kertminde by road.

Egeskov Slot is fairly easy to reach by public transport. The neighbouring village of Kværndrup is on the Odense–Svendborg train line, and the Faaborg–Nyborg bus stops outside the grounds.

Kerteminde

TIME FROM ODENSE: **25 MINS**

Art by the beach

At the narrow entrance of a fjord, Kerteminde is a snug coastal community with a walkable core of half-timbered buildings home to inviting cafes and restaurants. On the northern edge of town, the **Johannes Larsen Museet** *(johanneslarsen museet.dk; 120kr, under-18s free)* is a must for art lovers. Larsen was perhaps the most successful and prolific of the group of artists known as the *Fynboerne* (Funen Painters), who depicted vivid landscapes, naturalistic wildlife and scenes from everyday life at the turn of the 20th century.

Larsen's delightful home and studio are faithfully preserved, and inside an impressive modern gallery is a collection of his and other local artists' works. Larsen was an acclaimed painter of birds; appropriately the garden is chock-full of roving ducks and chickens. An excellent cafe-restaurant has terrace tables that look out across the road to **Nordstrand**, a white-sand beach that shows up in Larsen's paintings, and makes the perfect place to walk off a good lunch.

Tomb of a Viking king

Steps from the still waters of Kerteminde Fjord, a grassy mound hides within it the only known Viking ship burial in Denmark. Around the year 925 CE, a Viking chieftain was ceremoniously laid to rest on the deck of a longship, together

TOP TIP

Having a car or bike opens up more of the region, making it possible to explore the remote Hindsholm Peninsula, while also being able to overnight in great-value countryside B&Bs.

with weapons, tools, jewellery and sacrificial animals – four dogs and eleven horses.

Entering the low-lit, airtight burial chamber, the ship's ghostly remnants are revealed. Though the wooden hull decayed centuries ago, it left behind a perfect imprint, along with rivets, an anchor, iron curls from the ship's dragon-headed prow and bones of the sacrificed animals. According to archaeologists, the grave was plundered and the chieftain's body removed not long after the burial, for reasons unknown.

The experience begins at **Vikingemuseet Ladby** *(vikingemuseetladby.dk; 100kr, under-18s free)* which displays finds from the grave and a reconstruction of how the fully laden longship would have looked at time of burial. It's a short walk across fields to the burial mound. Just beyond, bobbing in the fjord, is a working reconstruction of the boat, built by enthusiasts using Viking-era techniques. Around the site, Viking-themed activities include spear-throwing and archery. These cost extra: purchase tickets inside the museum.

THE SPECTACULAR STOREBÆLT

Crossing the Great Belt strait that divides Funen and Zealand, the Storebælt Bro (Great Belt Bridge) was built in 1998 and still ranks among the world's longest suspension bridges. Spanning 18km, it's the largest construction project in Danish history, and replaced the Great Belt ferry service which launched its first car ferry back in 1930. Travel times have since been slashed from around 90 minutes to less than a quarter of hour, with a toll of 245kr for standard cars. To see the bridge on foot, you can join 10,000 runners racing over the Storebælt during **Broløbet**, a half-marathon from Nyborg to Korsør held every few years in early summer.

Exploring the Hindsholm Peninsula

Jutting north from Kerteminde, the sparsely populated **Hindsholm Peninsula** is rural Denmark at its most enticing. Narrow lanes wind through a patchwork of fields, linking together the tiny thatch-and-timber villages of **Viby** and **Måle**. You'll need your own wheels to explore – bicycle or car – and food supplies too, though in summer Måle's **Røgeri Hindsholm** has a cafe selling smoked salmon and charcuterie. Make a stop at the ancient burial mound at **Mårhøj** further north, en route to **Fyns Hoved** (Funen's Head), the peninsula's northernmost point. A looping 3km hike along a clifftop trail starts just over the narrow, windblown isthmus. Geographically, you're smack bang in the centre of Denmark, and yet surrounded by a panorama of sparkling sea, with views to Zealand in the east and Jutland to the west.

Nyborg

TIME FROM ODENSE: **15 MINS**

Medieval political powerhouse

Coming from Copenhagen, Nyborg is the first place you reach in Funen after crossing the epic Storebælt Bridge. The town is defined by **Nyborg Slot** *(nyborgslot.dk)*, an arresting 12th-century castle protected by extensive cannon-lined ramparts. For 200 years, it was the seat of Danehof, Denmark's medieval

Perfect for a special occasion splurge

EATING & DRINKING IN KERTEMINDE: TOP PICKS

Restaurant Rudolf Mathis: Elegant fish and seafood dishes make this restaurant one of Funen's top dining destinations. *noon-9.30pm Tue-Sat* **€€€**

Lulu's Cafe & Boutique: A ceiling of lampshades adds character to this cafe serving coffee and smørrebrød. *10am-5pm Wed-Mon* **€**

Boris Fisk: Fish and chips, hot smoked salmon and icy beers at this humble shack by the harbour. *11am-8pm Mon-Thu, to 3pm Fri, noon-8pm Sun* **€**

Skænkestuen: A pub since 1829, this time-warp place is hidden in one of the town's prettiest half-timbered courtyards. *10am-7pm*

Storebælt Bridge

parliament, and in 1282 the county's first constitution was penned inside its walls. The castle is closed for extensive renovation until 2028, but you can get a feel for the town's history by strolling through its historic quarters, starting at **Torvet**, the old town square. Overlooked by the imposing **Rådhus**, it's here that Nyborg celebrates its medieval roots during the **Danehof festival** in July, which brings jousting knights out on to the cobbles. **VisitNyborg**, the tourist centre on the square, has excellent walking maps that zero in on preserved stretches of the town's medieval city wall and **Borgmestergården** *(free)*, a former mayor's residence turned museum. Near the harbour car park, **Nyborg Cykler** rents out bikes from 150kr a day.

FESTIVALS AROUND FUNEN

Heartland Music Festival: *(heartlandfestival.dk)* In early June, Egeskov Slot provides the backdrop for this three-day event tailored to music lovers and foodies. International music acts play rock, electro and jazz, while top Nordic chefs serve up gourmet dinners.

Danehof Medieval Festival: A medieval jousting tournament takes place on Nyborg's town square in early July, and there are local food and drink producers hawking their wares along the narrow streets.

Øhavet Festival: *(oehavet.dk)* Taking place on the island of Ærø in July, Øhavet champions the Danish alternative music scene. Live bands, talks and children's activites.

Kerteminde Cherry Festival: *(kirsebaerfestival.dk)* Celebrating a beloved local crop, cherry-themed art exhibitions fill Kerteminde's galleries in July, and there are cherry tastings and musical performances.

EATING & DRINKING IN NYBORG: TOP PICKS

Consider booking a distillery tour

Jimbo's Kaffebar: Popular hangout, whether it's for a coffee or rounds of beer with friends. *10am-11pm Mon-Sat, noon-6pm Sun* €

Restaurant Remisen: Attached to Nyborg Destilleri, this restaurant serves international fare. *11.30am-midnight Thu-Sat, 10am-2pm Sun* €€€

Den Gode Smag: Overlooking the town square, this brasserie-deli has quality sandwiches. Kitchen closes 8pm. *noon-9pm Mon-Sat* €€

TOP EXPERIENCE

Egeskov Slot

Encircled by a moat and surrounded by 15 hectares of lavishly landscaped gardens, the 16th-century Egeskov Slot is a regal, romantic beauty. Extensive grounds are home to remarkable museums and play activities, while a roster of seasonal events includes a rock festival and Christmas markets. Pack a picnic and you can easily spend all day here.

TRABANTOS/SHUTTERSTOCK ©

Egeskov Slot

TOP TIPS

- Check the website for 'Open by Night' events (usually Wednesdays in peak summer), when the grounds stay open until 11pm and feature concerts and fireworks.
- Have a meal at **Brasserie Rigborg** on-site or grab a bite at one of the hot-dog kiosks. Picnics are permitted.

Castle & Gardens

Built in 1554, **Egeskov Slot** *(egeskov.dk; adult/child 265/160kr)* was updated to its current Gothic-meets-Renaissance styling in 1883. Part of the castle is still a residence for the family of Count Ahlefeldt-Laurvig-Bille, but you can explore 13 lavishly decorated rooms, filled to the rafters with weapons, paintings and antiques. The grounds are the real highlight, however. Many of the individually designed gardens are 21st-century creations. A garden-only ticket costs 225/145kr.

Museums

An astonishing array of exhibitions are on show inside the castle's former barns. Petrolheads will love the vintage cars, and there are dedicated displays of fire engines, motorcycles and fighter jets. A real gem is Europe's first **camping museum**, packed with life-sized dioramas that showcase covetous vintage camper vans, caravans and tents.

Family Activities

A smorgasbord of kid-oriented activities includes an adventure playground, a vertigo-inducing walkway high up in the old beech trees and a pedal-powered go-kart track. Inside the castle, **Titania's Palace** is a detailed dollhouse so vast it fills one of the chambers. Created in the early 1900s by an English painter, it's on long-term loan to Egeskov Slot.

Middelfart

TIME FROM ODENSE: **25 MINS**

A tale of two bridges

Nuzzling up against the Lillebælt (Little Belt), the strait that separates Funen from Jutland, prosperous Middelfart has a clutch of appealing sights and a watery backdrop dominated by the two Little Belt Bridges. Head first to the **CLAY Keramikmuseum** *(claymuseum.dk; 100kr, under-18s free, closed Mondays)*, a fantastic little museum that will get you all fired up over pottery and ceramic art.

Starting and finishing at CLAY, the 2.5km **Ceramics Trail** meanders through the half-timbered heart of Middelfart, taking in two history museums, a redbrick church with a whale bone-adorned interior, the handsome waterfront and around a dozen public art pieces. The route is subtly marked by blue ceramic tiles on the ground, but you should also pick up an accompanying trail leaflet in the museum. En route you'll pass the **M/S Mira III** *(mira3.dk; adult/child 210/150kr)*, a boat built in 1915 that embarks on two-hour whale-watching cruises on the Lillebælt, home to one of the world's densest populations of porpoises. The older of the Little Belt Bridges, built in 1935, offers **bridge walking tours** on top of its iron framework *(bridgewalking.dk; adult/child 325/265kr)*.

MORE ART BY FUNEN'S PAINTERS

The **Faaborg Museum** (p174) has an extensive collection of works by *Fynboerne*, as well as Kai Nielsen sculptures and Kaare Klint furniture. Works by the Funen Painters are also displayed in the permanent collection at **Brandts** (p161) in Odense.

FUNEN'S MUSICAL MAESTRO

The thunderous sound of duelling kettledrums from Carl Nielsen's best known symphony, *The Inextinguishable*, continues to fill international concert halls, but the acclaimed Danish composer had humble beginnings. Born in 1865, the Funen native was one of 12 children, raised in a poor but talented musical family. He grew up in Nørre Lyndelse, 15km south of Odense, and his **childhood home** *(barndomshjem.carlnielsen.org)* can be visited as a small museum between May and September. Nielsen drew inspiration from his native landscape, as seen in works like *Fynsk Foraar* (Springtime on Funen). In late August, Odense hosts a series of concerts for the Carl Nielsen Festival *(carlnielsenfestival.com)*, while the **Carl Nielsen Museum** is a hi-tech tribute to the composer.

EATING & DRINKING IN MIDDELFART: TOP PICKS

Holms Restaurant: Tuck in to pork-heavy Danish fare at Holms, looking like something out of Tolkien. *11.30am-8.30pm Tue-Sat* **€€**

Cafe Mauritz: Grab brunch fare, burgers and coffee at this sunny hangout next to the modern town hall. *10am-10pm* **€€**

Cafe Razz: A choice bar with outdoor seating. Brunch plates and smørrebrød can be washed down with wine. *10am-10pm or later* **€€**

Strib Fisk: Freshly caught fish and chips are sold from this appealingly rustic harbour hut beside the *M/S Mira III*. *9am-5.30pm Mon-Fri* **€**

Svendborg

FERRY TRIPS | BOAT-SPOTTING | LIVELY PUB SCENE

GETTING AROUND

Trains from Odense (40 minutes) arrive at Svendborg Station, centrally located and a stone's throw from the harbour and the Ærø ferry terminal. Regular bus services (1 hour) connect Nyborg with the bus terminal adjacent to the train station.

The town centre is small and easy to navigate on foot. From mid-May to early September, the vintage vessel *M/S Helge* sails a 2-hour scenic loop from Svendborg Harbour, with opportunities to hop off at various points.

Svendborg is connected to the islands of Tåsinge and Langeland by road, while ferries travel to the islands of Ærø, Drejø, Skarø and Hjortø.

Gateway to Funen's southern archipelago, the port town of Svendborg is a canvas of white sails in summer as Denmark's yachting fraternity spill out of marinas and into the lapis blue waters of the Svendborgsund. Historically a maritime hub, Svendborg grew to prominence as a shipbuilding centre and trade port. Global shipping giant Maersk was founded by a local father-and-son in 1904, and a commercial harbour still thrums with life – just out of sight of the seafront bars and moored schooners. In summer, a looping passenger ferry service putters south through the island-dotted estuary, stopping off at nearby beaches, wooded parks and sleepy maritime communities. Away from the waterfront, cobbled streets climb through the hilly town centre, passing cafes, shops and handsome half-timbered landmarks like Anne Hvides Gård, Svendborg's oldest house built in 1560. Other historic hotspots include a thought-provoking 'welfare museum' housed in Svendborg's old poorhouse.

Sailboats & Seafarers

Svendborg's maritime past and present

The cultural heartbeat of Svendborg's harbour zone is **Frederiksø**, a tiny island once home to begrimed shipyards and now mostly taken over by bars, cafes, artist studios and **Danmarks Museum for Lystsejlads** *(lystsejlads.dk; free, limited opening outside summer)*. Run by volunteers, the museum exhibits dozens of boats in a huge warehouse, including Olympic-winning dinghies, vintage yachts and *Stormy II*, which circumnavigated the world.

Stroll to the end of the quay for a glimpse of the dry dock where vessels undergo repairs – this is still a working harbour after all. Moored alongside Frederiksø are several vintage wooden sailing ships, all seaworthy and making regular sorties – with more across the water at **Sejlskibsbroen**, a historic jetty just west of the Ærø ferry terminal. In between,

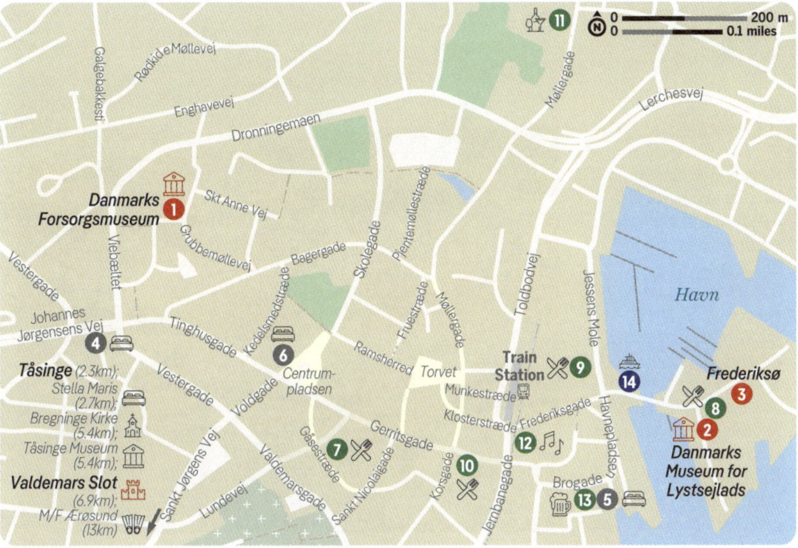

SIGHTS
1 Danmarks Forsorgsmuseum
2 Danmarks Museum for Lystsejlads
3 Frederiksø

SLEEPING
4 Danhostel Svendborg
5 Hotel Ærø
6 Hotel Svendborg

EATING
7 Børsen
8 Frederiksøens Madbar
9 Lolo Bakery & Bar
10 Salig Simons Gaard

DRINKING & NIGHTLIFE
11 105 Bar og Køkken
● Kammerateriet (see 8)
12 Rasmus
13 Strandlyst

TRANSPORT
14 M/S Helge

VisitSvendborg is a well-stocked tourist information centre housed in the yellow and-red timber workshop buildings. A sun trap on summer evenings, Frederiksø's **Strand Bar** is a fine spot to enjoy a drink or two and watch the world sail by.

Cruising South Funen

Messing about in boats

From mid-May to early September, the vintage vessel **M/S Helge** *(svendborg-havn.dk/en/ferries/ms-helge; 150kr roundtrip, 40kr single stop)* sets sail three to four times daily from Svendborg Harbour on a sightseeing loop around the Svendborgsund between the islands of Funen, Tåsinge and Thurø. Threading between a flotilla of sailboats, the

TOP TIP

To hire a bike, head to Svendborg Cykeludlejning on Frederiksø *(svendborgcykeludlejning.dk)*. Rates start at 150kr per day. The shop is owned by the nonprofit Cykeltutten, which brings together refugees and community members to build and repair old bicycles.

EATING IN SVENDBORG: TOP PICKS

Lolo Bakery & Bar: Tuck into pastries, Danish breakfast and sandwiches at this cafe facing the marina. *9.30am-5pm Wed-Thur, to 10pm Fri-Sun* €

Frederiksøens Madbar: Casual harbourside eatery serving fish and chips along with attractively presented seafood and salad boxes. *11am-9pm* €

Børsen: Hit up this gastropub for Danish classics, burgers, salads and a Sunday brunch buffet from 10am-1pm. *10am-11pm or later* €€

Salig Simons Gaard: French-inspired gourmet bistro in an atmospheric building. Three-course menus start at 350kr. *11am-11pm Tue-Sat* €€€

BIRCH JUICE ICE CREAM

One of the closest islands to Svendborg, minuscule Skarø has a gourmet secret: some of Denmark's best and most unusual ice cream. **Skarø Is** *(skarois.dk)* make their organic, deliciously textured creations, whether sorbet, dairy or soft ice, with sugar kelp and sap tapped from the island's birch trees. If you do visit the tiny ice cream cafe on the island, build up your appetite for a second helping by climbing Skarø's 'mountain' Vesterbjerg, which towers 9m above sea level. Even if you don't make it to Skarø, you can still taste its creations at gourmet delis and food shops around Funen.

cruise takes in a pretty landscape of green-forested shoreline dotted with tastefully-designed summer houses, no two the same. Stops include the popular beach area of Christiansminde, from where it's a 2km coastal walk back to Svendborg Harbour, and the old maritime village of Troense. The furthest stop is Grasten, on the horseshoe-shaped island of Thurø.

Close to where *M/S Helge* docks at Vindebyøre, on Tåsinge, **Nicus Nature** *(nicusnature.com)* offers SUP and kayak hire, and spear-fishing tours. A number of dive spots in the area include **M/F Ærøsund**, a wreck 7km west of Svendborg. See *dyk-sydfyn.dk* for more information.

Svendborg on a Shoestring

Discover the Danish Welfare Museum

A visit to **Danmarks Forsorgsmuseum** *(forsorgsmuseet.dk; 95kr, under-18s free)* leaves a lasting impression. A former workhouse where impoverished Danes lived from 1872 until 1974, this impactful museum recounts the institution's history while also exploring welfare and inequality in Denmark today. Once inmates stepped through the gates, they

DRINKING IN SVENDBORG: TOP PICKS

Strandlyst: True to its maritime heritage, this pub is adorned with ship paintings and hosts regular live bands. *3pm-2am Mon-Sat, to 7pm Sun*

Rasmus: Live music, jazz jams, karaoke and poker nights are on the calendar at this locals' favourite. *4-10pm Tue-Wed, to midnight or later Thu-Sat*

Kammerateriet: In a former warehouse on Frederiksø, this bar has live music and DJ nights on summer weekends. *10am-midnight or later*

105 Bar og Køkken: Hip little wine bar with a chalkboard tapas menu. Changing cocktail menus and Friday DJs. *5.30-11pm or later Wed-Sat*

TRABANTOS/SHUTTERSTOCK ©

Svendborg Harbour

forfeited their rights to vote, marry and have children. They were segregated by sex and classed as 'deserving' (the elderly and those with disabilities) or 'undeserving' (jobless vagrants and alcoholics). In exchange for a roof over their heads, they worked on tedious tasks, such as sorting lolly sticks and weaving straw mats. Shockingly, it was as late as 1961 before residents were re-enfranchised – all the more eye-opening given modern Denmark's reputation as an equitable society.

Cross the Water to Tåsinge

Villages, views and a grand castle

Facing Svendborg across the water is **Tåsinge**, an island joined to Funen by the 1224m-long Svendborgsund Bridge. On its northeastern shore, prosperous **Troense** has a perfectly formed marina and streets like Grønnegade and Badstuen that feel straight out of a time capsule. Just to the south, **Valdemars Slot** was built in 1644 for King Christian IV's son Valdemar Christian. Though closed to the public, you can still drive through the gatehouses and get a terrific view of the beefy castle buildings and gardens.

A worthwhile stop if you're en route to Langeland is the village of **Bregninge**, the highest point in the South Funen Archipelago. Clamber up the tower of **Bregninge Kirke** *(20kr)* for far-reaching views of up to 28 islands on the clearest of days. Across the road, **Tåsinge Museum** *(taasinge-museum.dk; 60kr, under-16s free)* is housed across five historic buildings and delves into local history, with a standout exhibition on the tragic story of Elvira Madigan and Sixten Sparre.

SOUTH FUNEN'S STAR-CROSSED LOVERS

He was a Swedish aristocrat and cavalry officer. She a beautiful tightrope artist in the circus. The love story of Elvira Madigan and Sixten Sparre was a sensation in its day. Sixten, who was married with children, became infatuated with the young Elvira after seeing her perform. They began a passionate love affair, conducted initially through letters, before running away together.

The couple eloped through Denmark, and in July 1889, checked into an inn on Tåsinge. Out of money and with no viable plan for the future, they decided to end their lives together in a nearby woodland. Sixten shot Elvira before turning the gun on himself.

The couple are buried at **Landet Kirke**, 10km south of Svendborg.

Beyond Svendborg

The south is where Funen shows off its most scenic side. Gentle hills, glittering coastline and an alluring archipelago await.

Places

In the calm Baltic waters, the South Funen Archipelago is the region's irresistible gem. Of more than 50 islands and skerries, around a dozen have permanent residents, ranging in size from tiny Hjortø (population: 7) to idyllic Ærø with around 6000 inhabitants. This low-lying archipelago was once a hilly region sculpted by glaciers until meltwaters from the end of the last Ice Age flooded the area. The resulting islands are some of Denmark's prettiest spots, many with summertime bike rental and overnighting opportunities. Outdoorsy travellers can swim, kayak, sail and fish, as well as hike Øhavsstien's fantastic network of trails and shelters. For more luxurious digs, a night in a traditional *kro* (inn) or castle makes a memorable stay.

GETTING AROUND

Tåsinge and Langeland are connected to Funen by road, but for most of the islands you'll need to take a ferry, departing from Svendborg or the historic port town of Faaborg to the west.

Ærø is the region's holiday hot spot, served by car ferries from Svendborg, Faaborg and Rudkøbing on Langeland.

For the more minor islands, Svendborg is the jumping off point to Drejø, Skarø and Hjortø, while Faaborg has boat connections to Lyø, Avernakø and Bjørnø.

Ærø

TIME FROM SVENDBORG: **55 MINS** 

Ærø escapades by bike

In keeping with the island's sustainable spirit, blissful Ærø really is best explored by bike, no lycra required. The gentle terrain, quiet lanes and well-marked routes are a dream for two-wheeled exploring. Charming vistas are served up by the bucketload, and at 30km long and 9km wide, Ærø is small enough to make the routes listed here doable on a long day trip to the island.

One irresistible ride takes in Ærø's northern side, connecting the villages of Ærøskøbing and Søby along a roughly 18km stretch of the Baltic Sea Cycle Route, also known as **National Cycle Route N8**. Follow signs marked '8' as you contour closely to the coast and then weave inland around tiny hamlets and farmers' fields, awash with wildflowers and butterflies in summer. Just 5km from Søby, briefly detour west to see **Søbygaard**, a photogenic manor house with a moat and drawbridge, where you can also clamber up 12th-century ramparts. In Søby, visit the harbour and thatched windmill, **Søby Mølle**. If you still have the energy, it's worth biking a further 5km to **Skjoldnæs Fyr**, a lighthouse with glorious sea views en route. Otherwise, catch the hourly local bus *(www.jesperbus.dk; free)* back to Ærøskøbing. Bicycles can be mounted on the bus, with some restrictions – see the website.

Ærøskøbing

TOP TIP

If travelling to Ærø with a car, it's wise to book your passage in both directions a few days ahead, or even a week or two for summer weekends.

Funen Cycle Route 92 makes another lovely bike trip. From Ærøskøbing, the 10.5km ride southeast follows a dead-flat, car-free coastal trail before country lanes bring you to seafaring town Marstal. Be sure to check out the **Marstal Søfartsmuseum** *(marmus.dk; 85kr, under-18s free)*, packed with model ships, paintings and paraphernalia from life at sea. For lovely views, pedal back via hilltop village Rise, making a pit stop at local brewery, **Ærø Bryggeri**, which also serves lunch in July and August.

Bicycles can be hired in Ærøskøbing, either at the petrol station on Pilebækken or from **Andelen Guesthouse** *(andelenguesthouse.com/cycle-rental)* next door. Pick up cycle maps from the tourist office just past the ferry terminal in Ærøskøbing, or download at *visitaeroe.com*.

FOR OUTDOOR ENTHUSIASTS

Funen is a top spot to get outdoors. Sailing trips, kayak lessons and bicycle hire can be arranged in **Svendborg** (p168). Read more about how to responsibly enjoy **Denmark's outdoors** (p282).

Bed down in wild nature

Get a dose of Nordic *friluftsliv* (outdoor life) by snuggling down in a sleeping bag at a wooden shelter. These range from architectural two-storey designs to floating pontoons reached by kayak, but the majority are simple, open-sided huts with raised platforms. Campgrounds are primitive, but typically have a fire pit and composting toilet. Funen is one of the first places where the concept took off, and the region has more than 100 locations including several pristine sites dotted around the

SUSTAINABLE ÆRØ

In 2021, Ærø was named the EU's most sustainable island. Thanks to wind turbines and solar parks, this eco-friendly isle produces more clean energy than it uses and adds the surplus to the grid. Homes are warmed using biomass and solar thermal heat. Built in Søby's shipyard, *Ellen* is a ground-breaking electric ferry that sails emission-free between Fynshav and Søby, charging its batteries with renewable energy. But Ærø doesn't plan to stop there, and its green goals go even further. The island is aiming to be net carbon neutral and energy self-sufficient by 2025.

coastline and countryside of Ærø. They're incredibly popular, so book a spot online (*bookenshelter.dk* and *naturstyrelsen.dk*) rather than simply showing up.

Faaborg

TIME FROM SVENDBORG: 1 HR (bus) OR 35 MINS (car)

History and art by the sea

The port town of Faaborg was once home to a sizeable fishing fleet, and still retains vestiges of its 17th-century commercial heyday. Rising up over Faaborg's cobbled lanes, the striking rococo **Klokketårnet** *(20kr, cash only)* is a bell tower missing its church. It was demolished after the Reformation, but the tower proved a handy means of directing naval shipping.

Under renovation in 2024, **Vesterport** is a step-gabled brick gatehouse dating back to the 15th century. In the main square, you'd be forgiven for doing a double-take at bronze sculpture **Ymerbrønden** ('Ymir's Well') – yes, that is a naked man sucking a cow's udder! Inspired by the Norse creation myth, local artist Kai Nielsen's work shows the giant Ymir being nourished by the cow Auðumbla who in turn brings the boy Búri into being by licking frosty stones. It was Búri's grandsons, including Odin, who created the Earth by slaying Ymir. The piece caused a stir when it was unveiled in 1913 – the sandstone original is now safely inside the handsome **Faaborg Museum** *(faaborgmuseum.dk; 100kr, under-18s free, closed Mondays)* which exhibits works by the Funen Painters.

Harbour strolls and seaside swims

Sleepy Faaborg wakes up in summer when the harbour bustles with sailboats and tourists. If you're brave enough to take a dip in the Baltic, head to the **Faaborg Harbour Baths** bathing area, or follow the coastal footpath east to the sandy **public beach** next to Klinten holiday complex. You can also hire SUPs and kayaks *(klintenoutdoor.dk)*. Opened in 2021, **Øhavsmuseet** *(ohavsmuseet.dk; 95kr, under 18s free)* explores the region's ancient geology and early communities. The harbour-front museum is also a visitor centre for South Funen's **Geopark**, which encompasses the surrounding region and archipelago. Download the app for information on geological and Stone Age sites *(geoparkoehavet.dk)*. Just outside town, the hilly woodland **Svanninge Bakker** has walking and mountain biking trails.

EATING & DRINKING ON ÆRØ: TOP PICKS

Restaurant MUMM: Ærøskøbing's top place has candles, dark-painted beams and dishes like fried scallops. *6-8pm Tue, noon-8pm Wed-Sun* €€

Ærøskøbing Røgeri: By the harbour, this place dishes up smoked-fish plates and plastic cups of Ærø beer. *11am-7pm, to 9pm in Jul-Aug* €

Restaurant Fru Berg: Views of Marstal's harbour from the covered terrace are a fine accompaniment to plaice, mussels and langoustine. *noon-9pm* €€

Ærø Bryggeri (p173): Ærø's craft brewery fires up the barbecue for summer lunches of grilled sausages. *noon-4pm Jul-Aug only* €

A SAILOR'S STROLL IN ÆRØSKØBING

With its pastel-coloured cottages and ship-in-a-bottle charm, Ærøskøbing is the nicest village on Ærø and a great base for exploring the island.

START	END	LENGTH
Ferry dock	Vestre Strandvej	2km; 2 hours

Only steps from the ferry you'll find the old shipyard, 1 **Det Gamle Værft**, which has activities for kids, such as metal hammering and rope weaving. Next up, stop at 2 **Flaske-Peters Samling** *(summer only)*, the former poorhouse now home to hundreds of ships in bottles. The remarkable collection is the life's work of Peter Jacobsen, a sailor born in 1873.

Round the corner, up Brogade is 3 **Ærø Museum** presenting an engaging snapshot of life on the island over the centuries. Next, step inside half-timbered 4 **Hammerichs Hus** *(open seasonally)*, a treasure trove of antiques and period furniture, with walls lined by thousands of Dutch tiles.

Continuing along Brogade, you'll reach the attractive town square, 5 **Torvet**. You may spot newly-weds around here – romantic Ærø is known as the 'wedding isle' after all. Stop at 6 **Den Gamle Købmandsgaard** for a coffee or light bite. An attraction in itself, this old grocer sells local produce, and in the courtyard you'll find 7 **Ærø Whisky**, a small craft distillery offering tastings.

Have a breather over a local Ærø beer on the square at 8 **Cafe På Torvet**, then loop along Søndergade and Vestergade back to the waterfront. Take the path past the yacht marina to see the clutch of photogenic beach huts lining 9 **Vestre Strandvej**.

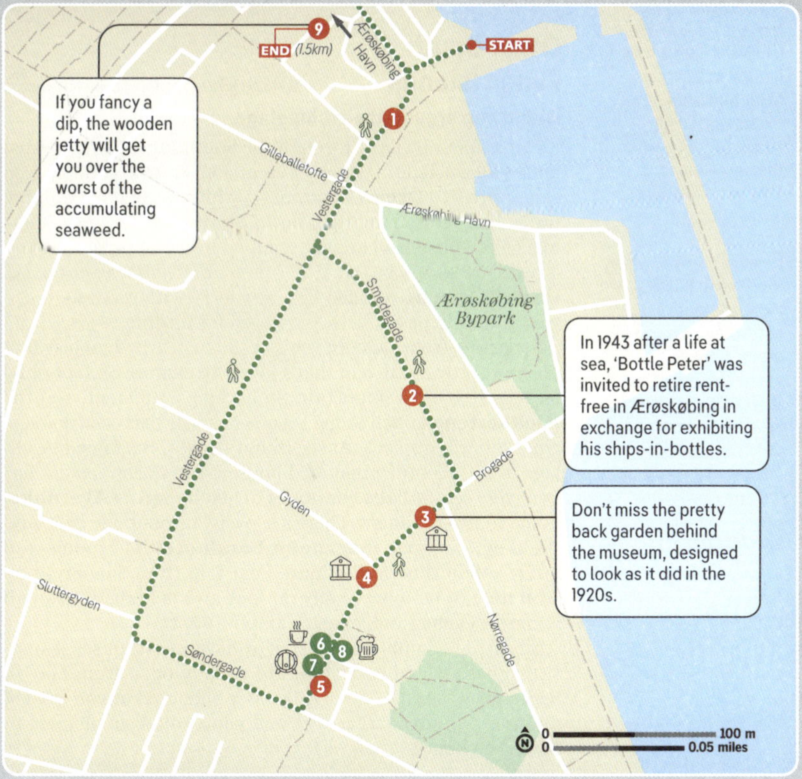

START

END (1.5km)

If you fancy a dip, the wooden jetty will get you over the worst of the accumulating seaweed.

In 1943 after a life at sea, 'Bottle Peter' was invited to retire rent-free in Ærøskøbing in exchange for exhibiting his ships-in-bottles.

Don't miss the pretty back garden behind the museum, designed to look as it did in the 1920s.

0 100 m
0 0.05 miles

LOCAL LIFE ON ÆRØ

Christian Stadager is CEO and master distiller at Ærø Whisky. *@aeroewhisky*

Ærø is a unique place where the islanders master the art of 'hurrying slowly'. A vibrant and thriving island community, here you will find peace, space and creative energy. The island itself is a special landscape created at the end of the last Ice Age. We islanders care about nature; what is close to us, and each other.

Summer is high season on Ærø, when the entire island is very busy. The Ærø Jazz Festival in week 31 (Jul/Aug) is a must for music lovers, while the Øhavet Festival is more alternative. All year round you can attend concerts and events; in December Ærøskøbing comes to life with an especially cosy Christmas market where you can find local artisanal takes on Danish specialities.

Hike South Funen's Øhavsstien

Hiking the **Øhavsstien** (Archipelago Trail) is an unhurried and enjoyable way to explore the best of the region's nature. Stage one of the trail starts just west of Faaborg at Faldsled, running through undulating hills, beech forests and along flat seashore. The well-signed and traffic-free trail weaves around farms, villages and castles, comprising 220km of trails in total, including branch routes that cross Ærø, Tåsinge and northern Langeland. Øhavsstien is divided into seven sections; download maps at *visitfyn.com/fyn/experiences/archipelago-trail*. Accommodation options along the way are plentiful and include campsites, shelters and guesthouses.

A Japanese garden in Funen

Halfway between Faaborg and Odense but straight out of Kyoto, **De Japanske Haver** *(dejapanskehaver.dk; 85kr, under-10s free)* is a delightful horticultural and aesthetic oddity. The extensive gardens, which include Zen-like raked sand, soothing streams and stepped paths, are the passion project of Danish landscape gardener Peter Dalsgaard, who studied garden design in Kyoto. An attached Japanese diner serves authentic lunch trays featuring teriyaki beef, katsu pork cutlet and tempura prawns. Best reached by car, the gardens are open to the public from 1 May to 30 September.

Other South Funen Islands

TIME FROM SVENDBORG: **35-80 MINS** 

Island hop around the archipelago

Flitting about by ferry through the South Funen Archipelago makes for a delightful summer excursion. From Svendborg, you can day trip to **Drejø** *(30 minutes)*, which is great for walking trails and nature, and then on to **Skarø** *(45 minutes)*, home to a snug village and an ice cream factory (see p170). The two islands are served by the *M/F Højestene (svendborg-havn.dk)*. Unspoilt **Hjortø**, reached by a tiny ferry with room for a single car and 12 passengers, is a haven for birdlife.

Departing from Faaborg you can sail to nearby **Lyø** just 7km offshore, a tranquil gem that's lovely to explore on foot or by bicycle. It was an important Stone Age settlement, and the **Klokkestenen** ('Bell Stone'), a precariously balanced dolmen, rings out when struck. At the island's centre is a fairy-tale village of 18th-century thatched houses. The *Ø-Færgen* car ferry *(oefaergen.fmk.dk)* continues to neighbouring **Avernakø**, home to 100 islanders. There's a lovely harbourside cafe, and the down-to-earth **Avernakø Landhotel** has rooms and a farm shop. Just a 17-minute boat trip from Faaborg, tiny **Bjørnø** can be toured only on foot and is home to a small winery, beaches and a basic camping spot.

All of the islands except Hjortø have guesthouses, campsites, shelters and cafes that are usually open from May to September, and most generally offer bike hire, or you can get a bike in Svendborg/Faaborg and pay a small supplement to take it on board.

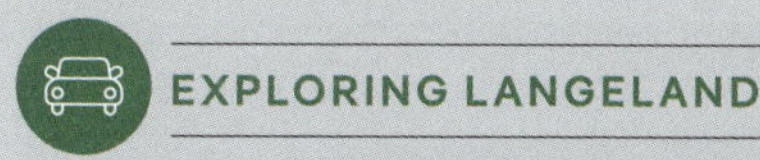

EXPLORING LANGELAND BY CAR

Home to windmills, wild ponies and intriguing cold war relics, the rural island of Langeland is well suited to a day-long road trip.

START	END	LENGTH
Rudkøbing	Tranekær	75km; 6 hours

The road from Svendborg delivers you to the red-roofed town of 1 **Rudkøbing** in Langeland's middle, where you can park in the port to wander through hollyhock-lined streets. Motoring on to the scenic south, the road winds through farmland dotted with creaky old windmills and towering turbines. 2 **Langelandsfort** is a former NATO military installation built in 1953 at the height of tensions between the Soviet Union and the West. The underground bunker and artillery complex is now a fascinating museum.

At the southernmost tip of the island, park up for an amble along 3 **Dovnsklint**, a row of sea cliffs where you might spot a herd of semi-wild Exmoor ponies. The nearby fishing harbour of Bagenkop makes a decent lunch stop - try the fish platter at 4 **Bagenkop Kro**. Return north to 5 **Skovsgaard**, a kid-oriented nature centre, cafe and organic farm in the grounds of a manor house.

In the northern village of Tranekær, a string of pretty cottages leads to 6 **Tranekær Slot**, a castle from the 13th century. Park by the castle for a wander in 7 **Tickon**, over 200 acres of lakeside grounds and woodland dotted with naturalistic art installations. Nearby, 8 **Medicinhaverne** is a beautifully manicured herb garden, while just to the north, 9 **Tranekær Slotsmølle** is a windmill from 1834 now home to a museum and cafe.

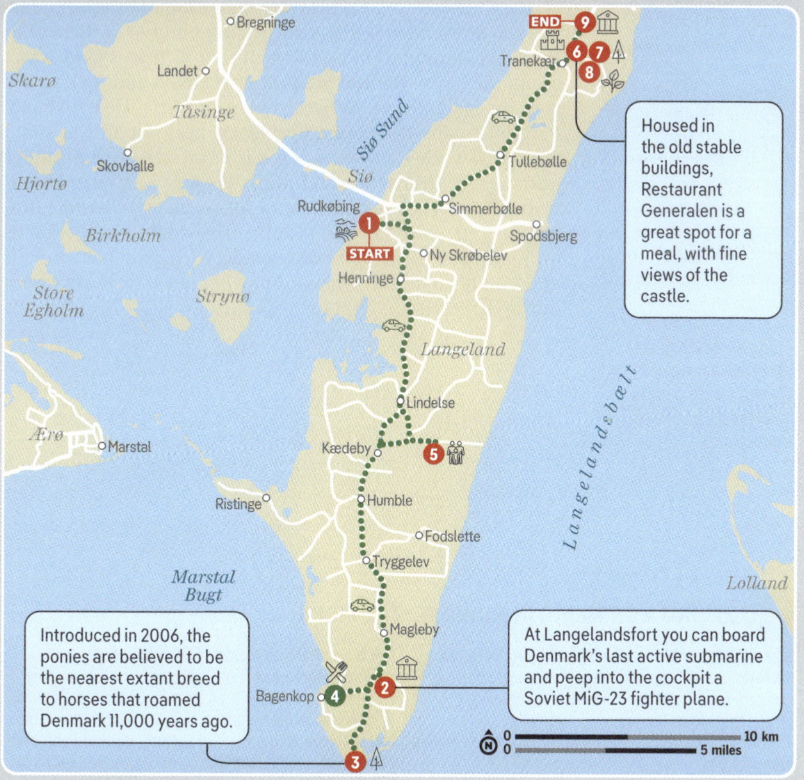

Housed in the old stable buildings, Restaurant Generalen is a great spot for a meal, with fine views of the castle.

Introduced in 2006, the ponies are believed to be the nearest extant breed to horses that roamed Denmark 11,000 years ago.

At Langelandsfort you can board Denmark's last active submarine and peep into the cockpit a Soviet MiG-23 fighter plane.

FAABORG FOR FOODIES

The old port town of Faaborg is a good place to taste several Funen specialities. Keep an eye out for *Fynsk rygeost*, a smoked cheese, in delis and supermarkets. Soft and spreadable with a smoky edge, it's a Funen original that some claim dates to the Viking era. For something even smokier, Faaborg's **Det Gamle Røgeri** ('the old smokehouse') is the spot for seaside staples like hot-smoked salmon fillets and smoked shrimp. Originating in Funen, Danish classic *brunsviger* is a sticky-sweet cake loaded with brown sugar and butter. It's traditionally served for birthdays, but you can enjoy a slice any time of year at **Vesterports Bageri**, a fantastic bakery-cafe beside Faaborg's old town gate.

Hvedholm Slot

Knightly nights on Funen

From minor medieval fortresses to Renaissance masterpieces, the Funen countryside is strewn with more than 120 historic castles and manors. A surprising number of them offer regal accommodation and fine dining at prices that won't break the bank. **Broholm Slot** between Svendborg and Nyborg is a magnificent, 700-year-old medieval castle with moat. Palatial rooms have open fireplaces, period paintings and antiques, while a museum wing is crammed with antiques and curious archaeological finds. West of Faaborg, **Hvedholm Slot** feels like entering an 18th-century costume drama with its spired tower, indulgently ornate dining rooms and lounges. Most bedrooms come with four-poster beds and kingly amounts of space. For a list of castle stays, check out *visitfyn.com*.

Make a night of it by booking a stay

EATING & DRINKING IN FAABORG: TOP PICKS

SOZE Kaffebar & Risteri: This cafe and roastery serves the best coffee for miles; stop for a sandwich or brunch. *10am-8pm* €

Spisehuset: Gourmet burgers skewered by a knife are served at this casual harbourside eatery. *11.30am-10pm Wed-Sat, to 4pm Sun* €€

Det Hvide Pakhus: Inside a harbour warehouse, Faaborg's top spot dishes up mussels, tapas, steaks and seasonal set menus. *11.30am-3pm, 5.30-8pm* €€

Falsled Kro: Gourmet inn 8km west of Faaborg serving set menus of locally sourced fare cooked with aplomb. Book ahead. *noon-3pm, 6-9pm Tue-Sat* €€€

Places We Love to Stay

€ Budget €€ Midrange €€€ Top End

Odense p158

Cabinn Odense € Centrally located, no-frills hotel with tiny rooms. Cheaper twins have bunk beds. Enjoy rooftop views of Odense from the top-floor breakfast buffet.

First Hotel Grand €€ Good value grand dame from 1897 with striking architecture and a central location. Some guest rooms due an update.

Villa A Hotel €€ Near the river and parkland, this spruced-up guesthouse has 15 uniquely furnished rooms, from compact singles to capacious doubles.

Hotel Odeon €€€ A short walk to HC Andersens Hus, this stylish bolthole has sleek modern rooms kitted out with designer furnishings.

Kerteminde p163

Danhostel Kerteminde € Classy, low-rise hostel in a quiet, wooded area on the edge of Holmeskov Forest, 700m southeast of Kerteminde Bridge.

Købmandsgaarden Kerteminde €€ Choose from minimalist doubles or an apartment in this half-timbered ensemble of 16th- to 19th-century merchants' houses set around a cobbled courtyard.

Tornøes Hotel €€ Creaky original stairs lead to two floors of rooms at this historic hotel overlooking the fjord-neck that divides the town centre.

Munkebo Kro €€€ Facing Kerteminde fjord but in the neighbouring town of Munkebo, this thatched inn has cosy old-world charm and an excellent restaurant.

Svendborg p168

Danhostel Svendborg € Central and with free parking, this sprawling hostel has spotless en-suite rooms, and dorm beds available in July–mid-September.

Hotel Ærø €€ Classic harbourside hotel with wood furnishings, a cosy lobby bar and traditional restaurant. Conveniently close to the Ærø ferry dock.

Hotel Svendborg €€ Central, modern business hotel with a neat if utilitarian design. Well-appointed rooms and a highly regarded restaurant.

Stella Maris €€€ Facing the Svendborgsund across sloping lawns, this grand 19th-century villa has been revamped into a splurge-worthy getaway.

Ærø p172

Andelen Guesthouse (p173) **€€** A century-old granary in Ærøskøbing has been transformed into a charming six-room guesthouse. Features include a small cinema and bike hire.

På Torvet €€ Meaning 'at the square', this boutique guesthouse and brasserie has chic, self-catering studios and an apartment-sized suite with lovely views of the square.

Femmasteren Hotel €€ Around a cobbled courtyard and facing the harbour, this basic but feel-good hostel has a stylish dining area with wood fire.

Vestergade 44 €€€ Elegant bed and breakfast in a beautifully updated 1784 house originally built by a sea captain for his daughter. Minimum two-night stay.

Faaborg p174

Danhostel Faaborg € Fairly new hostel with a fab location next to the elegant Faaborg Museum. Bright-white rooms (mostly twins) are shared between two historic buildings.

Vester Skerninge Kro €€ Between Faaborg and Svendborg, this 18th-century inn oozes charm and has neat rooms occupying a handful of traditional half timbered cottages. The restaurant is especially hyggelig.

Langeland p177

Tiki Camp € Glamping getaway with A-frame cabins and bell tents set amid leafy gardens and a grove of hazelnut trees. Eco-friendly features include composting loos and a vegan brekkie.

Bagenkop Kro €€ Book a great value half-board stay at this traditional inn in the south of the island and indulge in all-you-can-eat seafood with beer, coffee and dessert included.

Ribe & Southern Jutland

OLD TOWNS AND THE SEA

Tune in to the rhythms of the Wadden Sea, the clack of soles on cobbles and the distant cries of harbour seals.

Welcome to a region of mudflats, marshes, salty offshore islands, understated royal palaces and character-filled historic towns. The jewel in the crown of Southern Jutland is Ribe, the country's oldest town and historic Denmark at its most photogenic, where the night watchman still plods through antique streets, spinning yarns as he goes. Elsewhere, modern cultural treats come in the form of offbeat design museums, and edgy art and architecture.

Southern Jutland gets its personality from a few sources: the North Sea, naturally, but also from the south. It is the only part of Denmark connected to mainland Europe (by a 68km-long border), and in some places, you can feel the ties with Germany. Historically a disputed region, it was only in 1920 that Denmark was reunified and 'North Schleswig' became Sønderjylland (Southern Jutland).

The seasonal rhythms of the Wadden Sea dictate the appeal of this part of Denmark. Beach-going holidaymakers (many from Germany) fill the golden-sand beaches of Fanø and Rømø in summer, some taking it slow and easy, others harnessing the wind to whizz over sea and sand at extreme speeds. Spring and autumn brings an abundance of feathered friends (and their watchers), together with pods of fat harbour seals. Winter is the best time of year to hike over the mudflats on the hunt for oysters, mussels and nuggets of rare amber.

THE MAIN AREAS

RIBE
Denmark's oldest and most charming town. p184

KOLDING
Splendid castle and art museum. p194

For places to stay in Ribe & Southern Jutland, see p199

YORICK LEUSINK/SHUTTERSTOCK ©

Left: Harbour seal, Fanø (p190); Above: Ribe (p184)

Find Your Way

The best of Southern Jutland can be found along the coast. Go west for Ribe and the Wadden Sea islands, while on the opposite flank are the castle towns of Kolding and Sønderborg.

Kolding, p194

With its imposing royal castle, lively old streets and superb art and design museum, easy-going Kolding is worth a visit.

Ribe, p184

Ribe's 12th-century cathedral stands proud over Denmark's oldest town. It's a delectable slice of living history.

CAR

You need your own vehicle to get out to the Wadden Sea from Ribe. A car ferry connects Esbjerg and Fanø, and the adventurous can drive over the seabed to Mandø at low tide.

TRAIN & BUS

Southern Jutland's main towns are well connected by train and bus. It's only 35 minutes by rail from Ribe to Esbjerg and under an hour to Kolding. Local buses are primarily operated by Sydtrafik *(sydtrafik.dk)*.

Tirpitz Museum (p192)

Plan Your Time

After a couple of days exploring Ribe, strike out for the Wadden Sea via Esbjerg and Fanø, and soak up the island's charms for as long as you can linger.

Pressed For Time

- Get your bearings in **Ribe** (p184) by climbing the 52m cathedral tower. Wander the cobbles and make for the **Ribe Kunstmuseum** (p187), which has works from 19th-century 'Golden Age' artists, and **Museet Ribes Vikinger** (p187). Settle in at the historic **Weis Stue inn** (p186) for hearty Danish fare and beer before joining the night watchman on his evening rounds.

A Few Days to Explore

- After Ribe, make for the **Wadden Sea National Park** (p189). Sign up for seal spotting or oyster foraging and then catch the ferry to **Fanø** (p190). Swap your car for a bike and pedal to the idyllic village of Sønderho and spend the night at a rustic inn. Sail back to Esbjerg and then head to the compelling war museums of **Tirpitz** (p192) and **FLUGT** (p192).

Seasonal Highlights

SPRING

Spring breezes bring the fun to Rømø and Fanø's epic stretches of sand, as blokarts and surfers let rip.

SUMMER

Beaches and campsites swell with tourists, many from Germany. Folk music comes to Tønder.

AUTUMN

Bird-watchers flock to see the migrations. Starlings perform their 'black sun' routine in the marshes.

WINTER

Christmas markets and events inject hygge into Ribe. 'Tis the season for oyster hunting at the Wadden Sea.

Ribe

MAJESTIC CATHEDRAL | TIME-WARP ARCHITECTURE | NIGHT TOURS

GETTING AROUND

Ribe is a tightly clustered town, so it's easy to explore on foot. Almost all the sights (plus the train station) are within a 10-minute walk of Torvet, the central cathedral square.

Bicycles can be hired from Danhostel Ribe for 100kr/day. Ribe Cykellager, 3km north of the cathedral, rents out e-bikes from 200kr/day.

For parking, check the Danhostel north of the centre, which has four-hour parking, or drive a bit further on Saltgade for 48-hour parking.

Ribe is connected by rail to Esbjerg (35 minutes), where you can change on to direct trains to Aarhus and Odense.

You'd need a heart of stone to be unmoved by Ribe, Denmark's oldest and most delightfully crooked town. A host of half-timbered chocolate-box houses huddle around the country's first cathedral, a glorious hodgepodge of Romanesque and Gothic styles with a 52m-high tower looking out over marshes to the shimmering wetlands of the Wadden Sea. Such is the sense of living history in Ribe that the entire old town district has been designated a preservation zone. Sup a beer in one of Denmark's oldest inns, patrol the cobblestones after dark with the night watchman (a free nightly guided tour) and then bed down in antique lodgings with wonky floors and low ceilings. Throw in a fine art gallery that showcases Denmark's 'Golden Age' masters, and museums about Vikings and witches, and you've got the history part of any Southern Jutland tour all wrapped up.

Denmark's Oldest Cathedral

Romanesque jewel of the marshes

An important religious centre during the early Christianisation of Denmark, records show evidence of a bishop in Ribe as far back as 948 CE. The present cathedral, soaring divinely over the South Jutland marshland, dates from around 1225. Designed in the Romanesque style of the early Middle Ages, **Ribe Domkirke** *(ribe-domkirke.dk; free)* was constructed primarily from tufa, a soft porous rock quarried near Cologne and shipped north along the Rhine.

Later Gothic additions include the 52m-tall **Commoners' Tower** *(adult/child 25/15kr)*, which you can climb via a labyrinthine ascent through the cathedral's inner workings, each step soundtracked by the ferocious clicking of the 1696 clock. Up top, you're rewarded with inspiring views over red rooftops and flat green fields, the Ribe Å river tracing a winding course out to the Wadden Sea. A **museum** *(domkirkemuseet ribe.dk)* partway through the climb details the cathedral's construction history, explaining how an earlier tower collapsed

on Christmas morning in 1283, killing several townspeople. Allow 30 minutes to get up the tower and back down.

The Commoner's Tower was also used as a flood lookout. Over the centuries, tidal surges have burst through dykes and devastated Ribe. A mark on the pillar behind the pulpit shows the high-water mark in 1634, the worst flood ever recorded in South Jutland. Decorating the last two pillars on the northern side are faded remnants of **16th-century frescoes**. In striking contrast, the apse features 1980s stained glass and mosaics by Danish artist Carl-Henning Pedersen, nicknamed the 'Scandinavian Chagall'.

After exploring the cathedral, cross the south side of the square to **Kannikegaarden** *(free)*, a contemporary red-brick

TOP TIP

The 'Night Watchmen' tour isn't the only themed walk on offer in Ribe. In summer, weekly **ghost walks** depart from Museet Ribes Vikinger on Wednesday evenings, recounting tales like that of Maren Spliid, Ribe's most famous witch. Tours are in Danish and English.

THE BIG DROWNINGS

On the night of 11 October 1634, a monumental storm tide burst through primitive dykes and surged across the marshes towards Ribe. Reaching a height of around six metres above normal sea level, it killed hundreds of townsfolk and many more livestock. The cathedral, on a relatively high point in town, was flooded with almost two metres of water, interpreted by citizens as an act of divine punishment. The disaster became known as the 'Second Great Drowning'. The first happened in 1362 when an immense storm tide from the North Sea wiped out entire towns in Britain, the Netherlands, northern Germany, and Denmark, causing at least 25,000 deaths.

STIG ALENAS/SHUTTERSTOCK ©

Taarnborg

building that shelters the excavations of Denmark's oldest Christian cemetery. If visiting in summer, look out for classical music concerts held in the cathedral. At 8am, noon, 3pm and 6pm every day, the cathedral's carillon plays Danish folk ditties.

Ramble through Historic Ribe

See the town by day or night

Take any of the streets radiating out from Ribe's cathedral for a leisurely stroll into the past. On Puggårdsgade is a 16th-century manor house, the charmingly crooked **Taarnborg** with its brick spire, where a succession of Ribe bishops lived. Take Grønnegade to duck into narrow alleys that lead down and across pretty Fiskergade to Skibbroen and the riverfront. Here you'll find the **Johanne Dan**, an old sailing boat with a flat bottom that allowed it to navigate the shallow waters of the Ribe Å, fetching cargo from ships anchored out on the tidal flats. Close by, the **Stormflodssøjlen**, a wooden flood

EATING IN RIBE: OUR PICKS

Weis Stue: One of Denmark's oldest inns, this wonky spot serves meat-heavy mains, with smørrebrød for lunch. *11.30am-3pm, 5-9pm* **€€**

Sælhunden: This riverfront spot serves fish-centric Danish fare and smørrebrød on starched white tablecloths. *11.30am-10pm* **€€€**

Quedens Gaard: Start the day with Danish breakfast in the cobbled courtyard or snack on sandwiches, burgers and salads. *10am-6pm* **€**

Isvaflen: Get your ice-cream fix at this superior spot, served in cones or heaped atop pillowy waffles. *10am-10pm, from 11am Sun* **€**

column erected in 1920, marks the great deluge of 1634 that claimed hundreds of lives. Keep going along the riverbank and in 500m you'll reach the grassy earthworks and moat of **Riberhus Slot**, all that's left of a castle razed by Swedish forces in 1658.

On the lookout for floods, fires and ne'er-do-wells were the Night Watchmen, who made their rounds for centuries until the job was abolished in 1902. In the 1930s, they were reinstated as a tourist attraction, and the free **Night Watchmen Tour** remains a Ribe highlight. It's in both Danish and English but skews heavily to the former. Booking isn't necessary; just meet outside the **Weis Stue** inn at 8pm. The tour takes place nightly from May to the end of October (and during Easter and Christmas). There's also a 10pm tour from 15 June to 31 August.

Det Gamle Rådhus *(detgamleraadhusiribe.dk; 25kr, under-18s free)* runs 2½-hour guided tours of the town and cathedral, conducted in English. Check website for dates and times. The oldest town hall in Denmark, it hosts exhibitions on law and order amid handsome period interiors.

Ribe's Marvellous Museums

Vikings, witches and watercolours

In a grand mansion from 1864, the **Ribe Kunstmuseum** *(ribekunstmuseum.dk; 90kr, under-18s free)* has been around long enough to acquire some of Denmark's best works, including those by 19th-century 'Golden Age' artists such as Christoffer Wilhelm Eckersberg and the Skagen painters Anna and Michael Ancher. The gallery's riverside garden is a delight, and it connects with paths over the water to **Sankt Catharinæ Kirke**, the only other survivor of Ribe's dozen or so pre-Reformation places of worship.

Ribe is one of Scandinavia's oldest towns, and **Museet Ribes Vikinger** *(ribesvikinger.dk; 110kr, under-18s free)* does a fine job of unwrapping the history of the locale from its origins as a Viking trading post in the 700s through the thriving Middle Ages and beyond.

The compelling **Jacob A. Riis Museum** *(jacobariismuseum.dk; 95kr, under-18s free)* tells the tale of a boy from Ribe who emigrated to the United States in 1870 and went on to become a noted social reformer. Riis photographed the plight of New York City's poor, developing into a pioneer of documentary photography in the process. Theodore Roosevelt dubbed Riis 'the most useful citizen of New York'. Sharing the same

SEASON OF THE WITCH

Between 1572 and 1652, Ribe conducted 22 witch trials, but the most famous by far was against Maren Spliid, the wife of a tailor and a wealthy, respected citizen. After the trial was dismissed, her accuser, another tailor, albeit less successful than Maren's husband, approached the Danish king, who was more than a bit obsessed with magic and devilry. Spliid was tried a second time and acquitted once more, but then the case went to the Supreme Court where the king himself was the judge. Spliid was tortured and burned at the stake near Ribe in 1641.

DRINKING IN RIBE: OUR PICKS

Postgaarden: Building dating from 1580 with a charming courtyard and boutique microbrews on tap. *10am-5.30pm Mon-Fri, to 4pm Sat*

Terpager & Co: Lovely spot for nibbles and a glass of wine. There's a fine food shop attached. *11am-5.30pm Mon-Fri, 10am-4pm Sat*

Strygejernet: Called 'the iron', this pointy corner building houses a cosy little bar perfect for a quiet drink. *7pm-midnight Thu-Fri, from 2pm Sat*

Ribe Bryghus: Ribe's own craft brewery has eight regular beer styles on tap. *1-4pm Mon-Tue, to 6pm Wed-Thu, noon-6pm Fri, 10am-6pm Sat*

WHY I LOVE RIBE

Thomas O'Malley, Lonely Planet writer

Few historic towns feel as complete and unadulterated as Ribe, but this being Denmark, it's all so carefully and lovingly maintained, and the painted houses so perfectly wonky, that you almost start to wonder whether it's just a convincing film set. On a sunny day, try to snag a table on the cobbles outside Weis Stue, Denmark's oldest inn. The views of Ribe's magnificent Romanesque cathedral are a tonic for the soul, as is the beer, brewed to hoppy perfection by Ribe Bryghus, a local outfit operating out of an old train depot. Pair it with a hearty smørrebrød platter for the full effect.

Ribe VikingeCenter

space, **Hex! Museum of Witch Hunt** *(hexmuseum.dk; 110kr, under-18s free)* ramps up the fear factor with displays that put light and sound to ingenious use, but the exhibition could be improved. A combined ticket to both costs 155kr.

Ribe for Families

Hands-on fun and games

Kids can embrace their inner Viking at the **Ribe VikingeCenter** *(ribevikingecenter.dk; adult/child 145/75kr)*, a hands-on experience 3km south of town featuring costumed performers, traditional workshops and even 'warrior training'. There are archery and falconry demonstrations, and Viking-era crafts like pottery and leatherwork in a reconstructed 34m longhouse. An adventure playground is themed on Asgard and the Norse gods, but there's an even better one on the northern outskirts of Ribe. **Riplay** *(riplay.dk; free)* claims to be Denmark's largest playground, and features a 100m-long obstacle course among its many energy-expending fixtures.

Beyond Ribe

Lolling seals, oyster safaris and blokarts beckon at the Wadden Sea National Park and its salty offshore islands.

In the distant past, Viking ships launched directly from Ribe to Vadehavet (the Wadden Sea) and on to England and Frisia (a coastal region covering parts of the Netherlands and Germany). These days, the Wadden Sea doesn't see many Viking raiders and traders, but instead plenty of bird-watchers out to ogle the 12 million or so feathered critters that use the vast tidal mudflats as a feeding place or migratory rest stop. The islands of Fanø and Rømø, part of the UNESCO-listed Wadden Sea National Park, have clear-cut appeal for beachgoers, while out past the industrial city of Esbjerg, Denmark's western flank offers family-friendly sea swimming, WWII relics and superb museums.

Places

Wadden Sea National Park

TIME FROM RIBE: **20 MINUTES**

Wade out into World Heritage

Largest, flattest, wettest: three unlikely superlatives that sum up the UNESCO-listed **Wadden Sea National Park**, the world's biggest system of intertidal sand and mudflats. Twice daily at low tide, the seabed meets the sky, and birds swoop in to gorge at the tasty but temporary buffet of worms, cockles, crabs, shrimp and snails.

It might not sound like a bucket-list destination, but the Wadden Sea National Park offers plenty of outdoorsy fun, starting at slick **Vadehavscentret** *(Wadden Sea Visitor Centre; vadehavscentret.dk; adult/child 140/50kr)*, 10km southwest of Ribe. Check out the wildlife displays, marvel at the world's biggest oyster shell and, if the tides are right, catch the tractor-bus to the tiny island of **Mandø** (population: about 30). Hire a bike on the island and set off on the 10km looping trail to discover oyster banks, dykes, birdlife, sun-basking seals and cosy inns. You could drive your own car, but it's rough going along the seabed road, and there's a risk of being stranded if you don't pay attention to the tides.

If bivalve molluscs are your bag, sign up for an **oyster safari**. Participants don waders and schlep out past bobbing seals to harvest as many oysters (an invasive species here) as they can lug home. Purchase shucking knives, gloves and half-bottles of fizz at Vadehavscentret. Book tours at *vadehavscentret.dk*.

GETTING AROUND

Trains from Ribe run north to Esbjerg (35 minutes) and south to Skærbæk for Rømø (20 minutes) and Tønder (50 minutes).

The car ferry to Fanø departs from Esbjerg, taking just 12 minutes. A local bus service from the ferry dock runs about once an hour, connecting Nordby with Fanø Bad, Rindby Strand and Sønderho.

Rømø is connected to the mainland by road across a causeway. A ferry operates between Havneby and the nearby German island of Sylt.

TOP TIP

Wadden Sea activities and tours are popular and subject to the seasons, so book a spot well in advance *(vadehavscentret.dk).*

BLACK SUN OF THE MARSHES

Every spring and autumn, as the sun sets over the marshes outside Ribe and Tønder, a unique spectacle unfolds. Migrating starlings congregate in small groups as they decide on a place to roost for the night. On a rare evening, the starlings might eventually number in the hundreds of thousands, flying a balletic dance and forming patterns in mid-air that at times resemble a dense black sun (*sort sol* in Danish), especially if predators are in the vicinity. *Sort sol* occurs from March to April and between mid-September and late October. If you want to try your luck seeing it (not guaranteed), sign up for a spotting tour at *vadehavscentret.dk.*

Esbjerg

TIME FROM RIBE: **30 MINS**

South Jutland's biggest city

The industrial city of **Esbjerg** swaps Ribe's hallowed spires for chimneys and towering oil platforms, including Scandinavia's tallest at 250m. Esbjerg is as new as Ribe is old, once just a few farms until Esbjerg harbour was established in 1868. When fish stocks ran out, Denmark's youngest city reinvented itself as the country's main base for offshore oil and gas extraction. More recently, around 80% of Europe's offshore wind turbines come from its factories. Though chiefly of note for its ferry to Fanø, Esbjerg has enough for visitors to linger either side of the crossing.

Designed by Danish architect Jørn Utzon, **Musikhuset** is the city's main venue for cultural events as well as being home to the modern-art collection of the **Esbjerg Kunstmuseum** *(eskum.dk; 90kr, under-18s free)*. Next door, the handsome **Vandtårn** (water tower), built in 1897 but designed to be medieval in appearance, can be climbed for sweeping views of the port.

Fiskeri- og Søfartsmuseet *(Fisheries & Maritime Museum; fimus.dk; 175kr, under-18s free)* 4km northwest of the city has saltwater tanks teeming with local marine species, seal-feeding sessions (twice daily at 11am and 2.30pm) and **boat trips** in summer. Opposite is Esbjerg's most iconic landmark, **Mennesket ved Havet** *('Man Meets the Sea'):* four stark white, 9m-high, stylised human figures gazing out at the ships coming in and out of the harbour.

Fanø

TIME FROM RIBE: **1 HR** 

North Sea island haven

In just 12 minutes, industrial Esbjerg yields to the enticing island of Fanø, 56 sq km of beaches, dunes, heath and marshland, with two idyllic village settlements in **Nordby** and **Sønderho**. The ferry *(fanoelinjen.dk)* docks in Nordby, a strollable maze of sweet thatched-roof houses, blooming gardens and cobblestone streets lined with boutiques and cafes.

Hugely popular in summer, it attracts families and water-sports fans for the flat sandy beaches which are up to a kilometre wide in places. The best spot for bathers is between **Rindby Strand** and **Fanø Bad**, Denmark's first seaside resort opened in the 1890s. Further north is the vast sand spit, **Søren Jessens Sand**. South of Rindby, the beach is full of windsurfers, kitesurfers and blokarts. Get involved with **Club Fanø**

EATING & DRINKING IN ESBJERG: OUR PICKS

Industrien: Gastropub that mixes live music and late nights with mini burgers and cocktails. Try the gin variety. *5pm-2am Thu-Sat* **€€**

Sand's Restauration: Century-old spot serving Danish classics, paired with snaps (a shot of local akvavit). *11.30am-9pm Mon-Sat* **€€**

Dronning Louise: Restaurant, pub and club in one. Dine on sandwiches and steaks. Brunch served until 4pm. *10am-midnight* **€€**

Café Guldægget: Choice spot on the main square for breakfast pastries, coffee and smørrebrød. *7.30am-5pm Mon-Fri, 9am-4pm Sat* **€**

Blåvandshuk Fyr

(*clubfanoe.dk*), a company that hires various wind-powered vehicles designed for speed over the hard-packed sand. The outfit also organises **seal-spotting safaris** at Sønderho, where you can hike out for a mile or so at low tide to watch pods of seals basking on sandbanks. You might see common seals or the much heftier grey seal (males can weigh 300kg). A more leisurely way to spot them is aboard the **M/S Martha** (*marthasonderho.dk; adult/child 200/100kr*), which sails from Nordby's tiny marina out to **Langli**, an uninhabited island a few kilometres north of Fanø.

Blåvand

TIME FROM RIBE: 1 HR

Denmark's western edge

Head northwest from Esbjerg and you'll reach the appealing seaside community of **Blåvand**. Up on the dunes is **Blåvandshuk Fyr**, a 19th-century lighthouse with viewing deck that marks Denmark's most westerly promontory. **Blåvand Strand**, the beach running east of the lighthouse, is a beauty, with calm waters for kid-friendly swimming. Get out your phone to take photos of the curious beach 'wildlife': the **bunker mules** are WWII relics transformed by a British artist into equine form. It's a wily metaphor: the mule, unable to reproduce, symbolises an end to war.

ISLAND LIFE ON FANØ

Jakob Sullestad is the owner of Sønderho Kro, a traditional inn on Fanø.

Fanø is a creative, close-knit island with strong ties to the past. Every June in Nordby we celebrate Fannikerdagene, a folk festival where we honour the island's cultural heritage with costumes, dances and a traditional wedding.

If you come you should also experience our nature up close by setting out on foot or by bike, and don't forget those small stops along the way, such as a beer at the Fanø Bryghus. Micro-producers in Fanø have won awards for their quality produce, which you can taste at many of the island's restaurants and farm shops. And don't miss vibrant Sønderho, Denmark's most beautiful village. Historic houses, a natural harbour, special views over the water – it's a must.

EATING & DRINKING IN FANØ: ISLAND FAVOURITES

Sønderho Kro: Acclaimed restaurant showcasing local and seasonal specialities in a historic space. *noon-2.30pm, 6-8.30pm* €€€

HAVEN Fanø: Brunch on sandwiches, salads and sharing boards made with the island's own artisanal produce. Good coffee. *10am-3pm Mon-Sat* €

Slagter Christiansen: Nordby butcher known for its Fanø ham. Packed with local gourmet produce. *9am-5pm Mon-Fri, 8.30am-1.30pm Sat* €

Fanø Bryghus: Excellent craft brewery in Nordby. A resident food truck whips up tasty focaccia sandwiches and fries. *11am-10pm* €

FESTIVALS IN SOUTHERN JUTLAND

Rømø Motor Festival: *(romo motorfestival.dk)* Watch vintage hot rod cars and motorcycles race on Rømø's wide sandy beaches in summer. The festival originally ran from 1919 to 1924 and was reinstated in 2016.

Fanø International Kite Fliers: *(visitfanoe.dk/en/fanoe-the-island-of-kites)* Fanø hosts a photogenic kite festival in mid-June, when thousands of kites in all shapes and colours fill the skies over the epic sweep of beach lining the the west coast.

Tønder Festival: *(tf.dk)* Founded in 1974 and now regarded as one of the best folk music festivals in Europe, this four-day August event draws some 20,000 music fans. Expect to hear genres like Americana, bluegrass, Celtic and Nordic folk.

War on the shore

This corner of the coast was a strong point along Nazi Germany's 'Atlantic Wall' of coastal defences, and you can still find dozens of bunkers half-sunk in the sand. A patch of dunes near Blåvand Strand was only fully cleared of landmines in 2012. **Army of Concrete**, an exhibition at the superb **Tirpitz Museum** *(tirpitz.dk; 160kr, under-18s free)* just inland, puts a human face on life in the bunkers. The subterranean museum, designed by the celebrated Bjarke Ingels Group, is itself built into a bunker designed to house a Nazi mega cannon that could blow up battleships 55km away. Thankfully the war ended before it fired a shot. The museum also contains a beautiful collection of amber found along Jutland's shores, while **West Coast Stories** presents the saga of the coast from the Stone Age to the present. Don't miss the half-hourly '4D show' that brings the exhibition to life in stunning fashion.

In 2022, another spectacular Bjarke Ingels–designed museum opened. About 15km north of Tirpitz, **FLUGT – Refugee Museum of Denmark** *(flugtmuseum.dk; 160kr, under-18s free)* is housed in what was the country's largest refugee camp, taking in 35,000 German civilians who fled across the border towards the end of WWII. An innovative 5km-long audio walk transports visitors back in time to recreate a sense of the camp in what is now peaceful woodland. Inside the main buildings, half the exhibitions are about life in the camp, while the other half focus on refugee crises around the globe, giving a voice and face to those forced to flee their homes. It's an emotive, thought-provoking experience.

Rømø

TIME FROM RIBE: **30 MINS**

Whale bones and blokarts

A 10km causeway with road and bike lane connects the island of **Rømø** to the mainland. For most of the year it's windswept and sleepy, twice the size of Fanø but with far fewer residents. In summer, it swells with predominantly German tourists who gravitate to the wide, unbroken sand beach of the west coast.

Once across the causeway, continue straight to reach **Lakolk Strand**, the most popular holiday beach with huge campgrounds. Turn left instead and you'll eventually get to the main village of **Havneby**, passing the 18th-century **Rømø Kirke** with its maritime-themed interior and unique Greenlandic gravestones. In the southwest corner of the island, activity-rich **Sønderstrand** is a beach chock-full of cars, campers and wind-based racing vehicles like blokarts and kite landboards. **Rømø Adventures** *(romo-adventures.com)* offer instruction and hire.

The southernmost of the Wadden islands, Rømø has a range of nature activities, such as oyster safaris and seal-watching tours. Sign up at **Naturcenter Tønnisgaard** *(tonnisgaard.dk)*, but note that the tours are generally either in Danish or German.

The handsome thatched **Kommandørgården** *(natmus.dk; 60kr, under-18s free)*, 1.5km north of where the causeway joins the island, was the stately home of one of Rømø's

Horse riding, Sønderstrand

18th-century whaling captains. In the barn is the skeleton of a 13m-long sperm whale that stranded on the island in 1996.

Møgeltønder

TIME FROM RIBE: **50 MINS**

Village with royal pedigree

Despite its wee proportions, the tiny parish of **Møgeltønder**, less than 5km from the German border, has one of southern Jutland's largest churches: **Møgeltønder Kirke**, built around 1180. Inside the fresco-adorned interior is a baptismal font from 1200 and the oldest functioning church organ in Denmark. Check out the 'countess' bower', a balcony with private seating for the Schack family, who owned the church from 1661 until 1970.

East of the church, **Slotsgaden** is one of Jutland's prettiest streets, running for 400m to **Schackenborg Slot** *(schackenborg.dk)*, a 17th-century castle formerly home to Prince Joachim of Denmark. Check the website for info on guided tours and accommodation. From the castle grounds, you can pick up the looping 54km **Tønder Marsh Trail** *(toendermarsken.dk)*, if only for a short way to check out **Slotsfeltladen**, a historic barn to the south featuring Denmark's largest thatched roof – a truly fine head of hair.

For a royal feed, pop into **Schackenborg Slotskro**, a classy inn that dates from the 1680s. Halfway along Slotsgaden, **Mormors Lille Café** (Grandma's Little Cafe) is as cute as it sounds, serving old-school cakes and coffee.

The low-key town of Tønder 5km to the east has a treat in store for fans of Danish furniture. **Kunstmuseet i Tønder** *(msj.dk; 105kr, under-18s free)*, exhibits the chair creations of locally born Hans Wegner (1914–2007), one of Denmark's most famous furniture designers.

WEST COAST GOLD

If you go picking through the shallows on Jutland's west coast, you might strike gold and find a nugget of amber. A fossilised tree resin, amber was an important currency and trading commodity for early Danes. It comes from vast, extinct forests that spread across northern Europe 40 million years ago, and the west coast of Jutland has some of the largest deposits. Winter is the prime season for amber hunting, especially after a storm, as the rough seas churn up these precious nuggets. Amber is often found among seaweed, shells, and sometimes even under the watchful eyes of seagulls. The Tirpitz Museum displays some of Denmark's most stunning amber finds.

Kolding

ACTIVITY-RICH CASTLE | DESIGN MUSEUM | LAKESIDE STROLLS

GETTING AROUND

Kolding has excellent transport connections, with rapid rail links to most places in Jutland and east to Odense and Copenhagen.

Take bus 7 or 9 to get out to Trapholt from Kolding city centre. Buses leave from the bus station, which is next to Kolding train station. Bike hire is available at Kolding Hotel Apartments.

If you're driving into town, there's parking off Slotssøvejen, close to the library.

A small city with a crowd-pleasing mix of old and new, Kolding has two major drawcards in its hilltop castle and one of Jutland's best modern art and design museums. Visitors can find some outstanding hotels around town, and the old quarter is home to lively bars and restaurants, and one or two notable Renaissance buildings. Worthy modern additions include the town's library, Kolding Bibliotek, with its inviting chill-out spaces and art installations. Gastronomically, Kolding was an early pioneer of pizza in Denmark, and is known for its top-quality pizzerias.

The first castle in Kolding was built in 1268 to defend what was then Denmark's border at Kolding Fjord, the lands to the south ruled by the dukes of Schleswig. When King Christian III consolidated power in 1536, the former stronghold became a palace for the royal family in the west, and Kolding entered a new era of prosperity.

King of Kolding

Royal castle reborn

Standing proud over the lake, Kolding's showpiece castle was a smoking ruin after fire ravaged it in 1808. But **Koldinghus** *(kongernessamling.dk; 130kr, under-18s free)* rose from the ashes after a century of renewal that culminated in the award-winning work of architects Inger and Johannes Exner, who transformed the gutted south wing into a soaring architectural interplay of old and new – it really is a sight to behold. Spread over several wings, the castle is a delicious maze, crammed with fine oil paintings, gleaming jewels and exhibitions on the royal family. On summer weekends, costumed performers play music or act out period skits in various rooms. A generous array of **craft workshops** and dress-up activities keep kids entertained. Slog up to the top of the **tower** for panoramic views of the town and beyond to the mirror-like waters of Kolding Fjord.

Kolding's beautiful **Slotssøen** (castle lake) is a lovely place for a stroll. In **Kolding Bibliotek**, the town's inviting library,

TOP TIP

If you're not up for an icy dip in the fjord, there is an indoor swimming pool and waterpark, **SlotssøBadet**, by the castle lake.

HIGHLIGHTS
1 Koldinghus

SIGHTS
2 Slotssøen

ACTIVITIES, COURSES & TOURS
3 Kolding Bibliotek
4 SlotssøBadet

SLEEPING
5 Hotel Kolding
6 Kolding Hotel Apartments

EATING
7 Den Blå Bistro
● Madkælderen Koldinghus (see 1)
8 Rafaels

DRINKING & NIGHTLIFE
9 You'll Never Walk Alone Pub

look for the leaflet titled *Around the Lake*, which features a 3.5km guided walk taking in 16 sights. You can also download a PDF from *destinationtrekantomraadet.com*.

The Art of Design

Showcasing Danish creativity

Housed in another architectural wonder on Kolding's outskirts, **Trapholt** *(trapholt.dk; 140kr, under-18s free, closed Mondays)* is a terrific and capacious modern art museum showcasing everything from global art superstar installations to covetable mid-century furniture, including Denmark's largest collection of 20th-century chairs.

One of the museum's more intriguing exhibits is legendary Danish designer Arne Jacobsen's prefab summerhouse, **Kubeflex.** Standing outside on the museum's lawn, the innovative modular building is a prototype exhibited in 1970. Jacobsen died a year later and the summerhouse never went into production. Book a free 20-minute tour at Trapholt's information desk.

The museum's stylish restaurant, **Café Gustav Lind**, comes with gorgeous views of Kolding Fjord. If the water looks tempting enough for a dip, take a stroll down to **Badebroen Fjordvej**, a bathing area 15 minutes to the east along the water.

LIGHT SHOW

Every December, the **Kolding Light Festival** *(k-l-f.dk)* illuminates the town for three days, as public buildings and squares are transformed into light installations. The event attracts artists from across Denmark, who use the historic architecture as their canvas, bathing Koldinghus castle, the streets and the waterfront in colour and patterns. A Christmas market sets up along the cobbled streets.

EATING & DRINKING IN KOLDING: OUR PICKS

Rafaels: Kolding is famous in Denmark for its pizza joints, and Rafaels is one of the best in town. It also does pasta. *5-11pm Mon-Sat* €€

You'll Never Walk Alone: English-style boozer serving hearty pub grub paired with beers and big-screen football. *hours vary* €€

Den Blå Bistro: Fill up on French onion soup and steak frites at this grown-up bistro on a lively street. *11.30am-10pm* €€

Madkælderen Koldinghus: Upmarket restaurant housed in the atmospheric stone food cellar beneath Kolding's castle. *hours vary* €€€

Beyond Kolding

Head beyond town for more royal castles and the UNESCO-listed Christiansfeld, a religious settlement.

Places

You only have to travel 16km south from Kolding to reach one of Denmark's seven UNESCO World Heritage sites. The unerringly neat religious settlement of Christiansfeld, founded in 1773, was planned from the ground up as an egalitarian utopia. While the town probably won't blow your mind, it sets you up nicely to savour the more palatial lines at Gråsten Slot, the summer residence of the royal family, an hour south of Kolding by road or rail. Close by, the town of Sønderborg has its own splendid castle and acts as the gateway to Als, a low-key island with sheltered beaches and village vibes.

Christiansfeld

TIME FROM KOLDING: **30 MINS**

Piously perfect town

The planned 18th-century settlement of **Christiansfeld** was designed to represent the Protestant urban ideal, with parallel lines of homogenous, unadorned buildings centred on **Brødremenighedens Kirkeplads**, the church square. The democratic organisation of the Moravian Church (a nonconformist Lutheran congregation from Germany) is expressed here in its humanistic town planning – many of the residential buildings were communal. A good **visitor centre** stands across from **Salshuset**, the yellow stone church, and gives an overview of what makes this town special. Pick up a walking map that outlines the buildings and their functions, and sample the town's other claim to fame: delicious honey cake (*honningkage*).

Gråsten

TIME FROM KOLDING: **1 HR 5 MINS**

Regal summer retreat

For three weeks each summer, the sleepy town of Gråsten is abuzz when now-abdicated Queen Margrethe heads for some R&R at her summer residence, **Gråsten Slot**. When they're not staying, the lovely palace garden and richly adorned chapel is open to the public. The garden's seasonal closing times vary, from 4.30pm in winter to 8pm in summer. With a charming lakeside aspect on the banks of Slotssø, the palace was built in the mid-16th century but destroyed by fire on multiple occasions. In 1842, the main building you see today was con-

GETTING AROUND

From Kolding, you can make the short trip to Christiansfeld on buses 134 or 900X. Trains between Kolding and Sønderborg (1 hour, 20 minutes) stop at Gråsten en route. Buses 110 and 223 cover the 16km between Gråsten and Sønderborg.

For island-hoppers there are ferries connecting Fynshav on Als' east coast to the island of Ærø (*aeroe-ferry.dk*), and Bøjden on Funen (*alslinjen.dk*).

TRABANTOS/SHUTTERSTOCK ©

Royal chapel, Gråsten Slot

structed, and in 1935, the rights to the castle were handed to the royal family.

The best way to check whether the royals are in residence is to ask around (including at local tourist offices) or check online for royal family activity *(kongehuset.dk)*. In summer, signs are posted on the garden gates indicating the dates when the site is closed to the public.

Sønderborg

TIME FROM KOLDING: **1 HR 20 MINS**

War and peace

Sønderborg, nestled on both sides of the Als Sound, has a contemporary feel despite its medieval origins, thanks in part to some tasteful waterfront regeneration since the 2010s. In the mid-12th century, Valdemar I (Valdemar the Great) erected a castle fortress along the waterfront, and the town has since spread out from there. **Sønderborg Slot** *(msj.dk; 105kr, under-18s free)* is rich in lore, and nowadays it houses a museum of regional history as well as paintings from the Danish 'Golden Age'.

To some degree, the town has shaped Denmark, acting as the battleground for two wars against Germany in the mid-19th century. At the **Historiecenter Dybbøl Banke** *(1864.dk; adult/child 140/80kr)* you can get a glimpse into the bloody war of 1864 through demonstrations and storytelling. Close by, **Dybbøl Mølle** *(1864.dk; adult/child 60/30kr)* is a windmill that has been bombed twice and now stands as a revered national symbol. Exhibits cover the mill's history and explain the symbolism of the site.

Als well that ends well

Separated from Jutland by the narrow Als Sund, the island of Als is relatively untouched by large-scale tourism, and makes a good region for tranquil drives or bike trips (bus schedules can be erratic). Down south is where the best beaches lie (nice and sheltered – locals recommend the Kegnæs peninsula); up the

QUEEN MARGRETHE TAKES A BOW

In early 2024, Queen Margrethe II made history by becoming the first Danish monarch in nearly 900 years to abdicate. After a reign of 52 years, she stepped down on 14 January, 2024, citing long-term health issues and a desire to hand over to the next generation. Her eldest son, Crown Prince Frederik, took the throne as King Frederik X. Before her own ascension in 1972, Denmark had only ever had kings on the throne, but Queen Margrethe overcame initial scepticism to become a beloved figure in Danish society. Well loved for her sharp intellect, artistic flair and approachable manner, she is a polyglot and accomplished artist, even illustrating the Danish edition of Tolkien's *The Lord of the Rings*.

SOUTHERN-STYLE EATS

On your travels in the south, keep cash handy for roadside stalls selling farm-fresh produce like *jordbær* (strawberries) and *kartofler* (potatoes). The south has quality regional produce including *marsklam* (marsh-grazing lamb) and super seafood like mussels and oysters, which you can forage for yourself if you sign up for an oyster safari at the **Vadehavscentret** (Wadden Sea Visitor Centre; p189). Don't pass up the chance to indulge in a traditional cake buffet known as the *sønderjysk kaffebord* (southern Jutland 'coffee table'). Look out for *brødtorte*, a delicious layer cake made with rye bread.

Augustenborg Slot

east coast you'll encounter engaging little villages. **Augustenborg**, 10km northeast of Sønderborg along Rte 8 (take bus 223 or 224), is one of Als' more easily accessible and interesting villages – stop to wander around the gardens (including a sculpture park) of the grand yellow-and-white **Augustenborg Slot**.

Camping grounds are everywhere, heaving in summer with Danes and Germans, and there are also numerous holiday homes for rent, as well as B&Bs.

Padborg

TIME FROM KOLDING: **45 MINS**

Prisoners of war

The town of **Padborg** (population 4500), right by the German border, is the site of Frøslevlejren, an internment camp opened near the end of WWII following negotiations with Germany to keep Danish POWs in Denmark. During its nine months in operation, Frøslev held 12,000 prisoners.

Frøslevlejrens Museum *(froeslevlejren.dk; 75kr, under-18s free, closed Mondays)* tells fascinating stories of the Danish Resistance movement and daily prison life at Frøslev. If you've visited other German-run wartime camps, you're in for a surprise here: Frøslev had ample food, no torture and no executions (prisoners were even allowed one visitor per month). The only real horror was the threat of deportation across the border. Despite an agreement to keep Danish POWs in Denmark, some 1600 were deported to concentration camps in Germany.

Frøslevlejren is 4km northwest of Padborg Station.

EATING & DRINKING IN SØNDERBORG: OUR PICKS

Kislings: Stylish main-street cafe with a garden that serves super coffee and light bites. *8am-6pm Mon-Sat* €

Syttende: Modern Danish fine dining with a Michelin star. On the 17th floor of the riverside Alsik Hotel. *5pm-midnight Tue-Sat* €€€

Fox and Hounds: Cosy Scotland-inspired pub that serves game burgers, lamb stew and a large selection of whiskies. *5-11pm or later, Mon-Sat* €€

Bella Italia: Family-run trattoria that doles out big bowls of pasta and excellent thin-crust pizza, alongside veal, lamb and Italian wines. *5-9.30pm* €€

Places We Love to Stay

€ Budget €€ Midrange €€€ Top End

Ribe
p184

Danhostel Ribe € Skyline views, quiet location and a short walk into the old centre. Bike hire available. Occasional rambunctious school groups.

Hotel Dagmar €€ Billed as the oldest hotel in Denmark, Dagmar comes with sloping floors and cathedral views. Charming old-world tiling, artworks and antiques.

Weis Stue (p187) **€€** Eight small, wonky rooms above Ribe's oldest inn, all with creaking floorboards and bags of character. Shared bathrooms.

Den Gamle Arrest €€ Former jailhouse right on the main square opposite the cathedral. Bright, simple guest rooms, some using the old cells.

Hotel Backhaus €€ Cosy rooms plus restaurant in a quaint townhouse 100m from the cathedral. Good-value singles.

Ribe Byferie Resort €€€ Roomy self-catering apartments in a quiet holiday 'village' a ten-minute walk south of the centre. Rents out bikes and canoes.

Esbjerg
p190

Danhostel Esbjerg € Hostel in a grand old building with top-notch facilities 3km northwest of the centre. Rooms in newer wing have private bathrooms.

Cabinn Esbjerg € Denmark-wide chain offering tiny but functional rooms in a prime inner-city location. Just about the best value in town.

Hjerting Badehotel €€€ Delightful and luxurious, this century-old 'bathing hotel' is 10km northwest of town facing a wonderful stretch of beach. Classic old-school Danish hospitality.

Fanø
p190

Hotel Fanø Bad €€ Thatched inn set in former farm buildings on the outskirts of Nordby. Has a restaurant, cafe, lounge bar and small gym.

Sønderho Kro €€€ Known throughout Denmark, this 1722 thatched-roof slice of hyggelig heaven is the best place to stay on Fanø. Acclaimed restaurant in a steeped-in-time dining room.

Fanø Krogaard €€€ Historic inn on the Nordby waterfront renovated to a high standard in 2020. Cosy antique rooms and a large sunny terrace.

Rømø
p192

First Camp Lakolk Strand € Huge, family-friendly beachside campground set amid the sand dunes. Comes with all requisite facilities, plus cabins for rent.

Marsk Camp €€ Opened in 2022, this elegant glamping centre is actually on the mainland, 3km east of the Rømø causeway. Look for the unique sculptural tower.

Enjoy Resorts Rømø €€€ Not skimping on the creature comforts, this high-end resort of family holiday homes has a golf course, wellness centre and restaurant.

Kolding
p194

Hotel Kolding €€ Modern, business-like rooms in a super central location next to Kolding's swish library.

Kolding Hotel Apartments €€ Appealing lakeside complex of contemporary apartments set in wacky three-storey buildings. Parking costs extra.

Hotel Koldingfjord €€€ Grand, castle-like estate (a former sanatorium) out past Trapholt. Restful Scandi minimalism comes with first-class facilities including an indoor pool, cafe, restaurant and free bike hire.

Sønderborg
p197

Danhostel Sønderborg City € A classy budget offering, but dorm beds are available only from June to August. A 15-minute walk north of the town centre.

Hotel Bella Italia €€ Smart boutique hotel with stylish, crisply-decorated rooms and the added benefit of a popular Italian restaurant.

Alsik Hotel & Spa €€€ Tasteful Nordic design rules at this luxe tower hotel on the revitalised waterfront. Outdoor pools, sweeping views and a Michelin-starred restaurant.

For places to stay in Aarhus, Central & Northern Jutland, see p241

Above: Vestre Søbad, Silkeborg (p215); Right: Løkken (p238)

Aarhus, Central & Northern Jutland

PRISTINE COUNTRYSIDE, EPIC DUNES, BRILLIANT MUSEUMS

Denmark's largest region has some startlingly epic scenery, with fjords, forests and endless, dune-backed coastlines.

Welcome to Denmark's most varied region, with forests, dunes and lakes, a landscape wrought by ice, sand and time, where a slow pace and old-fashioned hospitality is the order of the day. Western Denmark only joined the eastern islands by bridge in 1998, and Jutland's bridge to Funen was built just over 50 years ago; before the bridges, the mainland (Jutland) was only connected by ferry. Jutlanders stem from hardy fishing and farming stock, and are proud of what sets them apart from urban Danes. Theirs is a world of windswept dunes, boat-packed harbours, glittering lakes and thatch-roofed villages, scenes that have inspired centuries of Danish art. This is also homeland to the world's most famous plastic blocks: Lego was born in Billund and is one of the region's biggest draws. Theme-park Legoland and play palace Lego House are a treat for kids of all ages. Between the exposed west coast – where surfers don wetsuits to ride North Sea waves – and the more sheltered east coast lie neat acres of farmland punctuated by the hills and forests of the Lake District, Rebild Bakker, Rold Skov and the Djursland peninsula. Here the Vikings left their mark at sites like Hobro's huge ring fortress and Aalborg's remarkable Viking cemetery. At sleepy, unassuming Jelling, relics of universal value reveal how the Danes turned to Christianity and modern Denmark was born. Add top-notch museums, the understated cool of Aarhus and up-and-coming Aalborg, and you'll understand why Copenhagen shouldn't be your only Danish destination.

THE MAIN AREAS

AARHUS
Denmark's culture-rich second city. **p206**

BILLUND
Capital of Children and home of Lego. **p219**

AALBORG
Museums and waterfront architecture. **p225**

SKAGEN
Art, sand and Danish high society. **p233**

Find Your Way

Central and northern Jutland encompass the lion's share of mainland Denmark. We've picked out the places that hold special appeal for travellers and can also serve as access points for deeper exploration.

CAR

Your own wheels allow freedom to stay at campsites and remote guesthouses – and explore Jutland's coastline. Roads are in great condition, traffic is light, and car-charging infrastructure is relatively well-developed. Electric cars get double the free parking time. For car-charging info, see *elbilviden.dk*.

TRAIN

The region is fairly well connected by rail, though you'll need to go by road if travelling in northwest Jutland. Billund (for Legoland) has no rail connection, but a good network of buses. The best website for planning rail travel around the area is *rejseplanen.dk*.

BUS

Most large towns and cities in the region are connected by bus, while summer sees seasonal bus services spring up in holiday hot spots. Airport buses are timed to sync with international departures and arrivals at Billund, Aarhus and Aalborg.

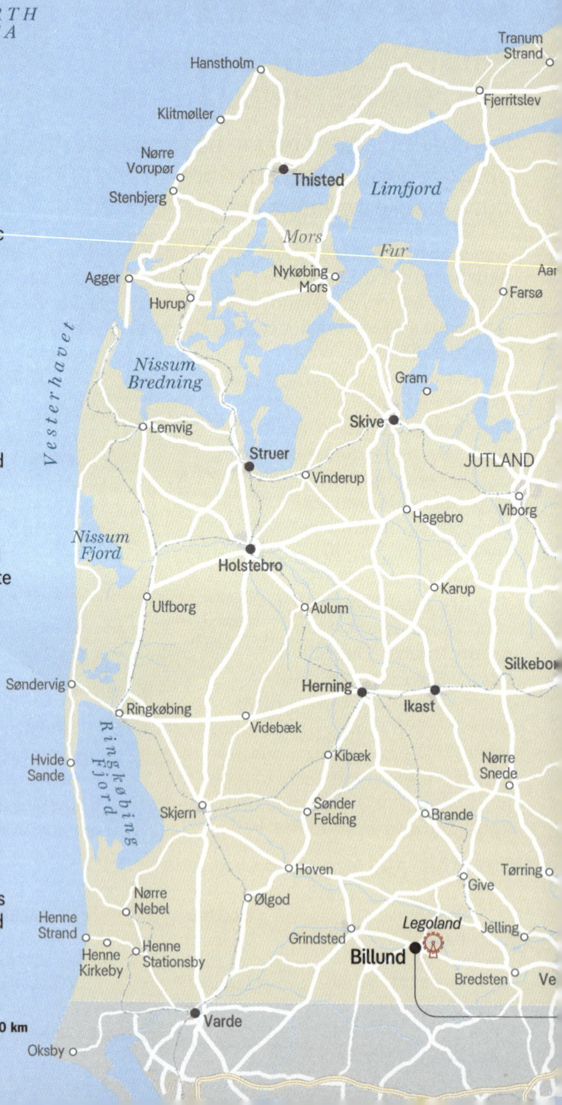

Skagen, p233
This far-flung, sand-edged fishing and holiday town popularised by the royals holds a place in the heart of Danes, immortalised by its 19th-century artist colony.
Aalborg, p225
This tranquil city is the gateway to Jutland's north, mixing striking, modern waterfront architecture with gems from the past.
Aarhus, p206
Denmark's youthful second city is like a mini-Copenhagen, with world-class museums and galleries, waterside fun and fabulous dining options.
Billund, p219
It's all about the kids, with Legoland and Lego House, plus Lalandia Water Park, and other family-friendly sights in the vicinity.
Skagen
Gammel Skagen
Kandestederne
Hirtshals
Ålbæk
Tornby
Sindal
Lønstrup
Hjørring
Frederikshavn
Østervrå
Sæby
Vesterø Havn
Læsø
Østerby Havn
Byrum
SWEDEN
Brønderslev
Hjallerup
Aabybro
Asaa
Nørresundby
Aalborg
Nibe
Hals
Støvring
Skørping
Rold Skov
Aalborg Bugt
Hadsund
Assens
Hobro
Mariager
Kattegat
Anholt
Handest
Fjellerup
Bønnerup
Cjerrild
Randers
Auning
Nimtofte
Grenaa
Bjerringbro
Djursland
Rønde
Tirstrup
Kalø Vig
Dråby
Ebeltoft
Lake District
Aarhus
Moesgaard Museum
Gammel Rye
Ry
Boes
Mossø
Skanderborg
ZEALAND
Odder
Hou
Sælvig
Horsens
Samsø
Ballen
Snaptun
Kolby Kås
Endelave
Juelsminde
Vejle Fjord
Fredericia
FUNEN

Plan Your Time

This region covers a wide area, so unless you have your own wheels it makes sense to base yourself somewhere central (eg Aarhus or Aalborg) and plan shorter trips from there.

BIGDANE/SHUTTERSTOCK ©

The 'sand worm', Grenen (p235)

If You Only Do One Thing

- Make for Aarhus, Denmark's second city, small, yet packed with sights, museums, galleries and more. Get high with a rainbow stroll on the roof of the **ARoS Aarhus Kunstmuseum** (p206) and experience its new underground wing. If the sky's clear, see harbour views from **Aarhus Øje** (p210), then delve into the past at **Den Gamle By** (p211), an incredible 'living museum' of Danish history, where reconstructed historic houses are brought to life by costumed actors and volunteers.

- Browse the boutiques and cafes of the cobblestoned **Latin Quarter** (p208), or hire a bike and head to **Moesgård** (p213) for deer-filled forests and sheltered beaches. Make sure you have time for the **Moesgaard Museum** (p212), a high-tech, hands-on wonder of prehistorical knowledge.

Seasonal Highlights

In summer this region comes into its own. Many places wind down later, but Aarhus and Aalborg hold year-round appeal.

APRIL

Spring weather sees theme parks, zoos and other outdoor attractions open up again after hibernation.

MAY

Late May is party time in **Aalborg**, when the biggest Carnival celebrations in northern Europe, including a grand parade, samba into gear.

JUNE

A great travel time, with sunny skies and fewer crowds than the midsummer peak. The Riverboat Jazz Festival comes to Silkenborg in the **Lake District**.

3 Days to Travel Around

● Zero in on Jutland's north by spending a few hours in **Aalborg** (p225), visiting its art museum and wandering the reborn waterfront, before crossing the Limfjord to **Lindholm Høje** (p227), Europe's biggest Viking burial ground. Make your way up the coast to **Løkken** (p238) for surfing and saunas, then hike over wild dune cliffs to **Rubjerg Knude** (p237) and its famous lighthouse, which was moved to avoid collapse into the sea.

● Finish up in Skagen to admire the evocative art on display at **Skagens Museum** (p233) and **Anchers Hus** (p234). Hire a bike and pedal out to the iconic **sand-covered church** (p236) – and don't leave without walking or taking the 'sand worm' tractor-bus to **Grenen** (p235), Denmark's northern limit.

If You Have More Time

● Start in **Billund** (p219) to nurture your inner child (and entertain your own children) at Legoland and Lego House. Stop for a crash course in Danish history at **Jelling** (p222) before finding your way to the beautiful **Lake District** (p214). Bike, hike and swim your heart out, take a boat trip on the world's oldest paddle steamer, then rest up in **Aarhus** (p206) for art, museums, fine Nordic cuisine and all-round buzz.

● Continue north to **Aalborg** (p225) to see a city in transformation, stopping at the extraordinary nuclear bunker, **REGAN Vest** (p229), on the way (having booked ahead), then head for the windswept northwest coast's idyllic beaches and surf spots en route to arty **Skagen** (p233), at Denmark's most northerly point.

JULY

Midsummer is peak holiday season for Danes, so expect campsites and hotels to be full-to-bursting. Book well ahead.

AUGUST

August sees an influx of Scandinavian fun-seekers, adding to crowds. The **Aarhus Festival** in late August features 10 days of cultural events.

SEPTEMBER

With summer over, the crowds depart – a good time for windsurfing and kiteboarding in coastal resorts like **Hvide Sande**.

DECEMBER

Cosy Christmas markets spring up everywhere. Seasonal family attractions like **Legoland** (p221) reopen for a brief burst of festive fun.

Aarhus

ART & CULTURE | GREAT MUSEUMS | GLORIOUS GASTRONOMY

Buzzing with students, vibrant, creative and full of gastronomic dining experiences, Denmark's second city is small but it packs in the attractions of a much bigger city. Aarhus (*oar*-hus) also goes by the nickname 'Smilets By' (City of Smiles), a slogan adopted in the 1930s that has stuck around – so nothing to do with those happiness indexes, even if Aarhus does tend to come out on top.

The city's earliest origins were in the Viking settlement of Aros ('mouth of the river'), roughly where the cathedral is today. Medieval Aarhus was more a city of frowns, wedged between feuding states and raiding tribes, but stability ensued from the 1500s and Aarhus flourished as a centre of trade, art and religion. In the 1930s, the city filled in its river and some questionable city planning saw a multilane road and fenced-in rail track block access to the waterfront. Thankfully the river was reclaimed in 1958, the road narrowed, and every year there are new attractions added.

As with elsewhere in Denmark, you can swim close to the city, and there are eating and drinking options plus fun activities along the waterfront.

GETTING AROUND

Aarhus' centre is compact and walkable, though you might want to use bike-share to reach the 'Lighthouse' (around 30 minutes' walk from the centre). If you don't plan on cycling (or driving) to sights beyond the centre, make use of Aarhus' extensive local bus network. Bus 18 runs out to Moesgaard Museum; buy tickets on board or by using the Midttrafik app. The Aarhus light rail (Letbane) has handy stops at Dokk1 and Risskov Strandpark for Den Permanente bathing beach.

TOP TIP

You can get to most city hot spots on foot, but to speed things up or go further afield, hook up with bike-share scheme Donkey Republic. Download the app to rent a bright-orange bike from locations around the city.

The Rainbow Over Aarhus

Aarhus' great contemporary art museum

The **ARoS Aarhus Kunstmuseum** *(aros.dk; adult/child 180kr/free)* is a great art museum before you even consider its magical rainbow crown – a technicolour walkway that's the work of Danish-Icelandic artist Olafur Eliasson. Topping the redbrick gallery, Eliasson's *Your Rainbow Panorama* is a 150m-long looping skywalk of multicoloured glass from which you can soak up dreamy, Kodak-filtered panoramas of the city – it's a wonderful thing to do, rain or shine.

Inside, the spiralling white architecture has NY Guggenheim vibes, and the art doesn't disappoint. *Boy* (1999) is perhaps

SIGHTS
1 Aarhus Domkirke
2 Aarhus Rådhus
3 ARoS Aarhus Kunstmuseum
4 Botanisk Have
5 Den Gamle By
6 Dokk1

SLEEPING
7 City Hotel Oasia Aarhus
8 SOFS Boutique Hotel
9 Villa Provence

EATING
10 Aarhus Street Food
11 Emmerys
12 Frankies Pizza Mejlgade
13 Greenilicious
14 Klassisk 65 Bistro & Vinbar
15 OliNico
16 Plant Food
17 Pondus
18 Restaurant Hærværk
19 St Pauls Apothek
20 Surdejspizzeria

DRINKING & NIGHTLIFE
21 ÅBEN Aarhus
22 La Cabra Coffee
23 Løve's Bog- & VinCafé
24 LYNfabrikken
25 Under Masken

ENTERTAINMENT
26 Institut for (X)
27 Musikhuset Aarhus
28 Øst for Paradis
29 Radar
30 Train
31 VoxHall & Atlas

SHOPPING
● ARoS Aarhus Kunstmuseum Store (see 3)
32 Flagstang Markeder
● Magpie Lane Vintage (see 8)
33 Salling
34 Vintage Divine

NUCLEAR POWER? NO THANKS!

Stroll down hip Vestergarde near Vor Frue Kirke (Our Lady Church) and you can't miss it: a mural of a grinning red sun on yellow background with the words: *Atomkraft? Nej Tak* – 'Nuclear Power? No Thanks'. The cheery image, known as the **Smiling Sun**, was designed in 1975 by Aarhus activist Anne Lund and became world-famous in the late 1970s and 1980s. Millions of Smiling Sun badges were sold in dozens of languages, the proceeds going to fund the anti-nuclear-power movement. Aarhus' activists were also instrumental in influencing Denmark's decision to rule out nuclear power plants in its future energy plans.

the most striking work here, an astonishingly lifelike sculpture of a crouching child by Australian artist Ron Mueck – his vulnerability is incredibly vivid, as the work is 5m tall. The basement is full of fun installations, including by Eliasson and American artist James Turrell.

In 2025, a new extension will open called the Next Level. It will feature a permanent artwork by Turrell entitled *The Dome, a Skyspace* in a circular indoor space. The new area includes an underground gallery devoted to contemporary art, and a public art square. You'll want to allow at least half a day here, or make an evening of it: ARoS opens until 9pm on weekdays (closed Mondays).

The Colourful Latin Quarter

Stroll through boho Aarhus

The Aarhus **Latin Quarter** (Latinerkvarteret) is a kernel of cobbled streets, lined by mustard-yellow and ochre-tiled-roof buildings. It's the city's prettiest district, with independent boutiques, cute cafes and creative bistros all competing for your attention. Comprising part of the city's old Viking core, this central area extends north and west from Aarhus Cathedral.

History hunters can dig up some handsome half-timbered merchant houses, especially along narrow **Mejlgade**. If you're headed westwards, make for idyllic **Møllestien**, a picture-book cobblestone street of pastel-hued cottages and rambling roses.

Denmark's Tallest Church

Views, music and frescoes

The tall, pointed tower of **Aarhus Cathedral** *(Aarhus Domkirke; aarhusdomkirke.dk)*, Denmark's longest and tallest church, is a city landmark. The original Romanesque chapel at the eastern end dates from the 12th century, while most of the rest of the church is 15th-century Gothic.

The whitewashed interior has surviving pre-Reformation frescoes, including a 1497 likeness of St George, where an almost cartoonish dragon lies on its back, vanquished by the saint, as its young snarl in a nearby cave – proof of the regeneration of evil. There's a stunning gilt altarpiece dating from 1479 by late-Gothic German sculptor Bernt Notke – it can be folded in five different ways to display different narratives, according to the time of year.

You can climb the **tower** *(closed during services; adult/child 20/5kr)* for a view over the city rooftops. There are also regular concerts held in the church; check the website for listings.

EATING IN AARHUS: BUDGET

Aarhus Street Food: Sprawling hive of global food-truck fare and bars in an old bus garage. Many dishes under 100kr. *11.30am-9pm* €

OliNico: Laid-back vibe, huge *moules-frites* (mussels and fries) portions, 175kr dinners. *noon-2pm & 5.30-9pm Mon-Sat, 5.30-9pm Sun* €

Plant Food: Vegan hangout in the Latin Quarter serving quinoa bowls and plant-based burgers. *noon-8.30pm* €

Surdejspizzeria: Excellent Neapolitan pizza at this friendly place, where you cut slices with scissors. *4-9pm Mon-Fri, noon-10pm Sat & Sun* €

Møllestien

PARTY IN AARHUS

Youthful Aarhus, with up to 44,500 students during term-time, loves a night out. Drinkers gravitate to the **Latin Quarter** for wine bars and hip hangouts; **Frederiksgade** for boisterous pubs and live jams; and **Frederiksbjerg** for craft cocktails and brewpubs. To drink like a local, get an 'Aarhus Set': a Ceres Top beer with a chaser of liquorice-like Arnbitter – both were originally created in Aarhus. And Aarhus has arguably the country's best music scene. Aside from the eclectic offerings of **Musikhuset Aarhus** and live-music events of venues like **Train**, you can easily find music in more intimate venues like **Radar** or **VoxHall**. Excellent arthouse cinema **Øst for Paradis** has a multilevel, suitably cinephile bar.

Design-God Town Hall

Mid-century modern icon

The grey-marble-clad Aarhus City Hall, the **Aarhus Rådhus**, codesigned by pioneer of Danish modernism Arne Jacobsen, was completed in 1942; it almost didn't have a clock tower until Aarhus' citizens looked at the plans and found them lacking.

You can pop inside to admire the clean lines, parquet floors and vintage elevators, or sign up for one of the weekly guided tours on Saturdays at 11.30am with **Aarhus Guiderne** *(aarhusguiderne.dk; adult/child 125/50kr)*.

Explore the Reborn Waterfront

Harbour transformed

Cut off from the city by a four-lane road and fencing for the railway, Aarhus harbour began redevelopment in 2010. The new layout was shaped by who else but Denmark's favourite architects, BIG.

Start your discovery of this exciting post-industrial area at **Dokk1** *(dokk1.dk)*, which houses Scandinavia's largest library. Here you will find hyggelig reading nooks, outdoor play areas for kids and a cafe, plus regional tourist information.

From there, head along the waterfront towards **Bassin 7**. Here there's **AWC** *(awc.co.uk; 1hr cable 300dk, 1½hr sauna 100dk)*,

EATING IN AARHUS: COSY CHOICES

Frankies Pizza Mejlgade: A young party crowd packs in for well-charred pizzas and cocktails by the jug. *4.30-11pm* €

Greenilicious: Bright riverside cafe (ground floor Magasin mall) for breakfast bowls, wraps, soups, salads with fresh ingredients. *10am-8pm* €

Frederikshøj: Michelin-starred, forest setting and gastronomic wizardry from Beirut-born Wassim Hallal. Booking essential. *6pm-midnight Wed-Sat* €€€

Klassisk 65 Bistro & Vinbar: Locals flock here for the prized hygge and a Danish spin on French country cooking. *5-11pm* €€

BEST SHOPPING

Salling: Central department store on the pedestrian street, with a good gourmet section and all the big local brands. Its rooftop garden has city views, a vertiginous viewpoint and cafe.

ARoS Aarhus Kunstmuseum Store: The ARoS gift shop has an extensive range of art books, homeware, accessories and nifty knick-knacks.

Flagstang Markeder: Scour Aarhus' monthly flea market for treasure; check the website for dates.

Magpie Lane Vintage: Treasures from retro wardrobes in great condition and with a fine range of accessories and clothing for men and women.

Vintage Divine: Another of Aarhus' great vintage shops, especially for dresses, shoes and accessories for special occasions.

KENNETH BAGGE JORGENSEN/SHUTTERSTOCK ©

Aarhus Øje (far right of image)

a gnarly wakeboarding park that uses a cable pulley to haul riders over jumps, after which you can have a sauna. There's also SUP rental and a Bjarke Ingels Group–designed **Harbour Bath** *(aarhus.dk/havnebadet; summer only; free)*, which is an enclosed sea-swimming area. Take it all in by climbing up the sculptural observation tower on the water's edge.

Bus 23 runs out this way, you can cycle or it's a 20-minute walk from the cathedral.

Panoramas from Aarhus' Skyscraper

Vast views from the Aarhus Øje (Eye)

Aarhus Øje, *(Aarhus Eye; aarhusoeje.dk; adult/child 149/79kr)* aka the Lighthouse, is a lone skyscraper on Aarhus' formerly industrial island. An anomaly at 142m and with 43 floors of glass and steel, Denmark's tallest building is designed by 3XN and houses expensive apartments. You can take a lift to the top, where the views are expansive but pricy for a five-minute visit. Included is an interesting exhibition on the harbour, for which you need to download an app and scan QR codes (handsets are available at reception). There's a restaurant as well, so the best way to see the view is to eat there.

The structure stands on around 1700 piles, including 28 concrete ones, 70m deep.

EATING IN AARHUS: BASSIN 7

Skovmøllen Ø: Superb spot with smørrebrød (open sandwiches) and fine dining. *11.30am-5pm daily, 6-10pm Thu, to 11pm Fri & Sat* €€

Bistro le Bleu: Classy French bistro with steak *frites, moules* and the like. Views over the water. *11am-11pm Tue-Thu, to midnight Fri & Sat* €€

Tipsy Ø: Californian and Mexican hybrid; with vegan options. *4.30-10pm Mon-Thu, 3.30-10pm Fri, 11.30am-11pm Sat, to 9pm Sun* €€

Street Coffee: Cosy, bottle-lined place for coffee, wine or artisanal beer in a waterfront cabin. *7.30am-6pm Mon-Fri, 8am-6pm Sat & Sun* €

Living History at Den Gamle By

Rebuilt historic buildings

Den Gamle By *(The Old Town; dengamleby.dk; adult/child 190kr/free)* is a brilliant day out – a small town that enables time travel within walking distance of the city centre. Some 80 buildings are arranged into a town that glides through four eras: 1864, 1927, 1974 and, the newest addition...2014, where you can visit a lesbian couple with three children, wonder at ancient tech like DVDs, or get into the vintage pub atmosphere of the Bent J Jazz Bar.

Elsewhere, you might go from chatting to a superstitious candlemaker to answering a rotary-dial phone in a gynaecologist's office. The immersive detail is hugely impressive and great fun, and it's real history, too: the buildings are mostly all original, transplanted from other parts of Denmark, while the museum itself has its origins in the Danish National Exhibition of 1909. There are horse and cart rides around the site, or to the neighbouring Botanic Gardens.

One highlight you might otherwise miss is **Aarhus Story**, which tells the saga of the city since the Viking age; you'll find it tucked away in the basement of the 1970s cinema.

Wandering the Botanical Garden & Science Park

Glasshouses, parkland and rare plants

Behind Den Gamle By is Aarhus' fabulous **Botanisk Have** *(Botanical Garden; sciencemuseene.dk; free)*, a green retreat of rockeries, rose gardens, hothouses and picnic spots. It's part of the Aarhus Science Museum. The dome-shaped walk-through glasshouses have Mediterranean, desert, forest and tropical habitats. The tropical house with its spiralling wooden staircase is at its centre, and it doubles as a fluttering butterfly house.

Serene Sea Swimming

Aarhus town beaches

For some fresh-air fun, Aarhusianers like to flock to **Den Permanente** *(6am-7pm Jun-Aug)*, a beachfront bathing arca north of town with its own changing facilities; Bellevue Beach, another popular spot, is a bit further on. Both are a breezy bike ride from the city centre; the easiest way to get a bike is via the app, **Donkey Republic** *(donkey.bike)*.

AARHUS FOR FREE

Botanical Garden: Tropical greenhouses with fluttering butterflies and outdoor gardens full of rare plants.

Infinite Bridge: Circular installation with views to the city and out to sea.

Salling Rooftop: Great city panoramas from top of the city's venerable department store; you can step onto a glass platform 25m above Strøget, the pedestrianised high street.

Aarhus Domkirke: The main church, with regular free concerts.

Harbour baths: Summer swimming pool in Bassin 7, in the clean water of the harbour.

Aarhus Rådhus: Mid-century-modern design deity, Arne Jacobsen's town hall – during the week, you can view its beautiful interior.

EATING IN AARHUS: NEW NORDIC

Restaurant Hærværk: Hærværk ('Vandalism') breaks the mould with sustainable menus that change daily. *5-11pm Tue-Sat* €€€

Substans: Michelin-starred, 11th-floor views, warm interior, work-of-art dishes with local produce. *6pm-midnight Tue-Thu, from noon Fri-Sat* €€€

Pondus: Substans' less fancy (but still pretty fancy) sibling, this is by the river and serves delicious organic Nordic cuisine. *5-11pm* €€

Gastromé: Michelin-starred gem north of town sources from its own 'mini-farm' for French-inspired Nordic dishes. *from 6pm Tue-Sat* €€€

TOP EXPERIENCE

Moesgaard Museum

Around 10km south of Aarhus, **Moesgaard Museum** is a dramatically modernist attraction that slopes into a grassy hillside. The exhibitions are just as spectacular: atmospherically lit, hands-on, interactive and thoughtfully bringing prehistory to life. Most thrillingly, they contain the Grauballe Man, who lay in a bog for over 2000 years before his secrets began to be revealed.

RICOCHET64/SHUTTERSTOCK ©

Moesgaard Museum

TOP TIPS

- If you don't fancy cycling from Aarhus, catch bus 18, or bus 100 for a 1km walk along beautiful Moesgård Allé.
- The surrounding countryside has plenty of picnic spots.
- Look for reconstructed historic buildings like a wooden stave church, the earliest of its type in Denmark.

PRACTICALITIES

Scan this QR code for more details and to book tickets.

I am the Bog Man

Stealing the show is the Grauballe Man, whose body was found in a peat bog near Aarhus in 1952, still looking much like he did when he died (albeit a bit more leathery) over 2000 years ago. The superb display is part history lesson, part true crime investigation. Was he a sacrifice to Iron Age fertility gods, an executed prisoner or a victim of murder? The broken leg and gaping neck wound suggest his death, around 290 BCE (give or take 50 years), was a violent one. His body and skin, tanned and preserved by the unique chemical and biological qualities of the peat bog in which he was found, are remarkably intact, right down to his hair and fingernails. As testing develops, more information has come to light about his health, even his last meal.

The Haul from Illerup Ådal

Another highlight is some of the 15,000 weapons, shields and armour found in the boggy valley – a former lake – at **Illerup Ådal**, dating from 200 to 500 CE. It's thought they were thrown there after victory in battle. A hoard of Roman silver coins, depicting Emperor Commodus, helps date the event.

The museum also has some fabulously decorative finds, beautifully lit. Look for an exquisite vessel dating to 3200 BCE, and a collection of 2800-year-old ornaments, including the Dancing Ring, a crown, so-called as it shows nine people holding hands and on the other side with fabulous half-horse, half-bird animals.

Cycling to Moesgård

Rural biking

With your own wheels, Moesgård, 10km south of the city centre, is a dreamy, coast-hugging route through old royal estates: stop off at the **Marselisborg Deer Park** *(aarhus.dk/marselisborg-dyrehave; free)*, just past the Insta-worthy Infinite Bridge. **Tivoli Friheden** *(friheden.dk; admission 175kr, rides band 120kr)* is a wholesome family theme park full of childhood favourites, like dodgem cars and a Ferris wheel, as well as newer, faster rides. It sits at the northern edge of the Marselisborg woods.

Don't miss the spectacular **Moesgaard Museum** and its ancient bog man. From here you can pick up a walking trail, the 4km 'Prehistoric Trackway', through fields and woodland to gorgeous sandy beach, **Moesgård Strand**, which is in a sheltered bay.

Meandering Around the Infinite Bridge

Circular sea boardwalk

If you walk or cycle 3km south of the city along the waterfront, you'll reach the **Infinite Bridge,** a circular boardwalk in the sea. It was created for the ARoS exhibition *Sculpture by the Sea,* in 2015. Originally a temporary installation between Varna and Ballehage Strand south of Aarhus, it proved so popular it became a semi-permanent fixture – the bridge is taken down in winter and then reconstructed in spring. It's here between April and October. It's a beautiful place to walk and sit, with views of the coast, beach, sea and the blue-green forest, and you can swim here, too.

There's free parking on the other side of the road from the beach.

AARHUS K

Aarhus K is an area of the city to the west of ARoS. It's a converted industrial zone devoted to creative enterprises, with a mix of stacked containers, forming workshops and studios, and including the renovated Godsbanen freight yard, which is an alternative cultural hub for the city; it's home to theatre stages, workshops and cafes, and hosts exhibitions, markets and events – it's well worth a look to see what's on while you're in Aarhus. Live-music venue **Radar** (p209) is here, with regular jazz, post-punk, pop and rock gigs, as well as **Institut for (X)** *(institutforx.dk),* a cultural centre hosting cultural and community events.

EATING & DRINKING IN AARHUS: OUR PICKS

St Pauls Apothek: Libations like 'Mr Hyde's Fixer Up' riff on vintage pharmacy stylings of this staple. *5.30pm-midnight Tue-Thu, to 2am Fri & Sat*	**Løve's Bog- & VinCafé:** Books, candles, wine in snug surrounds. Tapas too. *9am-11pm Mon-Wed, to midnight Thu-Fri, from 10am Sat, to 6pm Sun*	**ÅBEN Aarhus:** Craft beer the Danish way with perfect pours in cosy interiors. *2-8pm Sun, to 11pm Mon, to midnight Tue-Thu, 1pm-2am Fri-Sat*	**Under Masken:** Central but hidden reggae dive with a penchant for tribal masks and a devoted local crowd. *noon-2am Mon-Sat, 1-11pm Sun*
La Cabra Coffee: Line up for Aarhus' best coffee and cardamom buns at this perfectly formed cafe. *8am-6pm Mon-Sat, 9am-5pm Sun*	**Emmerys:** Homegrown cafe-bakery-deli chain good for coffee, pastries or sandwiches. Several locations. *7am-6pm Mon-Fri, to 5pm Sat & Sun*	**LYNfabrikken:** In a former factory – coffee, food, coworking vibes, views of the ARoS rainbow from its rooftop garden. *8am-10pm*	**Monk:** Great coffee and pastries on the harbourfront, with bay views from a minimalist interior. *7.50am-5.30pm Mon-Sat, 8am-5pm Sun*

Beyond Aarhus

Leave the city behind and go wild in some of Denmark's prettiest natural landscapes.

Places

Get ready to discover a loftier side to pancake-flat Denmark. The pristine Lake District (Søhøjlandet) is a lovely place to relax for a few days, with its chain of *søer* (lakes) – several joined by the Gudenå, Denmark's longest river. They're surrounded by lush tracts of beech forest, making the Lake District an outdoorsy crowd-puller with lots of great spots to go boating and swimming. The lakeside town of Silkeborg is a summer favourite with year-round appeal thanks to its galleries and cultural sights. West of Aarhus, the Djursland peninsula (Jutland's 'nose'), with its heather-clad Mols hills, is likewise within easy reach for day trips or longer escapes, a relaxing place to be for its family attractions and sandy beaches. It's a hot locale for Danish summer houses. Save a day or two for the old port town of Ebeltoft.

GETTING AROUND

Half-hourly trains connect Aarhus with Ry and Silkeborg via Lake District town, Skanderborg. Long-distance buses to Silkeborg stop next to the train station. Djursland has decent bus connections with Aarhus, but it's easier to explore by car.

It's great to take a boat trip with your bike (remember to book a space for the bike, no e-bikes), and then cycle back along one of the area's rural cycle ways, through forest and riverside.

Silkeborg

TIME FROM AARHUS: **45 MINS**

Vintage paddle steamer

The town of Silkeborg, meaning 'Silk Castle', only 45 minutes by train from Aarhus, feels like a different world. It's a slow-paced place ideal for water-based holidays, clustered around its riverside and harbour, where lake cruises launch in the warmer months. The venerable **Hjejlen Boat Company** *(hjejlen.com)* has been running cruises in the Lake District since 1861. Its main route connects Silkeborg's small harbour with the scenic lookout of **Himmelbjerget** (12km, 75 minutes).

It's a serene trip along the river, which opens out into the lake, with wooded banks on either side. From Himmelbjerget dock it's a 1km hike up to enjoy the views from the modest summit of 'Sky Mountain'. You can hop on and off at various piers along the cruise for lake swimming and picnics, and switch boats throughout the day. The jewel of the historic fleet is the *SS Hjejlen (return ticket to Himmelbjerget 260kr),* the world's oldest coal-fired paddle steamer still afloat, with a crew shovelling below deck. From Himmelbjerget you can take another boat as far as Ry (p217).

Boating, biking and walking the Lake District

Himmelbjerget must have been named by someone with a sense of humour. It was once thought to be Denmark's highest point at 147m. It might not be especially high, but it still

MADS MIKLADAL/SHUTTERSTOCK ©

Himmelbjerget

offers huge views of the surrounding forests and lakes from the 25m-high tower, erected in 1875.

If you're after a dip in the lakes, Almindsø (south of Silkeborg) is one of the cleanest in Denmark as it has no agriculture nearby. It has lovely bathing spots at **Østre Søbad** (by the main road) and **Vestre Søbad**, a short hike away on the north shore; both have jetties and changing rooms. A memorable way to experience the lakes is by self-guided canoe safari, with options ranging from one hour to several days. Enquire at **Silkeborg Kanocenter**, which has canoe *(150/500kr per hour/day)*, kayak *(200/600kr)* and motorboat *(350/1500kr)* rentals, and a range of flexible tour packages.

You'll also spot coloured trail markers leading hikers and mountain bikers deeper into the landscape. To rent your own wheels, book online with **Active Rental** or **Favoritten** *(cykelfavoritten.dk)*. The hilly forests of Nordskoven, east of Silkeborg, are crisscrossed with marked tracks, or take a guided mountain-bike tour with **MTB Guide** *(mtbguidesilkeborg.dk)*.

Bog man at Museum Silkeborg

Museum Silkeborg *(museumsilkeborg.dk; adult/child 85kr/free)*, is housed in Silkeborg Manor, one of the original buildings in the area that predates the town. It's across the river from the boat launch area, and houses an interesting town museum that is, incredibly, home to the 2400-year-old Tollund Man. Preserved by the unique, oxygen-free chemical balance of the bog, he is so well kept that the peat cutters who found him in 1950 thought they had stumbled upon a recent murder.

DENMARK'S HIGHLANDS

Until 1847 Himmelbjerget was officially Denmark's highest point, but after more precise surveying was done, that accolade passed to **Ejer Bavnehøj** (170m), a 30-minute drive south. Make the ascent and you'll find a lookout tower commemorating South Jutland's reunification with Denmark; a haunting sound installation; and a marked circular hike to another high point.

The Lake District's stumpy 'peaks' are really just false hills carved from Ice Age glaciers, but that hasn't deterred local enthusiasts from trying to conquer all its summits over 100m high. If you want to join in, check out *bestigbjerge.dk* (Danish only), an online game in which you score points each time you bag a mountain.

EATING IN SILKEBORG: OUR PICKS

Evald Brasserie & Cafe: Draught beer and dishes at renovated paper mill Papirfabrikken; riverside terrace. *11am-11pm Mon-Sat, to 10pm Sun* €€

Panorama Mad & Vin: Smart Scandi cooking, burgers, steak, excellent service at this town-square favourite. *11am-11pm Tue-Sat* €€€

Babba: Middle Eastern fare like falafel and meze, plus top cocktails. Shaded outdoor terrace. *11am-11.30pm Mon-Thu, to 1am Fri-Sat* €€

No 21 – Tapas & Vinbar: Bottle-lined waterfront tapas bar with cold cuts, wines, draught beer. *noon-10pm Wed-Thu, to 11pm Fri & Sat* €€

A SPIN AROUND THE DJURSLAND PENINSULA

Northeast of Aarhus, Jutland's 'Nose', the peninsula of Djursland pokes out into the Kattegat strait and makes for a lovely road trip.

START	END	LENGTH
Bellevue Beach	Memphis Mansion	107km; 1-3 days

Start at 1 **Bellevue Beach** and drive along Strandvej. Head inland through Astrup, then follow Studstraupvej until it turns into Vosnaesvej – you'll pass whitewashed manor house 2 **Vosnæs Gods** and end up back on the coast. Follow Strandvejen before turning through Rønde. Turn right through Molsvej into **Mols Bjerge National Park**. Lonely 3 **Kalø Slot**, a ruined castle built by Danish King Erik Menved in 1313, is on a small island accessed by a stony causeway. Get trail maps at the cafe by the causeway to hike through forests to ancient burial mounds and a long barrow. Drive to 4 **Jagtslottet**, a half-timbered mansion with hunting murals inside. It's 30 minutes to 5 **Grenaa**, with half-timbered houses and 7km of windswept sandy beaches. Stay the night and visit Svartlöga, a restored shipwreck hosting art exhibitions. Eat at wine-bar restaurant MundGodt or Skakkes Holm for a seafood buffet. From Grenaa, visit the area's best beaches, further north: 6 **Gjerrild Nordstrand**, good for spring raptor-spotting, and 7 **Bønnerup** and 8 **Fjellerup**, where you can hunt for amber. Drive inland from Grenaa to 17th-century 9 **Gammel Estrup**, a grand house with Lego-like architecture and the Herregårdsmuseet, an insight into baroque rural Danish life. From here it's a 20-minute drive to the bizarre 10 **Memphis Mansion**, an oversized Graceland replica.

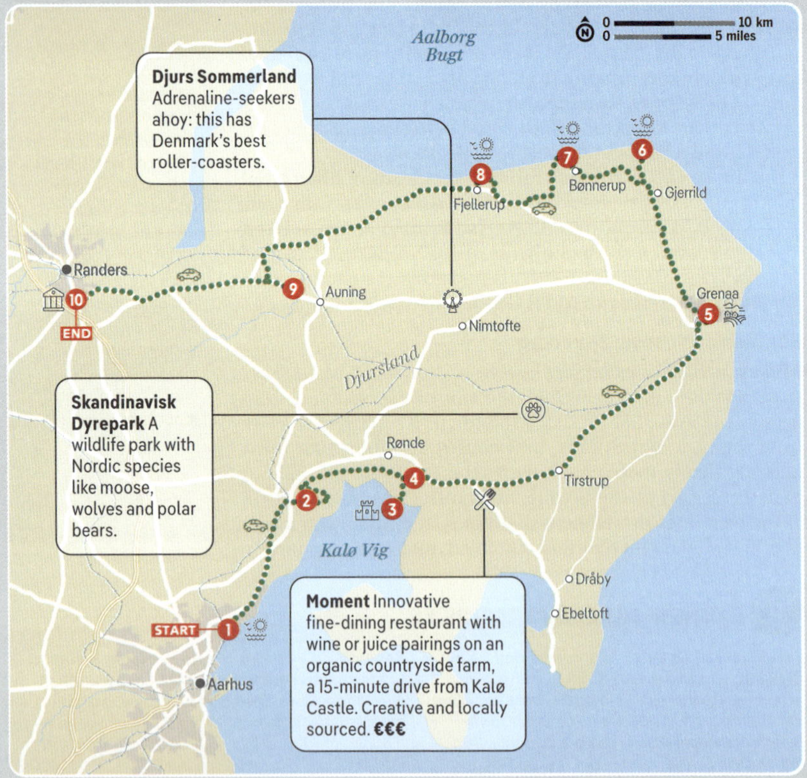

Djurs Sommerland Adrenaline-seekers ahoy: this has Denmark's best roller-coasters.

Skandinavisk Dyrepark A wildlife park with Nordic species like moose, wolves and polar bears.

Moment Innovative fine-dining restaurant with wine or juice pairings on an organic countryside farm, a 15-minute drive from Kalø Castle. Creative and locally sourced. **€€€**

You can even see the bristles on his chin. He had been buried with a leather rope around his neck – he had been hanged. It's not known why figures such as these ended up deposited in a bog rather than buried: theories include punishment or sacrifice. Fascinating displays show how the head was preserved, and how advances in technology have allowed more discoveries: his death has been radiocarbon-dated to 405 to 380 BCE. A figure has been created to show how Tollund Man might have looked when alive – he certainly seems slightly bemused.

Art-packed outskirts

Around 2km south of Silkeborg where lake boats stop, the **Museum Jorn** *(museumjorn.dk; adult/child 115kr/free)* is a terrific art gallery devoted to the stunningly prolific and well-connected Danish artist Asger Jorn. Jorn grew up here and so willed his works to the town. He was a mover and shaker in several contemporary art movements, and his work reflects that, ranging from splashy expressionism to *Stalingrad* – Jorn's 5m-wide abstract oil painting, is his *Guernica,* a meditation on the futility of war. On display from Jorn's own collection are works by Max Ernst and Le Corbusier. Your ticket price includes free rental of electric bikes (10am to 4pm); call or email ahead.

Ørnsø

TIME FROM AARHUS: **1HR 20 MINS**

An art-filled spa

Heading south from the Museum Jorn via Indelukket, a riverside park and marina, it's around 3km southwest to Ørnsø (about a 10-minute cycle) and another modern art gallery, **KunstCentret Silkeborg Bad** *(silkeborgbad.dk; adult/child 90kr/free),* housed in an early 20th-century lakeshore spa, which grew up around iron-rich Spring Arnakkekilden. The surrounding gardens are a kind of sculpture walk, and you can extend your ramble by doing the 4km trail around the lake. It's fun to seek out *Stærke Storm,* a wooden troll sculpture by Thomas Dambo hiding in the woods (subtle signs help guide the way). There are also 12 bunkers dotted in the woods, which were the headquarters of the German military in Denmark during WWII. The interesting **Silkeborg Bunker Museum**, crammed into one of the concrete hulks, has displays and artefacts dating to the occupation.

Ry

TIME FROM AARHUS: **30 MINS**

Relaxing in lakeside Ry

You can take a connecting boat from Himmelbjerget to the mellow town of Ry, which sits between Knudsø and Birksø (lakes) in the heart of the Lake District and is surrounded

WORLD'S OLDEST COAL-BURNING STEAMER

Silkeborg grew up around its paper mill, which burned down in 1864. Since reconstructed, today it's home to riverside restaurants, a theatre and music venue, and a papermaking museum. A reminder of its history is the world's oldest coal-burning paddle steamer, still taking passengers up and down the river and around the lakes. *Hjejlen* ('The Golden Plover') was built in 1861 by Baumgarten & Burmeister in Copenhagen. The paper-mill owners raised money to commission it as a tourist boat: it cost a whopping 10,000 rigsdaler at a time when workers earned around 150 a month. The expected tourists did not come, but the boat was renovated in 1900, and by 1932 began operating as a public mail boat.

EATING IN RY: OUR PICKS

Lakeside: Waterside pasta, steak, *moules-frites,* homemade Italian ice cream. *hours vary* €€

Restaurant Gastronomisk Institut: Top-notch cuisine – pigeon breast, veal rump. *noon-2pm & from 6pm Mon-Sat* €€€

La Vinya: Good, cosy sheepskin-furnished cafe with coffee, pastries and buns. *9am-5.30pm Sat & Wed, to 4.30pm Sun, to 11pm Thu & Fri* €

UNDER THE RADAR IN EBELTOFT

Joel Prudhomme, Maltfabrikken brewmaster, shares some favourite local spots. Instagram: *@brewpub_maltfabrikken*

Go Kaffe: Run by Bjarke who holds a morning salon with talks and songs on Fridays at 9am – a great opportunity to meet the locals. Coworking space for artists, writers and photographers too.

Aoife Coffee: Best coffee and cake in town, out by the pier among the fishing boats. Start the day with a sourdough bun and a cortado.

Sølballegaard: *(soelballegaard.dk)* Gorgeous renovated farmhouse in the Mols Bjerge forest, reopening in 2025.

Svartlöga: *(svartloga.dk/history)* Now in Grenaa, this shipwrecked boat was raised, salvaged and rebuilt by volunteers. It hosts art exhibitions when it's not sailing.

by quaint villages perfect for exploring. There are swimming beaches with jetties either at the edge of town at Sønder Ege Strand or on the eastern bank of the lake at Knudhule Strand. You can find **canoe hire** at the marina and cruise boats sailing to Himmelbjerget (p214). Or you can hike out that way on a pleasant **marked trail** (7km, 2 hours) and catch a boat back. The trailhead is on Munkedalsvej, which branches off Rodelundvej just south of Ry bridge.

Ebeltoft

TIME FROM AARHUS: **1 HR 20 MINS**

Picturesque summer getaway

Cobblestone streets lined with half-timbered houses, white-sand beaches and a classic warship attract large numbers of ice-cream-eating holidaymakers to beguiling Ebeltoft, and the pretty surrounds are now a national park. Thousands of summer visitors flock around white-sand **Ebeltoft Beach**, the town's tiny marina of sailboats and gentrified fishing-hut cafes. Most imposing is **Fregatten Jylland** *(fregatten-jylland.dk; adult/child 155/100kr)*, a wooden warship turned museum; once the pride of the Royal Danish Navy, it fought a major battle in 1864, the last time squadrons of wooden ships came to blows – you can still smell gunpowder inside the hull. From bow to stern it measures 71m, making it the world's longest wooden ship. It was launched in 1860 and played an instrumental role in Denmark's navy in the 19th century; today it's restored for visitors – step inside and experience the life of a crew member.

Next along, **Glasmuseet Ebeltoft** *(glasmuseet.dk; adult/child 130/30kr)* is a gallery devoted to contemporary glass art, with exhibitions of fragile beauty (tread carefully!) and an open studio where artists-in-residence blow and cast their creations in front of roaring furnaces.

One street inland is cobbled **Adelgade**, a delightful lane of pastel-hued houses and a tiny, half-timbered town hall from 1789. Take it slow and gravitate towards **Maltfabrikken** *(maltfabrikken.dk)*, the big red building at the top of town. This former malt factory has been thoughtfully revamped into a cultural and community hub, with a public library, concert venue, restaurants, seasonal street food, exhibitions and a skate park. Appropriately, the atmospheric brewpub malts its barley in-house. Climb the old chimney for views of the bay.

EATING IN DJURSLAND: OUR PICKS

Molskroen: Beautiful old *kro* (inn) around the bay from Ebeltoft, upscale Danish set menus. *noon-3pm Sat-Sun, 6-9pm Wed-Sun* **€€€**

Brasseriet: Also at Molskroen, a more casual restaurant with superb brasserie-style food. *6-9pm Wed-Fri, noon-9pm Sat, to 3pm Sun* **€**

Karens Køkken: On Ebelftoft harbour with views to the 19th-century *Fregatten Jylland*; great seafood. *hours vary* **€€**

Mellem Jyder: Charming, family-run restaurant in a 17th-century half-timbered house near Ebeltoft's old town hall. *noon-10pm* **€€€**

Billund

FAMILY FUN | CHILD-FRIENDLY ATTRACTIONS | LEGO

Billund is marketed as the Capital of Children, and this faintly surreal area is just that. It's best explored with little ones, unless you're a registered AFOL (adult fan of Lego). In 1932, Billund carpenter Ole Kirk Christiansen turned his tools to making wooden toys and came up with the name Lego, a contraction of *leg godt,* meaning 'play well'. The plastic brick was launched in 1958; by some estimates Lego will have produced a trillion of them by 2026. The company has given itself a deadline of 2030 to devise an eco-friendlier alternative.

Not only is Billund Lego-central, but there's a wonderful indoor waterpark, and ace zoo and safari park. Beyond Lego and other kids' stuff, there isn't that much happening in this quiet company town. Two to three days should be enough, allowing a day each at Legoland and Lego House, but an extra day means you can tackle Legoland at a less frantic pace. Your kids will remember it fondly forever.

GETTING AROUND

Legoland is less than 3km from Billund airport; a free shuttle bus runs to the park in July and August, timed to flights. Most regular local buses stop at the town centre (for Lego House), Legoland and the airport, and most accommodation is near Lego attractions. You can rent bikes from **Jupiter Cykler** in the town centre; however, Legoland, Lego House and Lalandia are all in easy walking distance, with trails routed through a verdant sculpture park. There's no rail service.

TOP TIP

Flights to Billund are often cheaper than to Copenhagen or Aarhus: this is Denmark's second-biggest airport (built by the Lego Group), bang in the centre of Jutland. Hotels are pricy so consider rural B&Bs and guesthouses outside town if you want to save.

Lego Heaven: Lego House

The ultimate Lego playdate

With a Bauhaus-esque exterior made from 21 staggered blocks, **Lego House** *(legohouse.com; adult/child 339/279kr).* is a wonderland for fans of the brick, and even if you're not, you'll likely get drawn in to building contraptions in its many creative zones. Kids aged between around five and 12 years are the perfect market. Families will delight at the wholesome, high-tech edutainment and Willy Wonka–style magic on offer. In the colour-coded 'Experience Zones' you can design your own Lego figure to express a mood (very *Inside Out*) then add it to a digital tableau, create vehicles and then race them, build Lego fish and launch them into digital tanks; and make a stop-motion film: you could spend a whole day here. There are also 13 outdoor terraces with some creative climbing frames and swings.

The Lego dioramas in **World Explorer** are glorious, packed with narrative detail. The central **Tree of Creativity** is 15.68m high, built of 6.3 million Lego bricks, and would take 12 years

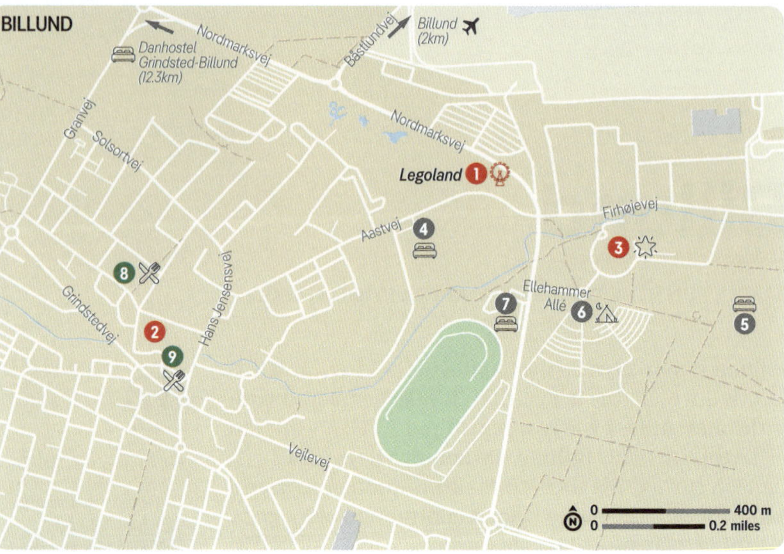

HIGHLIGHTS
1 Legoland

SIGHTS
2 Lego House
3 Lalandia Billund

SLEEPING
4 Hotel Legoland
5 Lalandia
6 Legoland Holiday Village
7 The Lodge

EATING
8 Billund Bageri
9 Billund Gastropub
● Mini Chef (see 2)
● Panorama Restaurant – Hotel Legoland (see 4)

FIVE LEGO HOUSE INSIDER FACTS

Stuart Harris, master builder at Lego House, points out insider features.

Wooden duck: In Ole's toolbox in Lego Square.

Ski Jumper In World Explorer.

New 'Mr T' Engraved onto the Tree of Creativity.

Wacky dance moves: In Moodmixer; when you plug in your creation.

Minifigure Tribute On Lego House's exclusive minifigure (a pirate, 30cm tall) .

to build if you were doing it alone. The **Lego Museum** in the basement tells the story of the company, which is still run by the same family.

Super fans can peek behind the curtain at the **Lego Factory** in Billund and visit Lego founder Kristiansen's house, but these limited tours sell out months in advance. Sign up online.

Splashtastic Lalandia

Superb, splashy family fun

Also within walking distance of Legoland and the Lego House are the thrilling slides, pools and lazy river of Aqualand at **Lalandia** *(lalandia.dk; day ticket 339kr)*. It's a waterpark, so nothing too classy, but brilliant all-weather fun. In the complex are other holiday-camp favourites such as crazy golf, and you can stay in cabins on site (room rates include admission to Aqualand).

WHERE TO EAT IN BILLUND: OUR PICKS

Mini Chef: 'Build' a boxed meal at Lego House, then collect it from robots. Book ahead. *11am-3pm Mon & Thu-Fri, to 6pm Sat, to 4pm Sun* **€€**

Billund Gastropub: Phew, something grown-up. Burgers, craft beer, classy dining space. *noon-11pm Tue-Thu, to 10pm Sun-Mon, to 2am Fri-Sat* **€€**

Billund Bageri: A long-running bakery that's ideal for breakfast or sandwiches. *5.30am-5pm Mon-Fri, to 4pm Sat & Sun* **€**

Panorama Restaurant: You can eat at this good-value buffet even if you're not staying at the Lego Hotel. Book ahead. *noon-3pm & 5.30-9pm* **€€**

TOP EXPERIENCE

The Original Legoland

Going strong since 1968, **Legoland** (see also p286) is the original, and some might say the best, of the genre, mixing retro appeal, Lego themes and interactive experiences with the latest tech. It's more of a family place than the go-to for stomach-flipping roller-coasters, though Polar-X-Plorer and Ice Pilots School supply faster thrills for bigger kids.

ALLARD ONE/SHUTTERSTOCK ©

Legoland

Miniland

Miniland is comprised of 20 million plastic Lego blocks snapped together to create whimsical, knee-high towns and cities, including the 5.5m Burj Khalifa. If you haven't time to visit them in person, at Miniland you can take a whistle-stop tour of Skagen, Ribe, Copenhagen's iconic Nyhavn waterfront and various royal Danish palaces, all rendered in Lego bricks (with obsessive attention to detail) at a scale of 1:20 to 1:40.

Duplo Land is for toddlers, and has flat rides including a small train ride, Duplo planes, mini Ferris wheel LEGONDOL, and Duplo playhouses, plus the new-for-2024 Peppa Pig Playground and giant Benny's Playship. Atlantis by Sea-life is a walk-through aquarium that's also great fun.

Family Attractions

Legotop, a 36m-high observation tower, offers views across the park. At **SEAT Traffic School** kids aged six to 13 can try driving (extra charge). Self-build Lego activities include building boats to race. In the **Arctic Basecamp**, prepare for a polar expedition by building your own vehicles. Western-themed **Legoredo** has a fun haunted-house-style attraction. **Pirateland** has Pirate Splash Battle and Pirate Boats. Dragen is a family-friendly roller-coaster at the **Knight's Kingdom**. X-treme Racers is not as extreme as the name suggests. In Ninjago Dark Ride you use hand movements to eliminate bad guys. Take that!

TOP TIPS

- To maximise ride time, save Miniland for the last hour when rides have closed.
- For full immersion, stay at the Legoland Hotel, which overlooks the park.
- Book online for almost half-price tickets and reduced queuing.

PRACTICALITIES

Scan this QR code for prices and opening hours.

Beyond Billund

Leave the Lego behind and surround yourself with history – or gear up for a watersports adventure along the coast.

Places

When you've had your fill of Lego fun (or maybe you entered Denmark via its second-busiest airport at Billund), there are some compelling destinations within easy reach for both kids and adults. The tiny town of Jelling, half an hour from Billund by car, played a starring role in Denmark's origin story and has earned UNESCO World Heritage status for its Viking burial mounds and runic stones.

To the north, the town of Herning is an unlikely hotbed of modern art – or go further afield to the central west coast and the fishing town of Hvide Sande where you'll find a world of watersports, windswept beaches and stunning sunsets over the North Sea.

GETTING AROUND

Bus 580 runs between Hvide Sande and Ringkøbing station (30 minutes) roughly hourly on weekdays, less frequently at weekends. Ringkøbing is connected to larger central Jutland towns like Herning and Skjern by train and bus, but it's easier with your own wheels. Consider hiring a car at Billund airport. Driving here is a breeze, with smooth, straight roads and cautious drivers. There are plentiful charging points for electric cars.

Jelling

TIME FROM BILLUND: **30 MINS**

Bluetooth's Rune Stone

Jelling, a kind of spiritual touchstone for Danes, is a tiny village amid the pea-green landscape of Jutland, but home to an extraordinary royal monument dating to the reign of 10th-century Viking King Gorm the Old and his son Harald Bluetooth.

In a clearing at the centre of town stand two huge **burial mounds** placed within the outline of a Viking ship (originally marked by stones), which would sail the deceased to Valhalla. Exactly between the mounds, and outside the door to **Jelling Kirke** *(jellingkirke.dk)*, is a boulder-sized **rune stone** installed by Harald that proclaims Denmark's transition from paganism to Christianity – the stone has been dubbed Denmark's 'birth certificate'. A second, **smaller rune stone** was made by Gorm in honour of his queen, Thyra.

When both of the mounds were excavated in the 19th century, no human remains were found, though people had long believed that the Northern Mound contained the tomb of Gorm. In the 1970s, archaeologists digging beneath Jelling Kirke found traces of three earlier wooden churches...and a burial chamber with human remains inside. Was it Gorm, relocated to Denmark's first church by his Christian-convert son Harald? Look out for the silver stripe on the church floor marking the burial site.

Next to the burial mound you'll find the excellent **Kongernes Jelling** *(en.natmus.dk/museums-and-palaces; adult/child*

SVENNOLINO/SHUTTERSTOCK ©

Ringkøbing Fjord

60kr/free, guided tour 45kr), a visitor centre with lots of interactive displays that vividly bring the story of the kings alive.

Ringkøbing Fjord

TIME FROM BILLUND: 1 HR

Natural beauty and watersports

Ringkøbing Fjord is, in fact, a vast lagoon (298 sq km) shielded from the North Sea by the long slender line of Holmsland Dunes. There's a breathtakingly beautiful road and cycle lane running along the isthmus – a fantastic drive, windswept walk or cycle. It's an otherworldly land and seascape, only an hour's drive from Billund. This is the largest of the West Jutland fjords, with shallow brackish water. Around Tipperne and Værnengene spread large salt marshes.

With its calm, shallow waters and strong coastal wind, the 'fjord' is a world-class destination for windsurfing and kitesurfing, and just 600m back across the sand you can surf in the North Sea waves.

There are lots of summer houses (the traditional Danish family escape) dotted around the area of the fjord, making this a great place to rent a house and get away from it all. Bird-watchers can look out for the plentiful migrating and local birdlife, including whooper and Bewick's swans, and most of the Svalbard population of pink-footed geese.

THE ORIGINAL BLUETOOTH

Harald Bluetooth was the son of Gorm the Old, a Viking dynasty originating from Jelling. He was king from 958 to 986, and not only united Scandinavia, but also converted it to Christianity. His father, Gorm, had begun the process, but Harald completed it. It's thought he gained his nickname because he had a rotten tooth.

In 1996, Intel, Ericsson and Nokia were planning new, short-range radio technology, working together to support connectivity. Bluetooth was a place-holding nickname that became its official one. The logo is the runes of the letters H and B, the king's initials.

EATING & DRINKING AT HENNE STRAND & RINGKØBING: OUR PICKS

Henne Kirkeby Kro: Two-Michelin-star gourmet splurge, south past Ringkøbing Fjord. *9am-3pm Mon, Wed-Thu, to 1pm Tue* €€€

Café Stranden: Beach brasserie at bijou resort Henne Strand; *moules frites* with sea views. *11.30am-8.30pm Wed-Fri, from 10am Sat-Sun* €€

Kræs Cafe: A modern restaurant at the marina, with lots of local seafood. *10am-5pm Mon-Fri, to 1pm Sat* €€

Stauning Whisky A/S: A whisky distillery that also offers tours and tastings. *10am-4pm Mon-Sat*

ACTIVITIES AT HVIDE SANDE

There's a well-stocked tourist office by the port. Ask about fishing trips with local anglers, and the fish auctions which visitors can see weekly in summer.

Westwind: Surf school with two fjord-side locations on either side of town. Instruction in surfing, windsurfing, kitesurfing and stand-up paddle boarding (SUP), plus gear rental.

Kabelpark: Try wakeboarding and water-skiing at this cable complex (beside the northern branch of Westwind), which uses a pully system to tow riders over jumps.

Vinterlejegaard Ridecenter: Riding centre about 10km south of Hvide Sande offering one-hour beach rides. Hvide Sande is perfect for viewing coastal sunsets on horseback.

SMIBO/SHUTTERSTOCK ©

Hvide Sande beach

Halfway down the isthmus, the fishing community of **Hvide Sande**, where vendors fry fish and chips at the old port, is the go-to place for watersports action, and there are plenty of restaurants and shops here, too.

Hvide Sande

TIME FROM BILLUND: **1HR 20 MINS**

Wind and seafood

Hvide Sande (meaning 'white sands') sits between the North Sea and the Lagoon, and owes its existence to the wind. Wind caused the sand migration that forced the construction of a lock here in 1931 to assure a North Sea passage for the port of Ringkøbing. And wind continues to be the big drawcard for the large number of tourists who come here for windsurfing.

Aside from wind, Hvide Sande is all about fish. It has a busy deep-sea fishing harbour, with trawlers, fish-processing factories and an early-morning fish auction. And it's a great place to eat seafood, obviously. There are also summer boat tours and outfits offering kitesurfing and windsurfing, as well as other activities: bike hire and boat trips are recommended.

The town has also had its moment in the Danish noir spotlight, with a recent murder-mystery series being filmed and set here (named *Hvide Sande*) that imagined a dark underbelly for the local cheery surfing community.

In early September, Hvide Sande hosts **Waterz**, Scandinavia's biggest watersports festival.

EATING AT HVIDE SANDE: OUR PICKS

Cafe Marina: Come for the harbour views, surf-and-turf burger and oven-baked lobsters with garlic mayo. Great value. *10.30am-9pm* **€€**

Nordsø Fisk: Fish and chips, or shrimp-, salmon- or fish-ball rolls. *9am-7pm Mon-Fri, to 6pm Sat-Sun Jul-Aug, shorter hours Sep-Jun* **€**

Slusegrillen: A kiosk at the edge of a car park by the water with top-notch fish and chips, and hot dogs. Cash only. *noon-4pm Tue-Sun* **€**

Lille K by Grantland: 1st-floor, window-lined spot with upmarket fish and chips, burgers, scallops; great sea views. *noon-10pm Wed-Sat* **€€**

Aalborg

ART & ARCHITECTURE | VIKINGS | HISTORIC SIGHTS

Aalborg, once an industrial workhorse known as a manufacturing centre for cement and akvavit (a vodka-like spirit), has been transformed, Danish-style, over the last few years. Dockside factories along the Limfjord, the long body of water that slices Jutland in two, have given way to bold architecture and leafy pedestrian zones, while the city's old core buzzes with cafes, bars and street art. It's worth making a day in your schedule to stop here on your way up north, especially as there are two incredible sights in the vicinity: a nuclear bunker and Lindholm Høje, Scandinavia's largest Viking burial ground. Aalborg was a big deal back in the Viking era, thanks to the Limfjord providing speedy access to the Atlantic for longboat raiding parties, hence its important burial site. In late May, the city overflows for the largest Carnival celebrations in northern Europe.

GETTING AROUND

Most traveller amenities are on the Limfjord's southern shore, save for the airport and Lindholm Høje. City bus 12 runs from Aalborg airport to the city centre; a taxi is around 100kr. For bike trips around the city, download the Donkey Republic bike-share app. Aalborg's tourist board has self-guided walks you can do with a smartphone. Go to *storyhunt.dk* or download the Storyhunt app and navigate to Northern Jutland (Nordjylland) for GPS-powered audio walks in English on street art and history, and a city highlights tour.

On the Waterfront

Architecture and activities

Aalborg's once industrial dockside has been reborn with new buildings and a broad boardwalk. The jewel in the harbourside crown is **Utzon Center** *(utzoncenter.dk; adult/child 100/60kr),* the last building designed by eminent Danish architect and Aalborg native Jørn Utzon (1918–2008). He died before it was completed and it was finished by his son. There are excellent temporary exhibitions, plus one of Aalborg's top places to eat. You may not have heard of Utzon, but you might have seen his most famous building: the Sydney Opera House.

The cubist **Musikkens Hus** *(House of Music; musikkenshus.dk)* is a futuristic-looking concert hall by Austrian firm Coop Himmelb(l)au – check out the interior (and what's on) as well.

Established for Aalborg's poorer residents in the 1930s, **Fjordbyen** is a beguiling hodgepodge of allotments and homes converted from former fishing sheds that's a contrast

TOP TIP

The outdoor cafe at **Salling** *(salling.dk)* has top views across the city's red roofs, and on a clear day to Lindholm Hoje. A bar on the floor above has an even higher viewpoint.

to Aalborg's contemporary waterfront. A short walk from Fjordbyen is landscaped **Vestre Fjordpark** with a beach-style swimming area, a diving pool with tower, playgrounds and a climbing wall. You can swim year-round, sail, kayak, play and picnic at the harbourside.

Baroque & Renaissance Riches

Pretty historic centre

Aalborg waved goodbye to substantial tracts of heritage when it industrialised in the early 20th century, but the old centre retains enough half-timbered buildings to evoke how it once looked. The five-storey **Jens Bangs Stenhus** and the **Jørgen Olufsens House** (now operating as an Irish pub), in particular, are two of Denmark's best examples of 17th-century residential architecture.

Budolfi Domkirke, a 12th-century cathedral (and Denmark's smallest), marks the heart of old Aalborg – keep an ear out for the hourly carillon of 48 bells. Across the cobbles you'll find the **Aalborg Historiske Museum** *(nordjyskemuseer.dk/u/aalborg-historiske-museum; adult/child 75kr/free)*, which counts among its treasures a bourgeois panelled drawing room from the Renaissance. Don't miss **CW Obels Plads**, Aalborg's most atmospheric old square, with cafes, restaurants and an ice rink in winter. An alley running off it leads to **Helligåndsklosteret** *(Monastery of the Holy Ghost; aalborgkloster.dk; guided tour adult/child 50kr/free)*, which dates to 1431; have a peek at the gardens or sign up for a guided tour of the interior. If you're after a night out, **Jomfru Ane Gade** is party street, jammed with bars, clubs and kebab joints.

Beautiful Alvar Aalto-Designed Art Gallery

Picasso, Léger and more

The **Kunsten Museum of Modern Art** *(kunsten.dk/en; adult/child 140kr/free)* is housed in a beautiful modernist building by the great Finnish architect Alvar Aalto, light-filled and with interesting spaces to display its fine collection. The art includes works and ceramics by Picasso and Fernand Léger, the joyful *Nana with Ball* by Niki de Saint Phalle, as well as great Danish artists such as Asger Jorn. Bus 15 does the trip, but it's also a nice walk – take the tunnel beneath the train station, through the green surrounds of **Kildeparken**, across Vesterbro and into a wooded area until you see the stunning white-marble building. In the basement is the excellent **Brasserie Kunsten**, ideal for light lunches or dinner, which opens onto a grassy lawn.

Scandinavia's Largest Viking Cemetery

Ship-shaped burials

In the northern suburbs of Aalborg is a windswept, lonely grassy hillock with a mesmerising sight: the largest Viking burial site in Scandinavia. There are 700 graves from the Iron Age and Viking Age at **Lindholm Høje** *(nordjyskemuseer.dk/en; free)*, once a high-status Viking village – 41 of the graves were burials, while the rest were all cremated. It's a place heavy with atmosphere, edged by a wall of beech trees. The oldest tombs are higher on the hill, and youngest at the foot. Many of the male burials are arranged in a 'ship setting' –

AALBORG'S SUPER STREET PARTY

Each year in late May, Aalborg is awash with colour, kicking up its heels to host Scandinavia's biggest **Carnival** *(aalborgkarneval.dk)* This enormous spectacle features gloriously elaborate costumes, with a different theme every year. The week-long event begins with a Battle of the Bands, with carnival bands from all over Europe joining an extraordinary International Parade.

The monster **Grand Parade** sees thousands of costumed participants dancing and parading Rio-style. There's a separate parade for kids, with storybook and animal costumes, entertainment, and stages for live music as well as open-air bar trucks aplenty. See the carnival website for the various levels of wristbands available, allowing access to different areas.

EATING & DRINKING IN AALBORG: BEST COFFEE

Penny Lane: Fairy-tale decor, Beatles theme and oodles of home-baked cakes to pair with coffee. *8am-6pm Mon-Fri, to 5pm Sat, 10am-5pm Sun*

Cafe Peace: Family-owned spot, with solid barista work, great breakfasts. *8am-10pm Mon-Wed, to 11pm Thu-Sat, 9am-5.30pm Sun*

Caféministeriet: Smart-casual hangout for hyggelig mugs of frothy coffee and brunch treats. *9am-11pm Mon-Thu, to 2am Fri-Sat, to 10pm Sun*

Behag Din Smag: A connoisseur's coffeeshop with next-level foam art. *7.15am-5pm Mon-Fri, 8.30am-4pm Sat*

A VIKING BURIAL

Viking burials at sites like Lindholm Høje offer valuable insights into the beliefs, culture and practices of the Norse people. There are few written records of Viking practices, although a description of a Norse funeral from 921, written by Islamic diplomat Ahmad ibn Fadlan, describes the horrifying ritual of burying an important man, including the sacrifice of a female slave alongside him. According to Ahmad, the rituals were fuelled by *nabidh*, a fermented drink made from dates and water. If death rituals were brutal, it reflected life at the time, but without collaboration, the accuracy of the account is unknown. What is certain is that there seemed to be differing trends in Viking burials, including cremation and burial. Rituals were simplified with the introduction of Christianity.

Lindholm Høje

the oval outline of a Viking boat – to sail the glorious dead to their eternal reward in Valhalla. Female graves are circular and oval. The shape and size of each setting relates to the status of the deceased.

The reason for the site's remarkable preservation is that at the end of the Viking era the whole area was buried under drifting sand, and only excavated in the 1950s. There's a good **museum** *(adult/child 100kr/free)* showing archaeological finds from its excavations, alongside exhibitions on daily life in the Viking Age.

Lindholm Høje is 15 minutes' north of central Aalborg via bus 13.

EATING & DRINKING IN AALBORG: OUR PICKS

Jørn: Superb Danish brunch and brasserie-style dishes in the Jorn Utzon building; harbour views. *11am-5pm Fri-Wed, to 9pm Thu* €€

Applaus: Great-value tapas-style Danish fare, with a 10-course 'social dining' menu for the ravenous. *5.30pm-12.30am Tue-Sat* €€

Mortens Kro: Lunch of smørrebrød, desserts with local berries; celebrity-chef spot. *5.30pm-1am Mon, 11am-3pm & 5.30pm-2am Tue-Sat* €€€

Pingvin: Innovative, small-plate dining that gives traditional Danish a globe-trotting flourish. *11am-10pm Tue-Thu, to midnight Fri & Sat* €€

Hos Henius: Trad spot named after an akvavit mogul; smørrebrød with Aalborg's famous spirit. *11.30am-5pm Sun-Wed, to 9pm Thu-Sat* €

Gedulgt: A fancy cocktail bar serving work-of-art concoctions. *6pm-midnight Thu, from 4pm Fri & Sat*

Irish House: Cosy pub in a 17th-century townhouse. *1pm-1am Mon-Wed, to 2am Thu, noon-4am Fri-Sat, 2pm-midnight Sun*

Søgaards Bryghus: Microbrewery on Aalborg's nicest square; meaty snacks. *hours vary*

Beyond Aalborg

Pack your wetsuit for a surfin' safari at Klitmøller. History hunters, take your pick from a nuclear bunker or Viking fortress.

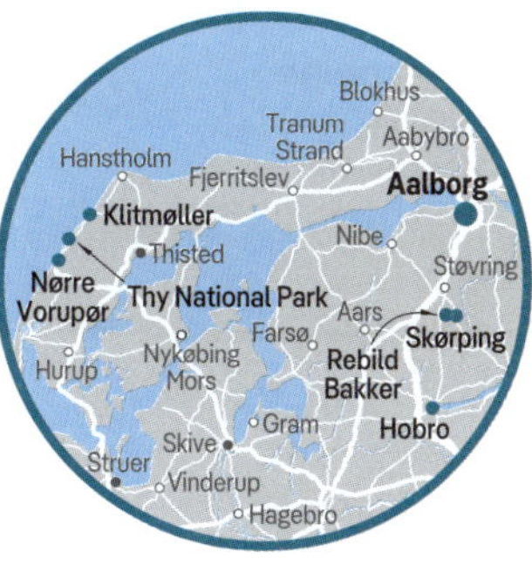

Centred on the narrowest crossing point of the Limfjord, Aalborg serves as the gateway into northern Jutland and its raw, alluring landscapes. Strike up and out for the coast and the surprisingly epic dunes of Thy National Park, which are 1½ hours away by car. This is Denmark's surfing country, home to scrappy seaside communities like Klitmøller (affectionately known as 'Cold Hawaii'); with your own wheels you can easily spend a few days roaming the coast.

Head south from Aalborg and you'll soon hit the Rebild Hills, part of an outdoorsy area of hiking and biking trails. Here too, hidden beneath a chalky hill is the Cold War nuclear bunker, REGAN Vest. Further on, the sleepy town of Hobro has Jutland's best Viking ruins: the UNESCO-listed 1000-year-old Fyrkat ring fortress: boats could sail right up to it on the Mariager Fjord.

Places

Skørping

TIME FROM AALBORG: **30 MINS** 

Underground nuclear bunker

Amid innocuous-looking wooded hills is a fascinating and foreboding secret: **REGAN Vest** *(nordjyskemuseer.dk; 285kr)* is a decommissioned Cold War–era nuclear bunker from the 1960s, hollowed out from a limestone and chalk hill. It feels like a post-apocalyptic film set, but it's real, and now a startling museum, which opened to the public in 2023. There's a splendid interactive exhibition to visit before your 90-minute tour underground, a chilling insight into the readiness of the Danish for impending nuclear war in the 1960s, it includes out-there hands-on activities such as a chance (virtually) to try out different nuclear weapons on the city of your choice.

The bunker was in use until 2012, though mainly decommissioned by 2002, preserved as if in amber. You also get to visit the nearby machinist's house, where the caretaker of the complex lived with his oblivious family. A 300m-long underground tunnel leads into the facility, where you will get to visit government 'situation rooms' hung with maps and outfitted with now-obsolete hardware. No photographs are permitted in the bunker.

It's a 30-minute drive south of Aalborg, or you can reach here by bus, but it's not direct and you have to walk (a scenic) 2km. Book well ahead to visit.

GETTING AROUND

Direct trains connect Aalborg with Hobro for the Fyrkat ring fortress. Disembark at Skørping for Rebild Bakker. Bus 53N takes you from Aalborg to Rebild Kommune, from where it's just over a 1km walk to REGAN Vest. Long-distance buses connect Aalborg with the town of Thisted, where you can pick up local connections to Thy National Park; having a car will make the trip easier and more fun, though: roads are light on traffic and well-kept.

TOP TIP

If you sign up for multiday surf camps in Klitmøller, you can usually arrange accommodation through the surf companies too.

LOWDOWN ON SURFING IN THY

Vahineura Itcher is a six-time Danish surfing champion and co-owner of the Cold Hawaii Surf Camp.

I've been surfing in Cold Hawaii for 17 years now. It's a great place for beginners to learn because there are always friendly waves to be found in different corners of Klitmøller's bay; my favourite spot is Klitmøller's reef – the best waves I ever caught there were at the outer reef. Klitmøller is a good surf spot all year, but you should always seek local advice before paddling out.

When I'm not surfing I like to go hiking in Thy National Park's beautiful nature, and hang out with my friends at my board shop.

Klitmøller

TIME FROM AALBORG: 1½ HR

Surf's up at Cold Hawaii

You might feel a tad underdressed without a board under your arm at Klitmøller, a far-out surf community facing a gorgeous sweep of the dune-backed North Sea. This was once a key fishing village on the route between Denmark and Norway, which saw an exodus after Hanstholm Harbour opened in 1967. It was in the 1980s that surfers began to come, discovering that the town's high-latitude winter storms created big waves, and the remote town turned into a major surfer magnet. More recently, it's become a popular escape from big city life, with some Copenhageners moving here to live permanently, a sea change signalled by the two workspaces and a Michelin-starred restaurant.

Windsurfing is big here in summer, while the surfing comes into its own in winter as the waves pick up. Near the beach, the **Cold Hawaii Surf Camp** *(coldhawaiisurfcamp.com)* will have you catching waves in no time, thanks to owners Mor and Vahine, both former Danish surfing champions. Across the road, **Westwind** *(klitmoller.westwind.dk)* is another long-established outfit with enthusiastic teachers.

Bikes can be rented *(coldhawaiibikes.dk)* along the main street. If you sign up for multiday surf camps in Klitmøller you can usually arrange accommodation through the surf companies too.

Thy National Park

TIME FROM AALBORG: 1 HR 40 MINS

Denmark's largest wilderness

There are marked hiking trails over the dunes that depart from Klitmøller into the wilds of **Thy National Park**. One of Denmark's handful of newly protected spaces, Thy National Park stretches 55km south along the North Sea coast from Hanstholm to Agger Tange, covering an area of 244 sq km of coastline, dunes, lakes, pine forest and moors. There are plenty of windswept, wide-open spaces to access: marked hiking, cycling and horse-riding trails, bird-watching opportunities, big waves, photogenic beaches, plus a good dose of history in fishing hamlets and WWII-era German bunkers.

Nørre Vorupør

TIME FROM AALBORG: 1 HR 40 MINS

Sea swimming and dunes

Around 13km south of Klitmøller is the small beach resort of **Nørre Vorupør**, where fishing vessels are winched up onto the sand. There's a sea pool here built into the North Sea shallows to enable safe swimming, which also has a ramp making it accessible for wheelchairs.

Nørre Vorupør is also the location of the **Thy National Park Centre** *(eng.nationalparkthy.dk)*, its stylish yet bunker-like concrete structure integrated into the dune landscape. Visit for its wildlife displays, books and hiking maps if you want to explore the extraordinary landscape of knobbly dunes topped with a green toupee of marram grass of Thy National Park. It's on the challenging West Coast Cycle Route, which runs from the German border in the south to Skagen.

Thy National Park

Rebild Bakker

TIME FROM AALBORG: **30 MINS**

Glacial playground for hikers

Rebild Bakker (Rebild Hills) is a protected area of muscular hills rising up over dense 'troll forest' (so named because of its twisted old beeches with multiple trunks), and one of Jutland's more unusual nature parks. A super visitor centre, **RebildPorten** *(rebildporten.dk)* has clued-up staff ready to furnish you with maps and intel on hikes, natural springs, mountain-bike trails (such as the 24km 'blue route'), fishing, canoeing and local folklore.

Hobro

TIME FROM AALBORG: **20 MINS**

Time travel to the Viking age

Since 2023, the 1000-year-old **Fyrkat Ring Fortress** *(visithimmerland.eu; adult/child incl entry to Vikingecenter Fyrkat 100kr/free),* 3km southwest of Hobro has been a UNESCO World Heritage Site, one of five such surviving fortresses built across Denmark by the embattled Viking king Harald Bluetooth around 980. It's a profound experience to wander around its grassy ramparts, now grazed by wandering sheep, and although only the traces of the structure remain, you can still see the fort's impressive scale and geometric circular design, with a diameter of 120m. It would have once

THE CURIOUS HISTORY OF THE REBILD HILLS

Held since 1912, Rebild Festival is a 4th of July celebration that's among the largest outside the USA, thanks to Max Henius who emigrated to the US in 1881. He raised money among fellow Danish-Americans to buy 200 hectares of land, founding the Rebild National Park in 1912. The group presented the land to the Danish government with the proviso that it would be open to all and accessible to Danish-Americans for the celebration of US holidays. This inspired the Danish forest service to acquire the adjacent Rold Skov, Denmark's largest forest and a great mountain-biking spot. It turned out to be a memorial sooner than Henius could have imagined: after presenting the deed to King Christian X, he drowned on his return voyage.

EATING IN KLITMØLLER: OUR PICKS

Tri: Michelin-starred, glass-fronted restaurant south of Nørre Vorupør, focusing on the local fjord seafood. *5.30pm-midnight Thu-Sun* €€€

Fiskerestaurant Niels Juel: Seafront terrace, good-value seafood buffet, cafe with fast food downstairs. *5.30-9pm Tue-Sun May-Sep* €€

Kesses Hus: Next-level crêpes, galettes, post-surf options like smoked deer. *11am-9pm Jul-mid-Aug, shorter hours Apr-Jun & mid-Aug-Oct* €

Good Food to Go: Wholesome takeaway place with dishes of the day based on fresh seasonal organic produce. *5-8pm Fri, 8am-8pm Sat* €

THE BLUETOOTH FORTRESSES

The five ring fortresses recently listed by UNESCO were constructed between 970 and 980 CE during the reign of King Harald 'Bluetooth' Gormsson. They're at Aggersborg, Fyrkat, Nonnebakken, Trelleborg and Borgring, all in strategic locations on land and sea routes. They're more than just remarkable for their uniform geometric circular design. They're also indicative of the centralisation and sophistication of power and connectivity during the Jelling period, built as a response to the threats from mainland Europe from German-Roman Emperor Otto II. The site at Fyrkat is one of the best preserved, equal to Trelleborg in Zealand – the forts are also known as *'trelleborgs'*.

JON ARNOLD IMAGES LTD/ALAMY STOCK PHOTO ©

Vikingecenter Fyrkat

held some 800 Vikings and their families in 16 longhouses. In the 1950s, a burial site was excavated beside the fortress, with around 30 burials, one of whom was interred with amulets and jewellery indicating that she may have been a *vølve*, a pagan sorceress.

A kilometre away is the excellent **Vikingecenter Fyrkat** *(nordjyskemuseer.dk/u/vikingemuseet-fyrkat)*, a re-created Viking-style farmstead where costumed staff and volunteers raise chickens and chop wood. Archaeologists believe such farms existed around the fortress walls, supplying encamped Vikings with fresh produce. The 33m **longhouse** here is particularly impressive – not to mention hyggelig, with its animal-skin blankets, crackling fire and sawdust aromas. One ticket covers both sites.

ON THE DEFENSIVE

Fyrkat is one of five Viking age ring fortresses, designated a UNESCO World Heritage Site in 2023; if you're a history buff with a yen to see more, the largest and best-known is the **Trelleborg ring fortress** in Zealand (p116).

EATING & DRINKING IN KLITMØLLER: OUR PICKS

Klitmøller Røgeri: Near the beach, this diner has house-smoked fish and a terrace for beers with a view. *10am-10pm Fri-Sat, to 4pm Sun* **€**

Haandpluk Kaffebar: Suitably DIY for a place like Klitmøller – a tiny microbrewery that also does tapas and coffee. *noon-6pm Thu-Sat* **€**

N151: Vahineura from Cold Hawaii Surf Camp has set up a fun coffee bar, with good coffee, home-baked cakes, authentic French pastries. *10am-5pm* **€**

Café Stalden: Rustic bodega on the outskirts. *11am-midnight Mon, to 4pm Tue & Sun, to 5pm & 8pm-midnight Wed, to 2am Thu, to 3am Fri-Sat*

Skagen

COAST | SEAFOOD | ART

At the northernmost tip of Denmark, the fishing port of Skagen huddles amid sand drifts. It's a curious mix of folksy yellow cottages with white-picket fences, a small, busy working port and upscale holidaymakers – the Danish Royal Family had a hand in popularising the town and it's something of a Danish Hamptons in summer, especially in week 29, when Lamborghinis and yachts arrive for their owners to drink rosé and eat the area's fresh seafood.

Two seas merge here, and the particular quality of natural light is a feature that drew a group of bohemian artists to the town in the 1870s. Fresh out of Denmark's Royal Academy, the 'Skagen Painters' were infatuated with the fabled 'blue hour', a time of evening when the mirror-like sea and sky merge as one. Skagen's three decades or so as an artist colony was its golden age; a big part of the town's appeal is discovering this history and the natural settings which inspired the painters. Bird-watching (around 350 species migrate through here, with most passing by in May); biking (of course) and walking are the other major pursuits.

GETTING AROUND

Skagen is small enough to get around on foot, but a bike is handy for Grenen and Gammel Skagen. Skagen CykelUdlejning, by the train station, has bikes for hire. Trains run to Frederikshavn roughly every half-hour or hour, where you can change for destinations further south. Buses stop outside the train station. Town bus S1 connects the sights between Grenen and the sand-covered church. Summer parking is at a premium. The 'sand worm' truck goes to Grenen, Denmark's most northerly point.

Skagen: Art & Fish

Skagen's artist colony

In the centre of town, amid buttermilk-yellow cottages, the handsome **Brøndums Hotel** (p241) was Skagen's hub of artistic activity during the late 19th century, and continues to host guests today. The **Skagens Museum** *(skagenkunstmuseer.dk; adult/child 125kr/free)* faces the hotel across the street, and has a great collection of the artists' work, which not only captures the area's extraordinary light, but also the people and life of the time. The artists painted local portraits and other subjects on the wood panelling of the hotel dining room where they met, and the entire room has been transferred to the museum.

SIGHTS
1 Anchers Hus
2 Drachmanns Hus
3 Kystmuseet Skagen
4 Skagens Museum

SLEEPING
5 Brøndums Hotel
6 Finns B&B

EATING
7 Jørgens Spisehus
8 Saxild
9 Skagen Fiskerestaurant

DRINKING & NIGHTLIFE
10 Havnekroen
11 Jakobs Café & Bar
12 Skagen Bryghus
13 Torst Cocktail Bar

TRANSPORT
14 Skagen CykelUdlejning

TOP TIP

Main street Sankt Laurentii Vej runs almost the entire length of this long, narrow town, from which it's never more than five minutes' walk to the waterfront. Lively street Havnevej, connecting the harbour and town centre, is great for an evening drink.

Exploring the Anchers' Artistic House

A preserved cultural landmark

Two of the most prominent Skagen painters were Anna and Michael Ancher (pictured together on the 1000kr banknote) who lived at **Anchers Hus** *(skagenkunstmuseer.dk; adult/child 90kr/free)* nearby. Their house has been preserved as if they have just popped out, with beautiful rooms brimful of curios and paintings. A combination ticket (along with the Skagens Museum) also gets you into the **Drachmanns Hus** *(skagenskunstmuseer.dk; adult/child 60kr/free)* on the western edge of town, the likewise charming and art-lined home of Skagen painter and poet Holger Drachmann.

Skagen's Seafaring Past

Shipwrecks and boats

To discover the region's fishing history, check out **Skagen Kystmuseet** *(kystmuseet.dk; adult/child 110kr/free)* a kid-friendly museum decked out with period dioramas, boats and fishing huts. One exhibition hall displays dozens of name-plates recovered from ships wrecked in the perilous Skagen waters, along with accounts of the brave locals who attempted rescues. Admission includes several other nearby coastal museums, at Sæby and Bangsbo.

Grenen, Where Two Seas Meet

Denmark's northernmost point

Heading north through Skagen, past the small **White Lighthouse**, the road ends 2km later at **Grenen** ('The Branch'), a tapering limb of sand, home to migrating birds of prey, grey seals and Denmark's most northerly point. This sandbar is sculpted by the collision of the Kattegat (an arm of the Baltic Sea) with the Skagerrak (part of the North Sea); you can paddle in the crisscrossing waves with one foot in each sea. Swimming is forbidden here, though, because of the ferocious tidal currents.

Getting to Jutland's northern tip means either a 20-minute hike along the seashore (longer if crossing the dunes), or hitching a lift on the 'sand worm' (Sandormen), a tractor-pulled bus that leaves the car park at Grenen from 10am daily, running all day. Cash only for tickets onboard, but the car-park machine takes cards.

War buffs can duck into the tiny **Skagen Bunker Museum** *(skagen-bunkermuseum.dk; adult/child 60/35kr)* by the car park, housed in one of many German bunkers left over from when Grenen was fortified during WWII.

The active **Skagen Lighthouse** (also called the Grey Lighthouse; *detgraafyr.dk; adult/child 85/30kr)* was built in 1858 and doubles as a bird observatory, with an exhibition on the many migratory species that rest up on the sandbar each year, plus, gorily, a fridge containing local roadkill. Entry also lets you brave the slog up 210 steps for inspiring coastal views.

Wandering Sands: Jutland's Dunes

Sand-drenched landscapes

It's not just the power of the sea that defines Skagen: sand drifts have menaced communities in the region for centuries.

PIONEERING ANNA

Anna Brøndum was born in Skagen, and her father owned Brøndums Hotel. Artists began to travel to Skagen in the 19th century, attracted by the simple, rustic lifestyle of the local fishing community, the soft northern light and unique qualities produced by the sea. Anna studied in Copenhagen, and met Michael Ancher in Skagen, where they settled. Anna, unusually for the time, continued to paint after marriage.

The Skagen artists' work was inspired by the Impressionists, breaking away from the more formal painting style of the past. Anna's work has a greater sense of realism than some of the more romanticised depictions of her peers, and her paintings offer a window to life at the time, with everyday subjects like families awaiting vaccination.

EATING IN SKAGEN: OUR PICKS

Blink: Top food using local ingredients in a superb location under the Grey Lighthouse. *10am-10pm Fri & Sat, to 4pm Sun & Tue* €€

Saxild: Delicious food like burrata with avocado on sourdough, in a yellow half-timbered building. *11am-3.30pm Wed-Fri, from 9am Sat & Sun* €€

Skagen Fiskerestaurant: Casual eatery at the port – lobster rolls, fresh oysters, fish soup. *11am-10pm May-Oct, shorter hours Nov-Apr* €€

Jørgens Spisehus: Danish dishes like *stjerneskud* (breaded and steamed fish on white bread), harbourside. *10am-7.30pm, from 11am Sat & Sun* €€

WHY I LOVE SKAGEN

Thomas O'Malley, Lonely Planet writer

Sagas that tell of shipwrecks and iron-willed fishing folk, a buried church, steely lighthouses, world-class art and the literal end of the road – what's not to love about Skagen?

Skagen had me the first time I wandered through its quiet, sandy lanes on a late September evening, admiring the picture-book cottages that were all warm and cosy behind their knee-high garden fences. And then, in the fading light, a pair of deer ambled across the street as though they owned the place, paying me no mind at all. It was magical.

Den Tilsandede Kirke

A fun 5km bike ride south of Skagen will take you to the sand-covered church, **Den Tilsandede Kirke**, which fell victim to drifting sand in the late 1700s. Only the tower protrudes from the landscape, the rest entirely buried. You can climb up the tower for a view across the trees, shrubs and sand of **Skagen Klitplantage**, a nature reserve with hiking trails. There's a kiosk and a car park.

Most of Jutland's shifting dunes have since been stabilised by planting conifers and dune grasses, but one was left to wander: Råbjerg Mile, 16km southwest of Skagen. Denmark's largest expanse of sand dunes, these undulating, 40m-high hills move at a rate of 15m per year and make for remarkable photos – you feel like you've swapped Skagen for the Sahara.

It was sandstorms that changed the fortunes of Gammel Skagen ('Old Skagen'), forcing many of its inhabitants to abandon the fishing hamlet and move across to the more-protected east coast. These days Gammel Skagen (aka Højen) has a touch of Cape Cod about it, with fine hotels and well-heeled summer residents. It can be reached by a pleasant 4km bike ride from Skagen proper.

DRINKING IN SKAGEN: OUR PICKS

Jakobs Café & Bar: Terrace usually heaving for early-evening drinks, DJs and live music later. Great spot to start the night. *11.30am-9pm*

Havnekroen: A popular local bar with relatively cheap beers and lots of convivial atmosphere. *10am-midnight*

Torst Cocktail Bar: Civilised cocktail den for a Skagen Sour with Nordic gin and hawthorn. *3pm-midnight Mon-Thu, from noon Sun, to 1am Fri & Sat*

Skagen Bryghus: Cathedral-like space with Skagen brews and thigh-slapping live music. Older crowd. *10.30am-6pm Mon-Thu, to 7pm Fri & Sat*

Beyond Skagen

Enter an elemental wonderland of sand, sea and spectral light shows. Even in the seaside towns, nature still calls the shots.

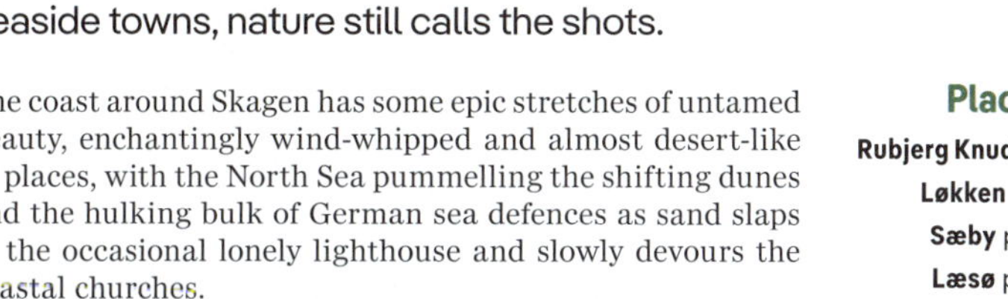

The coast around Skagen has some epic stretches of untamed beauty, enchantingly wind-whipped and almost desert-like in places, with the North Sea pummelling the shifting dunes and the hulking bulk of German sea defences as sand slaps at the occasional lonely lighthouse and slowly devours the coastal churches.

Punctuating all that brooding serenity are seaside towns: Løkken has surfer vibes and beachside saunas, while over on the less scenically dramatic east coast you've got Sæby, an unassuming Danish holiday resort that was inspiration for Henrik Ibsen's *The Lady from the Sea,* and ferry hub Frederikshavn – the latter most notable as the jumping-off point to the low-key island of Læsø.

Places

Rubjerg Knude Fyr

TIME FROM SKAGEN: **1 HR**

The lighthouse that moved

The primordial dune cliffs of Lønstrup Klint, wrought of sand and clay and battered by the waves, reveal Jutland at its most wild and elemental. The cliffs made of sand and edged by dunes appear contradictory against the blue of the sea. Spanning the 15km between Lønstrup and Løkken, they rise up to their highest point at **Rubjerg Knude** *(rubjergknude.dk)*, which is home to a famously long-suffering, and much revered, lighthouse.

Rubjerg Knude Fyr (see p239) was 200m inland when it was first turned on in 1900, but by 1968 heavy sand drifts had obscured the beam, forcing it to be closed. In 1980, the lighthouse opened as a museum – but had to close again in 2002 due to shifting sands. In 2016, the lighthouse was retrofitted with a new steel staircase so that visitors could once again enter and climb it...but by then erosion meant that it was in danger of tumbling into the sea. So in 2019, the entire 720-tonne structure was moved. It took 10 hours to transport the lighthouse 70m further inland, buying it another few decades of safety at a cost of 5 million kroner.

The lighthouse is a 1km walk through the sandy dunes from the car park. In summer, there's a *knuden* ('sand worm') truck for those who don't want to walk.

GETTING AROUND

The Danish train system doesn't extend to northwest Jutland, but in summer bus 99 runs a few times daily from Skagen down the northwest coast, taking in Gammel Skagen, Hirtshals, Tornby Strand, Hjørring, Lønstrup, Løkken and theme-park Fårup Sommerland, where it connects with bus 200 to Aalborg. Lonely roads, endless beaches and campsites make this part of Jutland prime road-trip country.

DUNE

The Little Ice Age in the late 16th century was a major climatic event, and impacted areas of the coast of western Europe. In both northern Scotland and western Denmark, large dune fields encroached on the land, burying and forcing several villages to be abandoned. Medieval deforestation had also contributed to the instability of the landscape. The sandy situation in northern Jutland was only truly brought under control with the Sand Drift Act of the 19th century, which set in motion the systematic plantation of grasses and trees to prevent the scale of drift. However, Råbjerg Mile was left: the word 'mile' means a high, naked, shifting dune in Danish.

Løkken

TIME FROM SKAGEN: **1 HR 10 MINS**

Surf and sand

Hugely popular with Danes, **Løkken** is the best base of a string of sandy, windswept towns situated along the west coast. The dunes provide a buffer between the bungalows and the beach; locals drive their cars out on to the hard-packed sand, which has distinctive rows of beehive-like white beach huts that get packed away for winter. Fishing boats come ashore right on the beach and sell fish directly from the day's catch, and in summer you can eat at food trucks serving the local seafood.

Glance up the shoreline to the north and you'll spot what looks like a lost city half buried in the sand, *Planet of the Apes*–style – the evocative ruins of a massive **German gun battery** from WWII that has gradually tumbled down from the eroded dunes above. If you walk along the coast you'll see several more that are dotted along the coast. Against the slow onslaught of the sand, even these hulking structures don't stand a chance.

Right by the entrance to the beach you'll find the **North Shore Surf School** *(northshoresurf.dk)*, offering lessons, gear rental, a cafe-bar, mobile sauna and its own fish-and-chips food truck.

Sæby

TIME FROM SKAGEN: **1½ HR**

Holiday home of Nordic literature

Halfway between Skagen and Aalborg on the sheltered north-east coast is genteel **Sæby**, lined with colourful half-timbered houses and with a boat-bobbing port, **Sæby Havn** (the old

Path to Rubjerg Knude Fyr (p237)

fishing port), amid yachts, seafood restaurants and ice-cream kiosks. Ibsen wrote *The Lady from the Sea* here, and a 6.85m high statue of the *Lady,* by Norwegian sculptor Marit Benthe Norheim, looms over the port.

From the marina, it's a pleasant walk into the centre, passing the imposing **Sæby Kirke**, which is all that remains of a 15th-century monastery – and the **Sæby Coastal Museum** *(kystmuseet.dk/en; adult/child 110kr/free)*, which is housed in a half-timbered farm building from 1800. It's a charming meander through the history of the monastery, and Sæby's subsequent reinvention as a holiday resort after an iron well was discovered in the 19th century – after this find, health tourists flocked here to take the waters. Your ticket also allows you admission to other local coastal museums, including at Skagen and Bangsbo.

A LIGHTHOUSE ON SKATES

In October 2019, a meticulous operation was carried out to move the 720-tonne Rubjerg Knude Fyr. Engineers first reinforced the structure to ensure it could withstand the move. The lighthouse was then lifted onto a specially designed set of skates and rails, enabling it to be shifted slowly inland. The engineers had estimated the weight to be 1000 tonnes, but it turned out to be lighter, making the process easier than envisaged.

Once the lighthouse was placed on the rails, it was pushed by machine along the track at a rate of about 12m an hour. The entire operation was a resounding success, with the lighthouse placed in a more stable situation – for now.

Læsø

TIME FROM SKAGEN: **2 HR 40 MINS** 

Salt bath island

Frederikshavn, 40km south of Skagen, is Jutland's busiest international ferry terminal, with connections to Oslo and

EATING IN LØKKEN: OUR PICKS

Huset Havs: Fun and funky bar-restaurant with a boat as a bar, and surf shop attached, run by the North Shore Surf School crew. *10am-5pm* €€

Restaurant Løkken Badehotel: Old-school Danish smørrebrød and *pandestegt rødspætte* (pan-fried plaice), by the main square. *9am-9pm* €€

Bolcheriet: Watch the candy being made at this colourful sweet shop full of toothsome treats. *10am-8pm Jul & Aug, shorter hours Sep-Jun* €

Slice of Life: Neapolitan-style pizza with fresh toppings; good beach takeaway choice. *5-8pm Thu-Sun Apr-Sep, limited hours Oct-Mar* €

LITERARY SÆBY

Sæby has literary chops. The town was the inspiration for both Herman Bang's 1902 novel *Sommerglæder* (Summer Pleasures) and Henrik Ibsen's 1887 play *Fruen fra havet* (The Lady from the Sea), which he wrote after spending six weeks in summer here. During Ibsen's stay, the 59-year-old author had developed an unrequited passion for Engelke Wulff, 40 years his junior, a resident who dreamed of escaping the small town. Their friendship helped inspire the play, whose themes share something of the spirit of *The Little Mermaid*, in longing to escape the sea while being drawn back to it.

LGIEGER/SHUTTERSTOCK ©

Horneks Odde, Læsø

Gothenburg, as well as boats to the time-warped Danish island of **Læsø**, with its sandy beaches, folksy traditions, radish fields and charming small communities.

The best thing to do here is take a salt bath – the island is famed for its salt – at **Læsø Kur** *(saltkur.dk; day 375kr incl towel and robe)*, a spa close to the ferry port, with hot tubs, warm salt pools, a sauna and steam rooms. There are various day-trip packages available, organised by the ferry company *(laesoe-line.dk)* that makes the 1½-hour crossing from Frederikshavn.

EATING IN SÆBY & LÆSØ: OUR PICKS

Slagter Tranholm: Cold cuts are this Sæby place's speciality; great for a takeaway sandwich. *9.30am-5.30pm Mon-Fri, 9am-2pm Sat* €

Jacobs Fiskerestaurant: Smart place with buffet or à la carte on Sæby harbour; downstairs kiosk serves fish and chips. *11.30am-9pm* €€

Frøken Madsen's Spisehus: Danish faves in a hyggelig building a block from Sæby's main street. *5-9pm Wed-Thu, to 10pm Fri & Sat* €€

Thorsen Fisk: Get local seafood from this excellent fishmonger on the main square at Læsø. *10am-1pm Mon-Sat* €

Places We Love to Stay

€ Budget €€ Midrange €€€ Top End

Aarhus p206

SOFS Boutique Hotel €€ Top pick for its excellent location, warm staff, rooms with Persian rugs, pretty garden oasis and relaxed, stylish ambience.

City Hotel Oasia Aarhus €€ A great city-centre choice, with Hästens beds (some of the most comfortable in the world) and light-filled, minimalist rooms.

Villa Provence €€€ Provençal country style dominates Aarhus' most charming boutique hotel. Superior rooms are larger but standard have the same attention to detail.

Silkeborg p214

Danhostel Silkeborg € Danhostels vary in quality but this is a good one: you can't beat the sweet riverbank location and private jetty for Hjejlen boats.

Villa Zeltner €€ Good-value B&B in the heart of Silkeborg, with a choice of small private apartments.

Knudhule Badehotel €€€ Just outside Ry, this smart lakeside hotel belongs to a top restaurant, Gastronomisk Institut.

Ebeltoft p218

Danhostel Ebeltoft € Excellent, if isolated, hostel (and a striking example of 1960s brutalism), half-hidden in green surroundings.

Ebeltoft Strand Camping € Pools, playgrounds and miniature golf, and cabins backing onto the beach near Ebeltoft.

Langhoff & Juul €€€ White-washed and red-roofed with Scandi-chic, neutral rooms with wood floors, big windows and balcony. Great location with views over Ebeltoft bay.

Billund p219

Danhostel Grindsted-Billund € Top-notch hostel 13km west of Legoland (with easy bus connections), well set up for families. Book well ahead.

The Lodge €€ In walking distance of Legoland, this more grown-up hotel still caters for families, with simple rooms and an indoor pool.

Lalandia €€ The smart chalets here at first glance seem expensive but you can sleep the whole family, plus you get free entry to the swimming pools and can self-cater.

Hotel Legoland €€€ Right next to Legoland, this is a dream place for Lego-lovers; pay extra for themed rooms that are not fancy but children will love.

Legoland Holiday Village €€€ This outstanding Lego-drenched 'village' incorporates themed motel rooms and a huge campsite.

Ringkøbing Fjord p223

Danhostel Ringkøbing € Hostel in a large sports centre, with spacious, light-filled rooms and plenty of socialising space.

Drivethru Surfcamps €€ In a converted farmhouse, this hyggelig hostel offers full board and multiday watersports courses. Sign up online.

Feriepartner Hvide Sande €€€ Agency that rents out state-of-the-art houseboats, plus apartments and summer cottages.

Aalborg p225

Kompas Hotel €€ Old seamen's hotel now a spic-and-span contemporary place near the waterfront. A nonprofit, its proceeds support a maritime welfare charity.

Pier 5 €€ Central hotel with tech-forward rooms, Limfjord views and a cocktail bar.

Klitmøller p230

Nystrup Camping € Popular with surf types; decent facilities here include cabins, bike hire and a playground.

Gaarden Klitmøller €€ Four guest rooms share a bathroom and living space at this colourful, homely guesthouse with garden terrace.

Skagen p233

Danhostel Skagen € A hive of activity, this hostel is modern, functional and clean as a whistle, if a bit away from the action.

Finns B&B €€ Fabulously quirky log-cabin-style home built in 1923 for a Norwegian count. Some rooms share bathrooms.

Brøndums Hotel €€€ This heritage hotel is a luxurious option despite shared bathrooms.

Løkken p238

Villa Vendel €€ Delightful option east of Torvet with four rooms (all with a bathroom) and two apartments. Classy old-world feel.

Cafehaven €€ Small country retreat overflowing with hygge; fresh, bright, well-priced rooms and studio apartments, incredible gardens.

The Faroe Islands

UNTAMED NATURAL BEAUTY AND SUBLIME ISOLATION

Discover life at the edge of the world, hiking routes across breathtaking mountains and a sense of undiscovered Europe you'll find nowhere else.

Wild and windswept, this 18-island archipelago possesses a raw and elemental beauty. Rugged basalt mountains rise above narrow sea straits, and towering cliffs teem with birdlife. Hundreds of kilometres from its nearest neighbours and home to just over 53,000 people, the Faroe Islands is a self-governing nation within the Kingdom of Denmark. Remote as these islands are, they're only a two-hour flight from London, and after many years off the radar, they are no longer a secret. The Faroes' international airport on Vágar has direct flights from London and New York as well as Scotland, France, Spain, Iceland, and several cities in Denmark and Norway. Travellers explore lonely lighthouses and timeless villages, hike mountain trails and go bird-watching, but you need to come prepared for unpredictable and weather like wind, rain and fog – it rains or snows more than 257 days a year.

It's thought Irish monks stepped foot on these islands first, followed by the Vikings, who settled more than 1000 years ago. Centuries of isolation have made the Faroese a resilient and independent people. Although their homeland is part of the Danish realm, the Faroese don't consider themselves Danes. Traditionally, they have lived from the sea, and even today, fishing and salmon farming drive the local economy. Discover this oft-forgotten world for yourself.

THE MAIN AREAS

TÓRSHAVN
The foodie, cultural, Faroese capital. p248

VÁGAR
A hikers and puffin-lover's paradise. p258

NORTHERN ISLANDS
Forgotten villages and unpaved roads. p263

SOUTHERN ISLANDS
Bird-spotting, yarn-bombing and solitude. p267

For places to stay in the Faroe Islands, see p271

Left: Suðuroy (p269); Above: Kallur Lighthouse, Kalsoy (p265)

Find Your Way

With the Faroe Islands' extraordinary network of tunnels and underwater roads, it's easy to drive and explore just about everywhere in a short stay; throw in a couple of epic hikes and a great dinner, and a week's stay makes itself.

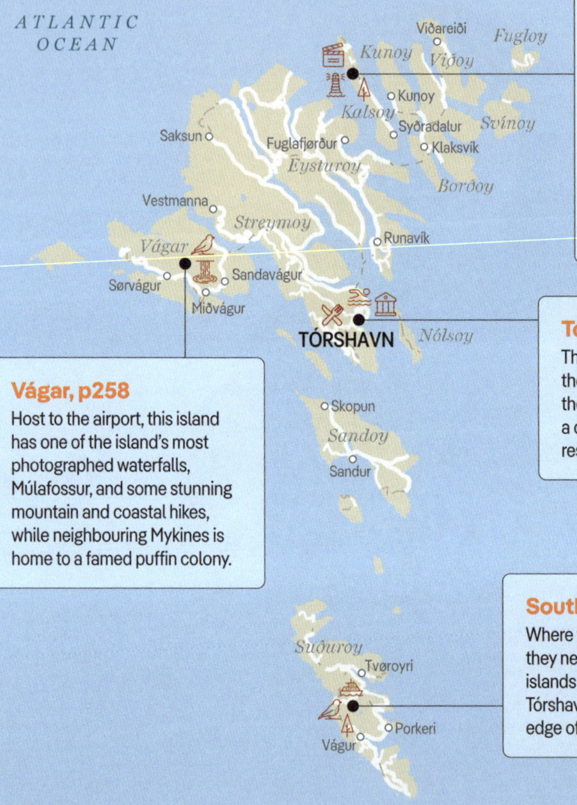

ATLANTIC OCEAN
Viðareiði
Fugloy
Kunoy
Viðoy
Kunoy
Kalsoy
Syðradalur
Svínoy
Saksun
Fuglafjørður
Klaksvík
Eysturoy
Borðoy
Vestmanna
Streymoy
Runavík
Vágar
Sørvágur
Sandavágur
Miðvágur
TÓRSHAVN
Nólsoy
Skopun
Sandoy
Sandur
Suðuroy
Tvøroyri
Porkeri
Vágur

Northern Islands, p263

A famous selkie statue, a lighthouse hike and James Bond's gravestone are three of the key attractions on the dramatic northern islands reached by ferry.

Tórshavn, p248

The old Viking capital of the islands is named after the god of war and is now a cultural hub with great restaurants to discover.

Vágar, p258

Host to the airport, this island has one of the island's most photographed waterfalls, Múlafossur, and some stunning mountain and coastal hikes, while neighbouring Mykines is home to a famed puffin colony.

Southern Islands, p267

Where the Faroese go when they need time out, these islands are two hours from Tórshavn by ferry and feel on the edge of the world.

PUBLIC TRANSPORT

The islands' bus network is good value for travellers. Four-day passes, including buses and ferries, cost 500kr; 7 days cost 700kr (children 7-15 half price). Check timetables closely, off-season routes are limited. The country's public ferry network runs from a ferry port near the main marina in Tórshavn.

CAR

Driving is the most convenient way to explore overall. Note: car hire can be pricy (book ahead). EVs are available. Many islands are linked by sub-sea tunnels.

LAURA HALL/LONELY PLANET ©

Bøur (p258)

Plan Your Time

Most of the archipelago's sights are within easy reach of the capital. With extra time on your hands, you can take a ferry to more remote islands.

If You Have Only 3 Days

- Make the most of the stunning scenery in **Vágar** (p258) by stopping in the village **Gásadalur** (p250) and the **Múlafossur** waterfall (p258). Hike to the coast at **Trælanípa** (p260) and feel the power of nature on a boat trip from **Vestmanna** (p255). Go for a Faroese culture fix in **Tórshavn** (p248), admiring art at **Listasavn Føroya** (p248) and eating local cuisine at **ROKS** (p250).

If You Have a Week

- Spend a day in **Vágar** (p258) and then visit the puffin colony at **Mykines** (p261). Devote time to **Tórshavn** (p248), calling at **Kirkjubøur village** (p253) and day-tripping to **Nólsoy island** (p253). Head north to hike to the lighthouse at **Kalsoy** (p265), summit **Klakkur** (p264) for panoramas and soak in the setting in **Saksun** (p255). Surf Atlantic waves in **Tjørnuvík** (p255).

Seasonal Highlights

SPRING

The islands teem with birdlife as puffins and other seabirds return to nest. Late April brings the **Flag Day** festival.

SUMMER

Longer days arrive, but the weather is a mixed bag. **Music festivals** get under way and locals celebrate **Ólavsøka**.

AUTUMN

Tourist season winds down and some attractions close. You might have popular sights to yourself.

WINTER

Dark nights draw in, but **Christmas** is cosy. Jazz and light **festivals in the capital** brighten the cold months.

Which Islands to Visit?

There are 18 islands to visit in the Faroe Islands archipelago, 17 of which are inhabited. They range from mysterious, fog-shrouded and wind-whipped, to green-edged and cultural. Off-the-beaten-track is a relative term here where everywhere feels virtually untouched; choose between islands with small occasional cafes and accommodation, and those where you're on your own, with a packed lunch and a hiking trail that seems known only to the local sheep.

Where to Go If You Like...

Bird-watching

Mykines Spot puffins waddling around on the cliffs, flapping frantically in the air and peeping out of their burrows on Mykines, the westernmost island of the group, which is known for its feathered friends. Peak action is in July.

Vestmanna bird cliffs A two-hour cruise from Vestmanna village takes you to secret cliff, dark caves and towering sea stacks, all thronged with sea birds in the summer months. Spot puffin, guillemot and kittiwake.

LAURA HALL/LONELY PLANET ©

Daring coastal walks

Viðoy At the northernmost point of the Faroe Islands, the hike to Cape Enniberg is extraordinary and extreme. Take a local guide – these paths are steep, dangerous and not often walked – and discover colonies of seabirds on the 754m-high cliff, one of the highest promontories in the world. Not for the faint-hearted, unprepared or those with a fear of heights.

Suðuroy Reached by a two-hour ferry crossing from Tórshavn, this island of just under 5,000 people, is driveable in a day. Hike barely marked trails to seabird-packed cliffs and stand overlooking the archipelago's southernmost point.

Film locations

Kalsoy This northern island, reached via ferry from Klaksvík, was used as the location for a Bond villain's lair in *No Time To Die*. It's an island of sharp peaks and tiny villages, full of myths and legends – particularly about its magical stones and its seal woman.

Tindhólmur The sharply point of Tindhólmur island featured in Disney's 2023 film *Peter Pan & Wendy* as Peter Pan's island. Other filming locations for the mist-wreathed and imaginative film include Risin & Kellingin, Trælanípa and Mykines.

Local food

Streymoy Head to the capital Tórshavn for fine dining, excellent seafood and traditional fermented dishes, plus casual fish 'n' chips and sushi joints. We'd recommend the local lamb and, for the adventurous, fermented meat and sea urchin roe.

Hanusarstova Meet a local farmer and her ridiculously photogenic sheep, and then eat dinner around the kitchen table at her farm. Hanusarstova is one of a number of local supper club options where you can eat with local people, known as *heimabliðni*.

JOSEK/SHUTTERSTOCK ©

Drangarnir (p259)

HOW TO

Plan your trip Visit in summer for the best bird-watching and hiking. Consider the shoulder months (May and September) for the best prices.

Book ahead Restaurants typically need a reservation. Check times ahead. Even in peak season, beyond the capital some may open only on a handful of days a week.

Budget It's typical to pay between 50kr and 200kr for access to local hiking trails. The situation is in flux with a tourist tax replacing individual fees (expected by October 2025).

Pack sensibly Expect bad weather and prepare accordingly. Check the weather – and local webcams – on *faroeislandslive.com*

Touring the Islands

Car rental is the obvious choice, giving you freedom to explore the winding roads and outstanding scenery of the islands at your own pace; second is taking the local bus for which there are discounts for multi-day passes. But there are plenty of other ways to explore the islands.

If you're short on time, the excellent 'Faroe Islands In A Day' tour with Guide to Faroe Islands *(guidetofaroeislands.fo; 1450kr)* is a six-hour minibus excursion of all the highlights, from Saksun to Tjørnuvík, with an expert local guide. It's also possible to see the Faroes by helicopter. Check out timetables and options on Atlantic Airways *(atlantic.fo)* and book way in advance – there are limited seats and priority is given to local people.

Cycling is another option: *rentabike.fo* in Tórshavn hires e-bikes and with quiet, scenic roads it can be fun. Note that there are significant hills. It is possible to bike pack the islands, staying in small campsites along the way.

Perhaps the most beautiful way to see round these islands is by boat. The website *boat.fo* offers a range of guided boat excursions, fishing trips and family sailing options; the most romantic way to get around has to be with the red-sailed wooden schooner *Nordlysid (nordlysid.com; 4-hour tours from 1095kr).*

Tórshavn

CULINARY DELIGHTS | FAROESE CULTURE | HARBOUR LIFE

GETTING AROUND

Tórshavn is best explored by foot and bus. Parking is limited. The SMS Mall offers two hours' free car parking. The harbour car park allows eight hours of free parking.

Free local buses operate around Tórshavn. Bus 300 has regular services from the international airport in Vágar. Taxis and shared shuttles are also available. From Tórshavn allow 45 minutes to an hour to transfer from the airport.

There are two ferry terminals in Tórshavn: a car ferry terminal for local ferries; and a larger terminal for international services to/from Denmark and Iceland.

In a land of wild mountains and scattered villages, Tórshavn offers something different. Around 14,000 people live in the Faroe Islands' capital, making it a relative metropolis. Delve into Faroese culture with a museum visit, taste local cuisine at a first-rate restaurant or go shopping for design, wool and other Nordic treats.

Many of the sights are close to Tórshavn's colourful waterfront, which brims with yachts and fishing boats. The city has the highest number of hotels, making it a common base for a longer stay in the country. Many of the archipelago's key sights are within an hour's drive.

At the southern tip of Streymoy, the harbour is divided in two by the Tinganes peninsula, home to a village-like cluster of charming cottages, tangled passageways and the prime minister's office. More than a millennia ago, Viking settlers founded one of the world's earliest parliaments in this very place.

Faroese History & Culture in the Capital

Tórshavn's museums and galleries

Get to know the Faroes' art scene at the national gallery **Listasavn Føroya** *(art.fo; adult/child 90kr/free)*. Housed in a bright space, the permanent collection of Faroese art spans from 1830 to the present day. Among the works are several paintings of brooding seascapes and poignant scenes from village life by renowned artist SJ Mikines. Check out Edward Fuglø's striking painting *Colony* and the sculpture *WhaleWar*, which explores the debate around *grindadrap* (whaling in the Faroe Islands; see p260). A mesmerising mirrored room, *The Deep Blue* by Tróndur Patursson is perfect for selfies. The gallery also puts on temporary exhibitions.

The displays at the national museum Tjóðsavnið *(tjodsafnid.fo; adult/child 80kr/free)* reveal insights into local history and Faroese traditions. Exhibits cover the archipelago's geological formation, archaeology and the importance of wool and seabird hunting. The collection itself is housed in three loca-

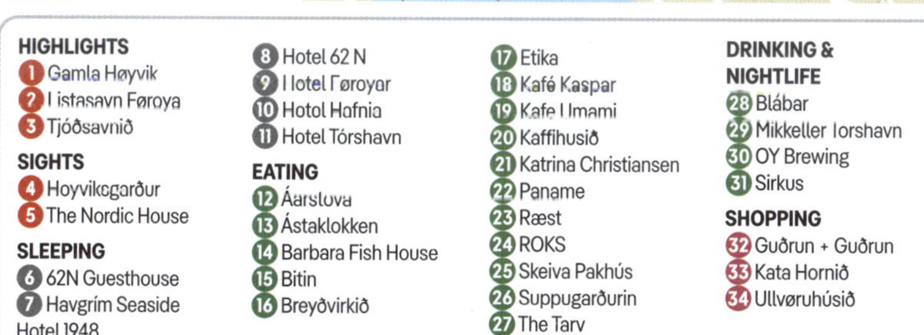

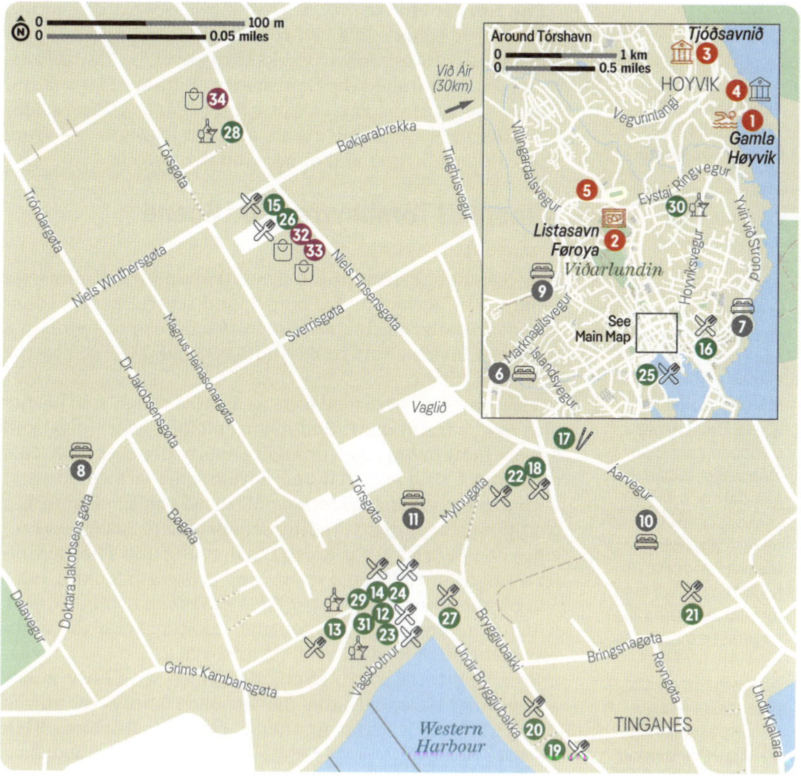

HIGHLIGHTS
1 Gamla Høyvik
2 Listasavn Føroya
3 Tjóðsavnið

SIGHTS
4 Hoyvíksgarður
5 The Nordic House

SLEEPING
6 62N Guesthouse
7 Havgrím Seaside Hotel 1948
8 Hotel 62 N
9 Hotel Føroyar
10 Hotel Hafnia
11 Hotel Tórshavn

EATING
12 Áarstova
13 Ástaklokken
14 Barbara Fish House
15 Bitin
16 Breyðvirkið
17 Etika
18 Kafé Kaspar
19 Kafe Umami
20 Kaffihusið
21 Katrina Christiansen
22 Paname
23 Ræst
24 ROKS
25 Skeiva Pakhús
26 Suppugarðurin
27 The Tarv

DRINKING & NIGHTLIFE
28 Blábar
29 Mikkeller Tórshavn
30 OY Brewing
31 Sirkus

SHOPPING
32 Guðrun + Guðrun
33 Kata Hornið
34 Ullvøruhúsið

tions: the main building; **Hoyvíksgarður**, a well-maintained historic farmhouse and collection of outbuildings; and the whaling station at **Við Áir**, a 30-minute drive away where large metal vats stand rusting on the edge of a quiet quay that once rang with noise, blubber and guts.

In keeping with the islands' focus on local tourism, visitors can participate in local traditions too. A charming three-hour knitting experience takes place a couple of times a week at a local home called **Skýming** *(guidetofaroeislands.fo; 1195kr)* where you can learn to knit in Faroese style, eat delicious local snacks and gain insights into local life on the islands.

TOP TIP

The Nordic saying 'there's no such thing as bad weather, only bad clothing' comes into its own in the Faroes. If rain halts play and you can't hike the route you planned, you'll find museums, bars, cafes and shops to browse.

SUSTAINABLE TRAVEL IN THE FAROE ISLANDS

From October 2025, the Faroe Islands' tourist board will institute a Nature Preservation Fund to protect the archipelago's unique and vulnerable nature. It is – in effect – a tourist tax, where 20kr per night on accommodation (capped at 200kr) is mandatory. Cruise passengers will be taxed 65kr; hiking fees – previously levied on private land by landowners – will be phased out unless a service is provided. All the income from these taxes will go directly to maintain hiking paths, support local tourism and protect nature. Specific hiking fees listed in this guide are therefore subject to change. 'Hiking in the Faroe Islands' *(visitfaroeislands.com)* is a great source of information for walkers.

The Nordic House *(nlh.fo; free)* showcases Nordic culture in the Faroe Islands in a turf-roofed building, and has a cafe and a series of stunning artworks to discover, including some whimsical metal sheep by Danish artist Bernhard Lipsøe and Faroese artist Hans Pauli Olsen's *Pilot Whale Killing* sculpture. Discover upcoming events and music evenings – from musicals to folk, jazz and dance – on the website.

A Taste of Tórshavn's Food Scene

Dining out in the capital

Tiny Tórshavn's restaurant scene truly punches above its weight. The scene has ballooned, and several good restaurants, typically offering set dinner menus, can be found in a cluster of historic turf-roof buildings around Gongin by the eastern harbour.

A feature of Faroese food is its fermented delights, in particular *ræst,* a traditional wind-drying method where meat and fish are hung out in small draughty huts to dry over time. This results in a dry, textured and flavoursome fermented meat with a musty edge. *Skeripikjøt,* air dried and aged lamb, is a traditional local dish. Finding somewhere to taste these reicpes can be tricky, but Ræst, OY Brewing and The Tarv offer a range of traditional dishes and are worth looking out.

Book ahead for **Ræst** *(raest.fo; tasting menu from 1500kr),* which combines modern gourmet cooking with the Faroese tradition of fermentation. **Áarstova** *(aarstova.fo; from 800kr)* exudes a warm hygge ambience with cosy nooks and vintage paraphernalia. Slow-cooked lamb is the star of its menu. With a seafaring theme, candlelit **Barbara Fish House** *(barbara.fo; from 750kr)* serves homely seafood dishes. **ROKS** *(roks.fo; from 650kr)* is a stylish restaurant serving sea urchin, Greenlandic snow crab and more – the sister restaurant to the former Michelin-starred Koks. Up the hill, **Katrina Christiansen** *(en.katrina.fo; from 199kr)* serves Faroese ingredients tapas-style, as well as summer weekend brunches. **The Tarv** *(tarv.fo; from 145kr)* is a smart surf-and-turf waterfront grill house popular with locals. For a break from traditional fish and lamb, try **Skeiva Pakkhús** *(skeivapakkhus.fo; from 495kr)* for Italian food with flair, inside a tastefully renovated harbour-front warehouse, or **Etika** *(etika.fo; from 129kr)*, the archipelago's only sushi restaurant, with three locations across town.

For budget-conscious options, head to **Kafé Kaspar** *(kaspar.fo; from 99kr)* for salads, bagels and burgers; **Suppugarðurin**

THE FAROES FOR FOODIES

The capital has a delicious dining scene, but for an authentic slice of Faroese fare in a down-to-earth setting, try *heimabliðni* (p254). The word means 'home hospitality', and visitors can sign up to enjoy a home-cooked meal at a local's house.

TÓRSHAVN PAST & PRESENT WALKING TOUR

Delve into the history of the Faroe Islands and experience the charm of their culture and architecture on this city meander.

START	END	LENGTH
Skansin	Kongaminnið	2.5km; 1 hour

Sweeping views over Tórshavn make the fort of 1 **Skansin** and its prominent lighthouse a great starting point to find your bearings. Head past the ferry docks and meander around 2 **Undir Ryggi**, part of the old town. Arc back to 3 **Gongin**'s cluster of traditional turf-roof buildings. Follow the Klettaskot footpath into the heart of the Tinganes peninsula and its village-like clutch of black-tar painted homes, then stroll to the historic former warehouses at the tip. These maroon wooden buildings house the rather understated 4 **prime minister's office** and several government ministries. Norse settlers established one of the earliest recorded parliaments here, called the Ting. From the early 9th century, meetings were convened every summer to pass resolve conflicts. Stop for a coffee at 5 **Kafe Umami** and then pop into the little art gallery of 6 **Smiðjan í Lítluvík** on your way to the atmospheric old cemetery 7 **Gamli Kirkjugarður**. Next, head for Tórshavn's 8 **Havnarkirkja**, a handsome cathedral erected in 1788. Nearby, the 9 **Ráðhús** (town hall) is made from dark basalt rock. The white timber house on Tinghúsvegur is 10 **Løgting**, the surprisingly low-key parliament building. Swing down Niels Finsens Gøta to window shop at the knitwear stores and at 11 **Marjun Heimá**, which displays Faroese national dress. Finally, wend your way to 12 **Kongaminnið**, an obelisk commemorating King Christian IX's 1874 visit that has superb city views.

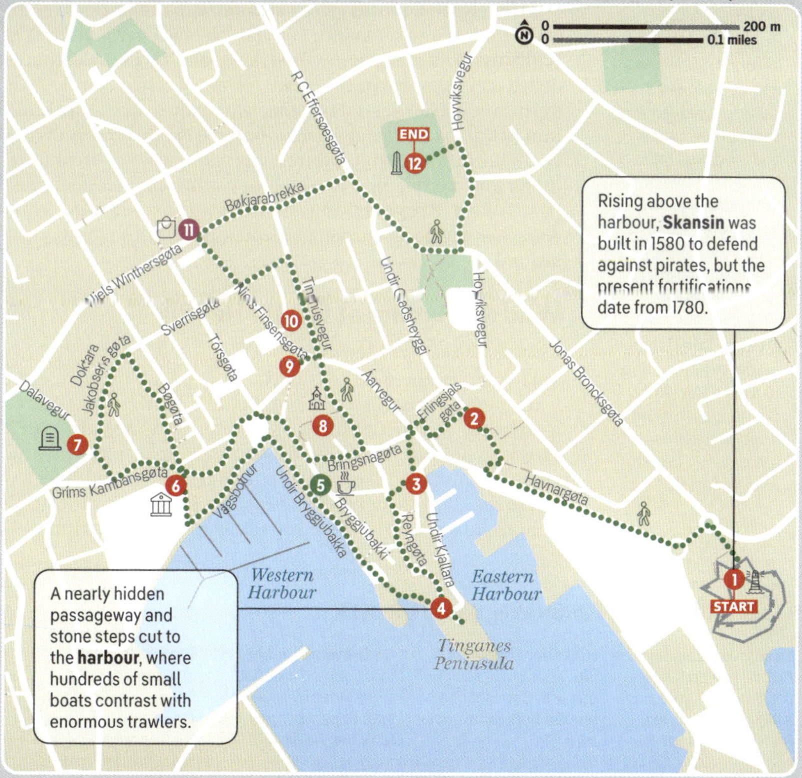

Rising above the harbour, **Skansin** was built in 1580 to defend against pirates, but the present fortifications date from 1780.

A nearly hidden passageway and stone steps cut to the **harbour**, where hundreds of small boats contrast with enormous trawlers.

WHO WERE THE FIRST SETTLERS ON THE FAROES?

The Faroese language is derived from Old Norse, a legacy of this island chain's Viking heritage. However, the first settlers on this North Atlantic archipelago may have been Celtic-speaking people from the British Isles. After studying DNA and faeces sediments from sheep, scientists dated the arrival of livestock to around 500 CE and deduced that a community must have been present 350 years before the Vikings arrived. Ancient Celtic grave markers, some place names and medieval texts lend further weight to this theory. Researchers also discovered barley grains on Sandoy that predate the Viking period. DNA analysis found that Faroese men belong to a predominantly Scandinavian gene pool, while women have mostly British Isles ancestry.

ITOMM/SHUTTERSTOCK ©

Tórshavn

(suppugardurin.fo; from 150kr) for tasty ramen in a black cottage; or **Paname** cafe *(paname.fo; from 45kr)*, a friendly all-day cafe/wine bar serving light bites next to a lovely bookshop. Daytime **Kafe Umami** *(facebook.com/kafeumami)* serves excellent brunch in a modern space by the harbour, and nearby **Kaffihúsið** *(kaffihusid.fo; from 35kr)* has a wide selection of delicious cakes. **Bitin** *(bbitn.fo; from 58kr)* has Nordic-style open sandwiches served on stoneware plates, and **Ástaklokken** *(astaklokken.fo; open seasonally, from 50kr)* is a divine, characterful pizza and natural wine cafe, serving breakfasts, lunch and dinner in a kooky, hippy atmosphere. For breakfast, bakery **Breyðvirkið** *(facebook.com/breydvirkid; from 45kr)* has the best sourdough bread and pastries plus a queue around the block.

Wild swimming at Gamla Høyvik

Dip into cold, clear water

Take a dip in the wild seas of the North Atlantic, where the water temperature is a challenging 8°C year round. There's a concrete pier with ladders down to the water at **Gamla Hoyvík**. Joining a tour by Rib62 *(rib62.com)* gives you access to a sauna, with essential oils, and a hot tub with a view out to sea. The water is super clear, and just around the headland there are rocks where you often spot seals reclining.

DRINKING IN TÓRSHAVN: BEST FOR BEER

Sirkus: Incorporating the Faroes' first craft beer bar, Sirkus is a young and lively bar. *4-10pm Mon-Fri, 10am-10pm Sat-Sun*

Mikkeller Tórshavn: A 500-year-old turf-roofed pub with Copenhagen-brewed beer on tap. *hours vary*

OY Brewing: Brewery, tap room and food hall surrounded by huge steel vats. Expect burgers and fun vibes. *hours vary*

Blábar: Popular jazz and blues bar with international and touring acts, and live music every weekend. *8pm-1.45am Thu, 5pm-3.45am Fri-Sat*

Beyond Tórshavn

Breathtaking scenery, challenging mountain hikes and captivating birdlife beckon visitors beyond the capital.

As many key attractions are a short drive from each other, if you rent a car it doesn't make much difference where you're based, opening opportunities to live like a local in a turf-roofed, lakeside cabin if you like. On Streymoy ponder the ruins at Kirkjubøur then head to its northern reaches for a boat ride to Vestmanna's soaring bird cliffs. Surf cold waves in sublime Tjørnuvík and soak in the spectacular setting of Saksun. Drive the world's first underwater roundabout from Eysturoy to the north to discover quiet roads and dramatic drives. To the south, a tunnel offers access to Sandoy with ferry options to Suðuroy.

Places

Kirkjubøur

TIME FROM TÓRSHAVN: **2 HOURS**, **14 MINUTES**

The Islands' historic roots

Just 11km from Tórshavn by road, the village of **Kirkjubøur** is one of the Faroe Islands' most historic, full of black timber houses with distinctive red window frames. In medieval times, it was the archipelago's religious and cultural centre. Constructed in the 1300s, **Kirkjubømúrurin** (St Magnus) is a roofless ruin, but the outer walls of the imposing cathedral stand 9m tall. Steps away, **Ólavskirkjan** (St Olav's Church) is the Faroe Islands' earliest church still in use. Dating from 1111, it's dedicated to one of Norway's first Christian kings. Unlike many Faroese churches, the door is unlocked, so peek inside. Next door, **Roykstovan** is an astonishing 900-year-old farmhouse and former bishop's residence that has been in the same Faroese family for 17 generations.

The best way to reach **Kirkjubøur** is to walk and then catch the bus back. From Tórshavn, a footpath follows a stream towards the **Okkara brewery**, from where a 7km cairn-marked trail snakes over the hillside. This straightforward hike takes roughly two hours, and has wonderful views of the nearby islands before descending steeply to the village.

GETTING AROUND

The best option to explore the area around Tórshavn is to rent a car. You can do this at the airport on arrival or in Tórshavn. Local buses also ply the routes but offer less flexibility. There are no trains.

TOP TIP

Some homes serve waffles and coffee to visitors. Look out for flyers on bus shelters and a Faroese flag displayed outside the house.

Nólsoy

TIME FROM TÓRSHAVN: **20 MINS**

Small island life

The island of **Nólsoy** *(nolsoy.fo; 40kr)* feels a world away from Tórshavn. A striking sperm whale jawbone marks the entrance to **Nólsoy village**, and you might spot fish hanging

HEIMABLIÐNI: DINING WITH LOCALS

Heimabliðni means 'home hospitality', and it's an experience offered on many of the Faroe Islands. Eating in a home is one of the most intimate ways to learn about the Faroese way of life and taste local food that's rarely offered at restaurants. Meals range from simple lunches with soup and cake to gourmet supper clubs held in farmhouses and B&Bs. Fish or lamb is usually on the menu, but you might try a little *ræst* (fermented meat) or be offered whale. *Heimabliðni* is not a cheap option (around 500kr for a multi-course meal plus storytelling) and you have to reserve ahead. A minimum of two to four people is often required. Check *eatlocal.fo* to book an experience or ask at local tourist offices.

Hikers, Streymoy

up to dry outside colourful houses. The tiny village museum, **House by the Well** *(nolsoy.fo; contact the tourist board for visits)* is a preserved 17th-century home, previously lived in by 10 generations of a single family, and the pretty 19th-century village church is painted an unusual white and green. The island's steep eastern side is rich with birdlife, including **puffins** and the world's biggest **storm petrel colony**. Check *jenskjeld.info* to arrange a guided visit.

In a wonderfully wind-blown spot on the island's southern end stands **Nólsoyar Viti**, a photogenic white lighthouse built in 1893, and you can hike across the island's wild hills to see it on an excellent 13km return walk from the ferry landing, which has tremendous views to Tórshavn. To find the trail from the dock, take the right-hand fork. The path is well marked with cairns and blue stakes. It climbs steeply, but soon levels out and then contours the grassy escarpment for much of the way. You'll glimpse another lighthouse to the right, but keep walking straight. The boggy path crosses a few footbridges as you near your destination. The beam from its huge 4-tonne lens can be seen for 16 nautical miles. Allow four to five hours for the hike. Check return ferry times before you set off.

Vestmanna

TIME FROM TÓRSHAVN: **46 MINS**

To the sea cliffs

Vestmanna is the starting point for one of the Faroe Islands' most exhilarating excursions, a boat trip to the spectacular seabird cliffs, known as **Vestmannabjørgini** *(puffin.fo; adults/children 398/200kr)*. From the harbour, the 90-minute tour heads up the strait to Streymoy's northern coast, where a towering rock face overlooks the Atlantic Ocean. High overhead, seabirds such as fulmars, kittiwakes and puffins nest. The waves can get choppy, and travellers are given hard hats as the boat weaves through narrow straits and into sea caves. Boat trips run daily from April to September. If the sea conditions are too rough, tours go to the rock pinnacle **Trøllkonufingur** and sea caves on Vágar's southern coast instead. **Fishing with Blástein** *(fishingwithblastein.com)* runs well-regarded angling trips from Vestmanna.

The town of Vestmanna itself has little to see. A tourist centre at the harbour has a cafe and a small history museum. The **Faer Isles Distillery** *(faer.io)*, which makes whisky, gin and akvavit, has opened a visitor centre, and offers tours and tastings *(bookings guidetofaroeislands.fo)*. Look out for the characterful **Kvívík Igloos**, two geodesic domes perched on the top of the hill above Kvívík, on your drive back to Tórshavn.

Saksun

TIME FROM TÓRSHAVN: **47 MINS**

Black sand beach

Tucked down a long single-track road in a far-flung corner of Streymoy, **Saksun** has a magical setting. Ringed by rugged green mountainside with tumbling waterfalls, the village overlooks **Pollurin**, a circular tidal lagoon with a black sand beach. This wild and achingly beautiful landscape in starkly contrasting colours is a photographer's dream, but Saksun's popularity is not without issue. Some locals are fed up with the influx of tourists, and it's important to be mindful that Saksun is a living community. Stick to designated footpaths when visiting and don't take photos into people's homes.

The road forks as you approach the village. Go right for **Dúvugarðar** *(facebook.com/duvugardar; adults/children 150kr/free)*, a small summer-only museum in a 19th-century turf-roof building, and Saksun's eye-catching white church. Taking the left fork brings you to a car park for the lagoon. It's a lovely walk to the fjord's mouth, and standing in this natural amphitheatre is absolutely awe-inspiring. You can also get a superb vantage point of the lagoon and the surrounding mountains by walking part way up the **Tjørnuvík trail**.

Tackle the trail from Saksun to Tjørnuvík

Escape the crowds and enjoy magnificent scenery on this 7km (approximately three-hour) hike to Tjørnuvík. As the route ascends diagonally out of Saksun's valley, the views over the lagoon and surrounding peaks are utterly breathtaking. Keep your eyes peeled for stakes marking the trail because several sheep tracks can make the way confusing. From the first cairn, the route turns east and gradually climbs around the mountainside. After crossing a midway ridge, northern **Eysturoy** and the rock pillars of **Risin** and **Kellingin** come into view. The path enters a green, sculpted valley and then descends to **Tjørnuvík**. This is a one-way route, so you need to arrange transport. Tjørnuvík has bus connections to Oyrarbakki, located at the bridge to Eysturoy, but Saksun has no bus services.

WHY I LOVE THE FAROE ISLANDS

Laura Hall, Lonely Planet writer

I can't help but come over all poetic in the Faroe Islands, this far-off archipelago where mist swirls, clouds sit on the shoulders of mountains, and myths and legends haunt the coast. It's a place for dreamers, hikers, thinkers and anyone who wants to feel a sense of awe in nature. At the same time, alongside this sense of Big Nature, there's a feeling of small wonders too: fluffy lambs by the side of the road, cosy cafes, and authentic and homespun tourism experiences, where you can eat or knit beside locals and hear all about their lives on the edge of the world. There's really nowhere else like it.

THINGS TO DO IN THE FAROES

Harriet Olafsdóttir av Gørðum is a fifth-generation sheep farmer and runs Hanusarstova, a farm, B&B and *heimabliðni* on Eyusturoy *(hanusarstova.com)*. These are her recommendations.

I really like **Sandoy** – it's my favourite island. It's just a bit different from the others: it's flatter and it looks distinct. For me, it's an example of the proper, unspoilt and raw Faroe Islands: a lot of people go to Saksun and Tjørnuvík but people often skip Sandoy. I also love **Suðuroy** – if you have the time, visit.

My other favourite thing to do is go to a nice cafe in **Tórshavn. Paname** (p252) and **Ástaklokken** (p252) are my favourites. I like that Ástaklokken serves raw milk from local farmers and uses Faroese herbs.

Catch a wave in Tjørnuvík

It's not quite Hawaii, but Tjørnuvík's U-shaped sandy bay still produces consistent waves, making it the Faroes' top surfing spot. Surfing had barely made a ripple until enterprising locals established the sport here a couple of years ago. **Faroe Islands Surf Guide** *(faroeislandssurfguide.com; from 1450kr)* offers board hire and classes for beginners. Don a thick wetsuit with gloves, boots and a head covering to keep the frigid Atlantic water at bay. The best surfing months are September to April. In summer, the outfit runs stand-up paddleboarding (SUP) and cliff-jumping tours; combined surf and SUP tours are also on offer.

Funningur

TIME FROM TÓRSHAVN: **43 MINS**

Hairpin bends

The largely single-track route from Eiði to Funningur takes in the best viewpoint of Risin and Kellingen, and winds in a wide zigzag down to the small collection of houses in **Funningur**, all in the lee of **Slættaratindur**. It's an epic drive, where sheep run across the road and views stop you in their tracks. Funningur has a little turf-roofed church and is known as the first settled town in the Faroe Islands. From the highest point in the road leading into the village, at an unpaved car park, it's an easy walk 15 minutes to **Hvíthamar**, a viewpoint over the fjord and village.

Climb Slættaratindur

Slættaratindur rises up from northern Eysturoy's rugged landscape. Its flat summit is often shrouded in mist, but on a clear day, sweeping panoramas take in the whole archipelago. This mountain is the tallest point in the Faroe Islands, but in 2012, it lost 2m in height after fresh measurements revealed it's actually 880m, not 882m. The trailhead to the summit begins at **Eiðisskarð**, on the road between Eiði and Funningur. From a small car park, the well-worn path ascends steeply for about 30 minutes. Captivating views of nearby peaks unfold as the trail quickly gains elevation. It then climbs diagonally left over the grassy stone-strewn slope. Higher up, the terrain is rockier, and the trail curves over the mountainside before suddenly switching right and circling back for the final steps to the summit. The hike takes about 2½ hours return. Be careful of ice and loose rocks. It's a Faroese tradition to hike to the top on 21 June, the longest day of the year.

Take a short walk around Gjógv

The town of **Gjógv** has a natural harbour and gorge packed with nesting **fulmars** and **puffins**, reached via another freehand sketch of a sheep-clogged road. A pretty river runs through the village through a wildflower meadow. Walk up past the little cafe and follow the path to a steep cliff. At the gate, pay 50kr to hike further up on the very steep route for stunning views of **Kalsoy** and look out for puffins that nest in the cliff, as you go. It's an hour or so to the top. You can take a different, less steep route overlooking the village on the way back.

LAURA HALL/LONELY PLANET ©

Funningur

If you only want a short walk, an easy footpath from the heart of the village leads to a good vantage point over a rocky reef. Wooden steps take you to a bench dedicated to Danish Crown Princess Mary, now Denmark's Queen Mary, with views of the sea, seabirds and cliffs, and Kalsoy beyond.

Join a traditional chain dance

For hundreds of years, islanders have been performing traditional chain dances. Dancers hold hands and form a circle, singing folk ballads without musical accompaniment.

Every Wednesday evening from June to August, the **Gjáargarður Guesthouse** *(gjaargardur.fo; adults/children 650/300kr)* in Gjógv hosts a weekly cultural night, when a buffet dinner is followed by musical performances and traditional dancing.

THE TALE OF RISIN & KELLINGIN

From Tjørnuvík and the Eiði–Funningur road, you can see a pair of strikingly tall sea stacks at the foot of Eysturoy's northern tip.

According to an old local legend, the two huge rocks are the remains of a giant and a witch who attempted to tow the Faroe Islands to Iceland. Kellingin, the witch, has two legs and a pointy hat and is the sea stack closest to land; Risin, the giant, is the solid stack.

The story goes that the giants in Iceland were jealous of the Faroe Islands and wanted to have them all for themselves. The witch cast a rope around Eiðiskollur mountain, and the stocky giant Risin pulled, to try to bring them closer. They struggled all night long but to no avail. When dawn broke, the sunlight turned them both to stone.

EATING BEYOND TÓRSHAVN

Fjørukrógvin: A canteen-like restaurant offering lunch and a buffet. *9am-5pm daily* **€€**

Muntra: Fuglafjørður's village restaurant makes hearty meals like lamb shank and local fish. *11am-10pm daily* **€€**

Rose's Café: In Ljósá, this cafe has a menu inspired by the owner's Ethiopian upbringing. *11.30am-2pm daily* **€€**

Hanusarstova: Farmstay offering waffles with homemade jam, cake and coffee, plus *heimabliðni* evening meals. *Book in advance* **€€€**

Vágar

MYSTERIOUS LAKE | MESMERISING WATERFALLS | PUFFIN ISLAND

GETTING AROUND

It's relatively easy to travel around Vágar by bus as long as you have time to spare. The bus stop is immediately in front of the airport, and car-hire companies are to the left. Buses run west to Sørvágur (300) and Gásadalur (350). Both go east through Miðvágur and Sandavágur en route to Tórshavn, and handily they pass close to Vágar's attractions.

Ferries to Mykines *(mykines.fo)* depart from Sørvágur throughout the summer, with a direct bus service from Tórshavn, and helicopter flights *(atlantic.fo)* operate between Vágar Airport and Mykines. Check updated timetables at *ssl.fo.*

The Faroe Islands' international airport is located on Vágar. Less rugged than its eastern neighbours, Vágar has stunning waterfalls, traditional villages and splendid hiking trails. During WWII, British soldiers based here built the runway, roads and harbour. While the northern half remains wild hill country, the south is home to about 3000 inhabitants. On the west coast, Sørvágur is the jumping-off point for trips to the island of Mykines to see the extraordinary puffin colony. The larger settlement of Miðvágur to the east has facilities like a petrol station and supermarkets. Rounding the headland, Sandavágur and its striking red-roofed church come into view. Built in 1917, the church contains a 13th-century rune stone dedicated to the settlement's Norwegian founder.

Timeless Villages & Show-Stopping Waterfalls

The Faroes' most beautiful waterfall

Four kilometres from Sørvágur, the coastal road arrives at the pretty village of **Bøur**, a snug collection of black-tarred, turf-roof cottages gazing out to the dark and dramatic seastacks, and islands out at sea. Further on, the road ducks through a mountainside tunnel and pops out at secluded **Gásadalur**, once one of the archipelago's most remote outposts and home to just 11 people. The hamlet only gained a road link to the outside world in 2006 when this tunnel was opened. Before then, villagers had to cross the mountain by foot or go by helicopter. Put yourself in a local's shoes by tackling the old postal route, a popular but challenging two-hour hike that zigzags steeply over the mountainside. Before entering the village, a wide 300m-long trail leads to one of the Faroes' most recognisable sights, the spectacular **Múlafossur** waterfall. Cascading over a cliff into the sea with the village and mountains as a backdrop, it's irresistibly photogenic. In the village, another well-marked path leads to a viewpoint overlooking Mykines island.

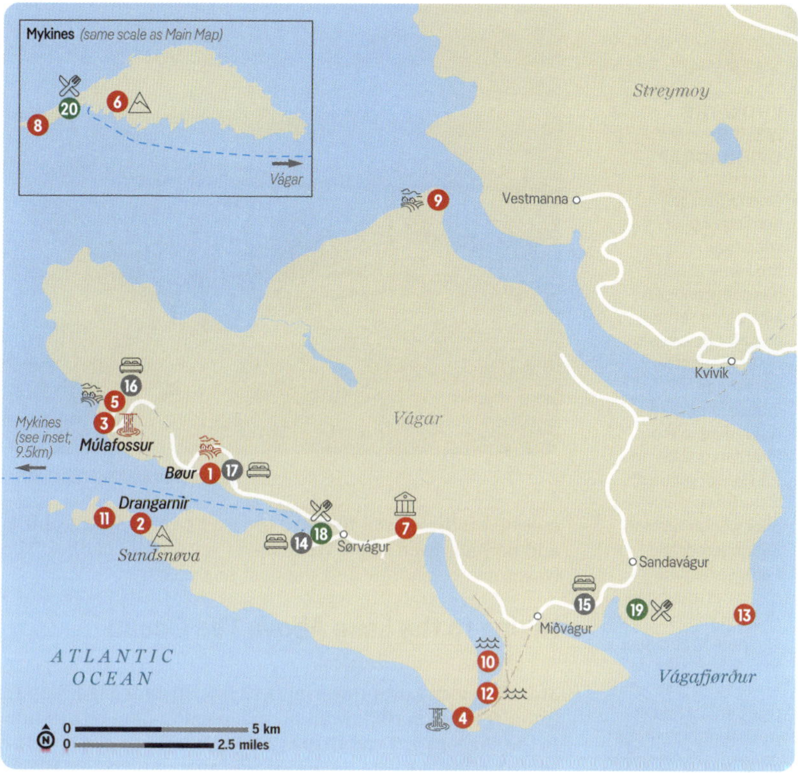

HIGHLIGHTS
1 Bøur
2 Drangarnir
3 Múlafossur

SIGHTS
4 Bøsadalafossur
5 Gásadalur
6 Knúkur
7 Krígssavnið
8 Mykineshólmur
9 Slættanes
10 Sørvágsvatn
11 Tindhólmur
12 Trælanípa
13 Trøllkonufingur

SLEEPING
Á Lonini Guesthouse (see 20)
14 Cottages by the Sea
Gásadalsgarður Cafe & Guesthouse (see 5)
15 Giljanes Hostel & Camping
16 Múlafossur Cottages
Mykineslon (see 20)
17 The View

EATING
18 Cafe Pollastova
19 Fiskastykkið
Gasadalur Cafe (see 5)
20 Mykinesstova Cafe
The Locals (see 20)

Spotting Sea Stacks & Seals

See the sights by boat

Seascapes are rarely more dramatic than the **Drangarnir** sea stacks and jagged teeth of the islet **Tindhólmur**. Drangarnir is actually two formations – a rock pillar and an angular arch – while Tindhólmur's serrated ridge juts 262m above the sea. The **Mykines ferry** passes these remarkable geological features on its daily voyage to the island; if you want to know more, take a small boat or RIB tour with **Blue Gate** *(bluegate.fo; 650kr)* or **Sea Travel** *(seatravel.fo; 1450kr)* whose trips sail right through the arch and get you up close for unbeatable views. Leaving from **Sørvágur**, it's a thrilling one-hour ride around the bay, first heading to Bøur and Múlafossur before

TOP TIP

As you drive from the airport towards Tórshavn, look out for a metal sculpture of a horse-like figure rearing up from a lake. It's a water creature from Faroese legend called the Nix, famed for luring unsuspecting people to their death in the water.

KNOW THE ISSUES: GRINDADRAP

Grindadrap, the hunting of pilot whales around the Faroe Islands, has come under increasing scrutiny, and bloody images of the slaughter have made international news. According to the International Union for Conservation of Nature, long-finned pilot whales are not endangered, and Faroese hunters slaughter around 850 of them annually (and sometimes dolphins too). They're driven ashore and then killed using spinal lances. Animal-rights groups condemn the practice as cruel and barbaric. Locals argue it's a sustainable food source and part of Faroese cultural identity. Controversy arose in 2021 when more than 1400 white-sided dolphins were killed. Following public outcry, the government introduced a quota of 500 dolphins annually, but there's no limit for pilot whales.

SCOTT ALAN RITCHIE/SHUTTERSTOCK ©

Trælanípa and Sørvágsvatn

crossing rolling swell to reach the islets. You'll spot seabirds and perhaps even seals. Wear warm waterproof clothes. The waves can be choppy and the boat has no cover.

Hiking to the Lake Above The Ocean

A walk to a visual illusion

Stunning views over towering sea cliffs, distant islands and a thunderous waterfall await on this popular 6km return hike to the clifftops at **Trælanípa** *(200kr/ free for under-14s)*. The route begins at a gate on the hillside above Miðvágur. Hikers traverse a well-maintained gravel trail overlooking **Sørvágsvatn**, the Faroes' largest lake (also known as Leitisvatn) before descending towards the headland. It's a unique looking lake – from the right angle at least – as it appears to be floating above the ocean. On foot, as you approach the angular 142m peak, sheer sea cliffs suddenly unfold, and the path forks. To the left, climb the wooden steps to the top for spectacular coastal views. If you're looking for the photographic illusion where the lake looks suspended above the ocean, this is the spot. The fork to the right leads to views of **Bøsadalafossur**, a 30m-high waterfall that tumbles into the sea. The hike takes about two hours. It's also possible to take a kayak tour of the lake with *guidetofaroeislands.fo*.

Vágar has several other worthwhile hiking trails. It's an easy 1km amble to a viewpoint overlooking the dramatic rock pinnacle **Trøllkonufingur** (Witch's Finger; p255) on Vágar's south coast. A car park is on the hillside behind Sandavágur, and from here, it's a roughly 20-minute walk east *(free)* along a paved and then gravel track.

A challenging 30km trek visits the abandoned hamlet of **Slættanes**, starting from the Á Hálsi car park near Sandavágur and finishing in **Gásadalur** (p258). It takes 12 to 15 hours, and some hikers choose to camp halfway. Find a detailed route guide in the *Hiking in the Faroe Islands* pamphlet *(visitfaroeislands.com)*.

Wartime in the Faroe Islands

A special British connection

Opposite the airport, the war museum **Krígssavnið** *(50kr, weekend afternoons only from May to September)*, tells the history of the Faroe Islands during wartime. After German forces invaded Denmark in April 1940, the British military launched Operation Valentine, a peaceful occupation of the Faroe Islands, and around 8000 British troops were stationed in Vágar throughout World War II. The war took a heavy toll on the Faroese, and more than 200 fishermen lost their lives at sea as they continued to fish through the conflict. The story is told through original photographs, mementos and personal stories. Labels are in English and Faroese.

Decades later, some British cultural quirks have stuck. The Faroese drink tea with milk and love battered fish and chips, and supermarkets stock brands like Typhoo tea, Cadburys chocolate and Tunnock's teacakes.

Visiting Mykines Island

On the trail of puffins

The archipelago's most magical island, Mykines, is a puffin haven with bewitching coastal scenery and quiet village life, and is reached via a ferry from **Sørvágur** *(mykines.fo; adults/children 150/60kr, twice daily in summer)*. Mykines also has a heliport.

Unique and unspoilt, the westernmost island of the Faroes can seem brooding and weather-beaten, but when the sun shines it's gloriously beautiful. Towering cliffs, teeming with seabirds in season, wrap around its coast, the small peak **Knúkur** rises in its centre and sheep pastures sweep along its gentler western slopes. A footbridge crosses to the islet of **Mykineshólmur**, which has a scenic lighthouse and squawking gannetry, but for many visitors the remarkable puffins are the stars of the show.

Ferry passengers disembark at a tiny harbour and climb the steep steps to the village, home to only 10 year-round residents. In May and August, all visitors are charged a 500kr hiking fee, payable online at *hiking.fo* – or at **The Locals** cafe on arrival. The boat tour is booked separately and runs daily between May and August, with limited options outside these months.

From the boat dock, it's more than 130 steps to reach the village. Mykines has only a handful of streets, and outside the village, there are only footpaths and tracks. The route to the puffin colony is marked by wooden stakes. Look out for notice boards with trail maps.

Around half a million pairs of Atlantic puffins breed in the Faroes each spring/summer season, but Mykines is not the only place to see them. Puffins are not year-round residents: they return to breed in late April and leave in early September. After years of decline, puffin populations are vulnerable. Researchers think food shortages, linked to rising sea temperatures and climate change, are a key factor. Adult birds must fly further to find food, leaving baby pufflings defenceless and hungry for longer.

Birdlife on Mykines has a special protected status, as do the flocks on Nólsoy and Skúvoy. It's important to follow visitor

FAROESE MUSIC

Grotto music: Listen to music in a sea cave aboard historic wooden schooner *Norðlýsið*. For schedules and tickets, visit *tn24.fo*.

Summartónar: Summer concert series held across the islands that showcases homegrown talent.

G! Festival: This July festival features local Faroese and Scandi indie and pop acts in the seaside village of Gøta.

Ólavsøka: The National Day festival is not complete without classical music, choral groups and communal singing.

Húsagongd: A tradition of singing unplugged in other people's living rooms is alive and well in the Faroes. A mini festival takes place in Sandavágur in May.

ARTISTIC INSPIRATION

Mykines has inspired many artists, including Faroese painter Sámal Joensen-Mikines (1906–79). His early works often depicted wild seascapes and dark scenes from daily life. After studying in Copenhagen, he settled in Denmark but visited Mykines every summer. See his art at **Listasavn Føroya** (p248) in Tórshavn.

EYESTRAVELLING/SHUTTERSTOCK ©

Lighthouse, Mykines

guidelines to minimise any disturbance to these delicate breeding grounds. Stick to marked paths and stay 2m from burrows. Keep your voice low and keep moving along the path. Do not point camera flashes into burrows or fly drones near nesting sites.

The main colony on Mykines nests in burrows along the cliff tops on its north coast. A footpath straight up from the village takes you there. A landslide closed the main trail west of the 1930s memorial, which meant parts of the nesting grounds and all of **Mykineshólmur**, including the bridge, lighthouse and gannet colony, were still off limits at the time of research. Even with the closures, you can see puffins in the cliff top area before the memorial. The walk to Mykineshólmur is wonderful, and if it does reopen it's not to be missed.

More time on Mykines

Stay in a traditional village

Stay overnight on Mykines for a taste of authentic village life after the crowds of day-trippers have gone. Meandering the handful of narrow car-free streets is a pleasure, and you have time to explore more of the island. Hike to the radio mast on **Knúkur**'s 560m summit for breathtaking views across Vágar and the length of Mykines. It's about 3km from the village over tracks and rough ground. A five-minute stroll across a field behind the helipad brings you to the **Kumlar viewpoint**, where you can see seabird cliffs. Find rooms at **Á Lonini Guesthouse**, **Mykineslon** and **The Locals** (p261).

EATING IN VÁGAR

Gásadalur Cafe: Atmospheric cafe with vegan options. The carrot cake is a must-try. *11am-4pm daily; reduced hours in winter* €

Fiskastykkið: Beautiful cafe in an old stockfish warehouse in Sandavágur, serving fish soup, cakes and coffee. *11am-9pm Wed-Sun* €

Cafe Pollastova: Local cafe with a menu of toasted sandwiches, brunch, nachos and more. *10am-8pm Tue-Sat, 2pm-8pm Sun* €

Mykinesstova Cafe: Cafe on Mykines serving homemade cake, soup and coffee. Ideal after a hike. *Open daily, various hours, May-September only* €

Northern Islands

SET-JETTING | DRAMATIC DRIVING | PURE SOLITUDE

The northern islands of the Faroes – Kalsoy, Kunoy, Borðoy, Viðoy, Svínoy and Fugloy – are where the feeling of remote island life kicks in. Once you're past the second largest town in the country (Klaksvík, population 5001), you're in a world of sharp-edged fjords lined with winding roads, narrow tunnels through towering mountains, and roads that lead on to a scattering of houses and the end of the world.

If you love this poetic feeling, it's worth a drive to Viðareiði, where the road runs out at a small historic church, with views of sea stacks on the horizon, or to the abandoned hamlet of Múli, a ghost town in the northern part of Bordoy which featured in the Nordic noir drama *TROM*. The last inhabitant left the village in 1992. If you prefer more blockbuster sights, Kalsoy island, which featured in Daniel Craig's final James Bond film, *No Time to Die*, is a must-see. If you plan to hike in this area, the best advice is to take a guide *(mountainguides.fo)* because it is rugged and isolated in the extreme.

GETTING AROUND

The most dependable form of transport is a rental car. Note: there are unpaved roads in the northern reaches of the islands. Bus options are very limited. Check the ferry times to Kalsoy closely; the timetable is irregular even in peak season, with large gaps in the schedule. You can find yourself waiting at the ferry port if you're not careful. To access the outlying islands of Fugloy and Svínoy, visitors have to travel by boat or helicopter. The ferry to both islands runs from Hvannasund on Viðoy with RITAN *(ssl.fo)*; the helicopter operation is run by Atlantic Airways *(atlanticairways.com)*.

Exploring Klaksvík

Culture, history and nature in the Faroes' second town

Much of Klaksvík's action centres on the port, where giant ocean-going trawlers come and go. In the early 1800s, it was a Danish trading station and became an important fishing hub. A modern four-star 81-room hotel is due to open here in spring 2025. The main reasons to visit Klaksvík include the **Norðoyastevna** rowing competitions in June, **Sailor's Day** celebrations and the **Summarfestivalurin** music festival in August.

Klaksvík is home to the islands' biggest brewer, **Föroya Bjór**. Founded in 1888 by a local farmer, it's one of the oldest Faroese companies and is still a family-run business. Steps away on the harbour, Klaksvik's new boathouse, designed by

TOP TIP

There are limited shops, cafes and restaurants in this part of the Faroes even in peak season; fill up on fuel in Klaksvík, and pack snacks and lunch for hikes as there is nowhere to eat further north.

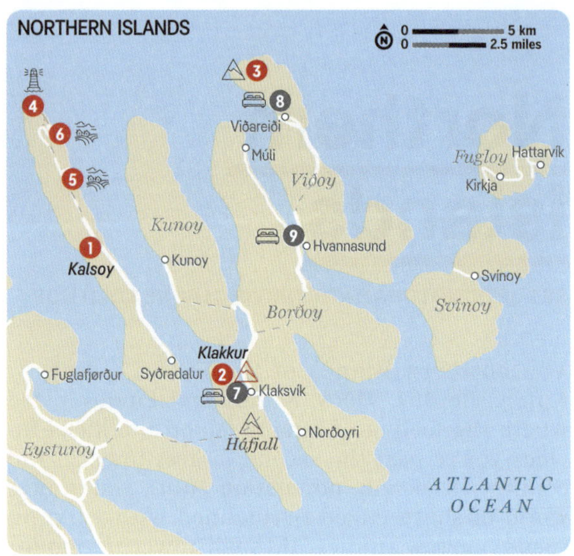

Faroese architect Ósbjørn Jacobsen, has been nominated for a Nordic architecture prize.

Klaksvík hugs a U-shaped fjord backed by steep mountains. There's a panoramic view of mountains and fjords from **Klakkur** (413m), and it's an easy one-hour hike from a small car park at **Hálsur**. Looking down over Klaksvík from this elevation, you can truly appreciate its unique setting, arcing around the fjord and surrounded by mountains.

EATING IN THE NORTHERN ISLANDS

Fríða Kaffihús: By the tourist information office, Klaksvík's best cafe makes appealing meals, with vegan options. *10am-7pm Mon-Sat* €

Kallur Lighthouse: At the lighthouse trail on Kalsoy, this small Thai spot serves plates of fried rice and pork. *9am-9pm daily in season* €

Café Edge: On Kalsoy in the village of Mikladalur, this cafe sells hearty soup, cakes and waffles with an incredible view. *noon-5pm Wed-Sat* €

Angus Steakhouse: Steaks, burgers and salmon in Klaksvík, served with American-style desserts. *11am-3pm, 5-9.30pm daily* €€

Set-jetting on Kalsoy

No Time To Die on Kalsoy

If you are looking for the ideal location for a James Bond villain's hideout, the steep dramatic slopes of **Kalsoy** fit the bill. It features in *No Time To Die* (near the end, blink and you'll miss it) and it's the final resting spot of Daniel Craig's James Bond. You can even take a selfie next to a mocked-up gravestone here, which reads 'The proper function of man is to live, not to exist'.

There's much more to the island than tourist baiting however: Kalsoy is a popular day trip with a stunning lighthouse trek, seabird cliffs with puffins in the summer, and a fierce selkie statue to visit. The car ferry from **Klaksvík** *(ssl.fo; 40kr return)* docks in **Syðradalur**, from where the road passes through four dark, single-track tunnels on Kalsoy's eastern side before reaching **Trøllanes**. Arrange a ticket for the car ferry well in advance – it's booked over a week ahead in peak season – or leave the car and go on foot, using the local bus when you arrive. From the car park, it's 30 minutes to Kalsoy's northernmost tip; local buses meet the ferry, but be aware that services are limited and with an irregular ferry service, you need to plan carefully to avoid a long wait for the ferry back. Look up routes and timetables on *ssl.fo*. It's also possible to **rent an electric bike** *(northern escapes.fo; 398kr per day)* at the ferry port and cycle to the two villages on the island.

Presiding over a magnificent vantage point, the solitary red-and-white **Kallur Lighthouse** is towered over by dramatic Matterhorn-like cliffs, with spectacular coastal scenery both east and west, including Viðoy's precipitous **Cape Enniberg**, and a scattering of sheep. The hike from Trøllanes takes an hour with a 200kr fee (pay at the shop before you hike); including time for the ferry and the drive to the start of the hike, allow around eight hours to visit Kalsoy. The hike is steep and not recommended for those with a fear of heights.

After retracing your steps, stop in Mikladalur on the return drive to see the statue of **Kópakonan** (the selkie, or Seal Woman) who, according to local legend, shed her seal skin and came ashore as a beautiful woman, but a local man hid her skin preventing her from returning to the ocean. Legend has it that the curse of the selkie is behind deaths at sea in the Faroe Islands. There are a lot of steps down to the beach where she stands powerfully backed by the mountains. There's also a pretty waterfall and probably the most scenic **cafe** on the islands to visit.

Thanks to its long, narrow shape and its mountains riddled with tunnels, the island is nicknamed 'the tin whistle'. Outside of summertime, there's nowhere to buy food beyond the snack-oriented kiosk in **Trøllanes**, so come prepared with your own; otherwise stop in **Mikladalur** for a cafe with a phenomenal view, or order **Thai food** at the foot of the lighthouse trail.

HIKING DOS & DON'TS IN THE FAROE ISLANDS

Most land in the Faroe Islands is privately held, and unlike in some countries, there's no 'right to roam'. Increasingly, landowners have introduced fees for well-known routes, but the public are allowed on old village paths. The excellent downloadable guide *Hiking in the Faroe Islands (visitfaroe islands.com)* details many free routes. The weather can change suddenly from sunshine to fog or rain, so wear warm, wind-resistant and waterproof clothing. Carry food, water, a map and fully charged phone. Some trails are remote or pass near crags or coastal cliffs, so put on proper footwear and tell someone about your plans. Help preserve the Faroe's fragile nature by sticking to marked paths and taking your rubbish with you.

DRIVING TOUR OF THE REMOTE NORTHERN ISLES

With your own set of wheels, three northern isles – Kunoy, Borðoy and Viðoy – can easily be explored.

START	END	LENGTH
Klaksvík	Hotel Nord in Viðareiði	38km; 1 day

From ❶ **Klaksvík**, drive to rugged Kunoy island, which is connected to larger Borðoy by a bendy causeway at Haraldssund. A tunnel cuts through the mountain to the west coast and Kunoy village. Park near ❷ **Kunoy church** and stretch your legs. Back in the car, continue along the road, coming to two back-to-back single-track tunnels. A causeway to the island of Viðoy connects the twinned villages of Norðdepil and ❸ **Hvannasund**. Not a single tree grows on Viðoy, but its name means 'wood' after the once common driftwood.

Emerge from a tunnel on the eastern side to find a lay-by, and a fantastic ❹ **viewpoint** to Fugloy and Svínoy. In a valley patterned by sheep pastures is the archipelago's northernmost village, Viðareiði. The ❺ **village church** presides over coastal views, and you can get out of the car for a three- to four-hour walk up Villingardalsfjall (841m), the country's third highest peak, from the ❻ **trailhead**. It's also possible to reach Cape Enniberg, which at 754m tall is one of Europe's highest vertical sea cliffs. This tough six- to-seven-hour trip requires good weather, and a guide is recommended *(hiking.fo)*. If you intend to tackle it, stay overnight at ❼ **Hotel Norð** in Viðareiði or Lokk-Inn at Norðdepil. Driving on, the old road contours Viðoy's western flank. There are views to the abandoned hamlet of Múli on the opposite banks, and waterfalls tumble down Borðoy's hills.

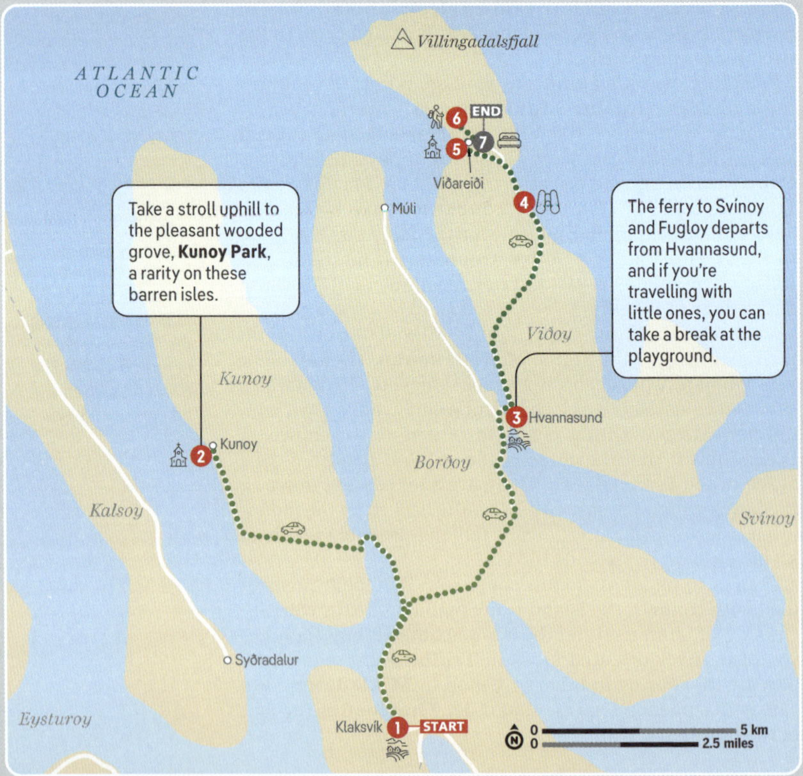

Take a stroll uphill to the pleasant wooded grove, **Kunoy Park**, a rarity on these barren isles.

The ferry to Svínoy and Fugloy departs from Hvannasund, and if you're travelling with little ones, you can take a break at the playground.

Villingadalsfjall
ATLANTIC OCEAN
6 END
5 7
Viðareiði
Múli
4
Viðoy
Kunoy
2 Kunoy
3 Hvannasund
Borðoy
Kalsoy
Svínoy
Syðradalur
Eysturoy
Klaksvík 1 START
0 5 km
0 2.5 miles

Southern Islands

LOCAL CULTURE | ISLAND ESCAPISM | BIRD CLIFFS

To the south of Tórshavn, the southern islands of Sandoy and Suðuroy beckon. Since 2024, Sandoy has been linked to Tórshavn by an underwater tunnel, making it just a short drive from the heart of the action. Even though it's easier to reach than before, it still feels unvisited, a world away from the drama of the island group's major sights. Sandoy is all gentle pastures, farms and sea views, low-lying and altogether calmer than the other islands. You can drive from north to south in about 30 minutes.

While a tunnel is planned to Suðuroy, a two-hour ferry is currently the only way to get there, putting it significantly more off the beaten track. It's an island of lush scenery, ending with bird cliffs and a lighthouse at its most southerly point. Hiking is divine, and even in peak season it's uncrowded. Views of the wild ocean and the unique cloud-topped uninhabited island of Lítla Dímun provide inspiration for artists and hikers alike. Stóra Dímun, another southern island, home to just one family, is only reachable by helicopter.

GETTING AROUND

Driving is the easiest way to reach Sandoy which, with the tunnel, is only a short drive from the capital. To reach Suðuroy, a car ferry runs from Tórshavn multiple times a day in peak season to Krambatangi dock, across the bay from Tvøroyri. There are local bus services on both islands. Bus 700 meets the ferry in Suðuroy and runs south to Vágur and Sumba, while bus 701 crosses to Fámjin and north to Sandvík. Exploring, especially if you want to take on some hiking, is however best done by car.

Exploring local art and culture in Sandoy

Outstanding painting and local traditions

With the inauguration of the 2023 tunnel to Sandoy, the drive from Tórshavn takes under 30 minutes, making it easy to explore this lesser-visited island. With rounded hills and lower elevation, Sandoy's landscape is less dramatic than its northern neighbours, and feels relaxed and mellow. It's a peaceful island to drive. In Sandur, the plain facade of **Listasavnið á Sandi** *(facebook.com/listasavn; 100kr)* belies the lovely light-filled interior. The two-floor gallery houses a superb art collection bequeathed by late Sandur native Sofus Olsen, including works by Faroese painters SJ Mikines and Ingálvur av Reyni.

Stop by **Bygdarsavnið Norðara Koyta á Sandi** *(Sandur Village Museum; sandsbygdarsavn.fo)*, inside a historic homestead, to see how people once lived. It's opposite the village kindergarten. Further south overlooking a beach, **Húsavík** is one of the

TOP TIP

Both islands can be done in a day trip; for a real sense of what it's like to get away from it all, a night or two on Suðuroy can't be beaten.

HIGHLIGHTS
1 Sandoy
2 Suðuroy

SIGHTS
3 Akraberg
4 Ásmundarstakkur
5 Beinisvørð
6 Bindisteinurin
7 Bygdarsavnið Norðara Koyta á Sandi
8 Dalur
9 Eggjarnar
10 Gallery Oyggin
11 Húsavík
12 Hvannhagi
● Listasavnið á Sandi (see 7)
13 Lítla Dímun
14 Lopra
● Ruth Smith Art Museum (see 23)
15 Salt Cultural Centre
16 Sandvík
17 Skopun
18 Stóra Dímun
19 Sumba
20 Sumbiar Bird Museum
21 Tvøroyri
22 Vágseiðið
23 Vágur

ACTIVITIES, COURSES & TOURS
24 Vágur Swimming Pool

SLEEPING
● Brim B&B (see 23)
● Café MorMor B&B (see 21)
25 Gist Guesthouse
26 Heima i Stovu
27 Mølin Guesthouse

EATING
● Bryggjan Filipino Buffet (see 23)
● Café'in á Mølini (see 27)
● Glasstovan (see 21)

Faroes' oldest villages and has several well-preserved historic stone houses. At the end of the road, **Dalur** is known for traditional chain dancing. In the north, the town of **Skopun** has a peculiar claim to fame: a 7m-tall giant postbox, which locals say is the world's largest. The drive down to the town is the highlight though, with rolling hills and expansive island views.

Between mid May and mid August, you can visit **Bindisteinurin**, the yarn-bombed rock at Bartalstrøð. Contact the local tourist information centre for its storytelling tours about this spot *(visitsandoy.fo; 80kr)*, inspired by a local story about a troll's cave and decorated in true Faroese fashion with wool. If you've ever wondered what a rock wearing a jumper would look like, this is your chance to find out.

Admiring the wild scenery of Suðuroy

Bird cliffs and black sand bays

The two-hour voyage aboard the Smyril ferry from Tórshavn to Suðuroy gets you off the beaten track. Sailing past the archipelago's southern islands, the ferry offers views to **Stóra Dímun**, and the archipelago's smallest and only uninhabited island, **Lítla Dímun**, often topped by a little hat of a lenticular cloud. The most southerly island of the archipelago, Suðuroy has a raw and rugged landscape with basalt columns in the mountains, zigzag roads and spectacular mountains.

The island is home to around 4600 people, but it has an air of remoteness. It's larger than Sandoy; driving from the northernmost point to the furthest south takes about 45 minutes. The ferry docks near **Tvøroyri**, a fishing port and the northernmost of two larger settlements. Further south is **Vágur**. Both have accommodation options, petrol stations, plus a handful of shops and places to eat; outside of these amenities, little harbour villages offer occasional cafes and tiny rural museums but little else.

Head north from the ferry port to the village of **Sandvík** for a short walk that leads to an observation point overlooking the sea stack of **Ásmundarstakkur**. If you have a car, you can park in a lay-by just before the farm buildings. There's no path as such, but keep your eyes peeled for the signpost and small wooden markers branching away from the farm track. There are clear views of cloud-topped Lítla Dímun island from the white-sand beach just outside the village.

To the south of the ferry port, Vágur is the main hub. Take the short drive or walk to **Vágseiðið** for a 200m cliff where seabirds whirl and a natural harbour surrounded by reefs was used in the 19th and 20th centuries. A storm took the boat sheds away from this isolated spot; for years it was an entry point to the rich fishing grounds just offshore, but now access is via the town instead. Near Vágur, a narrow zigzag track leads to the cliffs at **Eggjarnar**, the site of a British WWII radar installation and lookout over stunning coastal vistas of the west coast.

Then continue further to the south and the end of the road. Gazing over the vast Atlantic at **Akraberg** brings you face to face with the forces of nature. Suðuroy's southernmost point is an untamed and windblown place, guarded by a red-domed lighthouse and flock of slightly over-friendly sheep. Story

CLOSED FOR MAINTENANCE

Every April, the Faroe Islands closes for tourists for a weekend as it welcomes 100 international volunteers to carry out maintenance work at its tourist sites instead. The scheme began in 2019 and has been oversubscribed ever since with visitors from all over the world. Participants are randomly selected and pay their own travel costs, but they receive food and lodging while spending three days assigned to one of a dozen or so projects, including repairing and building footpaths or installing signposts and viewing platforms in various locations. Participants rave about the experience, making friends for life and developing a strong connection with the country. It's a clever initiative designed to show that tourism can bring all kinds of values to a country beyond financial; it's held up as an example of successful regenerative tourism all over the world.

BEST FAROESE KNITS

Guðrun + Guðrun: Tórshavn's avant-garde designer knitwear brand *(map p249)*, including Sarah Lund's jumper from *The Killing*. To die for.

Heimavirki: Local outlets across the Faroes sell handmade crafts and knitwear. It's all slow, local fashion.

Ullvøruhúsið: A celebration of Faroese handcraft *(map p249)* with beautiful knitwear for adults and children alike.

Káta Hornið: Creativity-packed shop in Tórshavn *(map p249)* selling ceramics, fashion-forward knits and preloved knitwear.

Ribarhús: Fuglafjørður-based craft shop with knitted garments and other goods inside a charming century-old grocers.

panels tell of the area's long history; today the only people living here are those who spend a week in the isolated summer houses at the end of the road. Bring binoculars for the bird cliffs, and if you want to know more, contact the **Sumbiar Bird Museum** in advance *(+298 218485, tgt1101@gmail.com)* as it's only open on request. To get here, take the single track road from Sumba or follow the hiking trail.

Suðuroy's west coast has several spectacular vantage points that are worth driving or walking to. Between **Lopra** and **Sumba**, jaw-dropping **Beinisvørð** is a sheer rock face reaching 470m. Drive the dramatic and steep Um Hestin road, one of the island's two most scenic Buttercup Routes, for hairpin bends and the best views.

The handy and downloadable guide *Hiking in the Faroe Islands (visitfaroeislands.com)* details two hiking routes: a 6km (two-hour) route to **Hvannhagi**, a geological wonderland in the hills immediately behind Tvøroyri, as well as an epic 42km north–south trek that sets off from **Sandvík**, taking in the whole length of Suðuroy before reaching **Akraberg** as the finale.

Suðuroy's cultural scene

Art and music inspired by the wilds

If it's raining, or if you feel like a change from hiking, there are a number of spots on Suðuroy where you can explore the cultural life of this southern part of the archipelago. In Vágur, the **Ruth Smith Art Museum** *(50kr)* has two rooms dedicated to the artist's life and work. Her colourful work is well-known throughout Scandinavia. The museum is open from Wednesday to Saturday from 3pm to 5pm from June until mid-August.

In Tvøroyri, the **Gallery Oyggin** *(100kr)* is open in the afternoon and is run by a local artist and former teacher Palle Julsgart whose impressive sculpture, *Freedom*, a basalt pillar topped with bronze black-backed gulls, sits outside next to the jawbone of a blue whale. The small gallery includes his colourful local landscapes alongside other Faroese artists. His other sculptures stand in the small garden. Julsgart also offers day-long art tours of the area.

Just around the bay, between **Tvøroyri** (p269) and the ferry port, the black church-like shape of the **Salt Cultural Centre** *(salt.fo)* is a beacon for music and theatre. The former salt silo is now a stylish modern concert space with great acoustics and hosts touring acts in the summer.

A nod for those with kids on a rainy day: **Vágur's Swimming Pool** *(adults/children 50/20kr)* has a 50m pool, water slide, hot tubs and saunas, and is open from June to mid-August.

EATING IN THE SOUTHERN ISLANDS

Glasstovan: Small coffee and lunch in Tvøroyri, Suðuroy, offering sandwiches, bagels, salad and brunch. *noon-6pm Mon-Sat* €

Café MorMor B&B: Bric-à-brac filled café in Tvøroyri, Suðuroy, serving hearty meals and good coffee. *11am-6pm Wed-Sat, noon-7pm Sun* €

Bryggjan Filipino Buffet: Filipino restaurant serving a buffet and fish and chips down by the harbour in Vágur, Suðuroy. *4pm-9pm daily* €

Café'in á Mølini: In Skálavík, Sandoy, this former general store is now a quirky cafe serving coffee and burgers. *noon-6pm daily* €

Places We Love to Stay

€ Budget €€ Midrange €€€ Top End

Tórshavn
p248

Hotel Hafnia €€ Characterful modern rooms with a bustling lobby bar in an unbeatable location close to the fort. Cottages – well priced and great for families – are available.

Hotel Tórshavn €€ City centre hotel next to the harbour with decent rooms – and a nod towards local art.

Hotel 62 N €€ Decent modern hotel in the heart of the town with a cafe that doubles as the breakfast room; plus advice on what's on in town.

62N Guesthouse €€ Guesthouse in the heart of the action with doubles, singles and simple family rooms with bunks.

Havgrím Seaside Hotel 1948 €€€ Classy boutique property with views to Nólsoy Island, excellent service and superb breakfast.

Hotel Føroyar €€€ The island's most luxurious hotel, with a new extension to its specialist Faroese-themed spa. On the outskirts of Tórshavn.

Beyond Tórshavn
p253

Dalur Campsite € Village campground with grassy pitches, tents and great facilities, including a common room.

Visit Homes €€ Lovingly put-together rooms at a cosy house in Leirvík run by an attentive host.

Gjáargarður Guesthouse (p257) **€€** Swiss chalet-like hotel in Gjógv with plain rooms, a decent Faroese restaurant and good breakfast.

Hanusarstova B&B €€€ Fabulous farm stay with supper club dining option 20 minutes from Tórshavn with charming hosts and lots of sheep.

Leisure Pearl €€€ Dreamy two-bedroom cottage in north Streymoy that's been tastefully renovated and overlooks the beach.

Vágar
p258

Giljanes Hostel & Camping € Welcoming community feel. Compact single-sex and mixed dorms, plus a handful of private rooms and a patch of grass for camping. Large kitchen/lounge. Cheap car rental.

Gásadalsgarður Guesthouse €-€€ Charming charred wood cottage with four double rooms to rent in the house either individually or together. Great location in the heart of the tiny charming village.

The View €€ Four classic Faroese turf-roofed cottages overlooking sea stacks at Bøur, in one of the country's most idyllic spots. Book well in advance.

Cottages by the Sea €€ Well-appointed, light-filled duplexes with Scandi vibes located on Sørvágur's waterfront.

Múlafossur Cottages €€€ Two-bed wooden turf-roof cabins in a serene riverside spot above Gásadalur.

Northern Islands
p263

Lokk-Inn Apartments €€ A wooden house with a series of compact 1, 2 and 3 bedroom studios with kitchens and washing machines beside the fjord in Norðdepil.

Hotel Klaksvík €€ Rather basic hotel in the heart of the town with 30 rooms.

Hotel Norð €€ Almost at the end of the road in far flung Viðareiði, this small, simple and rather rustic hotel feels well off the map.

Southern Islands
p267

Gist Guesthouse € 16-roomed simple one-storey guesthouse just off the main road in Suðuroy with a shared kitchen, rentable hot tub and hiking routes from the front door.

Brim B&B €€ Chic, minimalist-style, modern B&B with views of the harbour and mountains in a great location in the heart of Vágur, Suðuroy.

Café MorMor B&B €€ A homely double room in an annex of an 1890s building in Tvøroyri, Suðuroy, and one of the island's most popular cafes.

Heima i Stovu €€ Small guesthouse in a 19th-century house with a historic, doily-ed feel in the north of Suðuroy. Extras include private hiking guides and supper club-style dinners.

Mølin Guesthouse €€ Yellow guesthouse-hotel in Skálavík with neat rooms and an old-fashioned grandma-styled cafe on Sandoy.

HEERING
NYHAVN 17

Nyhavn (p65)

TOOLKIT

The chapters in this section cover the most important topics you'll need to know about in Denmark. They're full of nuts-and-bolts information and valuable insights to help you understand and navigate Denmark and get the most out of your trip.

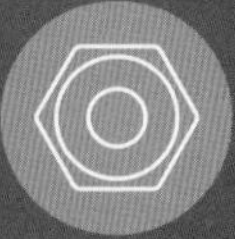

Arriving

Most travellers will enter the country at Copenhagen airport. Visitors pass cafes and shops before baggage reclaim, and there are more in the arrivals hall at Terminal 3, where all flights exit. It's only 8km to the city centre and takes less than 15 minutes by train or metro. Taxis take longer. International flights also arrive into Billund, Aarhus and Aalborg.

Visas

Schengen citizens can enter freely for any length of stay. Visitors from the UK, US, Canada, Australia and New Zealand don't need a tourist visa for stays under 90 days. Other nationals should check *nyidanmark.dk*.

SIM Cards

You can pick up a pay-as-you-go SIM card at WHSmith or 7-Eleven in the arrivals hall. Alternatively there is a vending machine inside baggage claim.

Wi-Fi

Copenhagen airport has good free wi-fi, and you'll find many locations across the city centre where you can log on free of charge, particularly in shops, bars and cafes.

Buying Travel Tickets

Purchase train tickets from the red machines in the airport arrival hall. Alternatively buy a *rejsekort* from the blue self-service machine, to take either train or metro.

Airport to City Centre

	Copenhagen	Billund	Aarhus	Aalborg
TRAIN	13min **around 36kr**	n/a	n/a	n/a
METRO	13min **around 36kr**	n/a	n/a	n/a
BUS	35min **from 23kr**	9min **free shuttle**	50min **126kr**	15min **22kr**
TAXI	20-30min **250-350kr**	6min **75-100kr**	40min **around 700kr**	10min **around 180kr**

LAND & SEA CROSSINGS

Made famous by the TV show *The Bridge*, the 16km-long Øresund Bridge connects Copenhagen with Malmö in Sweden, by both road and rail. Ferry routes to Sweden include Gothenburg–Frederikshavn, Varberg–Grenaa, Helsingborg–Helsingør and Ystad–Rønne on Bornholm. Denmark's only land border is with Germany; crossings are found near Padborg, Rens and Tønder in southern Jutland. Germany also has ferry links to Rødbyhavn on Lolland, Gedser on Falster, Rønne on Bornholm and Havneby on Rømø. Between Norway and Denmark, ferry services operate Oslo–Copenhagen, Oslo–Frederikshavn and Kristiansand–Hirtshals. The Smyril line sails between Denmark and Iceland, via the Faroe Islands.

FROM LEFT: FUSE/GETTY IMAGES ©, GEORGE MDIVANIAN/EYEEM/GETTY IMAGES ©

Getting Around

Denmark has excellent public transport links making it easy to travel around the country by bus and train. Car rentals are convenient, with safe, easy driving conditions on smooth roads.

TRAVEL COSTS

Car rental **400–600kr/day**

Petrol **13–14kr/litre**

EV charging **4.19kr/kWh**

Train ticket Copenhagen to Aarhus **Around 420kr**

Hiring a Car

The best rental deals are found on foreign booking sites. Several apps offer hourly rentals – Share Now has electric and petrol cars, and GreenMobility operates EV fleets. GoMore users rent cars directly from owners. Eon and Clever are EV charging providers, but you'll need an app.

Bringing Your Own Car

If you bring in a vehicle that is registered in a non-EU country, you must take out a border insurance policy. Requirements are outlined on the website of the Danish Motor Insurers' Bureau *(dfim.dk)*.

TIP

Download the *Rejseplanen* app. Enter your start and end points, and it will find the best routes, times and prices.

PEDAL POWER

Denmark is one of Europe's most cycle-friendly countries. Two-thirds of Copenhageners commute daily by bicycle, and it's usually the quickest way to get around. Copenhagen, Aarhus, Odense and Aalborg have *bycykler* rental schemes and there are numerous rental outlets. In villages ask at the local bike shop. In Copenhagen, Helsingør, Roskilde and Aarhus, Donkey Republic rents orange bicycles by the minute, and allows pick-up and drop off in different locations, all through the app.

Booking Trains

Train tickets can be bought from station machines, ticket offices or via the DSB website or app. There are early-bird discounts; check for orange saver tickets. Reservations are not free, however trains do get busy, so for longer distances it can be worthwhile.

Rejsekort

Fares are cheaper with a *rejsekort*. Similar to London's Oyster card, it's an electronic ticket system for travelling by bus, train, metro and water taxi. Purchase a card for 80kr, and top it up at blue self-service machines at stations. Remember you need to touch in and out, even on buses.

Flights

Denmark's main airport is Copenhagen, but Aarhus, Billund and Aalborg also receive international flights. SAS is the main carrier. Local airline DAT (formerly Danish Air Transport) flies to Bornholm. You can also fly between the centre of Copenhagen and Aarhus with Nordic Seaplanes.

DRIVING ESSENTIALS

Drive on the right.

Check cycle lanes before turning right.

Speed limit is 50km/h in built-up areas (40km/h in central Copenhagen); 60–90km/h on other roads; 110 or 130km/h on motorways.

Money

CURRENCY: DANISH KRONE (KR)

Credit Cards

Visa and Mastercard are widely accepted; American Express and Diners Club less so. Hotels, petrol stations, restaurants and shops may charge a fee for foreign cards.

Cash

Some cash machines exchange foreign currency. You don't need to carry much cash in Denmark as shops and services are increasingly cashless.

Taxes & Refunds

Denmark's 25% value-added tax, called MOMS, is added to goods and services. If you live outside the EU, you can claim a refund. Collect a form in-store, then present it with receipts, passport and purchases at the airport; there's a desk in Terminal 3 at Copenhagen airport.

Tipping

Hotels Usually 10-20kr is sufficient for carrying bags to your room.

Taxis It's not really expected, service is included in the quoted price.

Restaurants It's not expected, but tipping is becoming more common. Round up or add 10% when service is especially good.

HOW MUCH FOR A

Metro fare (central zones)
18kr

Bike rental
100-150kr per day

Museum entry
80-160kr

Ticket to Legoland
from 329kr

HOW TO... Save Money

Denmark is a relatively expensive country, but there are ways to save kroner. Seniors and students usually qualify for discounted museum and transport tickets. In general using a *rejsekort* gives lower fares on the bus, S-tog (trains) and metro. Book train travel early to bag an 'orange' discount ticket. If you're self-catering try the Too Good To Go app, to pick up bargain food deals and help save waste.

LOCAL TIP

If you're doing lots of sightseeing in the capital, consider the Copenhagen Card *(copenhagencard.com)*, purchased and used through an app (no wi-fi needed). It costs from 499kr depending on duration and covers entrance to almost 90 attractions and local transport.

DIGITAL DENMARK

Denmark is an increasingly cashless and digitalised society. According to the Digital Economy and Society Index 2022, it ranked second in Europe after Finland. It's rare that places won't accept credit cards. In fact it is more likely that shops or cafes are reluctant to take cash. Even hot-dog stands, market stalls and countryside honesty boxes ask for Mobile Pay, a local payments app available to Danish bank account holders only. Denmark's digitalisation goes far beyond money. Drivers licences and health cards can be carried on smartphones, and even correspondence with local government is via an app.

Accommodation

A Flock of Kros

The countryside inns known as *kroer* trace their origins to one travel-weary king named Erik Klipping, who demanded roadside inns to be opened at regular intervals way back in 1283. Amazingly, many survive today: some are stodgy (in both food and flair), while others have been brought up to date, becoming holiday destinations in their own right.

Hygge Holiday Cottages

Known as a 'summer house' *(sommerhus)* in Danish, holiday cottages are hugely popular, and many Danish families will spend at least part of their annual holidays in one. They are typically located in rural or seaside settings, and often rented on a weekly basis, which can represent good savings if you're travelling in a small group.

Bed Down on the Farm

At its core, Denmark is a land of fields and farms – so if you really want to get a sense for what's made life tick here for centuries, drop into one of around 30 farm stays connected to the National Association for Agricultural Tourism *(bondegaardsferie.dk/en)*. The farms vary from rural and relaxing to actively agricultural.

HOW MUCH FOR A NIGHT IN A

Rural castle
from 1250kr

En-suite hotel or kro
700–1500kr

Dorm bed
150–300kr

Noble Nights

Sleep like a queen – or at least some kind of baroness – in one of the many old castles and manor houses dotting the Danish countryside. The Danish Castle and Manor Association *(castles-manorhouses.dk)* keeps a list of about a dozen participating palaces. They're often used for weddings and group retreats, so book in advance.

Minimalist Hostels

There are plenty of budget hostels in Denmark. These are usually more institutional than funky or bohemian – often aimed at school/sports groups – but offer reliably clean and affordable lodgings. Danhostel *(danhostel.dk)* is the largest association, with around 60 hostels throughout the country. They are also a member of Hostelling International. Otherwise, larger cities all have private hostels to choose from.

CAMP OUT

Unlike Sweden, Denmark has no freedom-to-roam law *(allemandsretten)*, and camping on the beach is also forbidden. However, hundreds of serviced campgrounds offer sites for as little as 70kr. Plus there are over 1000 primitive campsites – the simplest are just a forest clearing with a fire ring. Check the map *(kort)* at *udinaturen.dk*. Serviced campgrounds take reservations, but primitive ones do not.

CLOCKWISE FROM TOP LEFT: CLEMMESEN/SHUTTERSTOCK ©, DREVS/SHUTTERSTOCK ©, LJUPCO SMOKOVSKI/SHUTTERSTOCK ©, CUNAPLUS/SHUTTERSTOCK ©, ANGELUS_SVETLANA/SHUTTERSTOCK ©

Family Travel

Trolls, fairy tales, Lego bricks – you'd be forgiven for thinking Denmark is a wonderland designed especially for little ones. Countless amusement parks, zoos, camping grounds and beaches whirr into life every summer for family holidays that are wholesome and worry-free. Where else in the world can you see rows of prams with snoozing babies parked outside cafes?

When to Go

The best time for families is May to September. Good weather is more likely, and all attractions and activities are in full swing. Your kids are likely to meet other kids (school holidays run from late June to early August) though attractions will be busy and charge peak prices. Many family hot spots (including Legoland) close in winter (November to April), but open briefly for Christmas.

Where to Stay

Camping grounds are a great bet in high season. Many offer family cabins, pools, playgrounds and activity programmes for kids. Hostels are another good option; rooms often sleep up to six (usually in bunks) and there will be a guest kitchen, lounge facilities and bike hire. Consider farm stays too; many are geared to families and offer play areas.

KID-FRIENDLY PICKS

Lego House (p219)
Little creators will delight at the hi-tech edutainment on offer.

HC Andersens Hus (p158)
The magical world of fairy tales, with a dress-up play town for little ones.

Sagnlandet Lejre (p115)
'Land of Legends' sees actors bring the olden days to life at this outdoor learning centre.

Tivoli Gardens (p56)
The place that inspired Walt Disney to found Disneyland.

Camp Adventure (p124)
Magical forest park with treetop attractions, zip lines and climbing.

Eating Out

As a rule, restaurants go out of their way to woo families. Many offer a *børnemenu* (children's menu), and if they don't, mainstays like burgers, *frikadeller* (meatballs) and pastries, along with hot-dog stalls, mean choosy eaters won't go hungry.

Baby Facilities

Most attractions and many cafes/restaurants have baby-changing areas. The Copenhagen metro has dedicated spaces for buggies, plenty of lifts and is free for kids under 12. Breastfeeding in public is a common sight and not taboo.

LAND OF PLAY

It should come as no surprise that Denmark's penchant for creative, inspiring and practical design extends to its playgrounds. No two play areas are the same, with the notion of swings, slide and climbing frame a thing of the past. Danish companies like Monstrum, founded in 2003, are the starchitects of play spaces, creating themed, art-forward, sustainable wonderlands (think giant creatures, marvellous machines and magical settings) that look stunning and stimulate free play. You can find their playgrounds at places like Lego House, Dokk1 in Aarhus, Copenhagen airport, and in urban, woodland and coastal settings throughout Denmark.

Health & Safe Travel

INSURANCE

EU citizens are covered by the European Health Insurance Card for most medical care, excluding non-emergencies or repatriation. Citizens from other countries should check for reciprocal health agreements, otherwise make sure you have adequate cover. A travel insurance policy that covers theft, loss of property and medical treatment is usually a good idea.

Health

Health risks are minimal and travellers don't need to take special precautions. Tap water is drinkable. Public healthcare is well functioning and pharmacies are widespread. Infectious diseases are not especially prevalent. Denmark emerged from the COVID-19 pandemic with few excess deaths, and was praised for its handling of the crisis. Vaccine take-up was high.

Safety

Denmark is one of the world's safest countries; the Economist Intelligence Unit named Copenhagen the world's safest city in 2021. The most common reported crimes are theft and vandalism. In the Faroe Islands, crime is virtually non-existent. Women travelling alone are unlikely to encounter problems, but use common sense if walking alone at night and avoid hitchhiking.

BICYCLE LANES

Danish riders are fast and bike lanes can be hazardous. In cities, the paving is differentiated, but they aren't necessarily marked or painted.

ONLINE WATER RATING (BADEVAND.DK)

Red Flag
Bad quality water, do not swim

Green Flag
Good quality water

Yellow Flag
No warnings given

Grey Flag
Currently closed

TICKS

Ticks are found across Denmark in forests and long grass, and are most active spring to summer. Most bites do not cause illness but ticks can transmit serious infections like Lyme disease and encephalitis. Campers and hikers should check themselves. If you find one, removing it quickly lowers the risk of infection. See a doctor if a rash develops.

Cannabis

Recreational cannabis remains prohibited in Denmark. You may see cannabis openly sold in places like Christiania, but it is not legal to do so. Support for decriminalisation has led to calls to trial more relaxed laws, but this has not taken place. Denmark has a nascent medicinal cannabis industry, but it is strictly licensed and controlled.

FROM LEFT: AFRICA STUDIO/SHUTTERSTOCK ©, ALEKSANDARNAKIC/GETTY IMAGES ©

Food, Drink & Nightlife

When to Eat

Morgenmad (breakfast; 6am to 9am) is a simple meal with coffee; the classic *bolle med ost* is a bread roll with cheese, or jam.

Frokost (lunch; noon to 2pm) is typically a smørrebrød (open sandwich) or cooked meal.

Aftensmad (dinner; 6pm to 9pm) is an evening meal at home; *middag* is a two- or three-course dinner. Danes eat early.

Where to Eat

Bakery Cheap breakfast and lunch option.

Coffee shop Simple food like bread rolls with cheese, croissants and pastries.

Cafe Casual sit-down lunch spots.

Vinstue/Bodega Old-fashioned pubs sometimes serving Danish classics like smørrebrød, breaded plaice or *stegt flæsk* (fried pork).

Kro Traditional inn. Classic danish fare is often elevated to gourmet levels.

Restaurant Smørrebrød at lunch and heartier dinners. Set dinner menus of five to seven courses are increasingly the norm at new Nordic-style places.

MENU DECODER

børnemenu kids' menu
dagens ret daily special
danskvand sparkling water
drinkskort drinks list
fadøl draught beer
fisk fish
flæskesteg roast pork
flaske bottle
forretter starter
hjemmelavet homemade
hovedretter main
hvidløg garlic
hvidvin white wine
kaffe coffee
kortmaskine card machine
kylling chicken
laks salmon
lammekød lamb
med with
mellemmåltid snacks
økologisk organic
oksekød beef
øl beer
ost cheese
regningen bill
ret dish
rødvin red wine
salat salad
sild herring
Skål! cheers!
sodavand fizzy drink
spisekort/menu menu
suppe soup
svinekød pork
te tea
vand water

HOW TO...

Order a Hot Dog

Travellers arriving at Copenhagen airport are greeted with the waft of *pølse* (sausages) as they wait in baggage reclaim. Danes love their hot dogs as much as Americans, and there's more than 100 years of hot-dog history. Though numbers have decreased, vendors are ubiquitous on street corners and town squares throughout the country. Hot dogs are a quick daytime bite or late-night snack, often with a bottle of warm chocolate milk.

To eat one the Danish way, order a classic *ristet hotdog* with everything *('med det hele')*. Its assembly must be precise. The sausage is placed in bread, then plied with mustard, remoulade and ketchup, topped with raw onions, then fried onions and sealed with overlapping pickled cucumber. An alternative is the *fransk* hotdog, a sausage with no French connection, but it's stuffed into a baguette-like piece of bread with a hole through the middle.

HOW MUCH FOR A...

Bolle med ost
32-45kr

Kanelsnegl (cinnamon pastry)
35kr

Cup of coffee
35kr

Beer
70kr

Glass of wine
80-150kr

Smørrebrød (one piece)
70-130 kr

Set menu at a city restaurant
350-600kr

Tasting menu at a Michelin-starred restaurant
2000kr + (excluding wine)

HOW TO... Smørrebrød

Smørrebrød, pronounced 'smuhr-bro', is simply an open sandwich with one layer of bread. It has long been a lunchtime staple and its earliest mention goes back to medieval times. At its most basic it consists of sliced rye bread topped with shrimps, pickled herring, egg or liver pâté *(leverpostej)*, plus garnish. But these days the smørrebrød served in restaurants are nothing less than elaborate art forms.

Butter Bread

Smørrebrød translates as 'butter bread' and became a Danish traditional lunch item among workers in the 19th century.

Eating smørrebrød is almost a ritual, and Danes are very particular about it. There's an unwritten law that governs the specific order, specific bread and the specific garnish that each serving must have. Smoked salmon goes with white bread and herring with rye bread.

Even the traditional Danish Christmas lunch on 25 December is a succession of open sandwiches, and don't dare deviate from the order! Lighter fish and prawn smørrebrød come first, before you advance to warm, meatier varieties. It's all accompanied by *akvavit* (Danish snaps) with a toast, then washed down with ale. To toast, raise your glass and say *skål!* (cheers!) while making eye contact with everyone at the table.

Cheap smørrebrød are available in bakeries or you can sit down for a multicourse extravaganza. Cafes usually offer individual items à la carte, or a choice of three servings at a set price.

GOING OUT

Danes love to party hard and most towns have a nightlife scene, whether you're seeking a casual beer at a pub, a more sophisticated cocktail or want to dance the night away.

It's not unusual for Danes to share a drink at home with friends before heading out and on sunny afternoons in summertime, groups of friends often hang out together in parks or along the waterfront, sharing a few cans of beer. For a casual drink you'll find plenty of options in towns and cities but, unlike places such as the UK, villages won't necessarily have a local drinking spot.

Bodegas are old-school pubs usually serving beer on tap. Smaller establishments are often rather smoky and among the few places indoors where cigarettes are allowed. The rise of craft beer has seen many brewpubs pop up. A lot of cafes and bars have pavement seating and even in wintertime Danes will be found outside huddled beneath blankets and heaters.

Don't mix up *vinstue* with *vinbar*. A *vinstue* is much like a *bodega*. A *vinbar* is a trendy wine bar found in cities. Usually the vibe is relaxed and low-key, and drinking *naturvin* (organic wine) is the thing to do.

Bar and pubs are usually open until 1am or 2am, even later on a Friday or Saturday night. Don't even think of going to a nightclub until well after midnight. Most places don't enforce strict dress codes and will still be going at 4am or 5am.

Responsible Travel

Climate Change & Travel

It's impossible to ignore the impact we have when travelling; Lonely Planet urges all travellers to engage with their travel carbon footprint, which will mainly come from air travel. While there often isn't an alternative, travellers can look to minimise the number of flights they take, opt for newer aircrafts and use cleaner ground transport, such as trains. One proposed solution – purchasing carbon offsets – unfortunately does not cancel out the impact of individual flights. While most destinations will depend on air travel for the foreseeable future, for now, pursuing ground-based travel where possible is the best course of action.

The **UN Carbon Offset Calculator** shows how flying impacts a household's emissions

The **ICAO's carbon emissions calculator** allows visitors to analyse the CO_2 generated by point-to-point journeys

Dine Sustainably

At the time of research 17 restaurants in Denmark had been awarded a Michelin green clover to highlight sustainable gastronomy. Copenhagen's **Høst** offers carbon-neutral dining, while **ØsterGRO** is a rooftop organic farm and restaurant.

Go Troll Hunting

More than a dozen giant troll sculptures are hidden across Denmark. Download the map *(trollmap.com)* and go treasure hunting! Danish artist Thomas Danbo made the trolls from recycled materials and reclaimed wood.

With Greenkayak you can sightsee for free and clean up local waterways by collecting rubbish as you paddle. The popular idea began in Copenhagen, and is now available at locations across Denmark.

Roskilde Festival (p113) has been non-profit since its inception in 1972, and aims to highlight environmental and social issues. Food stalls display their carbon footprints and the reusable cup scheme has slashed plastic waste.

TAKE GREEN TRANSPORT

Copenhagen's metro, S-tog (trains), local ferries and some buses are electric. Try Viggo's EV taxi fleet or Drivr, which has cabs powered by green hydrogen. Otherwise self-drive an EV with ShareNow or GreenMobility.

SUSTAINABLE DENMARK

In 2024, Denmark was the highest-ranked country worldwide on the Climate Change Performance Index, and earned top spot in the Environmental Performance Index (EPI), a global sustainability ranking by Yale and Columbia Universities. Read more about **Sustainable Denmark** (p303).

Hit the Hiking Trails

It really doesn't get more emission-free than walking. Denmark has some beautiful (and relatively flat) hiking trails. Try tackling South Funen's **Øhavsstien** (p176) or the 175km **Camønoen** (p146) on Møn.

Visit Europe's Most Sustainable Islands

In 2021, **Ærø** (p172) was named the most sustainable island in the EU. Meanwhile, only a year earlier, **Bornholm** (p132) and Samsø topped the list.

Stargazing on Møn

Brush up on your astronomy by going on a guided nighttime tour in the **Dark Sky Parks** (p146) of Møn and Nyord *(darkskymoen.dk/en)*.

Voluntourism

Each year thousands apply for the Faroe Islands' **Closed for Maintenance** (p269) scheme, which sees 100 volunteers spend three days helping with tasks like path-building and erecting signs at popular tourist spots across the archipelago.

Borrow from the Human Library

The Human Library in Nørrebro, Copenhagen, loans humans rather than books. Readers choose a title and sit in the reading garden for a conversation with a person who has a disability, a refugee or someone from a minority group, for example.

Tour Copenhagen's canals with **GoBoat** on a small boat that runs on solar power.

Cafe Exit *(cafeexit.dk)* helps released prisoners get a fresh start in Copenhagen, Aarhus and Odense.

On Your Bike

Ditch the car and bike like the locals do. Not only is it green, it's the most convenient way to get around city centres. Elsewhere, cycle routes and bike rentals are widely available.

RESOURCES

naturfonden.dk/english/
Find Denmark's nature areas with hiking trails and other activities.

frivilligjob.dk
Check Denmark's biggest portal for voluntary work.

danskretursystem.dk/en
How to recycle bottles, cans and containers, and get cash back.

CLOCKWISE FROM LEFT: LJUPCO SMOKOVSKI/SHUTTERSTOCK ©, AMENIC181/SHUTTERSTOCK ©, IDEA ROUTE/SHUTTERSTOCK ©, STOCKPHOTO-GRAF/SHUTTERSTOCK ©, ROLAND MAGNUSSON/SHUTTERSTOCK ©, SNEZHANA K/SHUTTERSTOCK ©

LGBTIQ+ Travellers

Denmark has consistently ranked among Europe's most queer-friendly countries. In 2024, the Spartacus Gay Travel Index placed it eighth worldwide. Historically Denmark has been a frontrunner on gay rights and anti-discrimination legislation, becoming the world's first country to recognise same-sex partnerships in 1989.

The Biggest Bash

Copenhagen Pride *(copenhagenpride.dk)* is the calendar's biggest event. Every August, a week-long festival of performances, debates and inclusive sports events culminate with a parade in the city centre – hundreds of thousands turn out. There's also a **Winter Pride** event in February, and the city hosted the 2021 World Pride and Eurogames. **Aarhus** *(aarhuspride.dk)* and **Aalborg** *(aalborgpride.dk)* have smaller annual pride events, and **Faroe Pride** takes place in Tórshavn in July. Held each October, **Mix Copenhagen** *(mixcopenhagen.dk)* is one of the world's longest-running LGBTIQ+ film festivals.

GOING OUT

Copenhagen has plenty of nightlife options, and most restaurants and bars are gay-friendly; the concentration of LGBTIQ+ bars and nightclubs in the old Latin Quarter make up the 'gaybourhood'. Beyond Copenhagen the nightlife scene is limited. There is a small handful of dedicated LGBTIQ+ bars and clubs in Aarhus, though the city is generally progressive, and fewer still in Aalborg and Odense.

Community

LGBT+ Danmark *(lgbt.dk)* is the largest and oldest national organisation, first founded in 1948 as Kredsen af 1948 (Circle of 1948). For information on the community in the Faroe Islands, try **LGBT+ Føroyar** *(lgbt.fo)*. LGBT Asylum *(lgbtasylum.dk)* is a volunteer-run NGO offering a social network and safe space for refugees.

FAROE ISLANDS

The Faroe Islands has a reputation for lagging behind Denmark's more progressive places, but it has an active LGBTIQ+ community and its attitudes are changing. Same-sex marriage and adoptions were legalised in 2017. While there are no specific queer venues, Tórshavn's main bars are generally safe and welcoming.

TOURISM

With a friendly, progressive attitude and a host of events and venues, Copenhagen is a popular destination for gay travellers. **Out and About** *(outandabout.dk)* has a free English guide with gay-friendly listings and information; it's available at LGBTIQ+ venues or tourist information. Author Bjarne Henrik Lundis leads one- to two-hour walking tours in Danish, English or German exploring Copenhagen's LGBTIQ+ history and society – see *visitcopenhagen.com*.

Oldest Gay Bar

In the heart of Copenhagen, and open at this very spot since 1917, Centralhjørnet is believed to be the world's longest-running gay bar. It stages popular drag shows and Sunday jazz, and classes itself as 'straight-friendly'.

Accessible Travel

People with disabilities shouldn't hold back from travelling in Denmark. Accessibility is improving and transport is usually designed to cater for wheelchair users and those with other impairments. However, you may encounter some older shops, museums and hotels that have not been updated.

Copenhagen Metro

All stations in Copenhagen's metro are designed for accessibility. Lifts link the street with platforms, there are no gaps between train doors and platforms, and the metro connects to the airport.

Airport

Airport assistance is booked directly through your airline. Copenhagen airport has a well-designed assistance centre and waiting room, found in Terminal 3 before security. Accessible toilets and lifts are located throughout the airport.

Accommodation

Modern hotels are usually designed with accessibility in mind, but some older hotels are not adequate. Search the God Adgang (Access Denmark; *accessdenmark.com*) website to check accommodation; *visitcopenhagen.com* also lists accessible hotels.

RESOURCES

God Adgang (Access Denmark; *accessdenmark.com*) awards a label to buildings, facilities and services that meet accessibility standards. A searchable database on the website details how different disabilities and impairments are supported.

Danish Association of the Physically Disabled (DHF; *danskhandicap forbund.dk*) has links for travellers.

Danish Association for the Blind *(blind.dk)*

Department of Transport *(dinoffentlige transport.dk)* has accessibility details.

ACCESSIBLE TOILETS

Public toilets are found throughout Copenhagen. To see the location of toilets that have disabled access, are supervised or both, check this map: *kk.dk/toiletter.*

Attractions

Some museums do not have ramps. Many old quarters have cobbled streets. Visit Copenhagen *(visitcopenhagen.com)* lists the most accessible attractions in the capital.

Transport

Copenhagen taxis accept collapsible wheelchairs; book ahead for powered wheelchairs. Trains and S-tog stations have lifts and (often) accessible carriages. Buses have ramps.

BE MY EYES APP

Designed by Danes, this free app for blind and visually impaired people worldwide connects to volunteers in over 150 countries to assist with everyday tasks, big or small.

Sølund Music Festival

Join 20,000 arts and music lovers for three days of musical performances in mid-June at the world's biggest festival *(solundfestivalen.dk)* for people with physical and mental disabilities. Running in Jutland since 1986, there's easy access for wheelchairs and quiet zones.

How to Plan a Trip to Legoland

The unquenchable popularity of Lego bricks, coupled with direct flights into Billund from destinations all over Europe, means more and more families are travelling to Denmark specifically to visit Legoland (p221) and the hi-tech Lego House (p219) play centre. If you're weighing up a family-sized pilgrimage to the birthplace of Lego bricks, this guide is designed to help you get the most out of your trip.

Check the Calendar

Legoland has a surprisingly sporadic opening schedule, so check carefully before organising a trip *(legoland.dk)*. The park winds down for the winter from around October until late March, but still opens on certain weekends, and for longer periods over Halloween and Christmas. In high season, Legoland claims that Tuesday and Wednesday see the most crowds, while Saturday is quieter. School holidays in Denmark end after the first week of August, so aim to go later than that for shorter wait times.

Get Cheap(er) Tickets

Buy your tickets for Legoland and Lego House online *(legoland.dk)* for a small saving. You'll also save if buying a combo ticket for both attractions. It's worth keeping an eye out for coupons, which sometimes appear in the Lego toy catalogue or on supermarket food products. A typical coupon offer is a free child's entry for every paying adult.

WHICH LEGO HOTEL?

Of the three official hotels, **Legoland Castle Hotel** has the most wow factor, with its cartoon castle architecture and rooms themed to knights, princesses and wizards. Legoland Hotel is closest to the park, with its own private entrance (but no early-hours access). A huge choice of themed rooms include Ninjago, Lego Friends and a *Lego Movie*–themed room, or more grown-up park-view rooms. Kids get a free Lego set. A great option is **Legoland Holiday Village** with its themed playgrounds and nature area. You can park next to your cabin and catch the shuttle bus into Legoland. For non-Lego options, see p241.

GOOD TO KNOW

- You can bring your own food and drink into Legoland. Pirateland has nice grassy picnic areas.
- It's a good idea to book Lego restaurants in advance, especially Mini Chef at Lego House and Panorama at Legoland Hotel.
- Download the official Legoland Billund app for live ride-queue times and e-ticket entry.
- Hire pushchairs at the park if you don't want to bring your own.
- Big family? Some Lego hotel rooms and cabins sleep up to eight people, or try the self-catering units at Lalandia.

ALLARD ONE/SHUTTERSTOCK ©

Nuts & Bolts

OPENING HOURS

During summer, attractions have longer hours, but may vary throughout the year.

Banks 10am–4pm Monday to Friday

Bars and clubs 4pm–midnight, to 2am or 5am Friday and Saturday

Coffee shops 8am–6pm

Restaurants noon–10pm (earlier at weekends for brunch)

Shops 10am–6pm Monday to Friday, to 2pm or 4pm Saturday, often closed Sunday (except supermarkets)

Smoking

Danes are surprisingly heavy smokers. Smoking is banned in restaurants, bars and clubs, but allowed in some small pubs.

Internet Access

Free internet is widespread. Log on at cafes, supermarkets, on transport and at public libraries.

Weights & Measures

Denmark uses the metric system. Decimals are indicated by commas, and thousands by points.

GOOD TO KNOW

Time zone
GMT/UTC +1 in winter, GMT/UTC +2 in summer

Country code
45

Emergency number
112

Population
5.8 million

Electricity

230V/50Hz

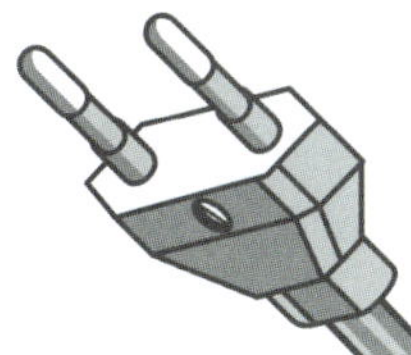

PUBLIC HOLIDAYS

Many Danes take their main work holidays during the first three weeks of July. Offices, shops and services usually close on the following holidays:

New Year's Day
1 January

Maundy Thursday
Thursday before Easter

Good Friday Friday before Easter

Easter Day Sunday in March or April

Easter Monday Day after Easter

Ascension Day Sixth Thursday after Easter

Whitsunday Seventh Sunday after Easter

Whitmonday Seventh Monday after Easter

Constitution Day
5 June

Christmas Eve
24 December

Christmas Day
25 December

Boxing Day (2nd Christmas Day)
26 December

New Year's Eve
31 December

Language

Many visitors to Denmark get around without speaking a word of Danish, but just a few phrases go a long way in making friends, inviting service with a smile, and ensuring a rich and rewarding travel experience – you could be invited in for some hygge, experience a sublime meal or grab that great shopping bargain.

Basics

Hello. Goddag. *go·da*
Goodbye. Farvel. *faar·vel*
Yes. Ja. *ya*
No. Nej. *nai*
Please. Vær så venlig. *ver saw ven·lee*
Thank you. Tak. *taak*
Excuse me. Undskyld mig. *awn·skewl mai*
Sorry. Undskyld. *awn·skewl*
What's your name? Hvad hedder De/du? *va hey·dha dee/doo*
My name is ... Mit navn er ... *mit nown ir ...*
Do you speak English? Taler De/du engelsk? *ta·la dee/doo eng·elsk*
I don't understand. Jeg forstår ikke. *yai for·stawr i·ke*

Directions

Where's ...? Hvor er ...? *vor ir ...*
What's the address? Hvad er adressen? *va ir a·draa·sen*
Could you please write it down? Kunne De/du skrive det ned? *koo·ne dee/doo skree·ve dey nidh*
Can you show me (on the map)? Kan De/du vise mig det (på kortet)? *kan dee/doo vee·se mai dey (paw kor·tet)*

Signs

Indgang/Udgang Entrance/Exit
Åben/Lukket Open/Closed
Ledige værelser Rooms available
Varm/Kold Hot/Cold

Time

What time is it? Hvad er klokken? *va ir klo·ken*
It's (two) o'clock. Klokken er (to). *klo·ken ir (toh)*
Half past (one). Halv (to) (lit: half two). *hal (toh)*
morning morgenen. *mor·nen*
afternoon eftermiddagen. *ef·taa·mi·da·en*
evening aftenen. *aaft·nen*
yesterday i går. *ee gawr*
today i dag. *ee da*
tomorrow i morgen. *ee morn*

Emergencies

Help! Hjælp! *yelp*
Stop! Stop! *stop*
Go away! Gå væk! *gaw vek*
I'm ill. Jeg er syg. *yai ir sew*
Could you help me, please? Kan De/du hjælpe mig? *kan dee/doo yel·pe mai*
Call ...! Ring efter ...! *ring ef·ta ...*
a doctor en læge. *in le·ye*
the police politiet. *poh·lee·tee·et*

Eating & Drinking

What would you recommend? Hvad kan De/du anbefale? *va kan dee/doo an·bey·fa·le*
What's the local speciality? Hvad er den lokale specialitet? *va ir den loh·ka·le spey·sha·lee·teyt*
Cheers! Skål! *skawl*
I'll have (a gin). (En gin), tak. *(in jeen) taak*

NUMBERS

1 **en** *in*
2 **to** *toh*
3 **tre** *trey*
4 **fire** *feer*
5 **fem** *fem*
6 **seks** *seks*
7 **syv** *sew*
8 **otte** *awte*
9 **ni** *nee*
10 **ti** *tee*

DONATIONS TO ENGLISH

One essential word thought to have Danish origin is 'smile'.

WORD STRESS

In Danish, stress often falls on the first syllable in a word. Compound words can have more than one syllable stressed.

Must-Know Grammar

Danish has a polite form of address, using the personal pronouns De and Dem. The words and phrases here are mostly in the familar form using du and dig, except where it's more appropriate to use the formal form. In general, use the formal form when speaking to senior citizens and officials, and the familiar form the rest of the time.

Five Phrases to Learn Before You Go

What time does it open/close?

Hvad er åbningstiderne? *va ehr āb-neengs-tee-thah-nah*

Opening hours vary throughout the year, especially for sights and activities.

Thanks for the meal.

Tak for mad. *taht for math*

After a meal you should always say tak for mad before getting up.

Which wine would you recommend?

Hvilken vin anbefaler du? *vil-gehn veen an-beh-fah-lah doo*

When Danes raise their glasses to you and say Skål! it means 'Cheers!'

Can I address you with 'du'?

Må jeg sige du? *mā yai see-yeh doo*

Danes generally only use the familiar form of address (du and dig) for everyone but senior citizens and officials.

Do you have plans for tonight?

Har du planer i aften? *hah doo pla-nah ee ahf-den*

Danish kitchens close relatively early: aim to eat before 10pm, before 9pm or earlier in smaller towns.

WHO SPEAKS DANISH?

The current international status of Danish is the legacy of its historical expansion. It's the official language of Denmark and has co-official status – with Greenlandic and Faroese respectively – in Greenland and the Faroe Islands, which are autonomous Danish territories. Until 1944 it was the official language of Iceland and today is taught in schools there as the first foreign language.

THE DENMARK

STORYBOOK

Our writers delve deep into different aspects of Danish life

Christiansborg Slot (p53)

A HISTORY OF DENMARK IN 15 PLACES

In the thousand years since Denmark was first unified, this tiny nation has had an outsized influence on the Scandinavian region, and the world beyond. It has undertaken a journey from paganism to Christianity, formed allegiances, fought battles and transformed from an absolute monarchy to a modern democracy. By Adrienne Murray Nielsen

IT WAS BACK in the 10th century when the name *Danmark* first appeared, carved in a rune stone. Viking ruler Harald Bluetooth had unified the Danes as a single kingdom and replaced their Norse gods with Christianity. Since then, over a thousand years of nation-building have shaped today's Denmark, in a story of conquest, religion, power and democracy.

Scandinavian Vikings were already making their mark. Norsemen had settled in Iceland, Greenland, the British Isles and Normandy, and their influence spanned Newfoundland to Baghdad. Among the last Viking rulers was Danish king Cnut, who reigned over a North Sea empire, encompassing Denmark, Norway and England.

Bloody battles and diplomatic allegiances cemented medieval Denmark as a regional power. A rivalry with Sweden repeatedly boiled over into conflict, as Danish Renaissance kings consolidated their wealth and power, adopted Lutheranism and established colonies on four continents. In the 19th century, brutal wars cost Denmark swathes of territory, resulting in a diminished state. Even so, cultural life flourished and it embarked on a new democratic chapter.

After WWII, the welfare state, universal healthcare and policies supporting women's equality, gay rights and the environment became cornerstones. In the 21st century, it's through softer powers that Danes continue to influence and inspire.

1. Stevns Klint

EVIDENCE OF DINOSAUR MASS EXTINCTION

Around 66 million years ago when dinosaurs roamed the earth, an asteroid violently struck the planet, causing what scientists believe was catastrophic climate change leading to mass extinction. The dinosaurs were wiped out and half of all species perished. In the chalk and limestone cliffs of Stevns Klint in southern Zealand, traces of ash have been found in a thin fossil-rich layer of clay. This has provided geological evidence supporting the theory of an asteroid's impact. The site was awarded UNESCO World Heritage status in 2014 and now has a state-of-the-art visitors centre.

For more on Stevns Klint, see page 121

2. Ancient Neolithic Dolmens

DOLMENS AND BURIAL MOUNDS

As glaciers retreated tens of thousands of years ago, humans first set foot upon Danish soil. The earliest settlers have been traced back to around 12,000 BCE, and eventually, communities were established. Today signs of early peoples are still scattered across the Danish countryside. There are thousands of ancient tombs, such as Neolithic dolmens and Bronze Age burial mounds in Jutland, Funen and Lolland, and some of the best-preserved are found on Møn. Kong Asgers Høj is a 10m-long chamber passage grave, and Klekkende Høj is a grassy knoll with a pair of burial chambers into which you can duck inside.

For more on Møn, see page 142

3. Bog Bodies

A HISTORICAL WHODUNNIT

Present-day Danish cultural and linguistic roots are thought to stem from a tribe that migrated from southern Sweden around 500 CE. However, there were scant records about the Iron Age inhabitants that preceded them until bog drainage and peat-cutting revealed the remains of hundreds of men, women and children. Among these ancient 'bog bodies', the most remarkable are Grauballe Man and Tollund Man, each over 2000 years old. Grauballe Man suffered a brutal and puzzling death, explored at the Moesgaard Museum near Aarhus. On display in Silkeborg, Tollund Man is so well-preserved that the whiskers on his chin are visible.

For more on the Silkeborg Museum, see page 215

4. Nationalmuseet

RAIDERS, TRADERS AND EXPLORERS

Think of the Vikings, and the imagination conjures up fearsome warriors in longboats, raiding and pillaging foreign lands. However, these Scandinavian seafarers were also farmers, traders, mariners and explorers. The Viking Age began when 'North Men' ransacked Lindisfarne Monastery on the coast of northeastern England in 793 CE, and went on to last about 250 years. During this time, opportunist raids evolved into organised conquests. Settlements were established in England, France, Iceland, Greenland and Newfoundland, while expeditions reached North Africa and the Middle East. Copenhagen's Nationalmuseet offers an unbeatable crash course in Viking history via its superb collections.

For more on Nationalmuseet, see page 59

Neolithic tomb, Møn (p142)

5. Vikingemuseet Ladby

DENMARK'S ONLY SHIP GRAVE

Hidden within a grassy burial mound is the only known Viking-era ship grave in Denmark. Believed to date from 925 CE, it's the tomb of an important king or chieftain, from a time before Denmark was a unified nation. Step inside the dimly lit burial chamber, and ghostly remnants of a magnificent longboat are revealed, as well as the bones of sacrificed animals, weaponry and grave goods, that were to accompany this powerful figure into the afterlife.

For more on Vikingemuseet Ladby, see page 164

6. Jelling

PAGAN KINGDOMS TO UNIFIED DENMARK

In the early 10th century, Jelling in Central Jutland became the cradle of Christianity for a new, unified Denmark. It was the seat of Viking King Gorm the Old, from whom a millennium-long chain of Danish monarchs has continued to this day. Ancient burial mounds rise up beside two enormous rune stones, often called 'Denmark's birth certificate'. One is engraved with the oldest representation of Christ in Scandinavia, and was erected by Gorm's son Harald Bluetooth. It reads: 'King Harald ordered this monument to be made in memory of Gorm his father and Thyra his mother, the Harald who won for himself all Denmark and Norway and made the Danes Christians.'

For more on Jelling, see page 222

7. Roskilde Domkirke

TOMBS OF DANISH ROYALTY

For centuries Roskilde was the capital of Denmark and this imposing cathedral encapsulates more than 850 years of Danish history. Beneath its vaulted ceiling, the royal mausoleum houses the crypts of 37 kings and queens from the Dark Ages to the modern day. There are no fewer than 11 spectacular chapels and crypts, including that of Denmark's first queen regnant, Margrete I. With the formation of the Kalmar Union in 1397, she ruled over all the Scandinavian kingdoms, Denmark (including Iceland and parts of Greenland), Norway and Sweden, an alliance that lasted until 1523, when the Swedes broke away, though Norway remained in Danish hands for another three centuries.

For more on Roskilde Domkirke, see page 111

8. Christiansø

BATTLES WITH SWEDEN

If you thought the Baltic island of Bornholm was the remotest part of Denmark, you'd be wrong. An hour's boat trip further east is tiny Christiansø, a 17th-century island fortress. During the 1600s, there was a succession of on-again, off-again wars between these Nordic neighbours. After suffering a humiliating loss in 1658, Denmark ceded the island of Bornholm and its territories in southern Sweden. Soon after, King Frederik III declared an absolute monarchy, which continued for the next two centuries. The now all-powerful king rebuilt the military, and his successor Christian V, transformed Christiansø from a fishing hamlet into an invincible naval fortress to monitor Sweden and stand ready for attack.

For more on Christiansø, see page 140

9. Christiansborg Slot

HISTORIC PALACE AND HOME OF DEMOCRACY

From Christiansborg's bell tower there are sweeping panoramic views over Copenhagen. It's a fitting location for the seat of Denmark's parliament, the Folketing. Simply known as Borgen (the Castle) to locals, it was first constructed as a palace in the 1730s by Christian VI, an unpopular, religious and authoritarian ruler, who was also a prolific builder of monuments and castles, largely funded by taxes and tolls from the Øresund. Christiansborg was partially destroyed by fire in 1794 then rebuilt, only to go up in flames again in 1884. The cornerstone of today's building was laid in 1907 by Frederik VIII, soon after the parliament moved in.

For more on Christiansborg, see page 53

10. Dybbøl Windmill

DEMOCRACY AND DEFEAT

When the 1849 constitution established an elected parliament, Denmark changed from an absolute monarchy to one of the most democratic countries in Europe. However, the law had also sought to declare the duchy of Schleswig as Danish territory, a move contested by Prussia. Two bloody wars followed, ending with a disastrous defeat that saw Denmark's map forever redrawn. A huge swathe of territory was ceded to Prussia, and remains German to this day, while parts of southern Jutland were only regained after WWI. The fierce fighting around Sønderborg, particularly at Dybbøl Mølle, made the mill a powerful symbol of Denmark's national identity.

For more on Dybbøl windmill, see page 197

11. Hans Christian Andersen's Birthplace

ENTER A FAIRY-TALE WORLD

Denmark's cultural scene flourished in the 19th century, with a wave of prominent artists, musicians and philosophers leaving their mark. Yet, no figure stands out more than Hans Christian Andersen. Known for his novels, plays and poems, Andersen authored over 150 fairy tales that captivated audiences worldwide. His life story is itself a tale of transformation, rising from a poverty-stricken childhood in Odense. At HC Andersens Hus his stories come to life, intertwined with the narrative of his own journey. The museum is centered around the humble cottage where Andersen was born, now a stunning complex of pavilions and gardens.

For more on HC Andersens Hus, see page 158

12. The Tirpitz Bunker

THE ATLANTIC WALL

When WWII broke out, neutral Denmark was invaded by German troops in April 1940, beginning a five-year occupation. The Danes retained some autonomy, running domestic affairs under Nazi supervision until 1943, when the Germans took outright control. Hidden in sand dunes north of Esbjerg, Tirpitz was a formidable Nazi bunker with artillery so powerful it could hit ships 50km off the coast. The site was part of Hitler's Atlan-

Freetown Christiania (p75)

tic Wall, a string of sea defences from northern Norway to the French-Spanish border, covering all of Jutland's west coast. Denmark was liberated in 1945, except for Bornholm, which Soviet forces held onto until 1946. The near derelict Tirpitz reopened a few years back as an innovative museum exploring the effects of war.

For more on Tirpitz, see page 192

13. Dansk Jødisk Museum

RESISTANCE AND RESCUE

Designed by leading architect Daniel Libeskind, the Danish Jewish Museum in central Copenhagen is an intriguing modern space inside a 17th-century building, that documents 400 years of Jewish history in Denmark, including a remarkable rescue during WWII. After taking full control of Denmark in August 1943, the Nazi occupiers planned to round up Jewish Danes and send them to concentration camps. In an extraordinary operation, the Danish Resistance managed to smuggle some 7200 Jews – about 90% of those left in Denmark – into neutral Sweden. In 2020, Frihedsmuseet, a new underground museum, also opened, telling the story of the Danish Resistance.

For more on Dansk Jødisk Museum, see page 63

14. Langelandsfort

COLD WAR PARANOIA

After its WWII occupation, Denmark abandoned its neutral stance and joined NATO. It was feared that if the Cold War turned hot, then this easternmost member state would be the first to be invaded by a possible Warsaw Pact army. In 1952 an extensive underground bunker complex was built in southern Langeland, remaining in service until the 1990s. Fortified with numerous gun emplacements, it both guarded the Baltic and acted as a listening post. Today visitors can wander around the gun emplacements, climb aboard a decommissioned submarine and see a Russian fighter jet. Denmark remains an active NATO member, sending troops to Iraq and Afghanistan.

For more on Langelandsfort, see page 177

15. Freetown Christiania

MODERNISATION AND COUNTER-CULTURE

Post-WWII Denmark pursued liberal social policies, introducing a social-welfare state with free healthcare and education, and later becoming a frontrunner on gender equality and gay rights. Though incomes reached new heights, the 1960s also saw disillusionment among the younger generation. Anti-establishment protests and a hippy counter-culture emerged, and there are few places more emblematic of this than Christiania. The free-living commune was established in 1971 after a group of young hippies and anarchists occupied an abandoned military base on the east of Copenhagen. Authorities allowed this 'social experiment' to continue, and recently Christiania celebrated 50 years. These days, however, its residents are no longer squatters but tax-paying landowners.

For more on Freetown Christiania, see page 75

MEET THE DANES

The Danish way of life ticks a lot of boxes, but there are also complexities to this Nordic nation. Adrienne Murray Nielsen introduces the Danes.

SOME FOREIGNERS COMPLAIN that Danes are hard to get to know. In my experience, they move in close-knit circles, but once you're introduced, Danes are rather sociable beings, fond of a drink or two. Of course, some stereotypes ring true. Danes are extremely punctual and organised. City-dwelling Danes are rather trendy and fashion-conscious, but the Nordic aesthetic is embraced in homes across the country.

In Danish society, family life comes first; by 5pm, most offices are empty. Books have been written about Danish parenting, with its emphasis on play. Kids are given room to take risks and are not overly sheltered. You might recall the international outrage when a giraffe was euthanised in front of school kids. Babies are practically born riding bicycles, and you'll see tiny kids pedalled around everywhere. Don't be shocked if you spot prams with snoozing babies left outside cafes as parents relax inside; trust is a part of Danish culture.

While Scandinavian languages share similarities, Danish is particularly tongue-twisting. Poking fun at Danes, Icelandic comedian Ari Eldjárn joked that to speak it, you 'need to have surgery done on your throat' and 'talk like you're being punched in the stomach'. Copenhageners have a staccato accent and don't pronounce the last letters of most words, making it tricky for newcomers to master. But most Danes are accomplished Anglophones – order a cup of coffee and they'll answer in perfect English.

Denmark's distinctive regional accents span from Jutland to Bornholm. But Denmark's urban-rural divide is stark in other ways too. There's more diversity and progressive attitudes in the capital. But it's also seen as elitist – a view that's often politicised.

However, during the COVID-19 pandemic, *samfundssind* meaning 'community spirit' became the latest Nordic buzzword. And perhaps there is something to it. Danes pay some of the world's highest taxes, and generally don't mind. Surveys often rank them (together with the Finns) among the 'happiest' people on the planet. In my view, 'happy' doesn't seem quite the right word, I prefer 'content'. There's low unemployment, plus social-welfare programmes, subsidised childcare, free education, universal healthcare and low crime and corruption. Inequality is low, and they're prosperous. All in all, this social cocktail makes Denmark a very liveable place.

Well, except for the brutally cold wind and bleak winters. However, Danes have a coping strategy: hygge. Usually, it translates as 'cosiness', but it's more than that; it's the simple joy of togetherness with family and friends.

However, this almost-perfect country does have a darker side. Racial and religious fault lines remain, and while Ukrainians fleeing Russia's invasion were welcomed with open arms, the last decade witnessed growing anti-immigrant and -refugee sentiment.

Who & How Many

Denmark is home to 5.9 million people; 5.1 million are considered of 'Danish origin'. Danes are high-income earners, with GDP per capita of US$69,270 in 2024.

I LIVE IN COPENHAGEN...

I was living on the other side of the world in Mumbai when I forged my first deep connection to Denmark. Though I'd been as a teenager and had later attended the Roskilde Music Festival, it was actually in India that I met my Danish husband. That was more than a decade ago. Turn the clock forward, and we've been settled in Copenhagen for five years, where we live with our young son. My husband hails from Funen, a place we visit frequently and to which we have strong family ties. We're among the many Nielsens of Denmark. It's the most common surname, followed by Jensen.

I'm also just one of more than 18,000 Brits who have made Denmark their home. Most foreigners choose to live in Copenhagen, which is becoming an increasingly cosmopolitan city. Denmark has an immigrant population of around 700,000, with the biggest group hailing from Poland, followed by Syria, Romania, Turkey and Germany.

DESIGNED FOR LIFE

A pared-back primer on Danish design. By Thomas O'Malley

EVERYONE RAVES ABOUT it, but what, exactly, is Danish or Nordic design? After a few days in Denmark, you start to get it. Functional, unadorned buildings with an impeccable finish. Clean lines and organic simplicity. Graceful, streamlined shapes. Warm wood tones and textures. An obsession with natural materials. Functionality first. Craftsmanship always. So many lamps. Minimalist interiors that are light and airy, yet cosy and comforting, a corrective for those heavy skies and long winters. It's design that doesn't shout but that feels natural, feels human. Design that makes things better.

Danish design has had an outsized influence on the way the world builds its public and private spaces, and on how it designs interiors, furniture and homeware. Its concepts have been applied to everything from concert halls to coffee pots to Lego blocks.

Though some would argue Danish design has its roots in the applied simplicity of Viking ships, it was the 1950s and '60s, or 'mid-century', that represented its Golden Age. Superstar designers and architects of the era, like Arne Jacobsen (buildings, furniture and homeware),

Aarhus Rådhus (centre of image, p209), designed by Arne Jacobsen

Hans Wegner (furniture, notably chairs), Børge Mogensen (furniture) and Poul Henningsen (buildings and lamps), took the earlier functionalist ideas of Kaare Klint, considered the father of modern Scandinavian design, and applied new industrial processes, technologies and social sensibilities. The new generation, having lived through WWII, believed that design could be used to improve people's lives.

Danish modern was the result, putting a Scandi spin on German Bauhaus simplicity and zeroing in on form as well as function. The world took notice, and furniture exports from Denmark rocketed. In 1959, construction began on Danish architect Jørn Utzon's design for the Sydney Opera House.

GRACEFUL, STREAMLINED SHAPES. WARM WOOD TONES AND TEXTURES. AN OBSESSION WITH NATURAL MATERIALS. FUNCTIONALITY FIRST. CRAFTSMANSHIP ALWAYS. SO MANY LAMPS.

Obsessive attention to detail, a quasi-philosophic process of refining and simplifying, even a touch of surrealism, were hallmarks of the period. Jacobsen and his contemporaries could spend months, even years, perfecting a single chair. Still, the results made the world sit up straight; in the 1950s *Time* magazine even devoted a cover to the phenomenon. Chairs of the period have names and personalities – the Ant, the Y, the Swan, the Egg, or Wegner's signature work known simply as 'the Chair'. Many are still in production. Poul Henningsen's PH5 lamp created in 1958 remains one of the most popular hanging lamps sold in Denmark today.

In Copenhagen's SAS Royal Hotel (now the Radisson Collection Royal Hotel), Arne Jacobsen designed not only the building but every item in it, down to the door handles, cutlery and the famous Egg and Swan chairs. Room 606 remains entirely as it was on opening day in 1960.

Danish design isn't fixed in time, of course. Trends come and go and come again, aesthetics evolve. While later designers remained influenced by the heroes of the 1950s, others challenged their hegemony, with fresh designs that were often bold, irreverent and avant-garde.

You only have to look at the industrial curves of Bang & Olufsen audio systems, or the elegance and craft of Georg Jensen silverware and jewellery. Furniture company Hay is a showcase of contemporary Danish designers, while the revered Bjarke Ingels Group (BIG) wins hearts and minds with their witty, unconventional and sustainable buildings.

Increasingly, Danish designers are looking outward and asking how design can improve the lives of people worldwide. The Index Project, a Danish nonprofit, is behind one of the world's foremost design awards, sometimes called the Nobel Prize of design, which seeks to reward design that solves problems and improves quality of life. It's evidence that the values of Denmark's Golden Age designers have endured. The notion, beyond all else, that design should make things better.

Bang & Olufsen's BeoGram 4004

FROM LEFT: KARL AAGE ISAKSEN/SHUTTERSTOCK ©, FREYA INGRID MORALES/BLOOMBERG/GETTY IMAGES ©

Statue of Hans Christian Andersen, Copenhagen

COLDSNOWSTORM/GETTY IMAGES ©

HAPPILY EVER AFTER

Fairy tales and folklore in Denmark. By Thomas O'Malley

ONCE UPON A time, there was a land of princes and princesses, of turreted castles and troll forests, wicked witches and goblins, stormy islands and sunken ships. And that land was called Denmark.

The likes of Thor, Odin and Loki, along with lesser beings of Norse mythology – all those mischievous dwarfs, elves, wights and trolls – served as a kind of proto-lore for Denmark in the time of the Vikings and early Northern Europeans, setting the tone for what would come later. Even after converting to Christianity around the 10th century, many Norse people clung to their pagan roots, their myths and folk tales trickling down through generations of retelling, morphing and adapting to the prevailing social climate of the day.

Myth, Magic & Mischief

Take the *nisse*, a short, bearded, gnome-like creature with a red pointy hat and a history stretching back to Norse mythology. A kind of animistic house spirit associated with the winter solstice, if treated well the *nisse* would protect the family from evil, but if wronged, he (and it was always a he) would play tricks and bring calamity. Early Christian belief disavowed the worship of pagan spirits like *nisser*, even going so far as to associate them with the devil. But all that changed in the 1800s and Denmark's romantic 'Golden Age'. Artists and writers were busy idealising nature, rural life and the folk traditions that derived from it. *Nisser* were rehabilitated, becoming the bearer of Christmas presents and the origin story of Denmark's take on old St Nick. Though the *nisse* is no saint – woe betide any household that forgets to leave a bowl of porridge in the attic for him at *jul* (Yule). Skip ahead another century and *nisse* gets demoted to an auxiliary role as a Christmas elf, and ultimately a plush festive figurine sold at Flying Tiger Copenhagen stores around the world. Them's the breaks.

Hans Christian Andersen

Hans Christian Andersen wrote about a *nisse* in his 1852 fairy tale, 'The Goblin and the Grocer' (*Nissen hos Spækhøkeren*), just one of more than 150 fairy tales he published during his lifetime. *The Complete Fairy Tales*, the definitive collection released a year before Andersen's death, is the most famous Danish book in the world, translated into over 160 languages. Chairman Mao was said to be a fan. Stories such as 'The Little Mermaid', 'The Emperor's New Clothes', 'The Princess and the Pea' and 'The Ugly Duckling' are embedded

Hear
H.C. Andersen
Talk

in the global literary consciousness like few others.

Inspired by the Brothers Grimm from Germany, collectors of old folkloric tales who published their volume a few decades earlier, Andersen's own stories were different, coming almost entirely from his imagination. Although simplified translations – and the saccharine filter of the likes of Disney – have turned many of them into quaint yarns for kids, Andersen's fairy tales are works of genuine literary heft that reward a close reading even today. And don't expect a fairy-tale ending – many are deeply pessimistic, tragic even. In Andersen's original telling of 'The Little Mermaid', the protagonist has her tongue cut out by the witch and endures an agonising transformation into a human, only for the prince to fall for someone else.

Andersen's own life had the arc of a fairy tale; born the son of a humble shoemaker, he set off to the city aged just 14 to make his fortune. Like the ugly duckling, Andersen only later became the swan – a world-renowned writer and member of high society. Critics agree that a strong autobiographical element runs through his work. A neurotic, sexually ambivalent, fame-driven, highly strung hypochondriac, by all accounts Andersen lived a troubled life, which might account for the malevolence at work in his tales, and all those unpalatable truths – love and loss, riches and ruin – that have made his stories so universal and timeless.

THE COMPLETE FAIRY TALES, THE DEFINITIVE COLLECTION RELEASED A YEAR BEFORE ANDERSEN'S DEATH, IS THE MOST FAMOUS DANISH BOOK IN THE WORLD, TRANSLATED INTO OVER 160 LANGUAGES. CHAIRMAN MAO WAS SAID TO BE A FAN.

Books by Hans Christian Andersen

Land of Fantasy

In his native Odense, the multimillion-dollar HC Andersens Hus is evidence of Andersen's enduring legacy, but it's in Denmark's landscape that the fairy tales really come to life, from the heather-clad dunes of Skagen to the deer-filled oak woods of Jægersborg Dyrehave. In the countryside, you can find Gisselfeld Kloster, the royal estate that galvanised the idea for 'The Ugly Duckling', and the fossil-rich cliffs of Stevns Klint, where Andersen wrote 'The Elf Mound'. Out and about, you might also chance upon trolls (which appeared in 'The Elf Mound' and several other stories), courtesy of upcycling artist Thomas Dambo who, since 2014, has installed giant wooden beasts in locations all over Denmark.

With its gingerbread-hued castles, unbroken line of kings and queens, cobblestone streets, mermaids and trolls (did you know those little troll toys with the up-combed hair were created by a Danish woodcutter in the 1950s?), Denmark can feel like the pages of a fairy tale – certainly that's a line the tourist board line likes to run with. And yet our understanding of what such a place might feel like is in part attributable to the imagination of Hans Christian Andersen. Call it Denmark's fairy-tale causality dilemma.

That the Danes (and much of Scandinavia) seem to have a predilection for fantastical tales shouldn't come as a surprise. After all, what could be more hyggelig than cosying down with a story at the fireside on a dark winter's night? And all of that happiness Denmark is famous for surely needs a counterweight, a corresponding darkness. In fact, the word *uhyggelig* means the opposite of cosy: it describes creepiness or dread, the sense of something sinister lurking in the forest. Proper fairy tales, like real life, operate in both the darkness and the light. And often, as the Danes well know, the most compelling tales of all don't end with a happy ever after.

SUSTAINABLE DENMARK

This small country has grown into a green powerhouse on a journey from fossil-fuel dependency to a renewable future. By Adrienne Murray Nielsen

AS POLITICIANS IN some countries waste time debating the very existence of climate change, Denmark has forged ahead with initiatives to tackle the problem. The country topped the Climate Change Performance Index (CCPI) in 2022, 2023 and 2024, and has one of the world's most ambitious climate strategies, though no country does enough to limit global warming to well below 2 °C, as outlined in the Paris Agreement.

Denmark has committed to reducing its greenhouse gas emissions by 70% (compared to 1990 levels) by 2030, and to reaching carbon neutrality by 2050. In comparison, the EU's 2030 target is 55%.

However, Denmark's green transition wasn't always inevitable. It was once heavily dependent on oil. So just how did it end up on this path?

In 1972 more than 90% of Denmark's energy use relied on oil. But when the price suddenly spiralled and financial shocks ricocheted around the world, Denmark was plunged into an economic crisis. It was these troubled times that became the catalyst for a change of mindset.

Car-free Sundays were launched, cycling was encouraged and Denmark began to harness its abundant wind. In 1978 its first large turbine was installed. Less than a decade later Europe's biggest wind farm was built, and in 1991 Denmark commissioned the world's first offshore wind farm. Public support for wind power has been strong and many small communities have invested in their own local turbines.

In fact, it was Danish high-school teacher and inventor Poul la Cour who, in 1899, designed what's considered the first modern wind turbine – he discovered that fewer rotor blades improved electricity production. Today, it's no overstatement to say that Denmark is a world leader in wind technology, driven by home-grown firms like Vestas and Ørsted. Denmark said no to nuclear in the '80s and ruled out new coal plants in the '90s. Today wind accounts for around half of the country's electricity needs, and solar and biomass are also growing.

Oil Commitments

What's less well known is that Denmark is one of the EU's biggest oil and gas producers. However, it has committed to ending North Sea oil and gas extraction by 2050. Just drive past the port of Esbjerg and you can't miss the stacks of enormous wind turbines being produced. This town was Denmark's oil and gas hub, but the transition from black to green is evident.

P
Zone

Sustainability is practised on a daily basis by Denmark's many cyclists. Nine out of 10 Danes own a bicycle and there are 12,000km of routes nationwide. In Copenhagen, almost half of all trips to work and school are done on two (or three) wheels, and the city has 400km of cycle paths, and several cycle highways and traffic-free bridges. It often tops lists of the most cycle-friendly cities. Meanwhile, cars are heavily taxed and expensive to own. However, recent trends suggest Danes are cycling less than they used to, prompting the government to pledge 334 million kroner on new cycle paths.

Public transport is also going green, with electrified ferries and buses. Car-sharing apps are commonplace, city taxi fleets are often electric and hydrogen-powered, and domestic flights are expected to be fossil-free by 2030.

Green Innovation

This small country is also a powerhouse of green innovation. At the huge data centre in Odense, waste heat from thousands of computer servers is captured and used to heat local homes. Denmark is also betting big on developing green hydrogen projects.

IT'S NO OVERSTATEMENT TO SAY THAT DENMARK IS A WORLD LEADER IN WIND TECHNOLOGY, DRIVEN BY HOME-GROWN FIRMS LIKE VESTAS AND ØRSTED. TODAY WIND ACCOUNTS FOR AROUND HALF OF THE COUNTRY'S ELECTRICITY NEEDS, AND SOLAR AND BIOMASS ARE ALSO GROWING

Solar and wind turbines, Holstebro

Danes are at the forefront of sustainable design, such as Green Light House, UN City and the regeneration project transforming Nordhavn's industrial area into a sustainable neighbourhood. In a world of fast fashion and consumerism, Copenhagen's Fashion Week stands apart. Participating clothing brands must meet strict sustainability rules, including waste reduction, green materials and ethical supply-chain practices. Among those to make the cut are Danish labels Ganni and Stine Goya.

Drink from a can or bottle and you might spot the 'pant' label. This means it can be recycled. In fact, 90% of cans and bottles get reused, thanks to the scheme's popularity and incentives. Shoppers simply return the used containers to a machine at the supermarket to get a small refund.

In the last two elections, climate change has been among the top issues for voters. Though Danish climate efforts are applauded overseas, the toughest critics are often at home. In fact, some feel their leaders aren't bold enough. As the 2030 deadline approaches, reports cast doubt on Denmark hitting its emission targets, prompting the government to introduce the highest corporate carbon tax in Europe.

Carbon Footprints

Among Denmark's major industries, shipping and farming still have significant carbon footprints. In the wake of Russia's invasion of Ukraine, European countries have scrambled to secure domestic energy supplies. For Denmark, that has meant postponing plans to take the last oil and coal-fired plants offline, and boosting North Sea gas production, albeit temporarily.

Yet Denmark's green ambitions have also been turbo-charged. Still to come is its most ambitious infrastructure project to date. The green light has been given to build a futuristic energy island in the North Sea, serving offshore wind farms. Denmark plans to establish colossal wind power hubs, capable of supplying electricity to millions of homes across Denmark and the EU, while the new centrist coalition government also wants to bring the country's net-zero goal forward to 2045.

Cyclists, Copenhagen

INDEX

The Danish language places the letters æ, ø and å at the end of the alphabet.

B

Map Pages **000**

Map Pages **000**

Map Pages **000**

“Marvelling at how parts of the South Sea Islands have as many vintage wooden windmills as modern wind turbines.”

THOMAS O’MALLEY

“I loved doing the bakery tour in Copenhagen, when my Danish guide-friend and I ate copious pastries in the name of research.”

ABIGAIL BLASI

FROM LEFT: OLIVER HOFFMANN/SHUTTERSTOCK ©, CLOUDY DESIGN/SHUTTERSTOCK ©

Mapping data sources:
© Lonely Planet
© OpenStreetMap http://openstreetmap.org/copyright

THIS BOOK

Destination Editor Amy Lynch

Production Editor Sofie Andersen

Coordinating Editor Tasmin Waby

Book Designers Megan Cassidy, Gwen Cotter

Cartographer Corey Hutchison

Assisting Editors Peterjon Cresswell, Kellie Langdon, Jennifer McCann, Mani Ramaswamy, Vicky Smith

Cover Researcher Kat Marsh

Thanks Ronan Abayawickrema, Imogen Bannister, Sasha Drew, Karen Henderson, Alison Killilea

Paper in this book is certified against the Forest Stewardship Council™ standards. FSC™ promotes environmentally responsible, socially beneficial and economically viable management of the world’s forests.

Published by Lonely Planet Global Limited
CRN 554153
10th edition – Jul 2025
ISBN 978 1 83758 364 5

10 9 8 7 6 5 4 3 2
Printed in China